CARRYING BRITISH MAILS OVERSEAS

... upon the coming
of the post to Dover

The coming of the post to Dover in the 1630s, showing a mounted postman with horn and bouget, and a packet-boat leaving upon the coming of the post. *Source:* Pen-and-ink drawing for the *Post Office Magazine* (December 1955) by E. A. Oldman.

CARRYING BRITISH MAILS OVERSEAS

BY

HOWARD ROBINSON

The ocean, with its vastness, its blue green,
  Its ships, its rocks, its caves, its hopes, its fears,
  Its voice mysterious, which whoso hears
Must think of what will be, and what has been.

KEATS

NEW YORK UNIVERSITY PRESS
1964

FIRST PUBLISHED IN 1964

© *1964 by Howard Robinson*

Library of Congress Catalog Card Number: 64-10621

PRINTED IN GREAT BRITAIN
in 11 point Ehrhardt type
BY C. TINLING & CO. LTD.
LIVERPOOL, LONDON & PRESCOT

FOREWORD

THE best-known event in Britain's postal development is, doubtless, the change in 1840 to uniform internal postage. It was based on weight instead of the number of sheets making up a letter, on pre-payment by the use of an adhesive stamp, and by a uniform penny rate no matter how far the letter travelled in the British Isles.

The writer, first attracted by this domestic innovation and its influence and economic and social changes found the study of the services overseas equally startling as the principles of 1840 were extended to mails abroad; they were of necessity overseas.

In Tudor times when the Government first began to carry private letters, the sending of mail across the narrow Channel from Dover to Calais or by way of Harwich to Holland was infrequent and slow. After King James succeeded Queen Elizabeth in the early seventeenth century he appointed the first 'Postmaster General for Foreign Parts.'

Progress was slow in the 1600s, but after the Restoration permanent regulations were put in force. Yet frequent wars between 1660 and 1815 interrupted, if they did not confuse, the transport of mails abroad. The eighteenth-century wars, moreover, were waged in regions far from home, becoming world conflicts as the European nations acquired distant colonies and extended their trading interests beyond the Atlantic into the Indian Ocean and the Pacific.

The migration from Britain to distant colonies of settlement soon created thriving centres of postal importance where the need for communication with 'home' would become ever more urgent. Today these colonies of settlement have become the chief part of a world-wide Commonwealth. And it has become closely linked with the United States, an outgrowth of the thirteen colonies that had left the Empire nearly two centuries ago.

In 1689 Falmouth was made the base for the first ocean mail packets, and it remained the only official port for the ocean services until the 1840s. By that time, the small Admiralty sailing brigs were already outdated. They soon gave way to steam-driven vessels belonging to powerful shipping lines, who found postal subsidies valuable as they extended their routes farther and farther beyond the Atlantic.

Since 1840 the advances in the services overseas have been continuous and impressive. The British Post Office has pioneered, not only in the introduction of domestic penny postage, but in the extension of cheap uniform postage overseas—'A Penny All the Way.' Shortly before the Second World War a comprehensive air-mail service abroad carried letters at a uniform rate without air surcharges. During the last war the Post Office devised the airgraph and later the air-letter form or aerogramme, which goes anywhere at a uniform rate. The air-letter form has been imitated the world over.

The title, *Carrying British Mails Overseas*, indicates the emphasis in this volume. It portrays the changing ways in which mail has been actually transported overseas, the ships and the routes they used, and the varied ways in which the mails were safeguarded and handled as the service has expanded during peace and war to its present world-wide position.

I have enjoyed the full use of the Post Office Records at the Head-quarters Building in London. In particular, I am indebted to Mr E. C. Baker, the former Archivist of the Post Office, for constant encouragement, for a careful reading of the whole manuscript, and for assistance in various other ways. Mr H. Thomas of Post Office Records has been very helpful as the manuscript was in its final stages, and Mr W. Disspain of the G.P.O. staff very kindly agreed to prepare the maps so necessary for realizing the spread of these world-wide services. R. H. Johnston of Wellington, New Zealand, and Dean S. C. McCulloch of San Francisco State College have examined the chapters relating to communications with the southern Commonwealths; the chapters are the better for their suggestions. Dr Boyd Shafer, until recently the Managing Editor of the American Historical Association, has shown a keen and helpful interest. Mr Robson Lowe, editor of the *Philatelist and Postal Historian* of London, answered a number of questions on the philatelic side, and Mr E. V. Dolby, Air Mail Adviser for BEA and BOAC, has made available material on the air-mail services.

In addition, my gratitude is due the American Philosophical Society for a grant-in-aid from the Penrose Fund, and the Social Science Research Council for another grant-in-aid; this assistance made possible the necessary research in the south Pacific on communications in that area.

I assume, of course, the responsibility for the emphases and interpretations in this account of Britain's mail services overseas both by sea and air as they have grown from feeble beginnings to a distinguished maturity.

The quatrain on the title page is part of a sonnet 'To my Brother George'. It was written about 1818, the year in which the poet's brother George Keats and his bride left Liverpool by sailing vessel as emigrants to America. See below, p. 116.

HOWARD ROBINSON

CONTENTS

FOREWORD   vii

1   *Beginnings of a Foreign Postal Service*   15

2   *A Postmaster-General for Foreign Parts*   19

3   *The Foreign Services—1660-1700*   23
The Dover Mails—Mails Cross the North Sea—Continental
Mails during the French War (1689-97)

4   *Rise of the Atlantic Services*   32
Packets to Spain and Portugal—The First Transatlantic
Services

5   *Atlantic Mails in Peace and War—1700-63*   39
Packets to Corunna and Lisbon—Transatlantic Routes

6   *The Packets during the American Revolution*   47
Peace-time Atlantic Services—A Colonial War

7   *Taking Stock—1783-93*   57
Corruption and Extravagance

8   *Trial by Battle—1793-1802*   66
The Falmouth Station—The Test of War

9   *The Handling of Sailing Packets—1803-15*   75
The North Sea and Home Stations—The Sailing Packets
out of Falmouth—Manning the Packets—Handling the Mails

10   *Mail Carrying Overseas during the Napoleonic
War*   89
The Peninsular and Mediterranean Routes—Services to the
Americas—Packet Warfare—The American War of 1812—
The Case of the *Montagu* and the *Pelham*

11   *Ocean Mails—1815-30*   105
The Admiralty Takes Over—Ship-letters—British Mails
Cross the Atlantic in American Vessels

12   *From Sail to Steam*   117
Steam Packets on the Home Stations—Steamships Cross
the Atlantic

A*

CONTENTS

13 *Mails on the North Atlantic Seaway* 129
Beginnings of the Cunard Line—Cunard Liners Face
American Competition

14 *Transatlantic Mails—Canada, the West Indies,*
South America 145
A Canadian Mail Line—The West Indies—The Pacific
Steam Navigation Company—Trollope Inspects the West
Indies

15 *Mails by Steam for India and the East* 158
The Overland Route—The Rise of the P & O—The P & O
East of Suez—The Journey across Egypt

16 *Mails to Africa—West, South and East* 172
The Union Steam Ship Company—Currie's Castles

17 *Australian Mails before 1870* 184
Early Mails—The Demand for Steam Communication—
Trial and Error—The Return to Steam Services—The
Suez Canal

18 *British Mails Cross the Pacific* 200
New Zealand Mail in the Days of Sail—The Panama Route—
Service via San Francisco

19 *The Handling of Ocean Mails a Century Ago* 217
Agents East of Suez—The Royal West Indian Mail—
Sorting at Sea

20 *The Carriage of Ocean Mail—1860-85* 234
The P & O versus the Orient Line—Atlantic Routes—The
Cunard Monopoly—The Blue Riband

21 *Ocean Penny Postage* 252
Elihu Burritt—The Lowering of Colonial Rates—The
Universal Postal Union—A Penny All the Way

22 *Changing Communications—1886-1918* 266
Cable and Wireless—Beginnings of Air Mail—Foreign
Services in War Time

23 *Mails Take to the Air* 279
The First Air Services—The Airship—Imperial Airways—
The All-up Scheme

24 *The Second World War and After* 295
The Airgraph—The Air-letter Form—The Revival of Peace-
time Services

CONTENTS

APPENDICES

    I *Packet Losses during the American Revolution*   308

   II *Packet Losses in the French War (1793-1802)*   311

  III *Packet Losses during the Napoleonic War and the War of 1812*   313

  IV *The Falmouth Packet-boats (1827)*   315

   V *Mail Carried by air (1950-62)*   316

  VI *Comparison of Air and Surface Mails Overseas (1939-62)*   317

BIBLIOGRAPHY   318

INDEX   323

ILLUSTRATIONS

1   The coming of the post to Dover in the 1630s   *frontispiece*

2   The Harwich packet-boat *Princess Royal*   *facing page 28*
    Drawings for the new 170 ton packet-boats, 1790

3   Weekly return of Benjamin Pender, the packet
    agent   *facing page 29*

4   James Bull and his son John   *facing page 64*
    Christopher Saverland

5   Two sailing packets at the time of the
    Napoleonic War   *facing page 65*
    Page from the log-book of the *Lady Mary Pelham*

6   Three Falmouth sailing packets of the 1830s   *facing page 128*
    The *Savannah*, the first steamship to cross
    the Atlantic, 1819

7   Two packet letters   *facing page 129*
    Two letters that crossed the Atlantic in the
    mid-1850s

8   Launching of the *Great Britain* at Bristol in
    1843   *facing page 160*
    The *Hindostan*, leaving Southampton in 1842

9   Anthony Trollope   *facing page 161*

10 Envelopes of two letters sent from Glasgow to
    Dunedin in the 1860s   *facing page 192*

11 The *Mataura*   *facing page 193*
    The Cunard *Arabia*
    The *Adriatic*

12 Elihu Burritt   *facing page 256*
    Sir John Henniker Heaton

13 A propaganda envelope on behalf of ocean
    penny postage   *facing page 257*
    Beechings Commemorative envelope

ILLUSTRATIONS

14   The Empire Flying Boat of the All-Up service, 1937   *facing page 296*

15   The Post Office promotes the airgraph, 1943   *facing page 297*
     Airgraph sent by Winston Churchill to General Smuts when the service to South Africa was opened

MAPS

1   Falmouth, the Atlantic Packet Port, 1689–1840   41

2   The Home Packet Stations and Their Early Connections   76

3   Mail Routes into the Mediterranean   90

4   The American End of the Atlantic Ferry   130

5   Packet Routes—the West Indies and Panama   150

6   Mail and Cable Routes in the Pacific   201

7   Mail Communication around Africa, through the Indian Ocean and on East   235

All photographs provided by G.P.O. Records are reproduced by kind permission of H.M. Postmaster-General.

I

BEGINNINGS OF A FOREIGN
POSTAL SERVICE

THE distinction between foreign and domestic postal arrangements has been clear cut ever since the start of regular mail services in the sixteenth century. Postmen on horseback carried the domestic mails along the main roads radiating from London, but those taking mails to Europe had to cross by boat to the Continent.

The need for these services overseas grew rapidly after Henry VIII came to the throne. His Government was drawn more and more into the power politics of the nearby Continent. The merchants and upper classes as well were increasingly concerned with matters European. The English upper classes were becoming great travellers in the sixteenth century, attracted by the literatures, the fashions and the finery of their European neighbours. Portia, in the *Merchant of Venice*, described her English suitor as one who had bought 'his doublet in Italy, his round hose in France, his bonnet in Germany and his behaviour everywhere'.

A postal service overseas that was distinctive and important grew up as a result of this mixture of motives. Couriers kept king and court, nobleman and merchant, in touch with the Continent. The messengers might take boat down the Thames as far as Gravesend, and thence travel overland to Dover, or go all the way from Dover to London on horseback, changing their mounts at the posting stations along the Dover Road. From Dover a boat carried a messenger and his dispatches across the Channel. At Calais or Dunkirk the mails would again go horseback by the established postal stations to Paris or Antwerp or to more distant centres. It is not surprising to learn that a vessel of the time, plying between Dover and Calais, was named the *Post Horse*, for the sea crossing was but another form of mail carriage. The postmaster at Dover furnished horses for the couriers on the road to London, and vessels for those going to foreign lands.

Early in his reign Henry VIII felt such need of an organized messenger service that Brian Tuke, his Clerk of the Signet, took on the additional duties of Master of the Posts. A dispatch from the Continent in August 1512 refers to the 'Master of the Posts in England', and by the end of the year Brian Tuke is mentioned with this title. It was no sinecure. When he accompanied the King to Flanders in 1513, for example, Brian Tuke took along thirteen messengers.

So important was the cross-Channel connection that the Dover Road was more and more travelled. A well-known letter that Tuke wrote to Thomas Cromwell in 1533, in defence of his services, declared that 'Except for the hakney horses bitwene Gravesend and Dovour, there is no such usual conveyance for men in this realme as in . . . France and other parts.' A few years later Brian Tuke reported that 'there are always ordinary [i.e., regular] posts betwixt London and Dovour'.[1]

Brian Tuke was not the first European Master of the Posts. The appointment was doubtless suggested by a practice already in use on the Continent, for the Holy Roman Empire had an Imperial Postmaster before the beginning of the sixteenth century. In 1480 the Emperor had selected a certain Francis de Tassis to supervise the Imperial postal services. When the Emperor Charles V—a contemporary of Henry VIII—combined in his vast holdings, not only Spain and northern Italy, but Germany, Burgundy and the Low Countries as well, the arrangements of Francis de Tassis were far reaching. On his death in 1517, the control of the posts passed to his nephew Baptista, and the family became hereditary Masters of the Imperial Post. By that time Antwerp had become the chief 'post exchange' for the northern territories. From Antwerp important postal routes radiated to France, Italy, Spain, northern Europe and the Channel ports. The successive Grand Masters of the Imperial posts, later known as the Counts of Tour and Tassis, were to control this important European service for over three centuries.

The couriers of Henry VIII, if he was on good terms with the Emperor, went by way of Flanders to the 'post exchange' at Antwerp, and thence to more distant destinations. If important, the royal dispatches might be carried all the way by an English courier. Brian Tuke, for instance, paid a certain William Thomas £13 6s 8d

---

[1] For reference to Brian Tuke as Master of the Posts, see *Letters and Papers, Henry VIII*, 2nd ed., I, nos. 136, 604, 885, etc. And for his letter to Cromwell, *Rep. Secret Com. on P.O.* (H.C., 1844), 32.

for coming from the Emperor's court with letters from the English Ambassador.[1]

Only gradually were the royal services extended to the general public. Sir Brian Tuke, who died in 1545, and his successor, Sir John Mason, were primarily royal postmasters. When Sir Thomas Randolph succeeded Mason in 1567, the reign of Queen Elizabeth had already begun—as well as a growing desire of the upper classes that they be allowed to share the royal posting arrangements. But this was granted only grudgingly. Vigilance was needed to guard against the unauthorized use of post-horses, and to prevent treasonous correspondence with Elizabeth's enemies on the Continent. When Sir John Stanhope became the Queen's Master of the Posts in 1590—two years after the sailing of the Spanish Armada—a Proclamation required the officers of town and shire to search 'all males [mails], bougets and other carriages' found on 'disavowed messengers coming in or going out of the realm with packetts or letters'.[2] Queen Elizabeth, who is well known for her caution, never seems to have given explicit permission for the general use of the royal postal services. The privilege, however, appears to have been tolerated, if royal needs were not hampered.

The merchants received the first concessions. Foreigners doing business in England, known as the Merchants Strangers, were allowed their own messenger, provided he was approved by the English Master of the Posts. The letters carried by their vessels, were to concern only the business affairs of the merchants. In 1568 the Postmaster of the Merchant Strangers, Christian Suffling, was succeeded by Raphael van den Putte, and on his death in 1603, the appointment was obtained by Matthew de Quester. This appointment was confirmed by Sir John Stanhope, the English Master of the Posts.[3]

The principal group of English traders doing business overseas, known as the Merchant Adventurers, had used their own messenger since early in the reign of Elizabeth. When this privilege was being questioned in 1626, they asserted that 'for some fifty years they had without interruption sent their letters and dispatches by a post of their own election'. Other groups of English merchants in foreign

---

[1] *Letters and Papers, Henry VIII*, 2nd ed., I, 1551, 1594; II, 1419; *Cal. S.P. Ven.*, III, 177, 226, 230.

[2] *Bouget* (later budget) was the French name for a small leather bag.

[3] See Charles, Lord Stanhope, *A Discourse* 'shewing the True State and Title of the Comptroller, or Postmaster-General of England, the Lord Stanhopes right to it, and consequently to the forraigne and inland Letter Offices' (n.d., *c.* 1637). Charles Stanhope was the son of Sir John.

trade had similar rights, but only to places where their 'factories are now settled'.

Although five main roads went out of London at this time, the only one that received the blessing of the Government as a foreign route was the Dover Road. It was well travelled. By 1582 a staff of ten couriers was carrying the mail via Dover to the Continent. They were called the 'forraigne Posts or Curriers, who by turn went to and from France, Flanders and Holland, with all Packets and Letters, both of the State and particular merchants'. A 'particular' merchant was one not in a group such as the Adventurers. In 1574 a correspondent in France wrote Lord Burleigh: 'The English post has gone out, and as the Dutch post might interrupt one I have for you, I enclose it in one to John Tyler, merchant.'[1]

By the end of the sixteenth century the royal messenger service overseas had expanded into a more general carriage of the mails. The merchants employed their own messengers, and the upper classes were permitted a limited use of the royal posting arrangements.

[1] *Acts P.C.*, June–December 1626, 303, 375; Stanhope, op. cit., 4; *Cal. S.P. Dom.*, 1561–90, 64; 1566–79, 445, 476, 482.

2

A POSTMASTER-GENERAL FOR
FOREIGN PARTS

WHEN King James succeeded Queen Elizabeth in 1603 he promptly re-issued the postal regulations of 'our sister deceased'. Six years later came another proclamation regarding the mails, with particular reference to the Dover Road. Merchants, both Strangers and others, were warned against employing unauthorized persons to carry their letters across the seas. They were to use only those messengers appointed by 'our Master of the Postes'. The postmasters at the various stations along the Dover Road were to record all the letters, to have ready two leather bags lined with cotton or baize to carry the mail, and to have horns for the postman to sound 'as oft as he sees company coming, or four times in every mile'. It was clear that the horsing privilege was for general use, including 'all strangers riding with horse or guide, by themselves or in company with our ordinary messengers or Postes for the Low Countreys or France'.

Matthew de Quester, who had succeeded as Postmaster for the Merchant Strangers in 1603, was soon given a more important office. In the next year he became one of the King's postmasters for beyond the seas. It seemed fitting. De Quester, born in Bruges, had come to England as a young man, had been naturalized, and all his family were English born, including a son Matthew, who was to share his father's interests. De Quester soon became the leading agent for the foreign correspondence. By 1610 the Venetian ambassador in England was using the post in De Quester's charge for his letters by way of Antwerp, paying his postal accounts to De Quester, and referring to him as the 'postmaster in London to the King of Great Britain'.[1]

A bitter quarrel ensued when Lord Stanhope asserted that this was an infringement of his control of both the foreign and domestic

---

[1] *Cal. S.P. Dom.*, 1603-10, 162, 397, 426; *Cal. S.P. Ven.*, XII, 15; XIV, 255; XV 586.

mail services. De Quester won out when letters patent in 1619 granted to him the office of 'Postmaster General for Foreign Parts'. A Proclamation of 1623 made this even clearer by announcing that De Quester's office was not subordinate to the Stanhope patent; according to the Proclamation, the two offices might well 'stand together, being of distinct places'.

Stanhope was reluctant to give in. When the postmastership of the Merchant Adventurers became vacant in 1625, Stanhope promptly appointed a Henry Billingsley to convey the letters. Billingsley announced that he would accept letters in London behind the Exchange at the sign of the George just beyond the Antwerp Tavern, and that they would be carried every Saturday by his postal service to Flushing and Holland, and the Hanse towns, and 'thereafter, if God spares his health and life, to other places'.

For a time Billingsley was allowed to carry letters for the Merchant Adventurers, but was warned against any general transport of foreign mail. Sir John Coke, one of the Secretaries of State, even questioned the right of the merchants to have their own postmaster. He shuddered to think what would happen 'if everie man may convey letters, under the cover of merchants, to whom and what place he pleaseth'. By that time, the Merchant Adventurers were the only group allowed their own postmaster, and he was to go only to Hamburg and Delft 'where the staples of cloth are now settled'.[1]

We get only a hazy view of the way the first Foreign Postmaster-General handled the mail. His couriers, who wore distinctive badges, not only carried letters between London and the Continent, but also delivered and collected letters in London. De Quester had a public office near the Exchange where two clerks kept a list of all letters sent and received. A table of schedules was hung up for the benefit of the public, but the rates have not come down to us. The office had writing desks for public use, as well as a table on which the outgoing letters were accumulated. Of this we know from an incident preserved in the correspondence of the Venetian ambassador. On one occasion his secretary 'writing in a room at De Quester's where the letters lie' stole a packet directed to Antwerp. It appeared that the secretary had been sent to the postmaster's office for this very purpose, using the writing of the letter as a ruse for taking the packet.

Mails were sent to the Continent about twice a week by the 'ordinary', and expresses were used for important dispatches that

---

[1] Stanhope, op. cit., 2; S. P. Dom., 1623-5, 131; 1625-6, 223; Hist. MSS. Comm., XXI, pt. 1, 330; Rep. Secret Com. on P.O., 50-51.

had to go post-haste. The Venetian ambassador, for example, wrote to the Doge of Venice in 1620 by an 'express courier', and he added that further details would follow by the 'ordinary' from Antwerp. Packets for a particular place were tied together with pack thread, and secured by the postmaster's seal. By the end of De Quester's tenure, he had nine ordinary couriers; three of these were used for letters to and from France, and six for mails via the Netherlands.[1]

A separate service for foreign mails appeared to be in good working order. However, it did not long remain with the De Questers. In March 1631-2 the office was transferred to William Frizell and Thomas Witherings, on the ground that Matthew de Quester, was aged and infirm. The new patent again emphasized the distinction between the domestic and foreign services, making clear that only the Postmaster-General for Foreign Parts was to have charge of mails going overseas. The Proclamation asserted that the secrets of the realm must not reach foreign nations, a condition not to be prevented 'if a promiscuous use of transmitting letters should be suffered'.[2]

Thomas Witherings, who soon became the sole foreign post-master, sought to correct the laxity of De Quester's couriers. They were accused of minding 'their own piddling traffic' rather than the service of the State or the merchants, and they were said to omit many 'passages by lying at tippling houses'. Witherings accused them of taking the incredible time of eight to fourteen days between London and Antwerp.

Instead of De Quester's leisurely service, Witherings proposed to introduce the use of fast and constant horse-posts, known on the Continent as the 'staffeto', by which mail was carried continuously by night as well as by day. Boats were to leave for Calais immediately upon the coming of the post to Dover. On reaching France, the captain of the packet-boat was to wait for the 'first packet that shall come by staffeto from Antwerp'. This new service, it was hoped, would lower the time between London and Antwerp to three days.

Witherings' conduct of the office in London did not differ greatly

[1] *Acts P.C.*, IX, 100; *Cal. S.P. Dom.*, 1631-3, 242; 1634-5, 389; *Cal. S.P. Ven.*, XVI, 186, 430; XVII, 111.

[2] See *Rep. Secret Com. on P.O.* for the Patent and the Proclamation. The calendar at this time was confusing. Until 1752 the year was reckoned in England as beginning on Lady Day (March 25th). The Gregorian calendar reform, already in use where the Catholic Church was influential, had changed the beginning of the year to January 1st, and had omitted ten days in March, in order to bring the vernal equinox into a correct relation with the sun. In England the date when De Quester lost his post, March 15, 1631-2, would be reckoned as coming near the end of 1631. On the Continent it would be March 25, 1632. The latter date corresponds with our present calendar.

from that of De Quester. A register was kept of all the writers, of those who brought the letters and of those to whom the letters were addressed. The mail was put in a budget or portmantle that was locked and sealed. When letters came from overseas, those for the Government and for the foreign ambassadors were delivered first, after which a 'roll or table of all other letters was to be set up in the office for every one to view and demand his letters'.

Witherings was so ambitious that he desired to control the inland services as well. A proposal of 1633 for setting up 'staffeto' posts between London and 'all parts of His majesties Dominions for the carrying and recarrying of his subjects letters' included the utterly impracticable proposal, in view of the state of the roads, that letters should be forwarded 120 miles at the least in one day and night. A patent of 1636 granted Thomas Witherings a monopoly of the inland office as well as foreign services. His grandiose plans did not work out. Even the 'staffeto' arrangements for the Continental services did not greatly improve. Sir John Coke wrote of them: 'Our foreign letters come with less expedition than they used to do.' In 1636, some Zealanders boarded the ketch that was carrying the mails and robbed the courier. In the same year Flushing freebooters stopped the mail-boat, taking money, apparel, provisions and the mail. 'If the Zealanders and the Callizians be not prevented,' wrote the Dover postmaster to Witherings, 'you will have nobody to serve.'[1]

Sir John Coke, who had much to do with granting the two postal monopolies to Witherings, retired early in 1640. Coke's successor was so unfriendly to the Postmaster-General that he lost his patents. For security reasons they were taken over by the Secretary of State, who granted their administration to a London merchant, Philip Burlamachi by name. Burlamachi had served the King as an agent overseas, and had made timely loans to a needy monarch. When civil war broke out in 1642 mail communications at home and across the Channel were so disorganized as hardly to deserve the name. Well established postal communications were not to be resumed until a decade had passed.

[1] *Cal. S.P. Dom.*, 1631-3, 583; 1633-4, 366; 1635, 398; *Hist. MSS. Comm.*, XXI, pt. 1, 230, 478; pt. 2, 6.

3

THE FOREIGN SERVICES—1660-1700

THE Civil War suspended any orderly carriage of the mails. It even became necessary to depend on French and Flemish boats, 'as an English vessel will not, in this time of danger at sea, adventure on that service'. In 1650, for instance, a Jane Shore wrote to her brother in La Rochelle: 'The jealousies of the time are great . . . All packets are stopped which is the reason you do not hear from me.'[1]

By the mid-fifties when more peaceful conditions prevailed, the Government of Cromwell revived regular postal services. Following an Ordinance of 1654, the Government farmed out the mail service to a John Manley. According to his contract, Manley provided packets to be 'employed weekly for the Foreign Posts, as hath been formerly used and accustomed'. But the grant of the postal service to an independent 'farmer' did not last long. Caution in the use of the mails seemed so important that history soon repeated itself. The Letter Office was again taken from the non-official contractor, and put in the hands of the Secretary of State. John Thurloe, who was also in charge of espionage, kept it until Charles II came back from the Low Countries.

The control of the postal services by Thurloe was based on the first of a long series of post-office Acts—passed by a Cromwellian Parliament in 1657. Not only was the Post Office to convey letters for the public, but it was also 'to discover and prevent many danger-ous and wicked designs . . . against the Peace and Welfare of the Commonwealth'. The public was to have postal communication only within the limits of security. Merchants could still send their letters of advice by 'Masters of any Ship, Barque or other vessel of Mer-chandize'. The Act included the rates for letters going to the Continent. The lowest was 6d for a single sheet; the highest, 1s. Letters containing two sheets were charged double, and those of

[1] *Cal. S.P. Dom.*, 1650, 71; 1652-3, 64.

'greater bulk' paid so much an ounce. The foreign letter rates do not seem high, as the charge for a single sheet was 4d to Scotland, and 6d to Dublin.[1]

When Charles II returned from the Netherlands in 1660, he and his followers regarded the Commonwealth and Protectorate as illegal governments. Consequently they set aside the Post Office Act of 1657, replacing it by a new Act in 1660 that 'legally' settled the Post Office. It became the foundation charter of an organization that was to continue henceforth without any break. As a matter of fact, the Act of 1660 is largely a restatement of the Commonwealth measure that it displaced. The domestic and foreign offices were united under one Postmaster-General, ending once and for all the concept of a sharply distinct foreign postal service overseas.

Foreign letters were charged four rates in the Act of 1660, for single, double and treble sheets, and by the ounce for larger packets. The cheapest rate to the French cross-Channel ports was 4d the sheet. A charge of 8d carried a single sheet to any place in Flanders and the Netherlands. A single-sheet letter to Italy via Paris cost 9d, the prepayment carrying the letters as far as Mantua. If a letter went to northern Germany via Hamburg, the charge was 6d as far as Hamburg. An exception to the charge per sheet was made for letters to Turkey and the Levant; they were permitted an additional free covering sheet for the long journey by land and water.

Two other terms of the Act dealt with foreign mail. One required that all letters sent out of England be carried in British vessels. A second repeated the provision of the Act of 1657 that all ship-letters —those that did not come to England on an official packet-boat— must be handed to the local postmaster at the port of entry. As no penalties were imposed for the non-delivery of ship-letters, this provision had little effect. Colonel Whitley, who had charge of the Post Office in the seventies, met the situation by giving the captain 1d for each letter or packet that he delivered to the postmaster at a port. 'This was so well liked,' wrote Colonel Whitley in 1673, 'that scarcely a letter escapes us.'[2]

---

[1] The charge for letters by the number of sheets had been included in the plan of 1635 when Thomas Witherings obtained his monopoly. Letters were sent without covers, as the enveloping sheet would have been subject to charge. Envelopes were not to come into general use for nearly two centuries, not until the postal charge by weight replaced the older practice.

[2] *Peover Papers*, I, 147, 231; II, 102, 394, 406. These manuscript letter books throw much light on post-office practices during the seventeenth century. The postmasters at ports gave the captains receipts for the number of letters handed in, and payment was made in London on the presentation of a receipt.

For a time after the Act of 1660 the Post Office was again farmed out, the first contractor being Colonel Henry Bishop. Before the end of the decade, however, the farm moved back once more under the direct control of the Government; Lord Arlington, the Secretary of State, became Postmaster-General in 1667. Since that time the Post Office has been a government department. By 1685 the services were under the direct control of the Treasury, with the Lord Treasurer as the Postmaster-General. During this period a deputy took over the direct supervision of the services, since Postmasters-General like Lord Arlington or the Lord Treasurer were too much concerned with other matters. Sir John Bennet, Andrew Ellis, Colonel Roger Whitley and Philip Frowde furnish the succession of actual 'governours' from 1667 to 1688.

Even though there was no postmaster for 'foreign parts', the overseas service was a distinct establishment. A comptroller headed the office staff, which included at first but four clerks and five London letter carriers. Instructions of 1662 indicate the priority given to official mail:

'On the arrival of the French and Dutch mails, Thomas Harper is to see them opened; to deliver the letters for the King and the Duke of York, the Lord Chancellor, the Secretaries of State and their servants, to such messengers as are waiting for them, or if there be none, to send down a servant from the office expressly with them; these to be delivered before those of any other person whatsoever; that no letters are to be given out till the window of the office is opened for general delivery.'[1]

One of the clerks had charge of the alphabet. It consisted of a 'long counter with all of the 24 [sic] letters marked against the wall, over against which are the letters of all, such as are to be called for'. The letter carriers for the Foreign Post Office delivered the letters 'that come from beyond the Seas to the several houses about the Towne as they are directed'. The Continental services went twice a week—to Calais for France on Mondays and Thursdays, to Dunkirk for Flanders on Mondays and Fridays, and to the Netherlands by way of Harwich on Tuesdays and Fridays. Thus, as an account of 1677 puts it, there were six mails, 'so many also to retorn weekly, but their arrivall being (as the weather) uncertain forceth the Clarkes to perpetuall Attendance'.[2]

[1] *Cal. S.P. Dom.*, 1660-1, 93; 1661-2, 239.
[2] Thomas Gardiner, *Generall Survey of the Post Office* (1677) in the *Dartmouth papers*, (British Museum, Harleian MSS., 7,356), pp. 24, 80, 85.

THE DOVER MAILS

The Dover packets were the only recognized carriers before 1660. They served the two principal European routes, going to Calais for the services to and from Fance, and to Flanders to connect with the widely spread Imperial posts of the Counts of Tour and Tassis. When the Post Office was granted to Colonel Henry Bishop in 1660 he negotiated a treaty with the head of the French Post Office. The handling of English mail by the French Post Office, it might be added, caused much dissatisfaction, both as to the proportion of the postage desired by the French, and as to the manner in which English letters were forwarded through France. English merchants doing business in Spain, were disgusted with the slow carriage of their Spanish letters. Colonel Whitley found that letters for Spain left Paris only every fortnight, instead of once a week as he expected. He threatened to change the course of the correspondence and send more of it through Flanders, adding that 'Diligence is the life of our business.'

The Flanders route by way of Dover went, at this time, to Nieuwport whence the mails were carried to Antwerp for eastern and southern Europe. On occasion Ostend was put to use because it was preferred by the Imperial Postmaster. The harbour of Ostend, however, was not so usable as that of Nieuwport 'during the bad weather of the winter season'.[1]

The actual boat service from Dover was in charge of a contractor, known as the Clerk of the Passage. It's service was hazardous, as frequent wars involved Channel shipping. French privateers were only too glad to seize Nieuwport packets when the Calais service was not running. Passengers crossing the Channel must have had unpleasant experiences entirely apart from the dangers of war. The Dover mail-boats of this time were small, only 20-30 tons burthen. In 1667 the Ostend packet-boat was 'cast away and thirty-five persons perished but the letters were preserved though much wet'. This may well have been an overcrowded boat, for 'poor soldiers' were carried free to the capacity of the packets. The fares were 5s for regular passengers to and from France, and 10s between Dover

---

[1] *T.L.B.*, 1686-94, 62; *Peover Papers*, I, 126; the *Cotton-Frankland Corresp.*, epp. of October 25, 1697, February 1, 1697-8, April 18, 1698, etc. This manuscript collection of letters was written by the two Postmasters-General of the time to their English representatives on the Continent. From 1691 to 1823, the Post Office always had two Postmasters-General instead of one. The first pair were Sir Robert Cotton and Sir Thomas Frankland.

and Flanders. During the winter the boats were far from full. The agent reported for a crossing in January 1675 that the boat for Calais had only 10 passengers, and that the one arriving from Calais on the same day carried only 2 passengers, 'one a Frenchman, and the other an Englishman [?] named Jones'.[1]

MAILS CROSS THE NORTH SEA

The second foreign route, between Harwich and the Netherlands, began as a regular service in 1660. At first, the Dutch used their own vessels for the mail service to and from England. They much preferred to send their letters by their own packet-boats rather than to trust them to the doubtful security of the Imperial post through Flanders.

The most convenient port in the Netherlands for a service to England was Helvoetsluis (Hellevoetsluis) on the south side of the island of Voorne at the mouth of the Maas. The Brill, some 6 miles away on the north side of the island, was also used on occasion. But Helvoetsluis had a much better harbour, a decisive reason with the mariners who sailed their frail craft on this North Sea route.

The port of Harwich on the Essex coast seemed the natural terminus on the English side. The land route from London to Harwich was almost the same distance as that from London to Dover—71 miles. If there was a war with France, the sea crossing between Harwich and Helvoetsluis was much safer than a route by way of Dover. The post road between London and Harwich had long been in use. As far back as 1635, the plans for 'staffeto' posts in England had included one that went to Harwich by way of Chelmsford and Colchester.

When Lord Arlington became Postmaster-General in 1667, just as the Second Dutch War came to an end, negotiations for a regular Anglo-Dutch service were renewed.[2] Representatives of both Amsterdam and Rotterdam came to London—Mynheer Blaauw on behalf of Amsterdam and ex-burgomaster Jacob Quack to present the case for Rotterdam. Blaauw sought special privileges for Amsterdam. Rotterdam, on the other hand, was in favour of collective action; Jacob Quack also promised a faster service than that of his rival by the use of the Brill pilot-boats. When Quack

---

[1] *T.L.B.*, 1686-94, 61, 79, 118; 1706-11, 64, 144; *Cal. S.P. Dom.*, 1665-6, 280; 1673-5, 515.
[2] The three brief wars with the Netherlands in the seventeenth century occurred in 1652-4, 1666-7, and the third and last in 1672-4.

came to London in December 1667 he found the envoy from
Amsterdam busy trying to obtain a monopoly of the letter service
for Amsterdam. Early in the next month Quack hastened back in the
hope of persuading the United Netherlands to common action. He
left Harwich early in January 1667-8, boasting that he would eat his
dinner next day at home, and thus demonstrate the speed of his
proposed service. He sailed despite a violent storm, so severe that
his vessel disappeared without leaving a trace. As a report from
Harwich a week later put it: 'There is no news of Mynheer Quack;
it is thought that he has miscarried.'[1]

An agreement was reached with Amsterdam in April 1668.
Mails were to leave London Tuesdays and Fridays, and take boat at
Harwich the following day. The letters for England were to leave
Helvoetsluis on Wednesdays and Saturdays. The postage went to the
country to whom the letters were sent. Amsterdam agreed to forward all letters from England to other parts of the Netherlands
without delay and by the shortest route. The most important part of
the agreement from the English point of view was the provision that
the mails should be carried in English packet-boats. This was made
possible only because Amsterdam was poorly located to maintain a
packet service based on Helvoetsluis. The three boats for the service
were to be 'proper Yachtes [yachts] or Galliott Hoyes'. If Dutch
vessels were thought more fit, they were to be 'naturalized'. The
hoys were to be of 40 to 50 tons with crews of six able seamen. The
service began with the mail of Friday, June 13, 1668.

An English packet agent resided in each port to take care of the
mails. John Payne, who was stationed in Helvoetsluis, saw to the
loading of the mails, checked the 'passes' of the passengers going to
England, and allowed 'poor soldiers' to go free to the capacity of the
boats. When it became clear in 1669 that Dutch hoys were best
suited for the service, three were purchased and 'naturalized', since
they were well fitted 'to avoid the shelves and sands of that coast'.

The journey must have been unpleasant in blowing weather as
hoys were generally used for the coastal trade. On one occasion
46 soldiers and 5 fare-paying passengers came over in one of the
packets. They may have carried numerous passengers, but the mails
were not large at this time. A mail of 1674, for example, had 77
single-sheet letters and 7 doubles; another of that year was made up

---

[1] *T.L.B.* 1667-8, 43, 61, 159, 168. Puns were inevitable. Andrew Ellis, the deputy
foreign postmaster for Lord Arlington, wrote to a friend: 'I esteem the town of Amsterdam above all the Quacks in Christendom.'

e Harwich packet-boat *Princess Royal* about to enter the Dutch harbour of Helvoetsluis
1794. She is flying the official postal flag of the time—a red ensign with a mounted
stman in the lower right hand quarter of the flag. See footnote, p.68. *photo:* The
therlands Postal Museum, The Hague. Watercolour by J. A. van Es.

Drawings for the new 170 ton packet-boats for the Falmouth ocean services, 1790.

packets Built 1790

"Length of the Keel for Tonage 61ft,6ins. • Breadth Extreme 23ft. • Burthen in Tons 172 $\frac{88}{34}$ "

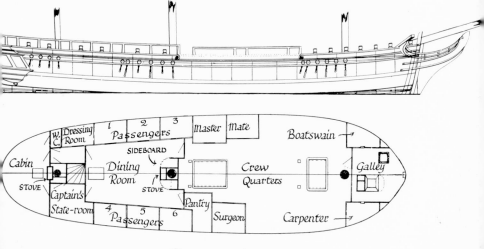

Plan of the Lower Deck

W. Disspain

A WEEKLY RETURN of His Majesty's PACKET-BOATS on the FALMOUTH Station Saturday July 10 1795

Station	Names	Commanders	Arrived	Sailed	Corunna	Lisbon	America	Leeward Islands	Jamaica	Captains on Leave	On what Occasion	Has been ashore since
Lisbon	Jane	Boulderson		July 5		—				Vigilance	to build a ship	July 6 1794
	Hanover	Todd	July	June 10						Judd	Do	April 7 1793
	George	Yescombe	June 15									
	Walsingham	Coyle	July 22 June 1			—				Coyle	to build a ship	Feby 21 1792
America and the West-Indies	Grantham	Bull	June 20									
	Sandwich	Dillon										
	Dashwood	Roberts	June 9	June 11						Rebeh.	to build a ship	Jan 25 1794
	Westmoreland	Wolfe	June 19	May 2								
	D. of Cumberland Drake	Jones	June 30							Drake	to build a ship	Sept 11 1792
	Chesterfield	Schuyler										
		Sharpe										
	Portland	Rogers		May 17						Rogers	No leave assigned	March 20 1794
	Princess Royal	Skinner		May 11								
		Caesar										
	Roebuck	Servante		July 16						Servante	McN.	Oct 20 1794
	Countess of Leicester Dodd		July 15	June 10								
	Halifax	Stanhope										
	Carteret	Taylor	July 22	May 2						Taylor	Private Business	May 2 1795
	Active	Clements										
	Jarvwin	Hocquard										
	Tartar	Ker	July	May 21						Ker	Private Business	May 14 1795
Corunna	Duchess of York	Jones	July	July 6								
	Prss of Brunswick. Bight			June 16								
		Totals	5	15	2	3	4	2	1	9		

B. Pender   July 24

of 96 single letters, 25 doubles and there were 11 packets weighing an ounce or more.[1] The new services via Harwich seemed in danger of collapse when the Third Dutch War broke out in 1672. Curiously enough, the Harwich service was not dropped but went on with little interruption. This strange arrangement is brought out in the numerous letters sent to Lord Arlington by Captain Silas Taylor, in charge of the naval stores at Harwich. He was certain, after the declaration of war, that 'our packets will not long continue their course . On the contrary, they were given passes by the Dutch 'so long as they [the Dutch] have an ambassador in England, and we [the English] suffer their packet-boats in quiet'. These protections were in general use during this brief war. The Dover as well as the Harwich boats had Dutch protections, and passes were furnished even by the King of France and the Governor of the Spanish Netherlands.

The Dutch Postmaster at Amsterdam throughout these years was Godbolt Muilman; he and Colonel Whitley exchanged frequent letters. At times Whitley encouraged the Dutch 'Mailman', as he was often called, in the hope that the mails might be speeded and true accounts rendered. At Christmas time, 1675, Colonel Whitley sent over a 'small present of two English cheeses', begging pardon for its 'meanness'. The reader may be surprised to learn that one was a Cheshire cheese weighing 100 lb., the other a 90-lb. Cheddar cheese. A year later he wrote Muilman: 'This day I sent two Rowles of Brawne (our English Sturgeon) in a box weighing 67 pounds . . . to pass by the first Boat to Mr Payne, who is desired to send it to you.' Whitley added in a postscript: 'Pray use some means to hasten ye Rotterdam letters.'[2]

CONTINENTAL MAILS DURING THE FRENCH WAR (1689-97)

The Revolution of 1688 brought a decided change in England's foreign affairs, for the coming of William from the Netherlands ended the tension between the Dutch and the English, and it led to a great European war with Louis XIV as the common enemy of England and the Netherlands. Since the war required King William's presence on the Continent for much of the time, the Harwich packet service was more important than ever.

[1] T.L.B., 1667-8, 427; Peover Papers, II, 147, 539; V, 7-16, 63, 115; T.L.B., 1686-94, 38, 127; 1690-1705, 98.
[2] Peover Papers, V, 123, 141; Cal. S.P. Dom., 1671-2, 262, 268, 284, 302. Mr Payne was the English packet agent at Helvoetsluis.

The English packet-boats, now four in number, often ran into trouble. The vessels were small, two were pinks, the *Francis* was a ketch, and the *Diligence* was a vessel of 85 tons. The *Francis* was taken by a French warship in 1691, and two of the others were captured later. They were replaced as soon as possible. The Postmaster-General wrote the Treasury in 1694: 'This morning sailed out of the River [Thames] another boat, which will supply the place of that lately taken into Dunkirk.'

In February 1693-4 King William suggested that the packets would be less liable to capture if they were small and unarmed, but built for speed. As one might expect, his proposal was adopted. The new vessels, built on plans prepared by Edmond Dummer, the Surveyor of the Navy, were in use by the summer of 1694. Neither freight nor ordnance was carried; everything was sacrificed to speed.

The crews disliked the change, believing that the vessels would be an easy prey to almost any privateer. A memorial from the Post Office to the Duke of Shrewsbury, a Secretary of State, puts the case vividly. As the vessels were provided with no defence 'they had to be extraordinary sailers to escape the Privateers. It was necessary that they should be low built, but by ye experience we have had of them we find that in Blowing Weather they take on so much water that the men are constantly wet during ye whole voyage and can noe ways go below deck to shift [change] themselves, being obliged to keep the Hatches shut to save the vessel from sinking.' The new packets may have been uncomfortable for their crews, but they did prove regular: 'In the whole of the late war not more than two packets were taken after Mr Dummer's model was followed.'[1]

When the war ended the uncomfortable packets were replaced by newly-built hoys of 60 to 70 tons in order to give more attention to the comfort of the passengers. This was necessary because the income from fares of the Harwich packets was being lowered by the competition from 'passage' [passenger] vessels; several had been 'lately sett up to go weekly between the River [Thames] and Rotterdam'.

The Dover services, as might be expected, were badly affected by the war. The runs to Calais ended, and French privateers out of Dunkirk kept the route to Flanders under constant peril. In addition, the mail services through the Spanish Netherlands to Italy and Spain were so hampered by the armies of Louis XIV that the

---

[1] *Cotton-Frankland Corresp.*, May 26, July 17, October 9, 1694; *T.L.B.*, 1686-94, 6, 47; 1691-9, 82; 1703-14, 106.

Imperial Postmaster even proposed to send letters from northern Europe for Spain by way of England.

By 1700 the postal arrangements overseas had already taken on the character they were to retain for centuries. One result of the numerous changes in the English Government during the seventeenth century was the conviction that the postal services should be in official hands. The danger of plots required watchful control of the mails. It seemed clear that the needed supervision could only be assured by keeping the packet services under government, and by requiring the carriage of mails in English vessels that were manned by native crews. By the end of the seventeenth century, the so-called 'Foreign Post Office', along with the domestic services, had become a department of government. The postal administration was already closely tied to the Treasury. The Post Office became a useful instrument for gathering revenue, as the mails grew ever larger and larger.

4

RISE OF THE ATLANTIC SERVICES

Colonel Whitley had suggested that packet-boats might sail the open Atlantic long before the service actually began in 1689. He had written the postmaster at Dover ten years earlier that Spanish letters could go by sea from western England 'to avoid the exactions of France'. In correspondence with the Imperial Master of the Posts at Antwerp, Whitley had suggested the use of 'ketches or Galliott hoyes . . . from Falmouth (or other western port) to ye Groine, or to such other places as you shall judge more convenient'.[1]

PACKETS TO SPAIN AND PORTUGAL

The service began in October 1689. Falmouth was chosen, after a consideration of Plymouth, as the port for the first packet service on the open Atlantic. It had the disadvantage of being farther from London than Plymouth—270 miles from London and 50 miles south-west of Plymouth. On the other hand, Falmouth had exceptional qualifications. The harbour, 5 miles long and 1 mile wide, was an excellent refuge for shipping, one of the best along the coasts of England. It was well protected from the full force of the Atlantic rollers, and could be entered even when the prevailing westerlies were blowing strongly up the Channel. In addition, Falmouth shipping was somewhat less exposed than that at Plymouth to French privateers in case of war.

Corunna, or the Groyne as it was usually called at this time, was the Spanish terminus of the service. It had a safe and spacious anchorage, so adequate that the Spanish Armada had finally left Corunna for the attack on England in 1588. Falmouth and Corunna were 450 miles apart.

The service began by the use of two vessels, but a third was soon added to ensure a fortnightly service. They were also used for carrying dispatches to the fleets in the Mediterranean. The agent

[1] *Peover Papers*, III, 309; IV, 9, 13.

at Falmouth, for example, received the following order in June, 1695: 'We send you herewith a Bagg with Dispatches, which Bagg with the Mayle sent you from here last Tuesday you are immediately to put on Board the pacquet Boat and order the commander to make the best of his way to the Groyne.' The captains on this service were directed to weight the mail if in danger from an enemy, and to sink it if the packet-boat was likely to be captured.

The mail-packets were permitted to take prizes, the prize money to be used as a partial offset for the expense of the new service. But there was so much grumbling by the crews that, in 1691, they were allowed the same rewards granted to the crews of naval vessels. It was understood that an enemy might be captured only if the packet-boat was on its direct course. At least seven prizes were taken during the war.

The packet crews on all stations received what was known as smart and pension money—for injuries while on duty and for payments to the widows and children of those who lost their lives in the service. The regulations were those of the Chest of Chatham, the name given to the fund for the regular Navy.[1]

Mail for the Falmouth service came by two land routes. The older south coast route from Plymouth was supplemented, and later replaced, by a road that left the route to Plymouth at Exeter, and went on to Falmouth by way of Okehampton, Launceston, St Columb and Truro. In fact, this inland route was set up especially to serve the packet service overseas. The Falmouth agent was notified in December 1704 that the new road was 'settled' and 'we have resolved that the mails to and from London be sent that way from Exeter . . . whereby they may be conveyed with more dispatch than by way of Plymouth.'[2]

The first agent at Falmouth was Daniel Gwyn. Francis Jones, who succeeded him in 1699, was followed by Captain Zechariah

---

[1] The seamen contributed 1s a month from their pay of 30s.
The annual smart payments were as follows:

For each arm or leg amputated above elbow or knee	£ 8
For each arm or leg amputated below elbow or knee	£ 6 13s 4d
For the loss of one eye	£ 4
For the loss of both eyes	£12
If the pupils of both eyes also were lost	£14

See *T.L.B.*, 1691-9, 12, 130, 226; 1699-1705, 72-75.

[2] St Columb on the inland route was the post town where Ralph Allen served his apprenticeship when the office was run by his grandmother. Reskemer Allen was the postmaster at St Columb in 1706-7, and he was followed for part of the next year by Gertrude Allen. Ralph Allen later became postmaster of Bath, and the most important eighteenth-century farmer of the internal cross-road posts. For Allen, see the writer's *Britains Post Office*, pp. 59ff.

Rogers, former commander of the packet-boat *Prince;* Rogers served until his death in January 1710-11. The agents received a salary at this time of £70 a year, and a small addition for acting as the local postmaster.[1]

The duties of the agent were exacting. For one thing, he had to be certain that the packet-boats sailed with their full complement of men, all of whom must be English seamen. The agent also saw to the furnishing of the vessels with 'ground tackle and standing rigging, shrouds, cables, sails and anchors, and all other naval materials'. He was frequently to inspect the stores, and to victual the vessels according to the rules of the Navy. A packet-boat on leaving was furnished with food and drink sufficient for the crew and passengers for thirty-five days. The victualling at this time was at the rate of only 7d per day per man.

When the mail was on board, the captain acknowledged receipt on the mail label as well as in the agent's journal, the receipt indicating the number and weight of the letters. A duplicate was sent to the agent abroad, and another to the General Post Office in London. The Falmouth agent also kept a journal of the winds for every day of the year, which were sent to London by every post. He also had to record the 'Names and Qualitys of all passengers, whether they shall pass as Whole, Half, or are transported as Poor.'[2]

The Treaty of Ryswick in 1697 brought peace, but it was brief, for Louis XIV, a few years later, accepted the throne of Spain for his grandson. The immediate effect of the War of the Spanish Succession was to bring to an end the packet service to Corunna. Falmouth, however, remained a packet station, as the vessels were diverted from Corunna to go down the west coast of the peninsula to Lisbon. It became a valuable route for communicating with the fleets in the Mediterranean, especially after the British strengthened the route by the capture of the Spanish Rock of Gibraltar in 1704.

At first three vessels were used on the Lisbon run, but it was soon found that a fourth was needed for a regular fortnightly service, and a fifth packet-boat was added in 1705 to furnish a weekly service.

---

[1] The other agents during the eighteenth century were William Rogers, who succeeded his brother for a few months to fill out the fiscal year; Joseph Durden, 1711-15; Joseph Penhallow, 1715-23; Stephen Banfield to 1747; George Bell from 1747 to 1778, when he was followed by his son Stephen. The list of agents in Susan E. Gay, *Old Falmouth* (1903) mistakenly lists Captain Roger's tenure as lasting three years after his death.

[2] *Fal. L.B.*, I, 57-59 where the duties of the office were listed for Captain Rogers in August 1705. The half fares were to pay for children and servants.

Sometimes more than one mail had to be carried by a packet-boat, but this was discouraged. In 1704 the Post Office informed the agent at Falmouth that they had received two Lisbon mails sent up express, but that the bag containing the Government dispatches was missing. 'When you have any packet to be sent with the mails,' they wrote, 'you ought to chain or tye the same to the Grand Mail . . . to prevent the like accidents in the future.' The Lisbon mail, although not large, might contain a variety of bags. A mail received in April 1705, for instance, included a bag of letters from Lord Methuen, the English Ambassador in Lisbon, 16 packets and letters 'for Her Majesty's Service', 290 double and single letters and 13 packets for London and Holland, as well as letters for Falmouth and Devonshire.[1]

THE FIRST TRANSATLANTIC SERVICES

Edmond Dummer, Surveyor of the Navy and designer of the small packet-boats used at Harwich in the previous war, urged the Post Office to increase the Falmouth services by sending vessels across the Atlantic to the West Indies. The transatlantic route was intended to meet a real need, for the British West Indian islands had long been of great value for their tropical products. Communications with the West Indies had depended on the fleets or by the sending of letters on merchant ships as opportunity offered.

The new route was opened in the summer of 1702, the Post Office using Edmond Dummer's ships, and paying him for the various charges that the new service required. His single-deck sloops were to go and return in about 100 days. Edmond Dummer was so confident of success, despite some losses, that he proposed in 1704 to carry on the service by contract. The voyages were to be monthly by the use of five two-deck vessels of 150 tons each. Each packet was provided with ten guns and a crew of thirty men. The contract allowed Dummer the freight of bullion and 5 tons of space for goods out and 10 tons home in each vessel. He was so sure of success that he agreed to run all risks, even to replacing vessels lost to the enemy. The postage, which had been the same as that on the Lisbon letters, was raised in 1704 from 9d a single letter to 1s 3d. This was not considered unreasonable by the Post Office in view of 'the great distance of this Conveyance' and the benefits that the merchants

[1] *Fal. L.B.*, I, 32, 50; *T.L.B.*, 1699-1705, 258-9; 1703-14, 17.

would receive from 'so regular and constant a Correspondence'. Edmond Dummer was a very sanguine contractor, even though his plan for a transatlantic mail service during war-time was thought 'impracticable by many of the best seamen in England'.[1]

Full instructions were sent to the postmasters of the six West Indian islands to be visited by the Dummer vessels. The postmasters of Jamaica, Barbados, Antigua, Montserrat, Nevis and St Kitts were to record the exact time of arrival and departure of each packet-boat. If letters for other islands were put on the packet, they were to go in separate bags. The island postmasters also received instructions for stamping outgoing letters:

'All letters to be sent for London [to] be Stamped with the name of the Place where they shall be first put in.' The instructions added: 'We have caus'd Stamps to be made for each Place, and do by this mail send you two Stamps for your Island with which you are to stamp all Letters . . . The best method of making use of them will be by nailing a piece of felt or a hat to a board, and wet the same with ink not too thin, whereby the Stamp being moisten'd will readily give an Impression of the Letters.'[2]

The first transatlantic packet service was doomed from its beginning, since the vessels ventured into waters infested by privateers. The capture of the first packet by a privateer out of Martinique was a warning of things to come. In fact, the West Indian packets completed only three round voyages in the first year, and two of those that returned safely had narrow escapes. There was also a deficiency from the letter postage and the passenger fares, which Mr Dummer asked to have charged on the next quarter, else he must fail and the 'business . . . will come to a full stop'. By the end of the first twelve months the postal income had reached only £5,000.

The service, far from improving, became less and less regular. A new contract that began in March 1707 made some concessions, but with little effect when the toll of vessels became greater than ever. Dummer reported in 1710 that the contract for five vessels in the West Indian service had required him to furnish three times that number: 'These misfortunes have always kept me building.'

---

[1] *T.L.B.*, 1699-1705, 208, 235, 241, 262. The contract was for three years from January 25, 1704-5, and could be extended 'if the war should continue so long'.
[2] *Fal. L.B.*, I, 53, 77.

Since French privateers swarmed along the route up the Channel, the packet-boats were allowed to make Bideford on the north Devon coast. The Post Office was even willing for the mails to leave from Bideford, and to return to such places as seemed most secure.

The end came through the insistence of Dummer's creditors. In September 1711 four of his five vessels—one at Falmouth and three on their return to Bideford—were taken over to pay his debts. Edmond Dummer's ambitious plan for a transatlantic packet service had come to a 'full stop' after it had been carried on after a fashion for nine years.[1]

This attempt at a long-distance packet service was so discouraging that mails once again went back and forth in merchantmen or warships. An official West Indian service was not to be tried out again until the mid-eighteenth century.

Although the colonies on the North American Continent were without a regular packet connection with the mother country, they had an intercolonial postal service. It was set up in 1692 by an Andrew Hamilton, who was the deputy in North America for the contractor, Thomas Neal. Towards the end of the century Thomas Neal, who had borrowed money from a Robert West, was unable to repay the loan with the result that his interest in the farm passed, in 1699, to Andrew Hamilton and Robert West. After Hamilton's death in 1703, the postal service was continued by West and Hamilton's widow. Three years later—Dummer's packets were then serving the West Indies—they asked for the right 'to erect Packet-Boats for the carrying of Letters and Passengers betwixt England and New York'. The petition was turned down.

Nor did anything come of an offer made in the same year by a Sir Jeffry Jeffrys. He had the *Eagle* of 180 tons at Cowes in the Isle of Wight that was offered for two round voyages a year. Jeffrys also wanted to carry freight 'according to ye rates set for Mr Dummer's Packets'. Although the Postmasters-General wrote the Treasury in favour of the *Eagle*, nothing came of the offer.

The growing interest in a possible packet service to New York led to an official report on this route by William Blathwayt, Auditor-General for the Plantations. In August 1706 he suggested that the packet-boats to the American mainland might go eight times a year, not monthly as was the schedule for the West Indian service, Blathwayt proposed that the charge for mail should be less than that

[1] *T.L.B.*, 1699-1705, 263, 1706-11, 6, 21; 1716-24, 31. Edmond Dummer died insolvent in 1713.

to the West Indies, as the inhabitants of the continental colonies were 'more numerous but poorer'. The governors of the mainland colonies added their plea for a regular mail route. Governor Cornford of New York, for example, wrote in 1708: 'I wish with all my heart that packet-boats were established to some port on this Continent.'[1]

The only result of the fervent desire for a packet connection with New York was a brief and inadequate service that began at the end of 1709. A William Warren of London proposed monthly voyages from Bristol to New York by the use of four vessels of 60 to 70 tons. No reply to Warren's offer has been preserved in the Post Office Records, but an advertisement by Warren has survived in the British Museum. The sheet announced that the Queen had granted him a monthly correspondence. His vessels were built 'of strength to resist the seas . . . and commodiously contrived for entertaining Passengers, who will be kindly Received on Board on Easie Terms'. The rates for the letters were set at 1s single.

William Warren furnished a service of sorts to New York just as the Edmond Dummer's efforts came to a sad end. Warren's *Royal Anne* is mentioned several times in the correspondence from New York. Governor Saltonstall reported an arrival in November 1710. By January next, however, we read of the 'uncertainty of the packets, for we have had none here since the beginning of November last'. Governor Hunter reported the *Royal Anne*, 'our third packet-boat', in June 1711. The service ceased in 1711 or 1712. The American mainland colonies were not to enjoy a regular packet connection until the mid-century.[2]

---

[1] *T.L.B.*, 1699-1705, 126-7; 1706-11, 33-35, 137; *Cal. Tr. P.*, 1702-7, 267, etc.; *Cal. S.P. Am. & W.I.*, 1708-9, 10. Jeffry's letter has been reprinted in Frank Staff, *The Transatlantic Mail* (1956), 114.

[2] See *Cal. S.P. Am. & W.I.*, volumes for 1710-11 and 1714-15. The *P.O. General Accounts* note payments made to Warren of £188 in 1710 and £252 in 1711-12. For the advertisement, see *Br. Museum*, 816 M 10, no. 60.

5

ATLANTIC MAILS IN PEACE AND WAR
—1700-63

THE reign of Queen Anne, almost wholly taken up with the War of the Spanish Succession, is notable for several postal changes. The union of the Scottish and English parliaments in 1707 was preliminary to a unified postal system for the whole of Great Britain. And in 1711, just as the reign was coming to an end, a general Post Office Act brought the postal arrangements up to date, and provided for the use of higher postal rates to help in meeting the expense of the long wars. The Act of 1711 was the most important measure since that which had 'legally' settled the Post Office in 1660.

The preamble of the Act justified the higher rates on the ground that 'Posts have at great charges been established by Packet-Boats between . . . England and the West Indies, and also on the Mainland in North America, through most of Her Majesty's Plantations and Colonies in those Parts, as also to divers Ports to which no Packet-Boats were till lately settled.' For the first time Parliament sanctioned rates on letters by packet to Corunna and Lisbon, a single letter costing 1s 6d, the same charge as for Spanish letters through France. Rates to the West Indies were made the same as those for Portugal and Spain. Letters to New York were charged 1s single, just as the short-lived Warren service out of Bristol was coming to an end. The charge for mail to Holland, France and the Spanish Netherlands was 10d single. Letters bound for Italy via Amsterdam or Antwerp cost 1s single. Letters for northern Europe were also 1s single, but only as far as Amsterdam.

The Act included the use by government of the postal income 'to carry on and finish the present war'. Each week the Post Office was to pay £700 into the Exchequer—over £36,000 yearly—and this was to continue for many decades after the death of Queen Anne. The ship-letter practice started by Colonel Whitley was now given parliamentary sanction—1d to the captain of a ship for every incoming letter and packet that he delivered at a home port. This practice brought in considerable revenue, since the ship-letter penny was added to the inland rate from the port to the destination for the letter. During the second half of the year 1708—to give a random illustration—the ship-letters numbered 43,709.[1]

Out of deference to Scotland, the Act of 1711 set up a mail route between Scotland and Ireland, the termini being Port Patrick on the west Scottish coast and Donaghadee at the entrance of Belfast Lough. At the time, Port Patrick had only a weekly communication with Glasgow by foot-post, and Glasgow and Edinburgh were also connected by a foot-post. The setting up of a horse-post in 1712 between Glasgow and Edinburgh, and of a twice-weekly foot-post to Port Patrick from Glasgow, made the packet route to Ireland somewhat more useful. It actually opened in 1713. The new route to Ireland never compared for usefulness with that out of Holyhead.

PACKETS TO CORUNNA AND LISBON

The Falmouth packet station became more and more important as the European nations of France, Spain and the Netherlands vied with Great Britain for colonies and commerce. The route to Corunna and its extension to Lisbon had served to meet war-time needs, both for civilian mail and for official dispatches for the forces outside and inside the western Mediterranean. So evident was Britain's interest in this area that both Minorca and Gibraltar were retained by the peace settlement of 1713.

The Corunna service never ran a very smooth course. After the Spanish Succession War, it was resumed, but again interrupted when a long trade war with Spain broke the connection for a decade. Its resumption at the mid-century was brief, for it was again closed as soon as Spain joined France in the Seven Years' War. That brought the Corunna mail service to an end. Henceforth all letters to north-western Spain and northern Portugal went by way of Lisbon. The Postmasters-General were glad to see the last of this service.[2]

The route to Lisbon was on an altogether different footing. During these years of alternating war and unsettled peace with

---

[1] *Rec. Gen. Entry Bks.*, vol. for 1703-14.
[2] *T.L.B.*, 1715-24, 79, 124 and *T.L.B.*, 1792-3, 117-23 for a full but somewhat inaccurate summary of the Corunna services when there was some interest in reviving the Corunna mail route as war with France was resumed following the French Revolution.

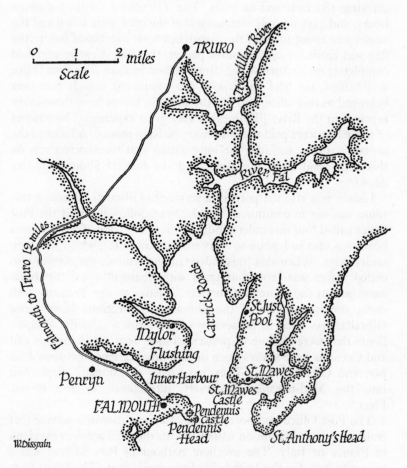

MAP 1. Falmouth, the Atlantic Packet Port, 1689–1840

Labels on the map:

TRURO

Tresillian River

River Fal

Falmouth to Truro 12 miles

Carrick Roads

St. Just Pool

Mylor
Flushing

St. Mawes

Penryn

Inner Harbour

St. Mawes Castle

FALMOUTH

Pendennis Castle

Pendennis Head

St. Anthony's Head

W.Disspain

0   1   2 miles
Scale

France and Spain, the relations with Portugal remained uniformly cordial. The packet-boats continued to ply across the Bay of Biscay, despite occasional losses to the enemy. Two packets were captured in the forties. The *Townshend*, when being used as an extra boat in 1740 to carry dispatches to England, fell in with a Spanish privateer carrying 180 men and 20 guns. The *Townshend* fought for seven hours, and gave up only after several of the crew were killed and the vessel was about to sink; the dispatches went overboard before the flag was hauled down. Another packet, the *King George*, vanished completely on a return voyage from Lisbon in 1746. The Post Office was baffled, for 'she was one of the completest vessels that ever belonged to this office, and but the summer before been thoroughly repaired in the River [Thames] at very great expense'. The widows of those lost were paid the customary pension money. A letter to the captain's widow includes the information that the shortest run on this route had been five days, and the longest about forty-five days.[1]

Lisbon was also the port for a service to Gibraltar, although this route was not in continuous use. In 1717, following what the Post Office called 'our misunderstanding with Spain', one of the Corunna boats was sent to Lisbon to carry mail to Gibraltar, which was then under seige. When this 'misunderstanding' ended, the service also ended. After war broke out again with Spain in 1739, two boats were put on the route to Gibraltar. A letter to the Treasury well states the importance of the Gibraltar connection: 'Ever since Gibraltar has been in possession of the Crown . . . the Pacquet Boats that were in time of peace stationed between Falmouth and and Corunna have always been in war time stationed between Lisbon and Gibraltar . . . They have been occasionally dispatched into the Mediterranean to carry intelligence to the British Fleet.'

The Post Office also bore the expense for a dispatch service that connected Port Mahon on Minorca with the mail services overland in France or Italy. The excellent harbour of Port Mahon was a favourite base for the British Mediterranean fleet. The Post Office objected in vain to bearing the cost of this service, since it carried almost no civilian mail. The dispatch boat made connection with the French posts at Marseilles, if the two countries were at peace, and with Genoa when Marseilles was closed by war. Port Mahon was taken by the French in 1756, but at the conclusion of the Seven

[1] *T.L.B.*, 1742-59, 56, 133-6; *Cal. Tr. B. & P.*, 1739-41, 502

Years' War it was returned to Great Britain, and a packet-boat was again put on this duty—until 1783 when Minorca was finally ceded to Spain.

TRANSATLANTIC ROUTES

The mid-century wars with France and Spain led to a revival of the transatlantic packet services, both to the West Indies and to the mainland colonies of North America. A revival of the West Indian services was considered early in the forties by the Government, although the Post Office was not in favour of renewal. 'We can see no occasion' according to a letter sent the Treasury, 'for any West Indian boats, which were the articles that so largely swelled the account' in the War of the Spanish Succession. Nevertheless, the Post Office was ordered to reopen the service. The first packet-boat left Falmouth about Christmas of 1745.

Experience with the renewed West Indian service seemed to justify the objections of the Post Office, for the postage obtained was even smaller than it had been thirty years before. In consequence, the second trial of a regular service to the Islands was given up in 1749. The total revenue from the mail carried on the last outward voyage was £39, and on the last one home, £48.[1]

When it became only too clear that another war with France was in the offing, the West Indian route was reopened in 1755. A contract was arranged with Richard Stratton and John Sargent of London for four vessels of 150 tons each. The contractors were to be paid nearly £9,000 a year, and the Post Office agreed to make good any loss or damage.

The third trial of a West Indian packet service was even more trying. The *New Duke* was taken by a French privateer even before the Seven Years' War officially opened. And other losses of packet-boats during the war added to the heavy expense. The Post Office was so exasperated that it put the situation plainly: 'This correspondence appears to us to have been originally set on foot with a view to the conveniency of the State in time of war rather than that of Commerce.' The packet-boats were stopped for a short time before the end of the war, but the route was reopened with the return of peace in 1763. At last it became a permanent line of transatlantic communication.

A packet service to New York seemed as imperative as had that

[1] *T.L.B.*, 1742-59, 81, 159, 180; 1760-1, 64; *Est. Bk.* for 1747.

for the West Indies when another war with France—the Seven Years' War—was in the making. In both cases, the packet route would furnish essential carriage for official dispatches. The New York service began in 1755, the same year that the West Indian route had been reopened. The Postmasters-General regarded the New York line as 'altogether new'. The feeble efforts of William Warren forty-five years earlier were so brief and irregular that they had been forgotten.

The 'new' route was started by the use of trial vessels so that the Post Office would have some experience on which to base a contract. One thing was sure, larger vessels would be needed on the rough north Atlantic than those going back and forth to the West Indies— the New York packet-boats were to be of 200 tons. The Post Office informed the Treasury that the first vessel, the *Earl of Halifax* (Captain John Morris) was to cost £700 for the round trip: Captain Morris reached New York in February 1756.

The cautious way in which the route was opened makes it possible to reckon the time taken by sailing vessels of the eighteenth century in crossing the Atlantic. The *Duke of Cumberland* made three round voyages, one of 93 days in 1762, a second of 132 days in 1764, and a third in 111 days. The *Pitt* took 93 days in 1762-3, but 155 days for a round trip in 1764. Normally the packet-boats remained in New York Harbour about three weeks. The voyages were intended to be monthly when the route was in full working order, but only four voyages were made in the first two years.[1]

At times, however, the packet-boats dallied in New York for much more than three weeks. In 1757, after the war was on, they were held up for months, as we learn from an account of a voyage that carried Benjamin Franklin to England: at the time he was Deputy Post-master-General for North America.[2] Benjamin Franklin went up to New York in the spring of 1757 to make the voyage to England on a mail-packet. Three were lying in New York Harbour when he arrived. Those that should have left for Falmouth after a delay of about three weeks, had been held back by the military commander, the Earl of Loudoun. He regarded the mail-packets as dispatch boats for sending information home in connection with a proposed

---

[1] For the revival of these services, see *T.L.B.*, 1742-59, 246-54; 1760-71, 47-48, 63-64; *Cal. S.P. Home*, 1760-5, 18-19; Butler, R. L., *Doctor Franklin Postmaster General* (1928), 61ff.

[2] Franklin had been postmaster of Philadelphia as early as 1737. In 1753 he was appointed Deputy Postmaster-General of North America jointly with William Hunter, the postmaster of Williamsburg. They succeeded Elliot Benger, the former lone holder of the office.

expedition to attack the French stronghold of Louisburg on Cape Breton.

Benjamin Franklin arrived in April, and waited over two months before Lord Loudoun permitted one of the packets to leave for England. Fortunately for Franklin, he was a passenger on the *General Wall* (Captain Lutwidge) that sailed for Falmouth at the end of June. The other two—one of them was the *Harriott* (Captain John Bonnell)—were forced, along with their transatlantic passengers and mails, to accompany the naval expedition on its way north. Lord Loudoun decided, after staying for some time in Halifax, to return to New York without attacking Louisburg after all, and the two mail-packets in his convoy went back to New York as well!

The *General Wall* that carried Franklin to England was regarded as a fast sailer: Franklin reported that she had gone once at the rate of 13 knots. Her speed was effective, for 'we were several times chas'd in our passage but outsail'd everything'. The *General Wall* left on June 25th, after waiting in New York for seventy-four days, and reached Falmouth in just over three weeks. Ten days later Franklin was in London; he had stopped to take a look at Stonehenge on the way.[1]

The mail-packets on the New York route were attacked again and again. The *General Wall* despite her boasted speed, was captured in 1758, and had to be ransomed. The *Harriot* was more fortunate. She behaved so courageously in a fight with a French privateer, that Captain Bonnell received £100 as a reward. This may well have been the vessel that carried orders to General Amherst; the captain to whom they were entrusted was warned that 'great care must be taken that they fall not into the enemy's hands'.[2]

The upkeep of this route had been a heavy burden. It cost about £9,000 a year, but the postal income was hardly a fifth of the expense. Yet there was no thought of discontinuing the New York packet-boats when peace came in 1763; the addition of Canada and Florida to the British colonies gave Britain the whole of the North American seaboard.

The pay for the sailors who faced the dangers of the sea and of war was astonishingly small. Throughout this half century the

---

[1] See *Franklin's Autobiographical Writings*, ed. Carl Van Doren (1946), pp. 754ff Franklin did not name the packet-boat, but positive identification has been furnished by the *P.O. Gen. Accts.* The vessel was named after an Irishman, Richard Wall, who spent most of his life in Spain where he took an active part in politics; for some years after 1748 he was Spain's ambassador to England.

[2] *T.L.B.*, 1760-71, 47; *Cal. S.P. Home*, 1760-5, 15-19, 244.

crewmen received only 1s a day, out of which 1s was reserved each month for the smart and pension fund. On the remainder they were expected to care for their families ashore. In 1760 the men complained loudly about their wages because of the high price of provisions for their families, with the result that the monthly 1s was not held back for smart and pension money. The crews were furnished food and drink at a rate that seems niggardly, to put it mildly; it remained at 7d or 7½d per man per day until 1763, when it was raised to 9d.

The Post Office should not take all the blame for this pinch-penny attitude, for the Treasury kept a constant watch on all expenditures, and its approval was needed for any changes that affected the postal income. Watchfulness was necessary since post-office funds were being diverted to other uses than the improvement and extension of the services, and a more liberal allowance to the crews. At this time, it was a source for preposterous pensions that had nothing whatever to do with mail carrying. In 1760 the pensions charged against the postal income were about £25,000 annually. And the Treasury was still receiving £700 a week from the Post Office under the terms of the Act of 1711.[1]

The less fortunate seamen, who sailed their small craft on the open Atlantic, deserve high praise. In the Seven Years' War, fourteen transatlantic packet-boats were taken by the enemy, and many more endured attacks but avoided capture, although there was often loss of life.

---

[1] *T.L.B.*, 1742-59, 162, 253; 1760-1, 265; and the *P.O. Gen. Accts.*

6

THE PACKETS DURING THE
AMERICAN REVOLUTION

THE Seven Years' War that ended in 1763 was so decisive a victory
for Britain that numerous territories were added to her transatlantic
holdings. The French gave up Canada. The West Indies where
Admiral Rodney had won a notable victory at the end of the war was
the scene of important changes. Dominica, St Vincent, Grenada
and Tobago were now within the Empire. Although Havana had
been taken from Spain just as the war ended, it was returned by the
treaty of peace. Spain, however, ceded to Great Britain the vast
region of the nearby mainland known as East and West Florida,
including the ports of Pensacola in the Gulf of Mexico and St
Augustine on the Atlantic seaboard.

The transatlantic additions to the Empire had much to do with
stimulating a new postal Act. According to the preamble, the Act of
1765 was needed because of increasing 'Trade and Commerce, and
the vast Accession of Territory gained by the late Treaty of Peace'.
The Act specified the charge on correspondence between the West
Indies and the mainland colonies; it was set at 4d the single sheet
and so on to 1s 4d per ounce for packets. It also listed inland routes
within the transatlantic colonies: the lowest, for single letters
travelling no more than 60 miles, was also 4d. The Act extended
ship-letter regulations to the colonies, no vessel being allowed to
'break bulk' before delivering letters to the postmaster at any port in
the British dominions.

PEACE-TIME ATLANTIC SERVICES

The Post Office had hoped to end the expensive service to the
West Indies with the coming of Peace—a premature decision, as it
was soon manifest that the packet routes should not be ended, but
lengthened to serve the new colonial additions. Canadian mails might

go by way of New York, but the southern mainland colonies, especially the Floridas, should be served from the West Indies. Charles Town in South Carolina—later known as Charleston—was chosen as the most suitable port for linking the mainland and the islands. When an Edward Lewis proposed a packet service to include the newly conquered territories in the Caribbean and the Gulf of Mexico, he obtained a contract in 1763. The packets were to stop first at the various Leeward Islands, then go on 1,000 miles to Jamaica, from there to Pensacola—another 1,000 miles—thence around Florida to St Augustine and on to Charleston. From this port they were to return directly to Falmouth. The chief drawbacks to this roseate scheme were the tremendous distances to be traversed by the packets, the all-too-frequent danger of hurricanes, and the almost complete absence of any passable land route between Charleston and New York, 1,500 miles to the north.

The first vessel to use the new route was the *Suffolk* (Captain James Bull) that left Falmouth in January 1765. The schedule proved utterly impossible with only three packets to make the numerous stops, and yet give a monthly service. By the end of the year Lewis was asking for two additional boats of 170 tons, to be used for 'so difficult and in the winter so dangerous a navigation'.

Soon a number of changes were necessary. Even five transatlantic packets were insufficient for a direct service that included Pensacola, St Augustine and Charleston. The Post Office, therefore, decided that the West Indian packet-boats should return directly from Jamaica to Falmouth, and that the mainland ports should be visited four times a year by smaller vessels of only 45 tons that would begin and end their voyages at Jamaica. Still another change was made when the home Government realized that a service for Charleston but four times a year showed too little regard for the southern mainland colonies. The result was an entirely new packet route between Falmouth and Charleston. This service, which was carried on by four packets, began in 1765, in the hope that the growth of the southern colonies would justify the expenditure.[1]

The regular schedule was difficult to maintain on the routes to the West Indies and the southern mainland. The trying conditions faced in those regions were feelingly described by the captains when they collectively petitioned in 1775 for larger crews. 'From the time

[1] *T.L.B.*, 1760-71, 88-90, 142, 262, 275-97; I (1771-8), 2-6, 24-27, 115. The volume of the *Treasury Letter Books* for 1771-8 began a new series; the serial number will be used hereafter.

we begin to approach the Southern Latitudes', they wrote, 'our People are seized generally with Disorders incident to these Climates . . . and sometimes more than half the Ship's Company are on the Surgeon's List.' The vessels were often so short-handed that it was even difficult to get up their anchors 'in passing from island to island which are in number nine'. In sailing from Jamaica, they usually encountered strong gales, and 'our Passage through the Bahama Islands is Tempestuous and so critical that we with great difficulty clear them'. And then came the change to colder weather on the homeward voyage: 'After passing through the tropical Climates which are so replete with noxious Vapous and Distemperatures of the Air, we very suddenly plunge into northern Climes which change the disorders from feverish to rheumatic Complaints.'

As to the New York service. When the war ended, the Post Office did not question its increased value, now that Canada was in the Empire. Although the income in postage on this route had not been encouraging, it was sure to increase, because of the great extent of the mainland colonies, the rapid growth in population, and their marked increase in wealth. Only four packets were used in 1763; a fifth was added in 1770 to assure a regular service.

The two deputy postmasters-general for North America at the time were Benjamin Franklin and Thomas Foxcroft. In 1764, they made an elaborate survey of the land communications in the hope of bringing such distant colonies as Quebec and the Carolinas into a regular connection with New York. Governor Murray in Canada and the merchants up the St Lawrence wanted a monthly service from New York immediately following the arrival of the packet-boat.[1]

The agreement for the hiring of a packet-boat was signed by the captain, even though he often had but a fourth or fifth share in the ownership. The agreements—a number have been preserved—were so elaborate that they furnish a good record of what the Post Office expected in the eighteenth century. The one made in 1768 by the Postmasters-General (The Earl of Bessborough and Lord Grantham) with Captain John Jones of Falmouth for the hire of the *Grantham* on the West Indian route will serve as an example.[2]

Captain Jones was to furnish 'one stout two masted double deck vessel . . . a prime sailer British-built and rigged and equipped in

[1] *Est. Bks.*, 1769, 1770. A Chief Central Office was set up at Charleston, under George Roupell; his region included the Carolinas, Georgia, the Floridas and the Bahamas.

[2] *Rec. Gen. Entry Bks.*, 1755-78, 200-6.

the completest manner and navigated by eighteen hands . . . all British subjects'. The Captain was to receive £1,572 14s 6d per year for the 'Hire Wear and Tear of the said Vessel and for Officers and Seamen's Wages and Victuals Port Charges Lights and all other Charges . . . in satisfaction of all risks hazard and damage . . . [by] the Sea Distress of Weather Fire Pirates or otherwise whatsoever.'

The contract required the *Grantham* to make two trips out and home every year. She was to sail from the home port within twenty-four hours of receiving the mail, wind and weather permitting. In her passage outward from Falmouth the captain was 'to deliver His Majesty's Mails and Packets of Letters or Expresses at the several Islands of Barbadoes, Granada [sic], Antigua, St Christophers and Jamaica as also at Pensacola . . . and shall return from Charles Town directly back to Falmouth.' If the vessel carried 'poor shipwrecked sailors . . . unable to defray their Passage home', the Post Office allowed the Captain 7½d per day for their victualling. On his return he was to send to the Post Office in London the journal of the voyage and a true list of the passengers, 'describing their respective Qualities'. The contract was for seven years.

It was agreed finally that 'upon the breaking out of a Rupture between the Crown of Great Britain & any Foreign Power the said John Jones shall have the option of either withdrawing the said Vessel . . . or of continuing it upon such conditions . . . as shall then be offered'. If the packet-boat was used during a war, the crew was enlarged, including among others a gunner and an armourer. If the vessel was taken, burnt or sunk by the enemy, the Post Office agreed to pay the captain the full value of the vessel. He was expected to bring another vessel into the service in place of the one lost. But if the hired packet-boat were merely stranded or damaged and could be repaired, the Post Office agreed to make good the necessary repairs, with such other 'Allowances as are agreeable to the Rules of the Navy in such cases'.

A COLONIAL WAR

By the mid-seventies a new war had to be faced by the packet services. It was not at the outset a 'rupture' with a foreign power but with thirteen of the mainland colonies in North America. The numerous grievances that led to this colonial revolt need not be detailed here. The revolt was partly the result of the comparative remoteness of the American colonies, the complete absence of regular communications before 1745, and the infrequent services after the mid-century. Open resistance began in 1775 in the neighbourhood of Boston. With the Declaration of Independence on July 4, 1776 the break was complete. When the colonists seemed likely to succeed, France recognized their independence (1777), and soon entered the war against Great Britain. The French were eager to avenge the humiliation, and to repair the losses, of the Seven Years' War. Spain followed suit, of course, and even the Netherlands joined Britain's enemies in 1780. A colonial revolt had become a general war.

It was essential to maintain the three packet routes across the Atlantic, since the packets, once again, would be useful for dispatch purposes as well as for the transportation of regular mails. And their speed should be increased, if possible, to meet war-time demands more effectively.

One device that became general at this time for increasing the speed of the packets was the sheathing of the bottoms of the vessels with copper. This gave a cleaner and smoother surface, guarding the wooden hulls from the teredo worms that were especially active in such areas as the West Indies and the Gulf of Mexico. When the Admiralty was found to favour the 'experiment', the *Thynne*, a West Indian packet, was sheathed with copper. This so increased the speed of the vessel that, in 1778, Lord George Germain, the Secretary of State for the Colonies ordered the Post Office, the owners, to 'sheathe them with copper with all possible Dispatch'.

Copper bottoms certainly increased the speed of the vessels. The agent at Falmouth wrote in 1778 that the *Hillsborough* had returned from Jamaica in fifty-two days after her bottom had been sheathed with copper:

'She never was esteem'd a remarkably fast Vessel, but by the Log Book kept on this voyage . . . and the Character given of her by all on Board . . . the Copper has qualified her to sail as fast any Ship.

Indeed Captain Rainier of the Navy and his Lieutenant who came home passengers in the *Hillsborough* gave an amazing account of her Celerity, and declared that she went 9 knot & 2 fathoms by the best time glasses, with the Weather Leeches of the maintopsail & mainsail shaking . . . I hope every Pb Bt on this station will be copper'd . . . as it will save seven or eight days by being always clean when those with fir sheathing or single bottoms must wait for spring Tides to clean.'

Stephen Bell, the agent at Falmouth, was certain that sheathed vessels 'would be prepared to go any place where worms abound . . . more particularly at this critical juncture of public affairs'. When the *Anna Teresa*, after a return voyage from Jamaica, was about to be sheathed, the agent wrote in November 1778: 'I verily believe that had the packets which have been taken been furnished with it, some if not all at this moment would be in the service.'[1] During 1776 'rebel privateers' were active on the sea lanes. Massachusetts shipping, in particular, was extremely troublesome. Over 600 letters of marque were issued by the Continental Congress to vessels belonging to Massachusetts, and a thousand more were 'legalized' by the General Court of the Colony. The privateers were excellent sailers, and went far afield. Even the Lisbon packet-boats were armed late in 1776 when the Post Office learned that several vessels had been taken in the Bay of Biscay by an American privateer. The North Sea packets were furnished armament after the capture of the *Prince of Wales* on a voyage to the Netherlands from Harwich in 1777, taken by a privateer with the appropriate name of *Surprize*.[2]

The first packet-boat to be captured was the *Swallow*, taken early in 1777 by a privateer named the *Reprisal*. Among the four packets lost in that year was the *Weymouth* when she was returning from Jamaica; she was captured by the *Oliver Cromwell* 'belonging to Connecticut'.

The year 1778 was discouraging, for five mail-packets were lost to the Americans and the French. In June, the brigantine *Nancy* of New London, Connecticut, took the *Le Despencer* when on her way to New York with dispatches and mails, and several passengers. The passengers gave their paroles. This loss may well have occasioned a letter that was sent from New York by Lord Carlisle; he had crossed the Atlantic as the head of a commission of peace. Lord Carlisle wrote: 'We are going to send away another packet, and if my advice is followed we shall send them all away, as we ought not

---

[1] *T.L.B.*, I, 120-8, 149-51, 346-7; *Fal. L.B.*, II, 29, 46, 48. It cost about £600 to copper a bottom, and took at least six weeks. The copper plates measured 4 feet by 14 inches.

[2] *T.L.B.*, I, 129-31, 145-7, 192; *Fal. L.B.*, II, 34. Over 3,000 British merchantmen were taken by the Americans during the war, according to G. W. Allen, *A Naval History of the American Revolution* (Boston, 1913). S. E. Morison, in *The Maritime History of Massachusetts* (Boston, 1921), notices this 'legalized piracy'.

to expect above one in four to escape our two enemies, the French and the Americans, who are now very powerful indeed at sea.'[1]

So great was the need for packet-boats that the Government decided to build them at its own expense. 'We have ordered two new packets', wrote Lord Germain, 'of 287 tons . . . to be sheathed and bolted with copper.' The haste in ordering the new vessels followed a criticism by Lord Howe of the 'bad sailing' of the *Swallow*. The new vessels were named the *Speedy* and the *Swift* in the hope that they might live up to their names. By the end of 1778 the building of new packet-boats by the Government had become a settled policy. Drastic action of some sort was needed, for three of the nine packets on the New York and Charleston stations had been taken by this time. Nor did 1779 prove a better year; eleven packets were lost. By the end of the year the *Speedy* and the *Swift* were ready, and gave hope that henceforth the service would be carried on 'with greater Credit and Dispatch'.[2]

Disappointment followed disappointment. Six more packets were captured in 1780. To everybody's amazement two of the victims were Holyhead packets that were used on the run across the Irish Sea to Dublin. The Holyhead postmaster wrote the General Post Office in London in March 1780:

'I am sorry to acquaint you that the *Hillsborough* and the *Besborough* [sic] packet boats have been taken by the *Black Prince* and [the *Black*] *Princess* . . . The *Hillsborough* left this port at eleven o'clock yesterday morning, with one mail and was taken at six o'clock in the afternoon. The *Besborough*, with two mails from Dublin, was taken this morning at eight o'clock, within six leagues of the Head [Holyhead]; the three mails were sunk, and the packets being ransomed, arrived here this evening. The crews of both privateers were Irish.'

In fact, these two 'American' privateers were commissioned by Benjamin Franklin, who was then in France as the representative of the revolting colonies. A third Holyhead packet, the *Le Despencer*,

---

[1] J. Fenimore Cooper, *History of the Navy of the United States of America* (Philadelphia, 1839), furnishes the name of the *Swallow*'s captor. The official British account of the loss of the *Le Despencer* records her capture by *two* American privateers after a hard fight. The American prize court, on the contrary, stated that the *Nancy* took the *Le Despencer*, without assistance and after a short engagement. See W. F. Middlebrook, *History of Maritime Connecticut in the American Revolution* (Salem, Mass., 1925), II, 166, and see below.
[2] *T.L.B.*, I, 345-7; II, 2-6, 57-59; *Fal. L.B.*, II, 72-73.

was nearly taken when she hastened to Dublin with the news of the captures. She just managed to get over the bar into Dublin Harbour with the privateers in full chase.[1]

Eleven more packet-boats were taken in 1781, and six in 1782 before the war came to an end. In July 1781 even the *Speedy* and the *Swift* were captured. Presumably they were taken while together near Barbados. The loss of two such well armed packets while in company should have been looked into, but nothing was done about it at the time. Six years later when a committee of the House of Commons was inquiring into certain abuses in the Post Office, the assistant secretary of the Post Office was asked if he had ever heard of packets being captured when not on their mail routes. He replied that he had heard insinuations 'no longer than two days ago' when a sailor called at the Post Office for his smart money. This former member of the crew of the *Swift* said that the *Speedy* and the *Swift* were taken by two disguised French frigates that had 'marked their ports' so as to look like Virginia tobacco ships. The two packets had chased the tobacco ships, only to be captured by the French. It was thought the packets were 'out of their course and that they ought not to have sailed so long in common together'.

A. H. Norway in his *History of the Post-Office Packet Service 1793-1815* (1896) relates at considerable length the capture of one packet that seems to have a remarkable likeness to the loss of the *Speedy* and the *Swift*. He wrote of one unnamed packet 'about the year 1780' which was running towards New Orleans—certainly well out of her prescribed route—when she saw two innocent looking vessels 'remarkably like sugar ships'. The packet proceeded to capture them, only to be taken by a disguised French frigate and her consort. Norway adds that the matter became known when a Committee of the House of Commons learned the true facts—when a sailor, formerly on the packet, called at the Post Office for his smart money, and gave the facts reluctantly. Norway's narrative looks very much like a disguised account of the capture of the *Speedy* and the *Swift*.[2]

---

[1] W. B. Clark, *Ben Franklin's Privateers* (Baton Rouge, La., 1956) for a full account of the privateering activity stimulated by Franklin. The *Black Prince* took numerous prizes, but no other mail-packets.

[2] No record of a packet lost in the manner related by Norway is to be found in the *T.L.B.* or the *Falmouth Letter-Books*. A. H. Norway was a Post Office man; he furnished no precise references, although he claimed that his volume was compiled from records 'chiefly official'. For the loss of the *Speedy* and the *Swift*, see *T.L.B.*, II, 216-7; *Walsingham Papers*, IV, 76, where some awkward questions were asked. The *10th Rep. Commrs. of Enquiry* (1788) declared that 'surmises attending the capture of these packets would have justified an inquiry which was never made'.

Occasionally a packet did succeed in capturing an American or French vessel. At least nine such captures occurred during the war, according to a report demanded of the agent at Falmouth, but the agent was unable or unwilling to furnish particulars. When the *Le Despencer*, captured in 1778, was taken into New London, Connecticut, one of the passengers wrote back to England that the engagement could have been avoided, but nothing came of the inquiry that resulted. It was never easy to obtain information from the Falmouth agent about what he called, with masterly under-statement, these 'inconsistent transactions'.[1]

When Lord Cornwallis surrendered at Yorktown in October 1781 the war on land was decided. Fighting at sea continued, Admiral Rodney winning a notable victory over the French in the spring of 1782 near the island of Dominica. Minorca was lost in that year, but Britain retained her hold on Gibraltar despite a siege of three and a half years. By the treaties signed in 1783 the Floridas were returned to Spain, and the thirteen revolting colonies were granted their independence. The short-lived Charleston service and that to Pensacola ended with the coming of peace.

Benjamin Franklin had been dismissed from his headship of the American colonial postal system before the war began, but both Roupell and Foxcroft remained loyal, and they continued to hold their offices during the war period. Foxcroft even came back from England to be the agent at Philadelphia when it was occupied by British forces, and he also served at New York for a time. Hugh Finlay, who had been the chief surveyor of the American colonial postal system, was promoted to Franklin's position. By the end of the war, however, Finlay was confining his attention to the northern colonies that remained loyal, where he was later to serve as Post-master-General of British North America. The chief task for Finlay was to develop communications between the St Lawrence seaway and the mother country, *without* sending letters through the United States.[2]

The packet service was harried more severely in the War of the American Revolution than in any previous war of the long series that began in 1689. Forty-three packets had been lost to the enemy during the war. Nineteen others had suffered so much damage that

[1] *T.L.B.*, I, 298; II, 242; *Fal. L.B.*, II, 60, 96, 190.

[2] For the letter dismissing Franklin on January 31, 1774, see the *American Letter Book* in the P.O. Record Room, London. See also *T.L.B.*, II, 14-26, 243, 249; *Walsingham Papers*, III, 379ff., 699.

they required extensive repairs. The expense from the loss of packets, from repairs needed for those damaged, and for building Government vessels was over £200,000.[1]

---

[1] See the Appendix for a listing of the captured packets and their captors; the list is believed to be complete. For the expenses, see *T.L.B.*, II, 122; V, 323. The *Walsingham Papers*, V, 1279-80 furnishes detailed costs of the packet services for each year.

7

TAKING STOCK—1783-93

THE war that ended in 1782 brought some changes in the trans-atlantic routes. Communications with the West Indies had even expanded during the war, two separate services going on occasion, to the West Indies. In 1793 the Post Office was using ten packets to carry mails to the Caribbean, five for the Leeward Islands, and five more for a direct service to Jamaica. The Jamaica packet left on the first Wednesday of the month, and a second vessel left on the third Wednesday, making its first call at Barbados, and then visiting the other Leeward Islands before its return to England. This fort-nightly service to the West Indies was supplemented by the use of small vessels to carry mail back and forth between the islands, and as feeders for the packets that crossed the Atlantic. Even the West Indian merchants could find no fault with these elaborate arrange-ments.[1]

The instructions sent to the head postmasters of the islands were full and precise. The postmaster, on the arrival of the packet-boat or the inter-island schooner, delivered the letters. If any remained in his hands more than three weeks, he was to return them to London with the reason for the non-delivery written on the outside, such as 'Not to be Found, Gone Away, Dead, Refused and the like'. Letters sent to other islands and to places in America and the United Kingdom were to be put in separate bags 'with a Tickett in each bag expressing the number of Letters'. A quarterly statement was to be sent to London giving the number of letters and the total amount of the postage.

The postmasters seem to have been very lax or lamentably ignorant of their duties, so much so, that John Palmer sent further

---

[1] *T.L.B.*, II, 249; *Palmer Papers*, Bundle IV, no. 107. John Palmer had introduced the mail-coaches in 1784, and was appointed Comptroller-General of the Mails in 1786. Until his dismissal in 1792, Palmer waged a largely unsuccessful battle for various improvements in the carriage of mails on land and sea. He and Lord Walsingham, one of the Postmasters-General from 1787 to 1794, were usually at odds. For Palmer's acitivites, see Ellis, *The Post Office in the Eighteenth Century* (1958), pp. 99ff., and pp. 164-6.

instructions in 1791. He required the postage to be marked on all letters sent to London. A pair of scales and weights, and proper stamps for postpaid and free letters were suggested. This brought some curious replies. Several of the postmasters wrote that scales, weights, stamps and ink could not be purchased in the islands, and asked that supplies be sent. The postmaster at Tortola, Macnamara by name, wrote to ask for more salary and added: 'I am intirely [sic] ignorant of the mode of charging letters & of the rates of postage a predicament in which I believe the postmasters of the West Indies are universally in.'[1]

John Palmer found the revenue from the West Indies imperfect and irregular. Reports were slow and infrequent. By 1788 the postmasters in the West Indies owed the London office more than £20,000, nearly half of which was due from Francis Dashwood, the postmaster of Jamaica. The mail carried by the transatlantic packets was not large, averaging at this time only about 6,000 letters a month for all the islands. Palmer proposed that the postage be raised to 1s 8d for single letters and that one packet instead of two be sent each month. Lord Walsingham regarded such an idea as preposterous, and Lord Walsingham had his way.

The New York route was resumed at the end of the war, as a matter of course. Connection with the mainland was important, for the young United States was growing rapidly in population and wealth.

The colonies north of the United States, colonies that had remained loyal and had received numerous United Empire Loyalists from the south, deserved more attention. The Post Office set up an all-British route by having the New York packet-boats stop regularly at Halifax in Nova Scotia for eight months in the year. They were not expected to make Halifax during the winter months. There was some thought of an overland route between Halifax and Quebec, but it was much slower for Canadian mail than the carriage of mail by way of the Hudson to Albany and then on to Lake Champlain. One object of the all-British route was to guard the 'security of the State Correspondence'. Both the Governor of Canada, Lord Dorchester, and Hugh Finlay, the Postmaster-General of British North America, felt that the mails were not always safe, even in sealed bags, if they included matters regarding

---

[1] *Walsingham Papers*, I, 233ff., being instructions sent in 1788 to the postmaster of Montserrat. The postmasters of the more populous islands received salaries; that for the postmaster of Jamaica, £150 per annum, was by far the largest. See also *Palmer Papers*, Bundle IV, no. 126.

boundaries, 'or in the event of a war with other Powers about which the opinion of Congress might fluctuate'.[1]

After the war the Lisbon packets gave a weekly communication. John Palmer questioned this unnecessary extravagance, proposing that they serve Portugal as they were serving Spain—through France. Lord Walsingham was horrified at Palmer's temerity. Walsingham was sure that neither the ministers nor the merchants would hear of it for a moment. Walsingham was right. The Falmouth captains were also partial to the Lisbon route, if not for the same reasons. The Lisbon route meant for them more frequent returns to the home port, and it was more lucrative in fares and in the freight on bullion than the West Indian service.

The Dover packet-boats carried mails to Ostend after France joined the revolting colonists in 1779. Because of the great value of the Dover-Ostend route—it connected with the Tour and Tassis posts—the Post Office had replaced the older packet-boats by cutters of about 70 tons. The fast cutters were in use by March 1781, and were so effective that but one was taken, whereas five of the earlier Dover packets had been lost to the enemy in the previous two years.

A treaty with France in 1784 renewed the postal connection with France after several years of interruption. It provided for a service from London every Tuesday and Friday, and from Paris for London on Mondays and Thursdays. The chief change that came with the Treaty of 1784 was the agreement that French vessels should carry the French mails to Dover.

The service out of Harwich seems to have gone on with little interruption during the war, since the Netherlands did not join the enemies of Britain until 1780.

The postal connections with Ireland saw some changes. The 'very inferior' boats between Port Patrick and Donaghadee were replaced in 1790 by packets of about 40 tons. This crossing of the Irish Sea continued to be unimportant postally. On the contrary, the service between Holyhead and Dublin, carried on by five packet-boats, was of prime value, so much so that it became a daily service (except Sunday) shortly after the Seven Years' War.

After the coming of peace in 1782, the Post Office set up a third route to Ireland. The new route across the Irish Sea joined Milford Haven in South Wales with Waterford in southern Ireland. This

[1] *Walsingham Papers*, III, 259, 379-99; *10th Rep. Commrs.* (1788), 19; *T.L.B.*, VII, 64-65.

additional service was sought chiefly by the commercial and trading interests in southern England and Ireland in order to replace the roundabout route by way of Holyhead and Dublin. The Post Office opposed the proposal because it was certain not to pay its way. It seemed unnecessary because passage boats sailed frequently between Milford Haven and Waterford as well as between Bristol and Cork. But the objections of the Post Office were overruled, and this line of communication was opened in 1786. It began as a tri-weekly service, but soon afterwards, the number of boats were raised to five so that this southern route to Ireland would have the same daily service as that by way of Holyhead. The Post Office had bowed reluctantly to the demands of the trading interests, for this service was far from a financial success. The Milford mails were light, and there were few passengers—one to every forty that crossed to Ireland by way of Holyhead. It would have been better for the packet-boats to use Bristol and Cork, or to have the mails carried by passage boats.[1]

By the end of the eighties the services overseas were numerous and expensive, much more so than ever before in peace-time. Twenty-three packets were based on Dover, Harwich, Port Patrick, Holyhead and Milford Haven, and twenty more used Falmough for routes on the Atlantic. The total expense was about £53,000 a year.

CORRUPTION AND EXTRAVAGANCE

The general disappointment in Britain caused by the heavy burden of another long war led to Government-wide investigations. Readers of Edmund Burke will recall his abiding interest in 'economical reform'. The younger Pitt was also concerned about the extravagance and waste that burdened the State. A general house-cleaning was overdue. If this examination of the Post Office shows a manifest need for the removal of abuses in the postal administration, it should not be inferred that the Post Office was more currupt or careless than other departments of the Government. An Act of Parliament in the mid-eighties (25 Geo. III, ch. 19) authorized three commissioners to examine *all* the public offices for any abuses that might exist. They were to add such 'observations as shall occur to them . . . for abolishing and regulating any of the fees, gratuities, perquisites and emoluments'.

Our concern is with the Tenth Report of the Commissioners,

[1] *T.L.B.*, IV, 241-7; VIII, 143-51; *Est. Bks.*, 1790-4.

made in 1788. This Report on the Post Office followed one made in the previous year of a committee that had reviewed Lord Tankerville's dismissal as one of the Postmasters-General. The Tankerville Committee had asserted that the management of the Post Office was 'notorious', and had urged an immediate inquiry. Lord Tankerville had been appointed during the 'ministerial revolution' of 1782. 'I always understood,' said Lord Tankerville, 'that it was Mr Pitt's wish that I should regulate and reform abuses.'[1]

The three commissioners appointed in 1788 made a thorough search for abuses, with considerable success. Their findings on the Post Office in general need not be examined here. Some examples of jobbery in the conduct of the packet services overseas will indicate the need for reform.

The Postmasters-General, in addition to their large salaries and the income from patronage, received as much again from an allowance based on their share of the freight on money carried in the packet-boats. Among their fees on commission was a payment of over £12 on the appointment of all postmasters, every agent abroad, and all captains of the packet-boats.

The Secretary of the Post Office—known today as the Director-General—was Anthony Todd. He had entered the postal service in 1738, and had been the Secretary since 1768. Anthony Todd had gradually accumulated an impressive income from varied sources. His salary of £200 was supplemented by a commission of 2½ per cent 'on the whole expenditure of the Packet Boats employed at Dover, Harwich and Falmouth'—amounting in 1784 to £1,170. He also received income from his part ownership of a number of packet-boats. To the Commissioners, this princely accumulation was shocking, since the Secretary was primarily responsible for an efficient and orderly management.[2]

There were also strange doings at the ports used by the foreign-bound packets, especially at Dover. When Mr Barham, the Dover agent, retired in 1774 because of ill health, his post was sought and obtained by John Walcot, the postmaster of Dublin, since the Dover Office brought better returns. John Walcot, it might be added, was the nephew of Lord Le Despencer, a Postmaster-

---

[1] *Rep. Com. Tankerville*, 9, 69, 100. The *10th Rep. Commrs.* (1788) was not printed until 1793 and then without the numerous appendices. They have not survived, but the *Observations* of the Post Office on this Report have been preserved. The end of the matter came in 1797 with the *7th Rep. Com. on Finance*, that inquired as to how the recommendations of 1788 had been carried out.

[2] For Anthony Todd's dominance of the Post Office after 1768, see Ellis, op. cit., pp. 91ff.

General at the time. John Lees succeeded to the post in Dublin that was vacated by Walcot. Some of the financial consequences were very curious. Mr Barham, the postmaster at Dover, who retired because of ill health—his death was apparently not far off—was allowed to keep his full income, including both salary and perquisites, as a reward for his long and faithful service. Consequently John Lees was to pay Walcot, the successor of Barham at Dover, the full income of the Dublin Post Office during the life of Mr Barham, save for £300 a year that he retained. Both Walcot and Lees naturally looked forward to the early passing of Mr Barham.[1]

This seemed bad enough, but the shift was used by Lord Carteret, one of the Postmasters-General, for his own purposes, and this was done with the knowledge of Lord Le Despencer and Anthony Todd. Lord Carteret, who was financially embarrassed, took advantage of the shuffle to obtain an annuity for one of his friends, who was referred to in the correspondence as A.B., but whose real name was Peregrine Treves. John Lees of Dublin agreed, on the death of Barham, to pay Peregrine Treves an annuity of £350. This payment would be a pure sinecure, for Treves testified before a parliamentary committee that he was a Jew and a foreigner, and that the annuity was given him 'from friendship only'. Peregrine Treves admitted that he had never done any work in the Post Office, yet he appears in the *Establishment Book* of 1779 as one of Anthony Todd's 'clerks'.

Everybody concerned looked forward to, and expected relief from, the approaching death of Mr Barham, who was supposed to be in 'a very precarious state of health'. But, like so many pensioners, the unworried Mr Barham lived on and on in the enjoyment of his large income. The shifts had occurred in 1774, shortly before the Report of the Commissioners of Enquiry brought this set of proceedings to the light of day. The real sufferer, as Lord Carteret saw it, was his friend A.B.—Peregrine Treves— whose annuity from Dublin was unduly delayed. This was temporarily replaced by the appointment of a Francis Dashwood as postmaster of Jamaica in 1782, on condition of his paying to A.B. £300 annually.

When Lord Tankerville brought to light this complicated set of arrangements he lost his position as Postmaster-General. Lord Carteret was responsible for the dismissal. The Committee of 1787 that investigated this treatment of Lord Tankerville gave the affair

---

[1] *10th Rep. Commrs.* (1788), 4-6; *Rep. Com. Tankerville*, 12-13, 58-59. The Le Despencer correspondence in the Bodleian (Edgerton MSS., 2,136) includes some Walcot letters. See Ellis, op. cit., 92, for Todd's care of the Walcots and the Dashwoods.

publicity. The Committee of 1788, in their turn, looked on the whole business that centered around A.B. as 'extremely reprehensible and improper'.[1]

Nor were the conditions at the Falmouth station above reproach. For nearly four decades before 1785 the agency at Falmouth had been held in succession by George and Stephen Bell, father and son. Stephen Bell, whose agency came during the American Revolution and the post-war period, had a salary of £230, but it was trebled by perquisites from the packet-boat captains. The owners of the wagons that carried to London the bullion and money that came by the packets gave Bell 10 per cent of what they received for the carriage. His total income was well over £800 a year. The office in London became so suspicious of various other abuses as well that they sent an investigator to Falmouth to make a personal report. Bell was found to have made forgeries of receipts, to have neglected to account for some of his takings, to have sold supplies intended for the packet-boats. By 1785 Stephen Bell was so far behind on his payments to the Post Office in London—he owed about £2,500—that he committed suicide.

Benjamin Pender, who succeeded Stephen Bell as the agent at Falmouth, received an income of less than £400, and he paid a pension of £100 a year to Bell's widow. Whatever the salary of the agent at Falmouth, he at least gave constant attention to his duties.

The Commissioners also found that the agents abroad and the postmasters in the colonies sent in accounts that were imperfect and irregular. At the time of the inquiry, the various West Indian postmasters owed over £20,000, nearly half of which was due from Francis Dashwood, the postmaster at Jamaica, who had come to Carteret's rescue by paying an annuity to Peregrine Treves. The postal officials heatedly denied that Dashwood had been permitted 'to avail himself of indirect means, as the Commissioners suggest, to enable him to pay this annuity'.[2]

One of the most serious accusations made by the Commissioners was the purchase by postal officials of shares in the privately-owned packet-boats. The Inspector of Packets, for instance, had shares for a time in some of the packets that he was supposed to inspect. The investigation showed that 'many of the officers of the Post Office were owners of Packet Boats'. Thomas Todd, an assistant secretary

[1] *T.L.B.*, III, 34, 316; *10th Rep. Commrs.* (1788), 24.
[2] Ibid., 17, 25; *Rep. Com. Tankerville*, 76, 124, 148; *Observations* of the P. O. on the Report of 1788, 5.

under Anthony Todd, had shares in two boats. Of the officials owning shares, the most important as to his position in the Post Office was Anthony Todd himself. He was part owner of several boats, including a one-fourth ownership of the *Grantham*. The Commissioners observed: 'So considerable an advantage obtained from a service over which it was in Part his Duty to superintend, and to check Expense, needs no comment; it is only surprising that the Continuation of this should have been permitted even to this Day'. The revelations of 1788 ended packet-boat ownership by postal officials—with one exception. Francis Freeling, who succeeded Anthony Todd as secretary in 1798, wrote the Committee of 1797 that 'no persons in the service of this office have shares in any of the Packets, excepting Mr Todd, who has a fourth share of the *Grantham* on the Falmouth station, and whose Failure of Memory alone will account for his having said that he had none when he was asked the question'. The Commissioners of 1788 concluded that careless administration of the packet services had led to expenditures 'so enormous as almost to surpass credulity'.[1]

Charges of smuggling lay against the packet-boats, especially those on the Lisbon run. It seemed almost impossible to prevent the members of the crew from taking out what were mildly referred to as their 'little adventures'. J. S. Buckingham relates in his *Autobiography* of his first voyage from Falmouth in a Lisbon packet when he was a small boy of nine, presumably in the nineties. He wrote that the captain had as much as £5,000 worth of goods on board to be smuggled into Portugal, the other officers possibly half as much, and ordinary seamen £1,000 worth on the average. 'My first adventure,' he wrote, 'was a very humble one, not exceeding in value £50.' And he added a diverting account of how the goods were sold on the quay at Lisbon. Buckingham, who was born and bred on the shores of Falmouth Harbour, and was the son of a packet-boat captain, asserted that nearly everybody in Falmouth shared in the smuggling, it being thought 'honourable throughout all the sea-coast of Cornwall'[2].

The crews on the West Indian packets were guilty of smuggling among the islands. In 1787 the *Greyhound*, a Government-owned packet, was seized by the customs at Jamaica for taking on forty-seven cases of gin at the Dutch island of St Eustatius where the

---

[1] *10th Rep. Commrs.* (1788), 5, 25, 34; *Observations*, 200; *7th Rep. Com. on Finance* (1797), 7, 129.
[2] *Autobiography* (1855), I, 30, 63, 73, 88, 172. Some of his statements seem much exaggerated.

Two sailing-packet captains of the Falmouth Station, James Bull and his son John. John Bull succeeded his father in 1798. *Source:* Gay, *Old Falmouth*, 1903.

...topher Saverland, Fal-
...h packet agent at a
...al time, 1810–21.
...: G.P.O.

Two sailing packets at the time of the Napoleonic War, the *Diana* (foreground) and the *Prince of Wales*. Photo: G.P.O.

Lady Mary Pelham Packet. *Thomas Ewing* Commander.						
	Arrived	Sailed	Stay Allowed		Actual Stay	OBSERVATIONS
From September to February inclusive.			Days	Hours	Days	Hours	The Captain will here state the Cause of any Delay that may occur in any Port abroad.
Falmouth ...		13 Oct.					
Madeira ...	31 Octr.	1 Nov.		24		26	
Orotava	6 Nov.	8 Nov.			3		
Bahia ...	1 Dec.	6 Dec.	7			26	
Rio Janeiro ...	14 Dec.	7 Janr.	14		24		
Falmouth ...	19 March 1814						
From March to August inclusive.							
Falmouth ...							
Madeira ...				24			
Orotava							
Rio Janeiro ...							
Bahia ...			Land the Mail and proceed				
Falmouth ...							Commander

In case of Detention, by contrary Winds, or other Causes, it must be stated here, and the Particulars given in the Journal; and when any Governors, or Commanders of His Majesty's Forces, may find it necessary for the public Service to detain the Packet under your Command beyond the usual time, and there is no deputy Postmaster or Agent appointed by his Majesty's Postmaster General, you are in such Case to request a written Order for that Purpose, which must accompany this Journal as a Justification of your Conduct

You are to be very attentive to the correct Delivery of the Mails at each Port where you touch during the Voyage; *and to take especial Care that the whole of the Mails you receive for England, are put into the Portmanteau, which must be secured from Wet by a Tarpaulin, and immediately landed on your Arrival.*

You will be very particular in stating, for the Information of the Postmaster General, the Names of His Majesty's Ships which you may speak with on your Voyage, and also those which you may find and leave upon your Arrival at, and Departure from, each Port you may touch at.

☞ No Passenger to be taken in at *Rio Janeiro* without the Agent's Passport.

By Command of the Postmaster-General,
FRANCIS FREELING, Secretary.

Page from the log book of the *Lady Mary Pelham* for the Brazil voyage of 1813–14, when the *Pelham* and the *Montagu* were engaged by the American Privateer *Globe*. *Source:* G.P.O. Records.

captain had called to pick up a pilot. The captain insisted that he knew nothing about the gin until it had been found by the customs officers in Jamaica. In the following year the *Queen Charlotte*, on reaching Jamaica, was also found to have gin on board. It must have come on board, according to the captain, when he was ashore at St Kitts with the mail—he, too, knew nothing about it until it was discovered. Other cases of smuggling could be cited, for it was a perennial problem. One is at a complete loss to know how captains could be ignorant of smuggled goods in vessels less than a 100 feet long.

The indictment in the *Report* of 1788 was severe. Many of its suggestions for eliminating waste and corruption were accepted, with the result that a new establishment was in the making after 1788. The Falmouth agency was checked more carefully after that time, the West Indian postmasters were required to make their payments every quarter, no one in the Post Office was permitted to own shares in the packet-boats. The *Report* had recommended the sale of all Government-owned vessels. When new packets were to be hired, there was to be public advertisement of the need. Of the five Government-owned packets at Falmouth in 1788, all but one were sold in the next five years. The *Greyhound*, for instance, was auctioned off in April 1789 for £650. When the auction occurred she was described as a 'Prime Sailer, River Built and Copper Sheathed, Burthen 240 Tons'. The Commissioners also believed that boats the size of the *Greyhound* were much too large for the mail service, even if they had to cross the Atlantic. They recommended that such large boats be replaced by packets built for speed and with a tonnage of no more than 150 tons'.[1]

The most thorough overhauling that the Post Office had ever experienced was almost too late, for another war with France began in 1793.

---

[1] *10th Rep. Commrs.* (1788), 36-37; *7th Rep. Com. on Finance* (1797), 55. For the auction sheet announcing the sale of the *Greyhound* 'by the candle', see *Britain's Post Office*, p. 85.

8

TRIAL BY BATTLE—1793-1802

THE French Republic declared war against Great Britain in February 1793, shortly after Louis XVI had been beheaded. The war began as a war of ideas, on behalf of peoples against kings. William Pitt was fearful of this enthusiastic French imperialism. Even Edmund Burke, who had favoured conciliation with the American colonists twenty years earlier, was aghast at French revolutionary ideas and activities.

The French armies and fleets ranged far and wide. The Low Countries were taken over by 1795. After Napoleon Bonaparte's return from Egypt, the French seized the neighbouring states where monarchies had collapsed before democratic enthusiasm and French imperialism. When Spain joined France in 1796, Portugal became even more valuable as a British continental outpost. The war, of course, affected the colonists, especially the West Indies where thousands of British and French soldiers and sailors became victims of an unfriendly climate. The first war against the French Republic was to come to an uneasy end in 1802.

The Report on the British Post Office made by the Commissioners of 1788, included among numerous suggestions that the packet-boats even out of the Falmouth station, be limited to 150 tons. To quote their own words: 'Vessels of this description are fit to go to any Part of the World, and may be navigated at small Expense—every idea of defence should be relinquished, and they should owe their safety to fast Sailing, for which they ought to be particularly fitted.' In the discussions that took place after 1788, Lord Walsingham strongly supported this recommendation. He proposed that all the packets should be of the same model, and they they be built according to the designs of Marmaduke Stalkard of Rotherhithe, the author of a highly regarded book on *Naval Architecture*.[1]

The Falmouth captains examined the plans for the proposed

---

[1] *10th Rep. Commrs.* (1788), 36-37; *Walsingham Papers*, III, 161ff. The volume appeared in 1781 under the name of M. Stalkartt.

packet-boats, and were not pleased. Nine of the captains signed a letter in May 1790 stating that larger vessels of 200 tons would be better fitted for the Falmouth station. They finally agreed reluctantly to the new design for the vessels, if the boats were lengthened some 3 feet, thus raising the burthen to about 170 tons. With this change, they believed that the packets would sail much faster, and be more easily handled. As to the armament for the packets in the event of war, the captains were in favour of the same armaments as in the last war, and only hesitantly agreed to smaller equipment—'four four-pounders to keep off Row Boats and make Signals, and small Arms for the men lest they should be boarded by any little Privateer they may meet'. It had long been the policy of the Post Office that the packets should not fight but trust to fast sailing.[1]

The plans for the 170-ton vessels show a trim looking three-masted and double-decked packet. The keel was 61 feet and 6 inches long, and the extreme breadth of the hull was 23 feet. The top deck was about 80 feet in length. The lower or covered deck had three passenger cabins on each side, separated by an open space called the dining room. The six passenger cabins were intended only as sleeping places, for they were 4 feet 4 inches by 6 feet 6 inches in size and without ports. A platform under the lower deck aft of the mainmast provided store rooms, including a mail room, a bread room, a fitting room and the magazine. Each packet carried two small boats—a cutter about 20 feet long, and a smaller jolly boat.[2]

Three of the new packets were ready when the war opened in 1793. They proved to be fast. The *Chesterfield* made a round trip to the West Indies in ten weeks, the *Westmorland* in seven.

The first packet captured in the war was out of Dover, as one might expect; the *Dispatch* was taken when on her way to Ostend. Both Calais and Ostend were soon closed to British mails after French armies overran the Austrian Netherlands. The mail for the Tour and Tassis posts was taken to Flushing.

In the meantime, Harwich was busier than ever. The French, however, could not be stopped; they soon occupied the Netherlands.

[1] *T.L.B.*, V, 328-31; VI, 156-8, 162.

[2] The boat plans were found in the *Palmer Papers*, Bundle IV, no. 122. The size of the packets may surprise readers familiar with the present-day gigantic passenger and mail vessels. Yet vessels under 200 tons were then in regular use for long ocean voyages. The well-known *Bounty* (Captain Bligh) went to the south Pacific in 1787 where part of the crew mutinied two years later and took refuge on Pitcairn Island. The *Bounty* had a top deck but 4 feet longer than the 170-ton packets, and its cutter, in which Captain Bligh and his companions were set adrift, was the size of a mail-boat cutter. Like the packets, the *Bounty* was a three-master. For plan of the *Bounty*, see *Natl. Geog. Mag.* (Dec. 1957). For the plan of the 1790 mail-packets, see illustration, facing p. 28.

This meant that the English mails were barred from Helvoetsluis. Even Harwich ceased to be a mail port when it became necessary to transfer the Harwich packets farther north to Yarmouth. From Yarmouth the mails were carried across the North Sea to Cuxhaven at the mouth of the Elbe. Later in the war a mail agent was also stationed at Bremerlehe at the mouth of the Weser so that the packets could make either the Elbe or the Weser. Even Heligoland was used on occasion for transferring the English mails to coastal craft.[1]

Yarmouth had the disadvantage of being considerably farther north than Harwich. As the war appeared to be nearing its end, the Harwich captains, who much preferred their old port, were told to make Harwich if possible, instead of Yarmouth. The war-time use of Yarmouth was justified by the comparatively regular service; only five of the North Sea packets were lost to the enemy in over eight years of war.[2]

The Channel Islands, near the French coast, had been without a regular mail connection since the close of the previous war in 1782. On the renewal of war with France in 1793 the islands received a regular service. A Post Office surveyor, Christopher Saverland, was sent to the south coast ports to make a recommendation as to the best home base. He favoured Portsmouth, even though Southampton had been the base for services in the previous war, and was the port most used by the Channel Islands trade. Weymouth, a third possibility, was somewhat closer to Jersey and Guernsey than Portsmouth or Southampton but much less accessible from London. Despite Saverland's recommendation, Weymouth was finally selected as the home port. It had been a popular watering place after George III, following an extended illness, had taken up residence there in 1789. Here Pitt came for long interviews with the King. Indeed, the choice of Weymouth seems to have been made by William Pitt 'with the least possible communication with the Postmasters-General'. In fact, Pitt and the Ministry rather than the Post Office were interested in the revival of this comparatively unimportant mail route.

---

[1] *See* illustration facing p. 28 for one of the Harwich packet-boats in use at this time. The *Princess Royal*, pictured as entering the harbour of Helvoetsluis in 1794, was soon transferred to Yarmouth. She was taken by the French in the next spring. This *Princess Royal* is not to be confused with a Falmouth packet of the same name, which was lost to the French in 1800. *See* App. II.

[2] *7th Rep. Com. on Finance* (1797), 117-21; *P.O. Minutes*, XIX, 124-6. Norway, op. cit, 41, 107, is in error in writing that the North Sea packets were free from attack in this war.

The other home services were not seriously affected by the coming of the war. The Holyhead boats went on their usual and uneventful course. The Milford contract was in the hands of Samuel Newport when the war began. On the end of his contract during the war, Newport gave notice that he would not renew at the former rate. Bids were then sought by the Post Office, but Samuel Newport was the only bidder at an increase of over 40 per cent. The Post Office had no option but to accept his bid because of the importance of the Irish mails during a war in which the French attempted to land in southern Ireland, and to arouse the Irish to rebellion. The Milford service was still so unproductive that the Post Office took over the station a few years later, in the hope that it could be run at less than the contract price.

None of the packets on the home stations, not even those going back and forth to the Channel Islands, was captured during this war.

THE FALMOUTH STATION

The troubles of the Falmouth station were in sharp contrast to the freedom from interference enjoyed by the services to the Channel Islands and to Ireland. The weekly service to Lisbon was very irregular; during 1798, for example, there were only twenty-seven voyages in a service that was supposed to be weekly. The loud complaints of the merchants led to the assignment of another packet to this run early in 1799, in the hope that five boats would give a weekly correspondence.

In the West Indies, the French kept control of Guadeloupe throughout the war, although the British forces had taken Martinique in 1794. Guadeloupe remained a constant threat to the British West Indian packets and the inter-island mail-boats. When the Netherlands were overrun by the French, the colonial holdings of the Netherlands came under British control. Thereupon Guiana and Trinidad (taken from Spain in 1797) were served by British mail-boats. These schooners had supplemented the ocean packet-boats even before the war began, going southward and northward on the arrival of the Jamaica packet at Barbados, and they brought mails from the various islands to St Kitts where the returning ocean mail-packet received them as she was about to return to Falmouth.[1]

---

[1] *T.L.B.*, VIII, 1-4, 50; X, 98, 110, 168-9; *Reps. P.M.G.*, XXII, 255.

During the war against the French Republic, the Falmouth packets won considerable praise for a number of courageous and successful engagements in the defence of their mails. Accounts of duels with French privateers will underline the perils faced by British mail carriers at the end of the eighteenth century.

A successful battle that received wide notice was fought in December 1793. The *Antelope*, homeward bound from Jamaica, was attacked off Cuba by the French privateer *l'Atalante*. The *Antelope* (Captain Kempthorne) was in charge of the Master, Edward Curtis, on this voyage. After a chase that lasted for three days, the privateer was close enough to open fire after hoisting French colours and the 'Bloody Flag'—a sign that no quarter was to be shown. The packet had but twenty-three men fit for service, including the surgeon, as four had died on the outward voyage and two were ill.

According to the report of the boatswain, John Pascoe, who took over early in the battle after the death of Edward Curtis, the *Atalante* 'clapped us alongside and grappled us in a very hot fire'. The privateer's crew of sixty-five men divided into two boarding parties and prepared to take the packet. In the attempted boarding Captain Curtis and two others were killed, and the mate badly wounded. John Pascoe reported the action in an account that was signed by his mark:

'She then made another Attempt to board us by cutting down the Boarding Nettings, Ridge Ropes, etc., but they all got killed in the attempt. Our loss this Sally was three more wounded; but they then tried to get off by cutting their Grappling Rope but were prevented by the . . . lashing of her Square Sail Yard to our Fore Shrouds. We directly after found her Fire slacken which greatly encouraged Us. We kept up a constant Fire for half an hour more when we had the Pleasure of seeing them cry for Mercy, but to all appearance they deserved none nor expected any as some of them jumped overboard and drowned themselves, for their Bloody Flag was nailed to the Masthead. They were then ordered to tear it down and we took possession.

According to Pascoe's report, fifty of the sixty-five men on the privateer were killed, wounded or missing, while on the packet only two of the crew were killed and four wounded. In addition, a French 'gentleman' passenger was killed, 'who with another French Gentleman was all that assisted the Ship's Company'. It was a most creditable action, particularly as the leader in most of the fighting was the illiterate boatswain, John Pascoe.[1]

The *Antelope* returned to Jamaica to refit, along with her prize. The Jamaican House of Assembly voted a reward for the crew. A London 'Committee for Encouraging the Capture of French Privateers' was so elated that it passed out lavish awards—50 guineas for the widow of Edward Curtis, the same for the wounded mate and another 50 guineas for the survivors of the steward. John Pascoe also received 50 guineas and a signalling whistle; each of the crew received 5 guineas.

Such liberality put the Post Office on its mettle, and led to further awards. Pascoe and the wounded mate were each given a pension of £20 per annum. The Post Office also persuaded the Admiralty to turn over the prize to the captors. They added, however, this cautionary word: 'But Mr Pender [the Falmouth agent] must let it be thoroughly understood amongst the officers and crews that these rewards are given only in consequence of the particular circumstances attending this glorious action . . . for the Postmaster-General by no means intend [sic] to depart from the Principle . . . of considering it to be the duty of the Packets to outsail the enemy and to avoid going into action whenever it may be possible.'

In the next year, 1794, the *Antelope* did not have enough speed to outsail a French squadron when she was on her way to Halifax. Captain Kempthorne, who was in command of his ship on this trip, died on board the packet soon after her capture.[2]

In the autumn of 1796 two separate actions of the *Portland* (Captain Taylor) were so outstanding as to deserve rewards almost as liberal as those given the *Antelope* three years before. In the second engagement off Guadeloupe the *Portland* was attacked by the *Téméraire*. When the French attempted to board the packet Captain Taylor ordered the privateer's jib stay lashed to the packet, and he then 'requested' the passengers to 'open their musketry which was done with great effect, as forty-one out of sixty-eight

---

[1] The packet carried a number of passengers; one of whom, a former midshipman named Nodin, published an account of the engagement on the return to Jamaica and gave himself considerable credit for the victory. John Pascoe turned in the official account. This battle received notice in the naval histories of James and Clowes. Clowes erroneously made Nodin a member of the crew and added that 'Nodin distinguished himself most.' Pascoe denied that Nodin gave any assistance. See *T.L.B.*, VIII, 81-95; Norway op. cit., 45-52; and Clowes, *The Royal Navy, a History*, IV, 482, where it is stated that the *Atalante* had been fitted out at Charleston, South Carolina.

[2] *T.L.B.*, VIII, 157-8; IX, 43-45. For the important place of Captain Kempthorne in the packet service, see Gay, op. cit., pp. 120-4.

were killed or wounded on board the Privateer'. Captain Taylor, according to the report, 'unfortunately lost his life in the moment of Victory by the enemy villainously firing after their Colours were struck and he humanely employed in preventing any unnecessary carnage among them'. The ten passengers, who prepared a memorial of the action, were a fortunate addition to the crew. Four of them were captains of various regiments, one being of the Old Buffs, and a fifth passenger was the surgeon of the forces at Antigua. As in the case of the *Antelope*, the Post Office responded handsomely. The mate, who succeeded to the command on the Captain's death, received 50 guineas, the surgeon 10 and so on down, each able seaman getting 3. Captain Taylor, who left no surviving family was to be married on his return to a Miss Angove, a mantua maker—a house had been furnished in anticipation. Miss Angove received 20 guineas.[1]

Only one later action in this war seemed deserving of award—a duel in June 1798 between the *Princess Royal* (Captain Skinner) and a French brig. Captain John Skinner was born at Perth Amboy, New Jersey. He took the Loyalist side in the American Revolution, entered the Navy in 1776, and lost an eye and an arm in the service. He became commander of the packet *Princess Royal* in 1794. The conduct of Captain Skinner in the action with the French brig in June 1798 so impressed Brigadier-General Murray in Halifax that he wrote the Postmasters-General about the action. The brig, *l'Aventure* by name, was met by the stern chasers as she was coming up, and a vigorous action followed, in which the captain and the crew were greatly assisted and encouraged by fifteen passengers, including a Major Murray, a Captain Hobbinson of the Royal Fusiliers, and Mr Sheldon of Lloyd's Coffee House. The packet's resistance to the attack was so telling that the privateer finally put out her sweeps and pulled off. The casualties on the packet were two men badly wounded 'and myself slightly from the blowing up of a powder horn'. During the battle, after all the 4-lb cartridges had been used, they were supplemented by 'the Captain's sister and her maid who set to work making new ones in the bread-room'. The usual rewards were distributed, 50 guineas to the captain and another 50 to the rest of the crew.

Three years later, Captain Skinner transferred to the Holyhead packet station, a deserved award for years of service on the open ocean. He had charge of packet-boats out of Holyhead for the next

[1] The *Portland* was taken two years later by a privateer carrying 20 guns and 140 men. For her fortunes and misfortunes, see *T.L.B.*, IX, 169-180, 341-2.

thirty-three years—until he was swept overboard in a storm as his packet was leaving Ireland for Holyhead.[1]

THE TEST OF WAR

By June 1798 when the *Princess Royal* had fought her successful engagement, enough time had elapsed to make possible a judgement on the new policy of using smaller packets carrying but a light armament. In 1797 four West Indian packets and one bound for Halifax had been taken. One of the victims was the *Grantham* under the command of Captain James Bull. He had not been in favour of the official armament, for Captain Bull had mounted at his own expense seven additional brass and carriage guns. It was of no avail, as the *Grantham* was taken by a privateer of fourteen guns and carrying over 100 men. During the two years previous to the successful engagement of the *Princess Royal* twelve of the Falmouth packets fell to Fench privateers, which helps to explain the liberal rewards passed out to Captain Skinner and his crew. It was in the West Indies that heavily armed 'Frenchmen', using Guadeloupe as a base, were most active. According to the report of one captain, there were as many as 150 privateers fitted out at Guadeloupe.

The West Indian merchants, always vocal as to the shortcomings of the service to the West Indies, showed much concern with the irregular communication. In the spring of 1798 they sent a long memorial to the Post Office, declaring that lightly armed packets were nothing but a temptation to the enemy, and that they were by no means the fast sailers they were supposed to be. The merchants added that the average passage from Falmouth to Jamaica in the last three years had been forty-five days, and from Jamaica to Falmouth fifty-three days. The merchants even favoured the use of royal cutters for the mails. They intimated that conditions were so bad that the packet service ought to be transferred to the Admiralty.

There was some point to the proposal, since there had been a serious lack of packets in the latter part of the war. The Post Office admitted, in September 1798, that 'we have only ten packets out of sixteen [on the West Indian and American stations] and three of these ten are temporary vessels'. Nine packets were being built at the time, but it took a year to build a packet. In the meantime the

---

[1] The action of 1796 received some publicity from an account in *The Times;* it was drawn up by Mr Sheldon of Lloyd's Coffee House, who, it transpired, was 'for the most part owner of the ship'. For the official report, see *T.L.B.*, X, 30-34. The *Princess Royal* was captured by a French privateer when returning from the West Indies in 1800.

captains were ashore, supposedly supervising the building. Even the Postmasters-General grew critical, since the packets seemed 'ill prepared either for fight or flight . . . It is disheartening that as fast as we can build or hire vessels for packets they are sure to be captured.'[1]

The reply of Francis Freeling, the Secretary of the Post Office, was that the Navy Board as well as the Post Office had approved vessels of 170 tons, lightly armed. He compared the losses to date with those in the American war. He concluded that the losses in this war were no greater and that the expense was less than half what it was when the packets were larger and better armed. Mr Freeling used the loss of James Bull's *Grantham* as an example of heavily armed packets that had to give in to the French. Captain John Bull, who had succeeded his father in 1798, was also in favour of larger vessels, as he had asked permission in 1801 to build a packet of 210 tons. His request was refused.[2]

Some of the captains used every excuse to stay on land during the war. By the end of 1799 Captain Lovell Todd had made only eleven voyages in seven years. Captain Dillon had an even worse record, for he made but two voyages in five years, and begged off from going on his packet in 1794, on the ground that he had had a shock two months before 'which left him in a state of debility'. The Post Office ruled about this time that captains who stayed home must furnish a commander for the packet in addition to the regular crew, and that the absentee captain should lose his share of the packet money.

During this war 46 packet-boats and 10 West Indian mail schooners were taken by the enemy. A Spanish privateer captured the *Duke of Clarence* in 1800; all the rest were taken by the French. The worst year was 1800, when the service lost eleven packets and mail-boats. The expense of keeping up the service, such as it was, came to £700,000. A full list of the captured packets and their captors will be found in the appendix.[3]

---

[1] ibid., IX, 295-303; *Reps. P.M.G.*, XVI, 79-81; XVII, 393.

[2] Captain James Bull, who had been a captain in the services for over forty years, retired in March 1798, and was succeeded by his son John. John Bull, who had been serving on packets for eleven years, was to become one of the best-known and intrepid commanders in the next three decades.

[3] For the losses and expense, see *T.L.B.*, IX, 304-13; X, 322; *Report on Agreement with Mr Palmer* (1797), 109. J. S. Buckingham's *Autobiography* gives a full account of the capture of *Lady Harriott*, taken in 1799, but it is inaccurate. He makes the engagement occur in 1796, and he gives his age as ten at the time. As he was born admittedly in 1785, and as the official records date the loss of the *Lady Harriott* after his birthday in 1799, Buckingham was over fourteen.

9

THE HANDLING OF SAILING PACKETS
—1803-15

WHEN war between Great Britain and France ended temporarily in 1802, the Post Office renewed the peace-time services. The Dover route was reopened, but the packets went only to Calais. The Harwich station was again the base for mail-boats that went to Helvoetsluis; the Post Office decided to keep open as well the route to northern Europe by way of Cuxhaven.

The uneasy truce ended in the next year when Napoleon picked a quarrel with Great Britain. Even the United States of America became embroiled in 1812. An end came to Napoleon's activities when he was defeated at Waterloo in 1815, and taken to live on St Helena in the south Atlantic. This war, the last of a long series that had disturbed the packet arrangements for over a century was the most severe trial of all.

THE NORTH SEA AND HOME STATIONS

The Dover station was again closed. The service between Harwich and Helvoetsluis was also interrupted. Either the Post Office was careless or it hoped that communications with Holland might be tolerated, for no less than three of the Harwich packets were captured *in* the harbour of Helvoetsluis during the summer of 1803. After that, the Harwich packets went farther to the north, even beyond Cuxhaven, as it, too, was soon closed to the British mails. The packet-boats used Husum in Slesvig whence communications were maintained with Hamburg so long as it was not in French hands. In the winter of 1803-4, however, it fell to the French; the packets then went on to Gothenburg in Sweden. This long voyage was such an unpleasant change for the Harwich captains, who also lost much in passage money, that they sought and received an additional grant as compensation. They disliked

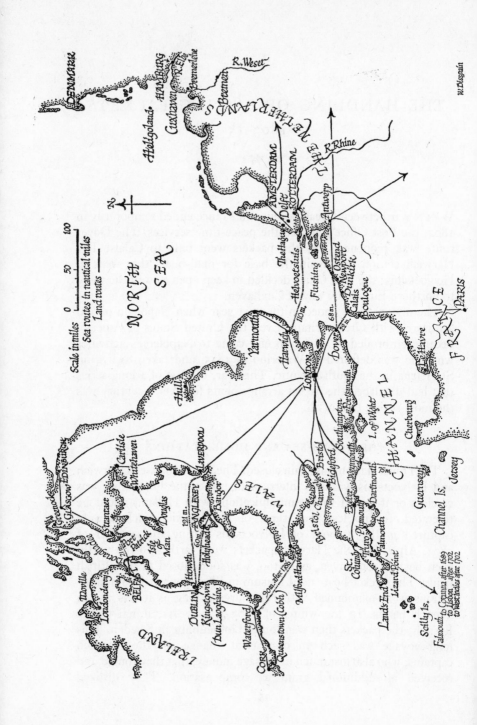

particularly entering the 'Cattegat during the Winter Season when no other Vessels scarcely attempt it'.[1]

The packet-boats serving Ireland and the Channel Islands carried on with little interference. The only one lost on these stations was the *Chesterfield* on the Channel Islands route; she was captured in October 1811 after a vigorous defence and the sinking of the mails. The loss of a packet-boat on the Weymouth station came as a great shock; it was the first on this route since it had begun some thirty years before.[2]

The war did not interfere with the Irish route, the packets peacefully carrying mail and passengers and gentlemen's carriages back and forth across the Irish Sea. Port Patrick was the base for four boats of 40 tons each; Milford Haven and Holyhead had five packets each. The service from Milford was irregular at best, on account of the strong contrary winds and what was called the 'influx' of the Atlantic Ocean. The service was even suspended occasionally during a succession of severe winters between 1804 and 1808. The Milford route was so unproductive that it should have been discontinued, were it not for its value, in war-time, for the Government. A sixth packet was put on the route towards the end of the war.

The Holyhead service was very profitable both for the Post Office and for the commanders, so much so that the packet captains sought it on account of the large income from passenger fares and because of its freedom from attacks by privateers. Captains would even leave Falmouth for Holyhead, and regard it as a promotion. Captain Skinner of the *Princess Royal* had transferred to Holyhead in 1799.[3]

THE SAILING PACKETS OUT OF FALMOUTH

The Falmouth packets became exceedingly important when a world-wide war with France began in 1803. The packet agent at the port until 1810 was Benjamin Pender. At that time the Post Office sent a surveyor, Christopher Saverland, to investigate the agency,

[1] *T.L.B.*, XI, 130-4; XII, 252.

[2] ibid., XII, 185; XIV, 154; XV, 168-9. In 1813 the Post Office dismissed Starr Wood, the *Chesterfield's* former Captain, for the 'grossest misdemeanor'. He continued to use his boat on this run, and gave the impression that his service was official by imitating the post-office flag. Each packet-boat had its distinctive flag; it was hoisted on approaching a port.

[3] ibid., XIII, 112-116; *Reps. P.M.G.*, XXIII, 123-9. Two other Falmouth captains who transferred to Holyhead were Captain Fellowes of the *Lady Hobart*, and Captain Stevens of the *Lady Mary Pelham*. For noteworthy voyages of these two packets, see the next chapter.

with the result that Pender was removed because of his alleged 'incapacity to control the procedures of this important station'. The postmasters-general sent Saverland back to take Pender's place. As a surveyor, Saverland had wide experience, was able, and had a keen sense of duty. His appointment was regarded as beginning a new era in the foreign packet services.

The Falmouth fleet numbered thirty-six packets in 1810 when Saverland took over. They were of two sorts, established and temporary packets. Twenty-one were established, their captains having met the conditions for permanent service. The temporary packets were so called because the shortage of established vessels required these additions, even if they did not exactly meet the requirements as to tonnage or accommodations. The Post Office no longer felt bound by the limit of 170 tons for an established packet. Only 5 of the 36 were under 180 tons, and 9 were over 190 tons burthen. The largest was a temporary packet, Captain Tilley's *Adventure* of 216 tons.

The established packets were usually named by the Post Office. The Falmouth agent wrote Mr Freeling in 1812, for instance, that Captain Stevens had called at the office to request that the post-masters-general name his packet, 'building at this port, as she was in a state of forwardness, and he wishes to order the appropriate head or bust'. His vessel became the *Lady Mary Pelham*. The packets usually bore the names of members of the royal family, or of the postmasters-general or of their wives.

The packets were commonly rigged as ships or brigs. If ships, they carried square sails. The more common rigging, that of a brig, consisted of square sails on the foremast, but the main mast, or the mizzen if the vessel was three-masted had a lower for-and-aft sail with a gaff and boom in addition to square sails. Another type of vessel increasingly popular at this time was the schooner. The schooner, which originated in America, was usually two masted with for-and-aft rigging and carried topsails as well. The British Navy was using schooners at this time, as we learn from a Saverland letter of 1813. When it was suggested that the packets should go to Halifax in the winter, he wrote London that the severity of the weather 'upon that coast' was such that 'square sail vessels are not so well adapted for the service as the Government schooners'.[1]

---

[1] *Fal. L.B.*, IV, 266; V, 49, 272, 293; VII, 133. The first schooner was launched about 1750 at Gloucester, Massachusetts by a Captain Andrew Robinson. For the American schooners, see the next chapter.

During these years Falmouth was frequently short of packet-boats, established and temporary. Saverland wrote the Secretary in London in 1810, for example, that ten vessels were absent on the Mediterranean and Brazil stations, and that only nine packets were expected back in that month; he added that it was very difficult 'to supply the needs of every month'. After the United States entered the war in 1812 and the packet losses sharply increased, Francis Freeling was in despair. He told the postmasters-general in November 1815 that ten packets were needed for the service of that month, but that only four were at Falmouth, two of them under repair and the two others in quarantine where they would have to remain forty days.

MANNING THE PACKETS

The crews of the vessels were a never-ending concern of the agent and the captains. In war-time, each vessel carried 28 men—the commander, master, surgeon, mate, carpenter, boatswain, gunner, cook, 18 able seamen and 2 'ordinary seamen'. In 1814 four more were added to the crew when additional armament was provided.

A constant cause of dissatisfaction among the crews was the small allowance for wages and food. Able seamen were paid 1s a day, and the allowance for food was set 1s 2d a day for officers and men alike. Additional food and clothing were permitted, if a packet was assigned to the bleak winter run to Halifax. When a packet-boat was about to be sent on that route, Saverland wrote Freeling: 'I have made inquiry among the commanders as to the allowance for the winter months . . . and find that a guinea was allowed for each man for warm clothing, and in some instances a great coat was given to each man . . . The best mode will be to buy each man a great coat [it cost 28s] to enable him to stand the deck [sic] in the inclement climate, for if you give him money he will spend it and go without.' As to rum, Saverland wrote that the allowance in the Navy 'is half a pint of spirits to each man per day mixed with water in such a manner as the commanders think proper'. This was made the basis for the allowance of rum, the commanders being advised to use the 60 gallons frugally, and not to begin 'until he gets into a severe climate'. At Halifax, he was to lay in the same quantity for the return journey.[1]

The seamen had been accustomed to take their 'little adventures' to sell in foreign parts, especially at Lisbon. This had been condoned,

[1] ibid., IV, 370; V, 79, 92; VI, 7.

even though a little adventure was likely to become a large one. In 1806, sailors about to leave on packets bound for the West Indies had gone ashore because they were forbidden to take out cheese and potatoes. The Post Office even tried to set a limit to a departing sailor's belongings by allowing him only the capacity of his sea chest—3 feet long and 14 inches broad— and a 'Cornish bushel of potatoes as sea stock'. In one instance when their boxes were opened —this was on the *Chichester*—the prying customs officials discovered snuff, iron spoons and knives, cotton handkerchiefs, and about 950 lb. of cheese. These goods, divided among twenty-eight men seemed so little that Saverland thought they should be permitted.

Now and again the customs officers found much more on the vessels returning to Falmouth. One of the worst cases was the *Nocton*, back from Brazil in 1811. When some smuggled tea was discovered on board, one of the ship's crew signalled to the sailors who had gone ashore that goods had been discovered, and they had better take care of themselves. The thorough examination revealed 188 lb. of tea, 113 lb. of tobacco, and 80 gallons of gin. The gin had been put in an empty water cask. As a result of the discoveries, some of the crew were impressed into the Navy. In 1816 Captain John Bull's *Duke of Marlborough* was impounded after a search revealed tea, spirits, pepper and other goods on board. Captain Bull had to go to London to get back his packet. He insisted he had no knowledge of these concealed goods.[1]

Shortly after Christopher Saverland had taken over the agency in 1810 he was faced by the 'mutinous state of the whole of the packet crews'; it was the result of the seizure of their adventures. The *Duke of Marlborough* had to be sent on its voyage to Lisbon with the assistance of sailors from H.M.S. *Experiment*, and the crews of the *Marlborough* and the *Adolphus* were imprisoned. When the *Dispatch* arrived, her crew was put on board a man-of-war to prevent them from joining the mutineers. When the sailors ashore gathered in front of the packet office, asking for the release of the imprisoned crews and for an increase in wages, they were dispersed by the reading of the Riot Act. Two days later the packet men gathered at the Seven Dials in Flushing—the village across the harbour from Falmouth—to unite against staffing the packets, and to obtain enough money to send two delegates to London to present their case to the Secretary, Francis Freeling. The two chosen delegates, Parker and Pascoe, left by coach for London the next day.

[1] ibid., III, 125, 341, 376; V, 523; VI, 207, 209; *Reps. P.M.G.*, XXVI, 230, 247.

Saverland anticipated their arrival by sending his version of the affair from Plymouth by the visual telegraph. He hoped that the two men would be imprisoned and made examples 'to prevent the recurrence of this dangerous spirit'. He wrote later, 'If force had not been used, it is very likely, after the detention of the mails for three weeks or a month, we might have *persuaded* the sailors to take the packets to sea at an advance in wages . . . and the next time that anything went wrong they would meet and demand still higher wages.' The two delegates were detained in one of the City of London prisons, but were soon released.

Instead of Parker and Pascoe being punished, the whole town of Falmouth was disciplined. The agency was removed to Plymouth where the naval authorities could compel obedience by the threat of impressment. The Government believed that the inhabitants of Falmouth should be made to feel 'the consequences of the late serious and disgraceful proceedings'. The removal to Plymouth was made early in November 1810. Soon the residents of Falmouth were promising to keep order, if only the packet business would return. It was the life of the port and of its 9,000 inhabitants. The packet services were finally resumed from Falmouth on February 15, 1811. The agent was able to report to Francis Freeling in the spring that the services had never been conducted so quietly 'as at present'. The town and the seamen had been humbled—and there was no increase in wages.[1]

Press gangs were busy during this war in all ports to keep up the crews of a Navy that numbered some 800 vessels. The incentive for serving on a packet instead of a merchantman was the supposed exemption of packet crews from impressment. When they were at home during the interval between sailings, the members of the packet crews carried protections, signed by the Falmouth agent. The press gangs, however, did not pay much attention to the protections.

Unpleasant incidents resulted. Saverland wrote in January 1813 that the steward of the *Princess Charlotte* had been impressed: 'He had my protection at the time, which he produced to the lieutenant of the gang.' Captain Slade of the Navy defended the action of the press gang in this case on the ground that the packet agent 'had no right to protect seamen for more than one month'. Christopher

---

[1] *Fal. L.B.* III, 4-20, etc.; *Pkt. Rep. Bks.*, I, 604-32. Norway, op. cit., 197-218 gives a full account of the mutiny, but makes the return to Falmouth January 1, 1811. It was not authorized until January 30th.

Saverland replied: 'Captain Slade has been very jealous about the number of packet seamen protected by me . . . Our seamen do not like to remain long on shore. If the packet be a month under repair, the men are always anxious to go to sea in another packet. There must always, however, be from twenty to sixty seamen without ships. These must be protected and our number being about 1,200 seamen there cannot be less.' In April 1813 a gang had impressed a packet seaman on the sick list. A mob in nearby Penryn was so infuriated that the lieutenant of the press gang was roughly treated; he had to return to Falmouth in a *chaise*. In October of the same year, Saverland reported that the packet seamen said, 'We may as well go into the merchant service and get £5 a month, as to be impressed with protections in our pockets.'[1]

Although the press gangs irritated Saverland, he was sure that the threat of impressment kept up the crews of the packet. 'I am of the opinion,' he wrote in 1812, 'that if it were not for the impress, the service would not be carried on at all.' An experience of 1814 seemed to justify this judgement. Ten men left the *Express* the day she was to sail. With the end of the war in sight, the search for men to keep up the crews of the Navy had relaxed; the press gangs were no longer active in Falmouth Harbour. Christopher Saverland reported that the packetmen now say, 'The press gang is gone and the H.M.S. *Experiment* is going and we don't care a d . . n for the agent and the captains.' There was a regular system of crimpage at the port. Seamen would enter on board a packet for protection 'and then run off as suits their convenience for higher wages on transports or merchantmen; crimps know where to find them'.

Yet the greatest loss by desertion took place, not in Falmouth or Lisbon, but in New York. The Falmouth agent wrote in 1812 that desertions almost altogether occur in New York, where the ships were frequently visited by crimps from the shore, 'inviting the seamen to their land of liberty with promises of high wages and plenty of grog'. The seamen who deserted in New York were always blacklisted, and their names given to Captain Slade of the Royal Navy 'to be impressed upon their appearance'. Saverland was told by a boatman at Plymouth that several packetmen were aboard the American frigate *President*, that even his own son belonged to her for two years, and that a former member of the *Walsingham*'s crew was quartermaster on the same ship at the time. The captain of the packet *Ann* had been told that 300 English seamen were in the

[1] *Fal. L.B.*, IV, 278-80, 288, 301. Many other instances could be cited.

crew of the *President*. It was a perplexing situation for the Falmouth agent; 152 seamen had deserted the service in New York in the three years before the United States entered the war.[1]

HANDLING THE MAILS

The log-book that each captain carried contained printed directions. He was to record daily the direction and strength of the winds, the distance sailed, as well as the latitude and longitude. On approaching a port the packet was to display 'the White Jack at the main-top-gallant-masthead—an English ensign at the peak—and the distinguishing flag of your ship at the fore-top-gallant-masthead'. The captain was charged to be very attentive with the correct delivery of the mails. If in danger of capture, he was to throw the mails overboard, having first weighted them to ensure their sinking.[2]

Bullion was often the most valuable part of the permissible cargo. According to a letter of 1811 from Saverland: 'The captain of a packet made an agreement with the shippers to deliver it safely in London at a percentage of from one to 2½ per cent, the dangers of the sea excepted . . . After the expenses of shipping, carriage on shore and to London, and the Bank fees were paid and deducted from the freight, the remainder is divided into three equal parts between the [Post] Office, the owners [of the packet] and the captain.' Bullion was not sent up to London by the relatively unprotected mail-coaches. When it arrived at Falmouth, the bullion was delivered to the Wagon Office, to be sent up to London in Mr Russell's heavily guarded wagons. When Russell raised the freight on gold and silver in 1811, the packets owners sought a cheaper conveyance, but they failed, as 'at present there is no other waggon directly to London but Mr Russell's'. The shipments of bullion were surprisingly large, one reason why the privateers sought out the packets on the Lisbon and West Indian runs. The King's share of the freight of bullion on the *Windsor Castle* from Jamaica—it arrived in December 1810—was £345. In the previous August the *Nocton* had brought in from Jamaica $27,000 and 948 doubloons. The *Francis Freeling* arrived from Lisbon in 1814 with £30,000 worth of coin on board. When a small tin box, not charged with postage, was discovered in the mail-bag from Antigua—it was

[1] ibid., III, 93, 235, 405; IV, 30; V, 61, 398, 442, etc.
[2] A few of the log-books have been preserved in the Post Office Record Room, principally some of those of the *Montagu*, the *Prince Ernest* and the *Lady Mary Pelham*—kept because they related to voyages that were investigated.

brought by the *Eliza* in July 1811—it was open and found to contain gold weighing about 22 ounces. If sent up in the mail-bag, it might have worked out, if sent by Mr Russell's wagon, the postage would be lost. The agent finally forwarded it in the special care of the guard on the mail-coach, charged with a *heavy* postage.[1]

As soon as a packet arrived from overseas, the medical inspector came out before the mail was landed, in order to give the packet pratique. As the log-book of the *Prince Ernest* put it: 'Came into Carrick Roads [Falmouth], made a signal with the gun for the Pratique Boat. At 4 a.m. the Doctor came and gave us Pratique.' If the packet arrived from the plague-ridden Mediterranean or the West Indies, the vessel as well as the mail might have to be fumigated. In that case, the packet might be out of service for forty days [quarantine] if it was sent for fumigation to Stangate Creek on the Kentish side of the Thames.[2]

If only the mail needed fumigation, it was sent to a floating lazaretto in Falmouth Harbour. Before the letters left the ship, each letter might be cut through in three places with chisels, or it might be done at the lazaretto if a large number of letters needed treatment. The work was in charge of Saverland's office at this time, the vessel used for the purpose being in a 'proper situation', that is, not so far away as to inconvenience the Packet Office. In 1816 the agent complained that the 'quarantine pool is four miles distant by water from this place', and that the quarantine officer was a 'waspish, petulant man'. The lazaretto was located in St Just Pool, across the harbour. In reply to criticisms that the letters were defaced, Saverland replied that the chisels used were too wide, even cutting letters in two, and that they were in 'improper hands'. He recommended smaller 'instruments for puncturing the letters'.[3]

The letters on the quarantine vessel were put in fumigating boxes where they were exposed to the fumes rising from one part of sulphur to two parts of powdered charcoal. This lasted for at least fifteen minutes. The letters were then taken out by tongs and dipped in vinegar before they were considered safe. Little wonder that the quarantine officer was waspish and petulant. Sometimes his treatment was not considered sufficient. Saverland reported in July 1813 that 'muriatic acid and nitre were afterwards used in my office during the sorting, which was never done before'. In this instance

[1] *Fal. L.B.*, III, 66, 123, 142, 220, 227, 250; V, 352; *Reps. P.M.G.*, XXVI, 156.
[2] *Log-Book* of the *Prince Ernest*, entry for November 11, 1813; *Fal. L.B.*, IV, 317, 479; V, 81, 148; *22nd Rep. Commrs. of Rev.* (1830), 338.
[3] *Fal. L.B.*, VI, 325, 350; VII, 22, 76.

the mail had arrived on the *Montagu* from Malta where there was 'disease'.[1]

Mail from overseas needed a good deal of routine attention before it was sent inland by coach. In sorting the letters, those for the cross-roads had to be separated from those going to London. In addition to seeing that all were properly taxed and appropriately stamped, Saverland's office had to keep watch for smuggled letters, attend to the separate charges for soldier's mail, take care that Government dispatches were sent to the proper officials, etc. His chief concern was over carelessly marked and unsorted letters. In June 1811 a large mail arrived from the Mediterranean with the 'letters from Malta neither tied nor wrapped up in paper, but all mixed indiscriminately together, the London and country letters so much together that the labels cannot be depended upon to ascertain their contents'. He found that occasionally paid letters came marked in black ink, when red ink should have been used to indicate pre-paid letters.

The Army mail from the forces in the Spanish Peninsula was a cause of much inconvenience. Saverland wished that soldier's letters from Lisbon could be sorted there, and put in two bags, one for London and the other for the cross-roads. In October 1813 he wrote that 'letters from Lord Wellington's Army were brought this morning without any money [for postage] or certificate of the money having been paid . . . and as the poor fellows may have paid the pence which are unaccounted for by the Army Post Office, I enclose the whole in the hope that they may be suffered to pass free'.[2]

Various stamps were in use at the Falmouth Office. Ship-letters—those not arriving on packets—were impressed with the ship-letter stamp. When a trunk from Brazil was opened, a number of letters were found: 'I have stamped the whole with the Brazil stamp and the inland postage and forwarded them.' He wrote in March 1813 to the head office in London that a great number of loose letters were put on board the packet in Jamaica: 'They are carefully picked out to receive the stamp here.' It was his regular practice to stamp foreign letters that arrived unstamped 'and for these I have different stamps according to the place they are supposed to come from'.

The Falmouth Packet Office regularly charged smuggled letters with the full postage. Saverland wrote in February 1812: 'The three

---

[1] ibid., IV, 479; V, 8, 99. A. W. Robertson, *A History of the Ship Letters of the British Isles* (1955-8), pp. 33-44, describes the disinfecting of mail.
[2] *Fal. L.B.*, III, 199, 207, 345; IV, 38; V, 48.

enclosed letters were sent to me this morning by the collector of the customs . . . taken out of a box of confectionary seized from the *Express* packet.' They were directed to Madeira. A year later he wrote that 'in searching for a dispatch for the Lord Wellington from the Admiralty to be delivered to Captain Slade, there were found ninety-three mercantile letters for different parts of Spain in the enclosed Army cover'. Such letters and all others not prepaid were returned to London. The agent reported that letters were returned almost every day to London because the postage was not paid.[1]

A constant worry of Saverland was the shortage of portmanteaus for the packets and the mail-coaches. In April 1812, bags of mail that had come from Halifax on H.M. schooner *Mullet* 'by not being enclosed in a portmanteau arrived here very wet, and the letters are rubbed and torn. They have been dried and put together in the best manner that I have been able to, except the enclosed parcel of fragments.' On another occasion, he wrote back to London that the mail-coach had brought Jamaican and American mails together with the Leeward Islands mail-bags, all enclosed in one portmanteau. This meant a shortage of cases; 'When these mails are made up, they become so large with the bye letters that they require four portmanteaus.' He suggested that they should be enclosed in separate cases on the mail-coach. In 1815 he wrote that the American mails as well as that for Jamaica can seldom be contained in less than four portmanteaus. When on board a packet the mail is necessarily obliged to be kept on deck, 'and although it is covered with a tarpaulin, no care can prevent the portmanteaus getting wet'.

The Falmouth Office took great care of the portmanteaus so as to get the maximum service from the expensive leather cases, but 'captures and the wear and tear from the mails being kept on deck exposed to the action of the sea, occasions a very large consumption and expense . . . In the winter they are carefully dried by the fire, looked over and repaired, and in the summer they are hung out of doors, but it frequently happens from the heat of the sun in a tropical climate and the exposure to seawater as before mentioned that a new portmanteau is spoiled and rotten in a single voyage.'

When the deputy comptroller of the Foreign Office in London complained that two mails arrived from Falmouth in one portmanteau, Saverland replied that the inland mails were always compressed in order to save the mail cases for the outward-bound packets. 'We have now twenty-seven packets absent abroad', he wrote, 'and if we

[1] ibid., III, 199, 411; IV, 45, 173; V, 98, 627, 659; VII, 161.

should have five packets arriving here upon the same day, and the order was to put each mail in a separate portmanteau, the mail-coach would not able to carry them.' Saverland suggested that the deputy comptroller of the Foreign Office must be ignorant of the great amount of business at Falmouth.[1]

In conclusion, mention should be made of a safeguard used at sea. When on a voyage the captain of a packet was expected to obtain the names of British naval vessels that he might speak. In order to learn whether an armed vessel was friend or foe, the captain made private signals known to the Navy and to the other packets—using flags by day and signal lights at night. If he did not receive a satisfactory reply, the packet cleared for action, and made every effort to outsail the stranger.

Mistakes occurred when packet signals were ignored by British naval vessels. In April 1812 the packet *Nocton* and H.M.S. *Psyche* had an 'unfortunate mistake relative to packet signals'. It was very unfortunate for the *Nocton*'s surgeon when a shot from the *Psyche* entered his cabin. He was wounded on the head by a splinter with the result that 'his faculties since have been totally deranged'. Another 'mistake' occurred, when H.M.S. *Harlequin* did not answer the signals from the *Queen Charlotte*.

The most serious action of a packet and a British naval vessel took place in March 1814 between the *Duke of Marlborough* (Captain John Bull) and H.M.S. *Primrose* (Captain Philliott). When the brig neared the packet, Captain John Bull showed the private day signal, hoisting a flag half yellow and half blue, but it was not answered. After dark he gave the night signal—two blue lights on each quarter —and again there was no reply. 'This is not a new thing', observed Saverland in his report, 'for the commanders of His Majesty's ships, particularly of the smaller class, not to answer the private signals made by H.M. packets.'

A battle ensued, and the vessels fought for two hours before they discovered that they were not enemies. Not until 9.20 was the packet hailed by Captain Philliott. But even then John Bull would not admit that his ship was a mail-packet, but replied that his vessel was H.M.S. *Vixen*. After private signals were once again given and

---

[1] ibid., III, 61, 281, 301, 477; VI, 18, 334. Portmanteaus were of three sizes, 3, 4 and 5 feet long, with ends of 1 foot 2 inches for the smallest to 1 foot 10 inches for the largest. They had stitched ends, stitched handles and double leather under the staples. The largest size cost £5 each. The portmanteau as a mail-case is not noticed in the O.E.D. It was a more modern form of portmantle. According to the *Dict. of Am. English*, the American Post Office paid the expenses of a prosecution in 1805 that included 'portmanteaus and mail locks'. For portmantle, see above, p. 22.

answered the engagement came to an end. Captain John Bull lived up to his name, for the casualties on the *Primrose* were 3 killed and 23 wounded; on the packet 1 passenger was killed and 4 seamen wounded. An inquiry at Falmouth acquitted Captain Bull of all blame, but the court martial at Falmouth only admonished Captain Philliott to be 'more circumspect in the future'.[1]

[1] ibid., III, 466; V, 304, 314, 637; *T.L.B.*, XV, 303; XVI, 318; *St Martins-le-Grand*, XXVI, 121-5.

10

MAIL CARRYING OVERSEAS DURING THE NAPOLEONIC WAR

THE sailing packets based on Falmouth faced war-time conditions for the last time during the twelve years that ended in 1815. Privateers and men-of-war endangered all their routes. The packets might even be pursued into home waters. On one occasion the *Duke of Marlborough* was forced to fight the enemy in sight of Falmouth. The successful resistance of Captain John Bull, in this duel, was watched by onlookers who crowded the nearby headlands.

THE PENINSULAR AND MEDITERRANEAN ROUTES

These routes were of the greatest value in the continental war against Napoleon. When one of Napoleon's brother's became King of Spain in 1808, the British replied by landing troops in Portugal. The Peninsular War with Wellington in command of the British forces, was a five-year effort to drive the French out of Portugal and Spain. Lisbon became the base for the war and for the penetration of the French commercial blockade.

The Post Office mail services proved absolutely essential for communication with the forces. Government dispatches went back and forth with the greatest possible speed. The agent at Falmouth wrote London in 1811: 'I wish that the coach might be kept to good time, particularly on Friday, in order that I may continue to dispatch the Lisbon packets always on Friday.' If, as sometimes happened, contrary winds prevented a packet from leaving, several mails might accumulate at the Falmouth office. Three mails might be ready to leave, for example, and but two packets were on hand. In that case, one packet-boat would take the first and third mails, and the other the second mail in order 'to prevent originals and duplicates being lost in case of the capture of either of the packets'. It was a general

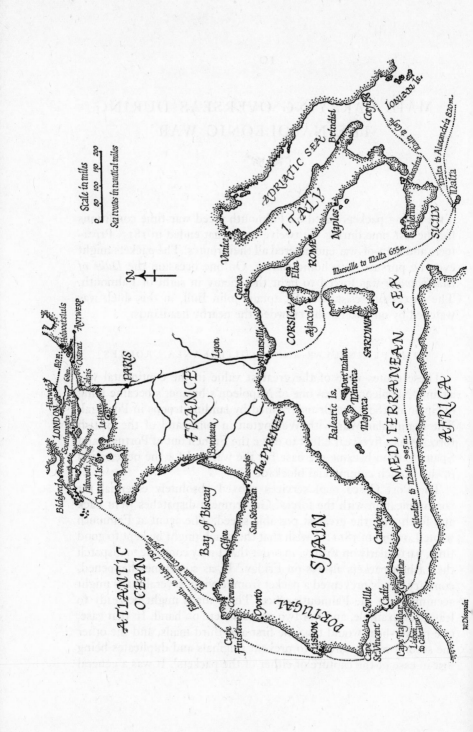

Scale in miles
0 50 100 150 200

Sea routes in nautical miles

ATLANTIC OCEAN

H.M.
Helvoetsluis
68m.
Antwerp
Ostend
Calais
LONDON
Harwich
Deal
Portsmouth
Southampton
Plymouth
Dover
Le Havre
Channel Is.
Bideford
Falmouth
Finisterre

PARIS

FRANCE

Lyon

Bordeaux
Bay of Biscay
The PYRENEES
985 m.
Gijon
San Sebastian
Pasages

SPAIN

Corunna
Oporto
Lisbon
PORTUGAL
Seville
Cadiz
Cartagena
Gibraltar

Cape Finisterre
Cape St.Vincent
Cape Trafalgar

Falmouth to Corunna 530 m.
Falmouth to Lisbon 800 m.
Lisbon to Gibraltar
Gibraltar to Malta 985 m.

Marseilles

Genoa
Ajaccio
CORSICA
Elba
ROME
Naples
SARDINIA
Minorca
Port Mahon
Majorca
Balearic Is.

ITALY

Venice
ADRIATIC SEA
Brindisi

IONIAN Is.
Corfu

Messina
Palermo
SICILY

MEDITERRANEAN SEA

AFRICA

Marseille to Malta 655 m.

Malta to Alexandria 820 m.
Malta

N

practice to send by the following mail copies of all important correspondence.[1]

Army dispatches and soldiers' mail greatly added to the load of the Lisbon packets. Although occasionally a messenger travelled by packet with government dispatches, the Army mail service had become so large by 1811 that the packet agent at Lisbon took over the management of the Army mail—to the entire satisfaction of Lord Wellington. Reynolds, the packet agent in Lisbon at this time, was even called the Army Postmaster.

The average time for the Lisbon packets was two weeks, depending much on the winds in the stormy Bay of Biscay, but the trip could be made in less than a week under favourable conditions. The *Princess Elizabeth* took four and a half days in July 1809, and but five days in March 1812. In May 1814 the *Francis Freeling* made a rapid voyage home in six days, explained partly by the value of her cargo and the stubborn but unavailing pursuit by a privateer. On her arrival at Falmouth the agent wrote to London by express: 'The Freeling brings no news, but as it is probable that the express [by horseback] may overtake the mail-coach of last night at Exeter and there is about £30,000 on board the Freeling, the safety of which the merchants will be glad to know, I have thought it right to forward the public letters without delay.'

Several other Peninsular ports were used by the Falmouth packets. Cadiz became a port of call when the Spanish Government had to retire from Madrid, and it was also a convenient port for communicating with the fleet patrolling the waters outside Gibraltar. Corunna was again in use for a time, but the gradual pushing of the French forces into north-eastern Spain by Wellington's armies made a stop at Corunna unnecessary. Instead, packets were sent to ports farther east along the north coast of Spain—to Gijon, San Sebastian and the nearby Passages. This was almost entirely a dispatch service. And when the British armies reached southern France, the packets proceeded to Bordeaux with the Army mail.

During the war the Falmouth packets carried mail regularly to Gibraltar, and, for the first time, into the Mediterranean. The service to Gibraltar and Malta was approved by the autumn of 1806, four packets being assigned to the new route. At the beginning the services were monthly, but two years later they were going into the Mediterranean every three weeks because of the increasing success

[1] For staggered mails see *Pkt. Rep. Bks.*, I, 386, 791; *Fal. L.B.*, III, 146; IV, 390, 505, etc.

in outflanking Napoleon's Continental Blockade. On the way to Malta the packets dropped mails at ports in Sardinia and Sicily.[1]

One of the best known Englishmen of that day, Lord Byron, used mail-packets in this war in order to visit the Mediterranean. In July 1809 he made his first journey to the Levant, where he spent two years on a grand tour. It was a region not commonly visited by English travellers, especially in time of war. Byron's journey was more than a grand tour, for his experiences bore fruit in the somewhat autobiographical *Childe Harold's Pilgrimage*. Lord Byron and his friend Hobhouse were passengers on the *Princess Elizabeth* (Captain Kidd) when the packet left Falmouth early in July. It carried nineteen passengers on this trip, including the wives of two British officers, three Portuguese gentlemen and various domestics. Lord Byron wrote his friend Drury: 'We sail tomorrow on the Lisbon packet, having been detained till now by lack of wind.'

The conditions on the packet were amusingly exaggerated:

> 'Now we've reached her, lo! the Captain,
> Gallant Kidd commands the crew;
> Passengers their berths are clapt in,
>   Some to grumble, some to spew.

> 'Hey day! call you that a cabin?
> Why, 'tis hardly three feet square;
> Not enough to stow Queen Mab in—
>   Who the deuce can harbour there?'

Fortunately for the passengers the voyage was unusually short: 'A very favourable passage of four and a half days.' But it was rough, for Byron wrote to a friend that he was 'seasick and sick of the sea'. He recalls the voyage in *Childe Harold*:

> 'And on the vessel flies, the land is gone,
> And winds are rude in Biscay's sleepless bay.
> Four days are sped, but with the fifth anon,
> New shores descried make every bosom gay.'

From Lisbon, Byron's party went overland to Cadiz, thence by H.M.S. *Hyperion* to Gibraltar. The next stage of the pilgrimage was on another packet, the *Townshend* (Captain Cock) that carried him

[1] ibid., III, 316, 372, 446; IV, 433, 507; V, 96, 236, 328; *T.L.B.*, XII, 318; XIX, 311.

to Malta. Lord Byron's further travels eastward were made in British war vessels, since packets were not yet going beyond Malta. After two years in the Levant he returned to England on a slow Government frigate that took six weeks for the voyage. It might be added that when Byron died in Greece in 1824, communication was still slow. The news of his death at Missolonghi on April 19th was transmitted with all possible speed by sailing packets, but it did not reach Hobhouse in England until twenty-five days later.[1]

The beginnings of a mail service into the Mediterranean initiated a route that was soon to grow to vast importance.

SERVICES TO THE AMERICAS

The oldest transatlantic route out of Falmouth was that to the West Indies, a route for which the merchants had been chiefly responsible. During the Napoleonic War, the packet-boats were busier than ever, for they visited the colonies won from France, the Netherlands and Spain. These included the Dutch colonies of Curaçao and Surinam, as well as Trinidad, St Croix and St Thomas. It was a difficult service because the ports of call were so widely scattered. By 1810 six West Indian mail-boats supplemented the packets that crossed the Atlantic. Communication from England was twice a month, but mails to Trinidad, Surinam and Demerara were less frequent, as the possessions lying to the windward of Barbados were difficult to reach by sailing vessels. The governments at Surinam and Demerara and the merchants trading with those mainland holdings petitioned for a direct packet service from Falmouth on the ground that the voyage across the Atlantic to Surinam might frequently be made in less time by direct packet than by way of Barbados and the mail-boat. By 1811 Surinam, Demerara, Trinidad and Curaçao had a direct packet.[2]

Another packet route that began during the Napoleonic War connected Falmouth with Rio de Janeiro in Brazil. It was the first time that the mail-packets had penetrated the south Atlantic. Francis Freeling was very doubtful of this venture because of the great distance and the consequent expense. Yet it was authorized in 1808 following the flight of the Portuguese royal family from Lisbon

---

[1] For the quotations, see 'Lines to Mr Hodgson' and *Childe Harold's Pilgrimage*, I, xiv. For his journey of 1809 see W. A. Borst, *Lord Byron's First Pilgrimage* (New Haven, 1948).

[2] The three British colonies of Berbice, Essequibo and Demerara now comprise British Guiana. Surinam, the present Dutch Guiana, lies just to the east. It was returned to the Netherlands in 1815.

to Rio at the time of the French occupation of Portugal. The voyages were monthly with the packets sailing by way of Madeira and the Canaries. Like the new Malta service, that to South America was to remain in use long after the war-time needs had ceased.

The time taken on this route was from two to three months each way. The *Diana* took 54 days in 1811, the *Sandwich* 77 days in 1813 for a return voyage, the *Lady Mary Pelham* 71 days in 1814. One cause for the permanent scarcity of packets during these years was the addition of the Malta services; another the great length of the voyages to Brazil.[1]

The chief port on the North American Continent was New York, although Halifax was in regular use during the summer months. It was the practice before the United States entered the war in 1812 to route the New York packets via Bermuda from November to February. By so doing they served the naval vessels that wintered there instead of at Halifax. The mail from Halifax and Canada either went from Bermuda direct by a British naval vessel, or was sent from New York. The packets out of New York in winter usually took the southern route that brought them much nearer Bermuda than Nova Scotia. Only when the port of New York was closed to British packets after the United States entered the war was Halifax visited the year round.

The time taken in crossing the Atlantic had been shortened with the gradual improvement of sailing vessels. The packets usually made better time returning from America than they could possibly make on the outward voyage, because of the prevailing westerlies. Eastbound packets from New York or Halifax, if sailing direct, could do the crossing in three weeks or less. In October 1810 the *Diana* reached Falmouth in 16 days, *Ann* took 21 days from Halifax in October 1814, but only 17 days on her next return in December.[2]

The return voyages of the packets from New York in the summer of 1812 were of particular importance, as the United States seemed likely to join in the general war against Britain. One of the chief causes for a warlike feeling in the United States was the impressment by British naval commanders of sailors found on American merchantmen, especially if the sailors were British by birth. And there were the galling restrictions on trade of the various orders-in-council, including the order to detain and search neutral vessels for contraband.

[1] *T.L.B.*, XII, 315; XIII, 33; XIX, 311; *Fal. L.B.*, III, 154, 341; V, 148.
[2] ibid., III, 1, 240; V, 522, 597; *Pkt. Rep. Bks.*, I, 46, 281, 525, 544.

On July 4, 1812 H.M. schooner *Bramble* arrived in England with dispatches and a mail from New York; she had left New York on May 31st and Bermuda on June 11th. The Captain reported that a long debate was to take place on June 1st as to whether the United States should declare war against Great Britain. It was believed that the vote in Congress would be in the negative. The packet *Lapwing*, arriving at Falmouth on July 6th—two days later than the *Bramble*— had much later news, for she had sailed from New York direct. The *Lapwing* brought news of June 14th, that 'the Senate had not decided the question, and the general opinion and the anxious desire of the people of New York was that there would be no war with this country'. The Senate actually voted on the question of war on the 18th, four days after the *Lapwing* had left New York. On the 16th, two days before the declaration of war by the American Senate, Lord Castlereagh had announced the withdrawal of the obnoxious orders-in-council. But the news of this action by the British Government, in the existing speed of transatlantic communication, could not have reached the United States until some time in July.

In mid-November after the United States had entered the war, the packet *Chichester* was sent to New York in the hope that her mails would be accepted. She was directed to proceed to Bermuda 'where after landing the mails for Novia Scotia and Canada you are to proceed with the letters for New York . . . with a flag of truce . . . and to return by way of Bermuda to England with such letters as may be confided to your care'. The *Chichester*, however, sailed back to England without any New York letters.[1]

Even before 1812 the Post Office was finding it more and more difficult to maintain the packet services. The Postmasters-General wrote to the Treasury as the war with the United States seemed likely, suggesting the need for more established packets. Christopher Saverland was exceedingly pessimistic after the United States joined Britain's enemies. He wrote Freeling in December 1812: 'We have thirty-nine packets but we must expect more to be captured.'

If packets were not available in Falmouth for important mails and dispatches to go overseas, naval vessels were put to use. In January 1812 the Post Office wrote the Treasury that fifteen naval vessels had been used in the previous eighteen months 'to take out mails which ought to have been dispatched by the packets'. In June 1813, for example, Captain Maples of H.M.S. *Pelican* carried the mails to

[1] *Fal. L.B.*, IV, 59, 68, 178, 191, 266; *Pkt. Min.*, I, 270, II, 109.

Jamaica and other ports in the West Indies, and brought back the mails to Falmouth. He was granted 50 guineas, and praised for performing so well an 'intricate duty'.[1]

PACKET WARFARE

How well did the sailing packets meet this long-drawn-out trial by battle that began in 1803, and was intensified by the American entry into the war nine years later?[2]

In the first year of the war—1803—the Falmouth station lost three packets, two by capture and the third by collision with an iceberg in the north Atlantic. All three are typical of the difficulties faced, and of the ways in which they were met.

The *King George* (Captain Yescombe) was captured at the end of July while *en route* to Lisbon. Despite the obviously superior force of a French privateer—fourteen guns and 100 men—the packet crew put up a vigorous defence. After a severe action, the packet was boarded and taken, the mails and dispatches being sunk before the capture. The captain and several others were severely wounded; they and the rest of the crew were taken into Vigo where the captain engaged a vessel to take them back to Falmouth. Captain Yescombe died on the return voyage. The Post Office was so impressed by the brave defence of the mails that a pension was granted to the captain's widow, and awards were made to the crew. It was the first of numerous awards for bravery made during this war.

The stimulus of awards had been used only occasionally in the French war of 1793. It now became a regular device for ensuring a courageous defence of the mails. In the previous war awards were made on only three occasions; between 1803 and 1815 they were granted over thirty times.

The second capture in 1803 illustrates the loss of a packet in which the commander and most of the crew were not inspired to a defence of the mails by either patriotism or the incentive of an

[1] *Fal. L.B.*, IV, 197; *T.L.B.*, XIV, 83-87, 166-8; *Pkt. Min.*, I, 100, 113, 134, 203; and numerous other references.

[2] Apart from manuscript records, the only full account of the packet fortunes and misfortunes in this war is in Norway, op. cit., A. H. Norway was in the postal service, and based his account on official records. It was published in 1895. Mr Norway was Secretary of the Irish Post Office in Dublin prior to the Irish 'Troubles' of 1916. Inquiry of his son, the well-known novelist, Nevil Shute (Norway), as to his father's papers, brought the reply that they were destroyed in the burning of the Dublin Post Office in 1916. Mr Norway was so impressed by the record of the packets that he was largely responsible for the monument to the packet service, its captains, crews and agents, that now stands on the Town Moor in Falmouth. It was erected in 1898.

award. The *Duke of York*, also on the Lisbon route, discovered an enemy in pursuit. When the French privateer used her sweeps and it was certain that the packet would be overtaken, the commander called a conference of his officers and crew to whom he stated that it was obvious that resistance would be in vain. All except the gunner and another seaman agreed. The *Duke of York* did not even fire in the course of a long chase, although there was always a chance that a few shots might have discouraged or disabled the pursuer. The Post Office decided that the commander and the crew, with the exception of the two who were willing to fight, should never again serve on a packet-boat.[1]

The third packet lost in 1803 is one of the best-known packet casualties of the early nineteenth century. The *Lady Hobart* (Captain Fellowes) sank after striking an iceberg off Newfoundland. She had left Halifax June 24th, and kept well to the northward after clearing Sable Island in order to avoid French cruisers. Two days later, however, the *Lady Hobart* was attacked by a French privateer, whose captain thought the packet was a merchant brig. The packet won the battle and sent back the *Aimable Julie* to Halifax with a prize crew. Later the French prisoners, save Captain Rossé and two others, were put on two British schooners, also bound for Halifax.

All went well until the early morning of the 28th when the packet, sailing by the log at a speed of 7 knots, struck 'an island of ise [sic] that appeared to hang over the ship, forming a high peak . . . and we suppose the length of the island to have been from a quarter to half a mile'. After the collision, the cutter and the jolly boat were launched, and some provisions hastily thrown into the boats. Three women passengers and fifteen men, including the French captain, were assigned to the cutter. It was so overloaded that its gunwales were within 7 inches of the water. The smaller jolly boat held eleven persons, and was attached by a tow-rope to the cutter. Before abandoning the packet, iron pigs of ballast were lashed to the mail and it was thrown overboard—a needless precaution as the packet sank shortly after it was abandoned. The boats then put off for Newfoundland, estimated to be 350 miles to the north-west.[2]

A gruelling experience followed. The captain read divine service

[1] *Reps.*, *P.M.G.*, XXII, 273; XXIII, 23-27, 166-74; *T.L.B.*, XI, 90, 97. A Mr Fenner was the commander in the absence of Captain Deake.

[2] One is reminded of another and more famous collision in much the same area, that of the *Titanic* in 1912. Both collisions took place south-east of Newfoundland on the edge of the southern limit of the icebergs. The *Titanic* also carried mail. See below, p. 270.

D

every day to keep up their spirits. On the third day the jolly boat separated from the cutter, and was soon lost in the fog. The next morning the captain discovered a sail. As his log-book has it: 'Great joy. Hoisted a lady's shawl on the boat-hook. Found it was the jolly boat. Threw out a tow-rope and bore away to the north-west.' On the sixth day, the fog continued to be so thick that they could not take bearings, but when it cleared later they were overjoyed to see the shore of Newfoundland but a mile away. The passengers and the crew, six days at sea, and weakened by the freezing, foggy weather, had reached land. The only casualty, apart from some frozen toes, was the French captain, who had jumped overboard in a fit of delirium the day before. According to Captain Fellowes: 'The raw spirits to which he had not been accustomed produced the most dreadful intoxicating effects and hurried on the fatal event.'

Captain Fellowes had received an appointment to the more lucrative Holyhead service about the time the *Lady Hobart* collided with the iceberg. As his promotion was not an award for his conduct after the collision, Captain Fellowes and his crew received £200 for their 'almost unexampled discipline, fortitude and resignation'. So much interest was aroused by their experiences after the collision that the Captain published a full narrative of the loss of the *Lady Hobart*; it was dedicated by permission to the Postmasters-General.[1]

The French captured two packets in 1804, both in the West Indies. Five more were captured in 1806. One was taken in 1807 near Barbados after Captain Dyneley and three seamen were killed; the survivors of the *Duke of Montrose* received awards.

A remarkably courageous and successful packet action in 1807 was a duel between the *Windsor Castle* and a French privateer that was reported as having 14 guns, and 90 men in the crew. As the packet-boat was nearing Barbados, an enemy schooner gave chase and an engagement followed that lasted for over two hours. The packet's crew put up so stubborn a defence that the privateer attempted to sheer off, but she was unable to do so as the rigging of the two vessels had become fouled. At this point, William Rogers, who was the acting commander of the *Windsor Castle* on this voyage, decided to board the privateer. The French captain was killed and the survivors of the privateer's crew were driven below deck. The casualties on the packet were 3 men killed and 8 wounded;

---

[1] *A Narrative of the Loss of His Majesty's Packet, the Lady Hobart, on an Island of Ise in the Atlantic Ocean* (1803, 45 pp.). It went through several editions. *Reps. P.M.G.*, XXIII, 123–29; *T.L.B.*, XIII, 327; XVI, 182.

on the privateer, 31 killed and 34 wounded. So great was the joy over the successful engagement that Rogers was recommended for a permanent command, received a sword from the inhabitants of Tortola, and later became a freeman of the City of London. Public subscriptions for the crew were collected in most of the islands. The Post Office, not to be outdone, made liberal awards in addition to paying £400 for the repair of the *Windsor Castle*.[1]

The records for the years 1809 and 1810 show no captures and few actions, explained in large part by the British occupation of Martinique in 1809 and of Guadeloupe in the next year. Only two packets were lost in 1811 and the first half of 1812—before the United States entered the war. The request of Captain Rogers of the *Chichester*, following an engagement in 1811, will give an idea of what might have to be done to escape the enemy. He wrote:

'On my homeward voyage, being off Finisterre, I fell in with and was chased by a large vessel which I had every reason to believe from the appearance of her sails and hull was an enemy as well as for her not answering the private signals . . . Finding her to come up with me very fast, I was obliged for the preservation of the packet and to prevent the loss of H.M. mails and dispatches, to knock out the stanchions, throw overboard the long boat, and run off my lee gun amidships in order to expedite the sailing of the vessel, which I an happy to say had the desired effect, and after a hard chase of thirty-six hours we escaped . . . I shall be much obliged by your communicating to their Lordships [the Postmasters-General] my humble request that the long boat which cost £25 may be replaced.'[2]

THE AMERICAN WAR OF 1812

When the United States declared war, it brought a change for the worse so far as the packets were concerned. Although the Americans had an insignificant Navy, many private vessels were fitted out as privateers in such ports as Gloucester, Salem, Boston, New Bedford, New York, Philadelphia and Baltimore. Privateers received commissions from the President, authorizing them to prey on the enemy's commerce. The takings were divided half in half between the owners of the vessel and the crew. Privateering offered such rich rewards that over 150 American privateers were on the

---

[1] ibid., XII, 176, 204-6, 215; *Pkt. Rep. Bks.*, I, 3-4, 131-3.
[2] *Fal. L.B.*, III, 215.

high seas in less than two months after war began. In the three-year war over 600 American privateers were commissioned. Of these, over 150 came out of the ports of Massachusetts. New York privateers were also active, and the clippers fitted out in Baltimore were especially noted for their speed.[1]

The first packet-boat taken by an American privateer was the *Prince Adolphus*, on the way from Martinique to Falmouth. Captain Boulderson gave up the packet without resistance, later explaining that this was because he did not know of the war with the United States. But the committee of captains at Falmouth that sat on the case decided that the packet should have been defended. The commander was dismissed, and payment for the packet—sent into Philadelphia by the captain of the *Governor McKeen*—was refused.

The first actual engagement between an American privateer and a packet-boat was in September 1812 when the *Princess Amelia* surrendered to the schooner *Rossie* of Baltimore after the packet's captain, the master and a seaman had been killed. In the same year, the *Townshend* (Captain Cock) was captured off Barbados by two American privateers, the *Tom* and the *Bona*, also out of Baltimore. When the master and several others had been killed, Captain Cock surrendered after throwing over the portmanteaus. When most of the valuables in the packet had been removed, the *Towshend* was returned to the captain for a ransom of $6,000. According to the American account of this action, the portmanteaus did not sink, and were later picked up by the crew of the *Bona*. This does not appear to have been known to Captain Cock or the Falmouth agent, for, if reported, it might have prevented the grant of an award for the courageous but unsuccessful defence of the mails.[2]

Another capture of the mails, in May 1813, caused much concern. The *Mary Ann*, returning from the Mediterranean, was attacked by the *Governor Tompkins* of New York. Although resistance seemed hopeless, the packet surrendered only after a sturdy defence, and after the two portmanteaus went overboard. Unfortunately, they did not have time to sink 'before the privateering people caught

---

[1] Use has been made of two accounts of the American privateering during this war. George Coggeshall, *The History of the American Privateers during Our War with England* (N.Y., 1861) is rambling and patriotic, but it has value as it was written by the captain of a privateer. E. S. Maclay, *A History of American Privateers* (N.Y., 1899) is more competent. See also, S. E. Morison, op. cit., 199-202, for the part played by the privateers of Massachusetts. Maclay gives the total number of prizes as 1,346. One American privateer, the *America*, took over twenty-six prizes (one was a packet-boat) that netted over $1,000,000 for the owners and the crew.

[2] *T.L.B.*, XIV, 321; XVI, 253-60; *Fal. L.B.*, IV, 285; V, 415, 423; Maclay, op. cit. 307, 451.

hold and took possession'. Captain Caddy had received the customary two pigs of iron before sailing from Falmouth, and they were attached to the mails. The Captain was mortified at their capture: 'I had never heard of an instance when a portmanteau had floated.' Some boxes in the mails were thought to have given them too much buoyancy.[1]

THE CASE OF THE 'MONTAGU' AND THE 'PELHAM'

An action between an American privateer and two mail-packets in November 1813 aroused so much controversy over the conduct of the two packets that elaborate inquiries followed. Two brigs, the *Montagu* (Captain Norway) and the *Lady Mary Pelham* (under Acting Commander Pering) left Falmouth a week apart for Brazil, but both reached Funchal in Madeira a few hours apart. From Funchal they proceeded together towards the Canaries, being followed by an American privateer, the *Globe*. The *Globe* attacked the two packets on November 2nd. Captain Norway took charge of the defence, as he was the senior commander and had the larger brig. He decided that the *Pelham* should keep close ahead of the *Montagu*, which was to take the brunt of the attack by the privateer. The *Montagu* was soon boarded, preventing the *Pelham* from firing at the privateer. Captain Norway, the surgeon and two other men on the *Montagu* were killed as well as several of the attackers who had climbed over the boarding nettings. The privateer then sheered off. Watkins, who had taken command of the *Montagu*, was soon wounded and taken below, whereupon the mail was thrown overboard and the flag hauled down—apparently on Watkins's orders.

At this point the *Pelham* came into action, and succeeded in doing much additional damage to the privateer. According to the American account: 'While we were thus engaged with the first brig, the other one bore up, and passing athwart our bows gave us a terrible raking fire, which completely cut up our sails and rigging. This broadside, added to the injury we had already received, rendered our schooner for a time unmanageable.' It was at this point, according to the *Globe*'s version that the larger brig struck her

[1] *Fal. L.B.*, IV, 425-6; *Pkt. Rep. Bks.*, II, 114; Coggeshall, op. cit., 117. The American account states that the spoil included $60,000 in gold and bullion. When several more boxes were found in a later mail that arrived from the Mediterranean, Christopher Saverland ordered the commanders, 'whenever you suspect the mails to contain boxes', to open the mail and take them out. According to Cooper, op. cit., II, 204, the frigate *Essex* on capturing the *Nocton* in December 1812, obtained specie to the value of $55,000. Privateering was profitable business. See illustration facing p. 65.

colours, when 'the other brig was pouring in on us broadside after broadside within half-pistol shot distance'. The *Globe*, nevertheless, attempted to take possession of the *Montagu* 'when to our surprise she again hoisted her colours'. After some further exchanges the privateer was obliged to haul off, and the two packets got away.

They then proceeded to Orotava on Tenerife; the *Pelham*, five days later, left for Brazil. The *Montagu* remained somewhat longer for repairs, not leaving for Falmouth until January 2, 1814. When near the Scilly Islands the *Montagu* had a further battering, this time by a gale, and was driven ashore. After further repairs the *Montagu* finally limped into Falmouth Harbour after a very frustrating voyage. She had lost her mails, her captain and four others by death, and eleven of her crew were still on the invalid list.

The *Pelham* reached Rio without further delays. During the voyage Captain Pering was confined to his cabin, as he had been injured by a musket ball in the thigh. The return voyage started January 7, 1814. Ten weeks later, in mid-March, the *Pelham* came to anchor in Falmouth Harbour, after an absence of five months.

Meanwhile, early in March, a committee of captains examined Watkins and the other members of the crew of the *Montagu*. The committee concluded that the crew were justified in throwing the mail overboard, that the colours were not struck but were shot down, and then re-hoisted. The crew asserted that the *Pelham* gave the *Montagu* no assistance. Watkins became a captain as the result of the inquiry.

When Thomas Pering returned he naturally objected to an investigation in his absence, even declaring that he would lay the whole matter before Parliament through his brother. A second inquiry followed, when the previous findings were considerably modified. The Captain of the *Montagu* was held unwise in ordering the *Pelham* to her position at the opening of the action; the *Pelham*, it was decided, did her duty after entering the engagement; and it was the opinion of the committee that the *Montagu* would have been taken by the Americans but for the *Pelham*. One of the *Montagu*'s crew declared that he had hauled down the colours on the order of Watkins, whose evidence was found to differ widely from his own Journal.

Much feeling was aroused over the matter in Falmouth. It was the more bitter because of Captain Norway's death, and because Thomas Pering, who was in temporary command of the *Pelham*, was not in the regular packet service. Captain Pering's threat to appeal to Parliament resulted in a Parliamentary *Return* of fifty folio pages, giving documents regarding the case. In addition, Pering published in 1815 an *Inquiry into the System of the Post Office*, in which he defended his own conduct, and sharply attacked Francis Freeling for the handling of the packet services.[1]

The war ended in 1815. The last packet to be taken was the *Windsor Castle* on her outward voyage to Halifax in March. The crew of the packet defended her *five* mails in no less than three distinct actions. The colours were struck when the crew of the American privateer were in the act of boarding. The packet Captain feared that the packet would be taken 'before we could destroy the mails, having five very large portmanteaus to sink'.

The mail service had faced trying conditions. From 1803 to June 1812 when the United States entered the war, 13 Falmouth packets were captured, 7 more based on Harwich and Dover, and 1 out of Weymouth. In addition, sixteen of the inter-island mail-boats in the West Indies had been taken by the enemy. From June 1812 to the end of the war three years later, 22 Falmouth packets were captured and 4 more mail-boats. Before the United States entered, the average of losses on the high seas was less than two a year; after June 1812 it was seven a year. During the long war against Napoleon 25 packet seamen lost their lives and 115 were wounded. The crews of fifteen packets received awards for the courageous defence of the mails, even though it was in vain.[2]

Reflections on the record were only to be expected after the coming of peace. Francis Freeling wrote a long letter in 1819 on the best class of vessels for the service. He now believed that a limitation of the packets to about 180 tons held down their speed. 'It is generally understood,' he wrote, 'that the American schooners of from 250 to 300 tons are the fastest vessels that go to sea . . . I believe there is not a single instance in the last war in which a packet escaped from a French or an American privateer by dint of sailing.' Mr Freeling concluded his long summary by stating that 26 actions

[1] See *Parl. Ret.*, 151/1815. An acting captain was put in charge of the *Pelham* because of the transfer of Captain Stevens to Holyhead after his packet had been assigned to the voyage. The two American accounts make it clear that the Americans never learned the names of the two packets. *T.L.B.* XV, 247, 257, 272, 295 states that the privateer lost thirty-three men; the American accounts state that the packets lost twenty-seven killed and wounded. Both seem to have been exaggerating. A. H. Norway's account, op. cit., 254-62, is very biased in favour of Captain Norway and the *Montagu;* the *Pelham* is even accused of 'cowardly actions', and Pering's name does not appear in Norway's account. He implied that the official papers were 'bulky' and that duels would have followed their publication.

[2] See the Appendix for the list of the thirty-five captured packets based on Falmouth.

had been fought, 22 mails had been lost, and 21 packets [I make it 22] had been taken after the Americans entered the war. His proposed remedy was to increase the packet tonnage to about 220 tons, but not on any account 'to exceed 230 tons'.

Francis Freeling, apparently, believed that another war with the United States might be in the offing. On the contrary, a long period of peace was to give Great Britain an opportunity to increase her industry and commerce as never before, to develop new and thriving colonies, especially south of the Equator, and to transform the mail services to meet ever-growing demands.

11

OCEAN MAILS—1815-30

WHEN peace finally came in 1815 the Post Office reduced the number of Falmouth packets to thirty, with crews of only twenty-one men. At the same time, the size of the packet-boats was increased to 230 tons, in line with Francis Freeling's opinion that greater tonnage would provide 'better sailing'. Larger vessels meant more passenger accommodation as well. The arrangements on a packet-boat, as described at this time, consisted of a 'mess room in which are 6 or 8 inclosed Sleeping-Cabins, with a sliding door and a Bull's-eye [window] in each'. There were also 'four open bed-places' in the after-cabin, and cots could be slung on emergency for more accommodation. The sleeping-cabins were far from spacious—6 feet long and 3 to 4 feet wide. At the forward end of the mess room, near the recess for the sideboard, were two small dressing rooms.[1]

Arrangements for a packet's departure were somewhat improved. By 1820 the London mail was reaching Falmouth in mid-afternoon and every effort was made to get the packet away before dark. When the vessel was scheduled to leave, the signal for sailing was hoisted and answered, the topsails sheeted home, and only the captain with his boat's crew were allowed to remain on shore; they were to take away the mail as soon as it was bagged. The portmanteaus were never made up until the wind became 'fair'.

Another improvement came in 1820 with the addition of a bag for 'loose letters'; it was meant for mail brought on board after the mails had been made up at a port abroad. When leaving Falmouth, the captain was not allowed to take any letters save those that were in the portmanteaus. The reason for the loose-letter bag was the danger that loose letters might be left about the vessel 'in the steward's pantry, in the captain's trunk or other improper place,

---

[1] *Fal. L.B.*, VII, 9; *Pkt. Min.*, 447L/1860. Passage money at the time for such accommodations was not cheap—13 guineas to Lisbon, 25 to Gibraltar, 50 to New York and 80 to Brazil.

D*

where they were generally forgotten and perhaps not delivered into my office until a week or more after the arrival of the packet'.[1]

Some changes occurred in the routes. A proposal of 1818 to send the Malta packet on to Corfu in the Ionian Islands did not appeal to the Post Office, for it would lengthen the voyage of the Mediterranean packets by two or three weeks. Sending a boat to Corfu seemed essential, however, as it was the seat of the British High Commissioner of the Ionian Islands. The islands had been taken from Turkey in 1815 and entrusted to British administration. The objection of the Post Office to this addition to the route was overruled; packets began visiting Corfu in 1819. It was almost wholly a dispatch service.

The sailing arrangements to the West Indies were somewhat simplified with the return to the Netherlands of their former island holdings. The Jamaica packet and that for the Leeward Islands continued to leave Falmouth two weeks apart. Both made the first stop at Barbados. The Jamaica packet, on her homeward journey, sailed by way of the Bahamas to pick up mail at Crooked Island. The Leeward Islands packet moved from island to island on the way to St Thomas. Although belonging to Denmark, St Thomas was useful because of its excellent harbour; then too, the Government of Denmark was glad to have a regular service from St Thomas. Eight days after this packet had left Barbados, a mail-boat followed the same course to gather the last letters for the packet that had reached St Thomas. Another mail-boat came with collections from the Windward Islands and also from Trinidad.[2]

The number of mail-boats circulating in the West Indies was increased from five to seven in 1823, and three more were added five years later.

In 1818 an offer was received that would have carried the mails among the West Indian islands by steam vessels at a considerable financial saving. Francis Freeling was not at all impressed with the offer. He cautioned the Postmasters-General: 'Your Lordships will pause before you will consent to entrust His Majesty's mails and dispatches and the lives of His Majesty's subjects to steam vessels, recollecting how little they are used, and the circumstances which have befallen them.' The Secretary of the Post Office was sure that

[1] *Fal. L.B.*, VIII, 77, 153, 269, 271.
[2] ibid., VI, 48, 234; VII, 86, 401; VIII, 55, 109, 244. Trinidad was not returned to Spain, and has been held ever since. The Ionian Islands however, were voluntarily ceded to Greece in 1864.

even a 10 per cent saving would not 'justify your opening the public interests to such Hazards'.[1]

The packet service to North America was difficult to arrange. Halifax, New York and Bermuda are located approximately at the points of an enormous equilateral triangle with sides 700 to 800 miles long. The earlier practice had been to sail from Bermuda to New York, and then on to Halifax. A winter service to Halifax was not regularly attempted until the War of 1812 made it indispensable. In November 1816, the *Francis Freeling* was taking out General Wilson to take over the command of the forces in Canada. He was to go overland from New York to the St Lawrence. As to the mail, the Captain of the *Francis Freeling* received these instructions: 'You will be charged with the mail for the United States and for Halifax and for Quebec, the whole of which you will deliver to Mr Moore, His Majesty's agent for packets at New York, the mail to be forwarded to Halifax by the first opportunity, and the Quebec mail to go through the United States according to the former practice in time of peace.' When a parcel was received at Falmouth for Quebec in January 1818, Saverland wrote the sender that he had no means of forwarding it farther than New York unless it was sent as a letter; he suggested that it go direct to the St Lawrence in the spring of the year 'as the conveyance to Quebec is very uncertain'.

The winter journey on the north Atlantic was not inviting. The passengers were few, the expenses great, and the 'wear and tear greater than upon any other voyage'. Like the Brazil route, it was not required of a packet captain twice in succession. Newfoundland was so out of the way that it did not as yet receive a direct service. A separate bag had been made up for Newfoundland since 1815, and regularly forwarded to Halifax, but the agent assumed that there was no communication with Newfoundland 'after the month of October'.[2]

By 1820 Halifax seems to have been regularly visited by the New York packets, as the result of requests by interested merchants in England and trading firms in Halifax; among the latter was Samuel Cunard & Company. The Government at home was assured that the harbour of Halifax 'is as accessible to the packets in winter as in summer . . . and that the great and increasing correspon-

---

[1] ibid., VII, 175; VIII, 18; *Pkt. Rep. Bks.*, II, 94,460. After the war, the packets on the Brazil run stopped at Bahia and Pernambuco as well as Rio de Janeiro. The captains did not care for this long and unrewarding route, and were not required to go to Brazil twice in succession.

[2] *Fal. L.B.*, VI, 186, 199; VII, 147, 295, 303; VIII, 18, 222.

dence with Nova Scotia and Canada makes it desirable that the packets should proceed to Halifax in every month of the year'. When the packet captains were consulted they agreed that the harbour might be open all the year, but they were still unwilling to go to Halifax in the winter months. As Bermuda still had its attractions, the packets were ordered to proceed by the southern passage to Bermuda, and 'with the usual wind they would fetch about New York and from thence proceed to Halifax'. The growing importance of British North America certainly justified a direct service from the mother country. The need for better services between England and North America was soon to be met by vessels much more adapted to face the north Atlantic than sailing packets of 230 tons.

After the war the Post Office attempted to extend the packet service to the Cape of Good Hope, and thence to India, a part of the world to which mail-packets had not yet penetrated. The long route around Africa had been a closed monopoly of the East India Company for 200 years, until the Charter Act of 1813 opened India to British private traders. Previously British mails that went via the Cape had been carried by the Company's vessels. They had been accustomed to touch at Table Bay long before Cape Colony became a permanent British possession in 1815. As there was no post office, the letters left at Table Bay were carefully wrapped and put under a stone or hidden near by. Inscriptions crudely graved on the stones gave the needed information. The Company's captains were instructed that on arriving at Table Bay 'you shall make search for letters and in like manner at your departure leave behind you in writing fitt remembrance of all matters useful'. When a vessel arrived at Table Bay from England, for example, there would be an accumulation of letters to be sent home. Instead of carrying them all the way to India, they were left at the Cape to be picked up by the next Company's ship bound for England.[1]

The massive East Indiamen were large and slow merchant ships with kettle-shaped hulls; they have been described as a cross between 'a castle and a floating warehouse'. The *Earl of Abergavenny*, for example, which was wrecked by a pilot's incompetence off Portland Bill in 1805, was an East Indiamen of 1,200 tons, and loaded with a cargo valued at £300,000. The captains, like the

[1] The South African Museum at Cape Town has a number of these 'Post Office Stones'. The one in the vestibule of the G.P.O. in Cape Town reads: 'THE LONDON ARIVED the 10 OF M[arch] HERE. FROM SURAT. BOUND FOR ENGLAND AND DEPART. THE 20 DICTO 1622 RICHARD BLYTH. CAPTAIN. HEARE UNDER LOOKE FOR LETTERS.' See *Annals of the South African Museum*, XIII.

packet commanders, had the passenger fares, but also rich rewards from their own trading interests. These 'floating warehouses' obviously could not provide for the regular and rapid transmission of the mails.[1]

Saverland suggested in 1814, the year after India was opened to general trade, that the Post Office set up a packet route to the Cape. He proposed that the Brazil packets sail four times a year from Rio to Table Bay where they would meet packets from the East Indies. At the Cape the mails would be exchanged, and the packets would turn about and carry back the mails they had received. It should bring in considerable postage; he pointed out that, in one year recently, India House had collected and sent out 280,000 letters in addition to their official dispatches.

The necessary authority for the new route was granted by an Act of 1815, the rates to India were set at 3s 6d single and 14s the ounce, with charges to the Cape at half the charge for India. Mails were to be monthly. Falmouth packets might be used, but the Post Office could employ other vessels, even those of the East India Company or vessels in private trade. Mail for the Far East was not included, since the East India Company still retained a monopoly of the trade with China.[2]

In October 1815 H.M.S. *Iphigenia* conveyed the first official packet mail to India. 'She is viewed', as the Post Office put it, 'in the light of a packet, and the commander is not to take charge of any letters not contained in the regular mails.' At the end of twelve months the Post Office had sent out sixteen mails. Despite this favourable beginning, the new route was shortlived. The East India Company, in particular, opposed the postal invasion of its territory, and the public objected to the high charges. An Act of 1819 (59 Geo. III, ch. 111) repealed the packet provisions of four years earlier so far as they related to India.

THE ADMIRALTY TAKES OVER

The idea of transferring the packets to naval control had occurred to Lord Melville, the First Lord of the Admiralty, before the end of

[1] Sir Evan Cotton, *East Indiamen* (1949), 44, 47, 128-39. John Wordsworth, the younger brother of the poet William, was Captain of the *Earl of Abergavenny*. Captain Wordsworth, who lost his life in the wreck, had planned soon to retire to Grasmere, and use his life savings to set the poet 'free from wordly care'.

[2] Act of 55 Geo. III, ch. 153. See A. W. Robertson, op. cit., pp. D21-25, for this service and for the hand-stamps in use. Letters could be sent along this route in ships not used as packets, at one-third the rate charged for packet letters.

the war. In 1814 he had talked with Francis Freeling, the Secretary of the Post Office, on the possible transfer. Francis Freeling had countered by describing the complexity of the service and the probable reduction of the number of packets with the return of peace. Mr Freeling wrote the Postmasters-General after the conference: 'I think it is not very probable that your Lordships will hear more of this matter.'[1]

Freeling was mistaken. In 1819 Lord Melville wrote a confidential letter to Lord Liverpool, the Prime Minister, on behalf of the transfer, now that the Navy was on a peace basis. If mails were sent by naval sloops, there would always be an effective force 'in and about the chops of the Channel'. In the event of war, the vessels carrying the mails would be less likely of capture, and fewer mails would be lost by being thrown overboard from endangered post-office packets. Then, too, the switch to Admiralty control would stop smuggling. It had revived noticeably after the war. Saverland wrote in 1816 that smuggling 'prevails here to a most alarming extent'. Lord Melville also asserted that the number of mail packets could be reduced from thirty to twenty-six.[2]

Francis Freeling made further efforts to head off the transfer, citing the contracts with the captains, who had built their vessels especially for the service. Six hundred 'prime seamen' were now used in the packets, who would probably be lost to the country 'and find their way to America', if the Navy took over. The captains supported the Post Office with a memorial of their own. They at least won the concession that their contracts would be honoured if the change occurred, that sloops of war would be used only to supplement the present agreements. They and the Post Office were

---

[1] *Pkt. Rep. Bks.*, II, 326. Freeling's report to 'your Lordships, the Postmasters-General', was to the joint holders of the office. Ever since 1691, when Sir Robert Cotton and Sir Thomas Frankland held the office jointly, there had been two Post-masters-General. They were usually unimportant save when one of the holders, such as the Earl of Tankerville or Lord Walsingham, made the post something more than a sinecure. This two-headed arrangement was to end in 1823. In that year, the Marquess of Salisbury died, and the other holder of the joint office, the Earl of Chichester, continued as the sole Postmaster-General. Since that time, many of the Postmasters-General have been more influential than the joint holders before 1823. For the list of Postmasters-General, see my *Britain's Post Office*, pp. 280ff.

[2] Viscount Melville, who was First Lord of the Admiralty from 1812 to 1827, was a highly respected administrator. See ibid., IV, 640, 644, and *Pkt. Min.*, 447L/1860. For references to smuggling, *Fal. L.B.*, VI, 409; VII, 96; VIII, 160, 169, 197. The *Chesterfield* from America was caught carrying a quantity of tobacco, concealed appropriately underneath 'the coals in the coal hole'. The *Diana* came back from the Mediterranean on one voyage with nearly 400 lb. of pepper, 124 gallons of brandy and 17 lb. of tapioca. The prying officials discovered another packet carrying a water-cask full of rum 'except for a bladder of water carefully inserted in the bung-hole'.

assured that the station would remain at Falmouth, and that the packets would be refitted at Falmouth as well. The Admiralty took over the responsibility for carrying the Falmouth mails on April 6, 1823.[1]

The immediate results of the transfer were slight. In 1824 the Admiralty extended the Brazilian services from Rio down the coast to Montevideo and Buenos Aires. The West Indian packet routes were also lengthened to include La Guaira, Cartagena and Vera Cruz. In 1824 the Falmouth agent found it necessary to have hand-stamps for the new stations. For the extended West India services he suggested a stamp marked 'Mexico' and another for 'Columbia' [sic] to be used for La Guaira and Cartagena mails. The packets soon began to stop at Havana as well.[2]

Lord Melville was badly mistaken as to the number of Admiralty sloops that would be needed; a few years after the change, thirty-nine packets, not twenty-six, were in use. Seventeen were privately owned post-office vessels, the remainder naval brigs. 'At present', according to a history of Falmouth published in 1827, 'there are thirty-nine packets employed; the first five on the list are on the Lisbon station, being those of the senior commanders; all the others take their turns for the various voyages, according to the time of their arrival home'. An additional naval brig was stationed in Carrick Roads, Falmouth, as a guardship, and to provide provisions and stores as they were needed. The establishment as a whole was under the command of Captain William King, R.N.[3]

SHIP-LETTERS

Only an occasional mention has been made of ship-letters—mail brought in or sent out of the British Isles by vessels other than Government mail-packets. The regulations regarding ship-letters go back to the seventeenth century, when Colonel Whitley began

[1] Christopher Saverland, the efficient Falmouth agent, had died in 1821 after thirty-four years of service as postal inspector and packet agent. Francis Freeling paid him high tribute, writing in 1821 that 'he has not left his equal'. T. M. Musgrove succeeded Saverland at Falmouth, and he was followed in 1824 by William Gay. See Gay, op. cit., 139.

[2] La Guaira was the port for Caracas, the capital of the present-day Venezuela.

[3] R. Thomas, *History of the Town and Harbour of Falmouth*, (Falmouth, 1827) for the packet list; it will be found in Appendix IV. The senior captain was John Bull. The two oldest packet-boats at the time were the *Walsingham* and the *Prince Ernest*—they had been carrying mail for twenty-seven years. A confidential statement, made in 1824, declared that Captain King suggested the transfer, but that the Admiralty had kept this quiet 'lest he should be hanged and burned in effigy at Falmouth'.

the practice of giving captains a penny for every letter and packet delivered to the local postmaster at a port.

In 1780 the Post Office attempted to increase the income from ship-letters by putting an additional tax on those coming in, and arranging for a supervision of letters going out of the country on private ships. Following a suggestion by Frederick Bourne, a clerk in the Foreign Office, an Act of 1799 set up a Ship-Letter Office. The gratuity to ship captains bringing letters into the country and delivering them at the port was raised from 1d to 2d. Such mail was to be charged 4d per single letter, in addition to the inland charge from the port where the letter was landed.

Bourne's suggestion for outgoing mail was that it be brought to the Post Office to be stamped and bagged, and then sent by private ship overseas. The Post Office was to receive half what it would have cost if sent the same distance by packet-ship. The Post Office even sought the aid of coffee-house keepers by offering them salaries to become postal agents. This proposal for handling outgoing ship-letters did not prove at all attractive; the coffee-house proprietors were not interested, and the general public could not see the advantage of sending to the Post Office their mail that was to go out of Britain by private ships. According to Francis Freeling, not one in eighteen of the letters going overseas in private ships came to the Post Office to be stamped and bagged.

In 1814, as an expensive war was coming to an end, the Government tightened the law. The rate for the sea-postage on incoming letters was raised from 4d to 6d, to be collected when the letter was delivered. Since the charge of half the packet rate was not bringing *outgoing* ship-letters into the Post Office, the law was changed to permit them to go at one-third instead of one-half the rate charged if going out by packets. But this concession had little if any effect.

Since more revenue was possible from letters brought into the British Isles, the needy Treasury raised the so-called sea-postage charge on incoming ship-letters to 8d for a single letter, raised it in 1815 only a year after it had been increased from 4d to 6d. And this very high charge for incoming ship-letters remained in force even after internal penny postage was granted in 1840. Rowland Hill's campaign for cheaper postage was only on behalf of mails that were posted and delivered within the British Isles.

It was all very confusing and may well be to the reader—separate ship-letter rates for India letters, and high charges for those coming from colonies other than India and from foreign countries when brought to Britain in private or foreign vessels. The Falmouth agent was even baffled in 1824 when a box and a bag containing India letters was brought in by Captain Kemp of the *Bombay Merchant* that had foundered in the south Atlantic. The crew, passengers and mail were carried into Rio, and brought to Falmouth in the Government mail-packet. The Falmouth agent, Mr Gay, was in doubt, so much in doubt that he forwarded the letters to London with the explanation that Captain Kemp would call at the Post Office in London on his arrival 'for whatever fee may be due him for their conveyance from India'.

Even the lowering of the charge from a half to a third of the packet rate for the *outgoing* letters when brought to the Post Office for stamping and bagging did not add much to the revenue. The Commissioners of Revenue asked Francis Freeling in 1829: 'If you knew a bag of letters was on an American packet, could you prevent her clearance?' He replied that the Post Office had no power of search. A further hindrance to making a success of the charge on outgoing letters was the strong objection of the merchants. They insisted it would 'fetter trade' if they had to forward letters to the Post Office to be enclosed in bags after stamping. Nicholas Vansittart, Chancellor of the Exchequer from 1812 to 1823, was so much influenced by the mercantile interests that he had 'thrown open the whole of the conveyance of letters outward'. Letters went out of England in any way the writer found convenient, despite the Act that has been cited. So universal was the avoidance of the official ship-letter bags at Liverpool, for example, that Mr Freeling declared: 'We have not one letter in one year for America from Liverpool.'[1]

BRITISH MAILS CROSS THE ATLANTIC
IN AMERICAN VESSELS

The mails to America, after the war that ended in 1815, were usually carried in the so-called 'American packets', and not in the official packet-boats that sailed out of Falmouth. An American packet service in American vessels had started just after the close of the war. New Yorkers were eager to make their port the chief one on the east coast, more important than Boston or Baltimore or Philadelphia. The establishment of a number of fast sailing packet lines out of New York to Liverpool, London and Le Havre did much to

[1] *22nd Rep. Commrs. of Rev.* (1830), 393, 587-9.

insure New York's primacy as a port. The idea of fixed sailing times for these American sailing packets might well have come from the example of the Falmouth packets, for they had been calling at New York for many years before the United States entered the war in 1812. The Falmouth packets used fixed sailing dates, but they carried no freight. Besides they were small, with passenger accommodations that were distinctly cramped. And they were slow. In March 1816, for instance, two of the Falmouth packets arrived in New York on the same day, although they had left Falmouth over a month apart. The *Princess Charlotte* had taken eighty-one days to bring the January mail, the *Osborne* forty-five days with that of February.

The use of scheduled sailings between New York and British ports by fast packets that carried mail, freight and passengers began in 1818. The Black Ball Line of American packets advertised in the previous October that 'frequent and regular conveyance' of goods and passengers between New York and Liverpool would be provided by packets that sail 'from each place on a certain day in every month throughout the year'. The *Courier* left Liverpool on January 1, 1818 to begin the service. Four days later the *James Monroe*, 424 tons, sailed from New York. The last bit of cargo for this packet was the mail-bag; it had hung for some days in the Tontine Coffee House to receive letters for England and Europe. The charge for single letters was 25 cents of 1s. In addition, the captain received the ship-letter gratuity of 2d for each letter that he delivered to the postal authorities in Liverpool. Harriet Martineau, who returned to Liverpool in 1836 on one of these packets, mentioned in her account of the voyage that the 'post-office boat' came out to meet them as the ship entered the Mersey.[1]

Monthly packets on a regular schedule proved so popular that they soon increased in numbers. The Red Star Line started a competitive service in 1822 with departures about the 24th of each month. The Black Ball Line countered with a second monthly service that left New York on the 16th, and the Swallowtail Line added a fourth monthly crossing, also in 1822. This provided a weekly departure both ways between Liverpool and New York. There was also a fortnightly service between New York and Le

---

[1] *Autobiography* (1877), II, 499. The passenger service provided by these 'liners' was the fastest and most comfortable crossing of the Atlantic up to that time. Fresh milk was available, as every vessel had its cow. The unfortunate animal was kept in a special deckhouse aft, with padded sides. For a chatty account of these services, see Basil Lubbock, *The Western Ocean Packets* (Glasgow, 1925).

Havre, and another to London, also fortnightly. The London liners stopped at Cowes or Portsmouth to take on or put off passengers and mails. Some years later Boston was connected with Liverpool by regular sailing liners.[1]

Little wonder that most of the mail for America from the busy industrial centres sent their mail to Liverpool rather than Falmouth, and that the Post Office bag in Liverpool was empty when a Black Ball or a Red Star or a Swallowtail mail-bag was hanging conveniently at a coffee-house to receive letters. These American liners became the main means of communication between the Old World and the New. They carried most of the transatlantic mail between 1815 and the beginning of the Cunard steamship service in 1840, including most of the British Government dispatches as well. The average run from Liverpool was about thirty-five days; the faster eastward journey usually took three weeks or less. These ships were capable of doing as much as 12 knots under full sail. So completely had they taken over the mail service to and from the United States that the Admiralty brigs out of Falmouth ceased calling at New York after 1828.[2]

Passengers were allowed, on occasion, to examine the addresses of the letters when the mail-bags were emptied on deck for the purpose of sorting out the letters for delivery in New York. Harriet Martineau, who crossed on the *United States* in 1834 wrote: 'It is pleasant to sit on the rail and see the passengers gathered around the heap of letters, and to hear the shouts of merriment at an exceedingly original superscription.' Government dispatches, however, were sent in special bags, and often under the care of an official messenger. The westbound mails, according to the British Post Office, were carried chiefly by the 'New York private packets' and went in sealed bags and boxes that were delivered to the Post Office in New

[1] The service out of New York four times a month became more frequent in 1838 when E. K. Collins started his Dramatic Line; it was so called because of the names he gave his liners—*Shakespeare, Garrick, Seddon, Sheridan* and *Roscius*. The *Roscius* was the first liner of over 1,000 tons. Other vessels on the competing Lines bore the names of famous persons and regions, such names as the United States, John Jay, Albion, Liverpool, Europe, England, George Canning, Wellington and Victoria. Both the Duke of Wellington and Queen Victoria visited the American packets that bore their names. Famous builders of these fast liners were W. H. Webb of New York, and Donald McKay of Newburyport and Boston. McKay, who was a native of Nova Scotia, designed and built many famous clippers. For a full account of these regular sailing packets, see *Queens of the Western Ocean* (Annapolis, 1961) by C. C. Cutler, ch. IV, and pp. 376ff. for lists of the ships.

[2] R. G. Albion, *Square Riggers on Schedule* (Princeton, 1938) is excellent. Tyrone Power, *Impressions of America* (1836), I, 1-43 gives an account of his voyage on the *Europe;* it took thirty-five days. For his untimely death in 1841 when crossing on a steamship that disappeared in the mid-Atlantic, see below, p. 131.

York. The eastbound mail was not handled with such care, but 'is given to the captain of the packet or to the passengers upon whom there is no check whatever'. The Postmaster-General suggested to the Treasury in 1838 that the correspondence with the United States was so extensive that it should be put on a 'more secure and regular footing'.

What was desirable, of course, from the British viewpoint was a faster official service. This was to result from the employment of steamship companies as carriers of British mails to all parts of the Atlantic. It was high time, since the emigration to far distant colonies and to the United States was increasing, along with an amazing growth in manufactures and commerce. Great Britain was well fitted by her location—near but not of the Continent—to take the lead in world communication, provided the postal communications could keep pace with the growing commercial and colonial expansion.[1]

---

[1] The quotation on the title-page relates to this period. John Keats was very conscious of 'The ocean, with its vastness . . . its hopes, its fears' when he wrote the sonnet 'To my Brother George'. Shortly after George's marriage in 1818 the young couple went by coach to Liverpool whence, late in June, they emigrated to America on a sailing vessel. John Keats accompanied them to Liverpool but he left for a walking trip in Scotland before they sailed. After a 'rough voyage' George and his wife reached Philadelphia. John Keats wrote from Scotland to his younger brother in London: 'I should think by this time they must have landed.' But westward crossings often took more than a month, as shown by two protracted voyages of packet-boats in 1816 (see above, p. 114). George's first letter to John—it has not survived—was written shortly after the young couple landed in Philadelphia. The letter did not reach John Keats until mid-October, three and a half months after George and his wife had left England. In Philadelphia they bought a carriage and horses to take them over the mountains to Pittsburgh whence they journeyed by boat down the Ohio to the 'back settlements' of America. George Keats died in Louisville, Kentucky, in 1841. See *Letters of John Keats*, ed. M. B. Forman, 4th ed., 1952, pp. 159, 201, 212, 223, 341.

12

FROM SAIL TO STEAM

THE Post Office still had considerable packet business after the transfer to the Admiralty in 1823 of the services using Falmouth as their home base. Two of those left in care of the Post Office went out of Dover and Harwich. Another connected the Channel Islands with England at Weymouth. Three routes continued to serve as carriers of the Irish mails—from Port Patrick, Holyhead and Milford Haven. All of these services can be conveniently reviewed together, for it was on these short routes that the Post Office pioneered in employing mail-packets driven by steam engines. It was the beginning of a revolutionary change in postal communication.

Dover packets were again crossing the Channel as soon as peace negotiations started, both to Ostend and Calais. Harwich had never ceased to be a packet port. Following the war seven packets maintained regular mail services with Helvoetsluis, Cuxhaven and Gothenburg. Mails for the Harwich service were made up in London twice a week for the packets going to the Netherlands and Germany, and once a week for the service to Gothenburg.[1]

The Channel Islands were kept in touch with England by three packets during and after the war. The service was twice weekly. The boats had a good passenger business and surprisingly large mails—larger than those on the Milford station.

The mails for southern Ireland were carried between Milford Haven and Waterford by seven packets, and extra packets had to be called on frequently when all the regular packets were absent from port because of 'unfavourable weather'. This route suffered from the competition of passenger boats between Bristol and southern Ireland. The Milford station caused the Post Office more concern than any other home station.

The four mail-boats between Port Patrick in Scotland and Donaghadee were intended for a daily service. But it did not always

---

[1] *22nd Rep. Commrs. of Rev.* (1830), 357, 396, 400, etc., and the *Pkt. Rep. Bks.*, 1820-4, 176. Sweden bore half the cost of the Gothenburg service.

work out that way, as the vessels were often delayed by adverse weather. The interruptions to this service had resulted in much of the correspondence between Scotland and Ireland going by way of Holyhead. The Port Patrick route also suffered from the competition of passenger vessels plying between the Clyde and Belfast Lough.

By far the most important of the Irish home stations was Holyhead. It took care of the English mails whether they came from London or Birmingham, Manchester or Liverpool. By the mid-twenties Thomas Telford had not only made over the Holyhead Road, but had built the famous Menai Suspension Bridge—opened in 1826— that connected the Island of Anglesey with the mainland. Elaborate harbour improvements had been carried out at Holyhead and at the port of Howth to the north of Dublin Bay. Howth had replaced the landing place at the Pigeon House near the mouth of the Liffey.

The mails were carried back and forth daily by the use of seven packets, two more than had been used during the war. The Holyhead agent was concerned, not only with the regular running of the packets, but he was also in charge of the extensive repair sheds at Holyhead. They were used by all the home stations, even by packets based on Weymouth.[1]

STEAM PACKETS ON THE HOME STATIONS

But all was not well. The marine engine had been sufficiently developed by the end of the war to make the steamboat useful on the Irish Sea. In 1819 the New Steam Packet Company began running passenger steamboats between Holyhead and Dublin. The results were likely to be disastrous for the passenger business of the sailing packets, whose captains depended much on passenger fares to supplement their contracts. The steamboats did the journey more quickly and with greater regularity than the Government sailing packets. The Post Office was forced, in consequence, to consider the possibility of introducing steam where passenger steamboats were likely to furnish competition.

An efficient steam engine had been in the making for two centuries before it began to revolutionize manufacture, the carriage of goods and the transport of passengers and mails. The decisive advance came in the mid-eighteenth century when James Watt of Greenock on the Clyde so improved the older pumping engines that they could be used in various ways. When James Watt joined with

---

[1] *22nd Rep. Commrs. of Rev.* (1830), 7, 48, 57, 105-8, etc.

Matthew Boulton of Birmingham in 1774 to form the firm of
Boulton & Watt, their factory became the chief source for the
newer engines. William Symington ran a steam tug on the Clyde as
early as 1802—it was powered by a Boulton & Watt engine. Robert
Fulton, an American inventor, who had been much in Britain and
France, made his memorable journey in the *Clermont* up the
Hudson River from New York to Albany in 1807. The first use of a
steamboat for a sea voyage was in 1818 when the *Rob Roy*, of 90
tons and 30 horsepower, began to ply regularly between Greenock
and Belfast. About the same time, the *Robert Bruce* started a service
between Glasgow and Liverpool.

In the spring of 1819 Thomas Boyd of the New Steam Packet
Company wrote Sir Francis Freeling that they were about to
establish steam vessels of 'great power and size' between Holyhead
and Howth, vessels that included 'all the late improvements made
in adapting steam vessels to the navigation of open seas'. Boyd
predicted that the crossing would take less than ten hours, and he
hoped that the Post Office would make use of his steamboats.

The trials were successful. Boyd's *Talbot* of 150 tons and the
Ivanhoe of 170 tons averaged less than ten hours for a trip across
the Irish Sea. They had cut in half the time usually required by the
sailing mail-packets. In 1820 the Holyhead packet agent even went
across to Ireland on the *Talbot* to find out how a steam-driven
vessel acted. The voyage took eight and a half hours; the sailing
packet that started about the same time took twenty hours. The
agent was pleased with his experience both going and returning;
the weather was moderate, the vessel had very little motion, no one
was sick, and he even enjoyed a comfortable breakfast. He added:
'There is a tremulous vibration in the steam packet occasioned by
the action of the [paddle] wheels which . . . counteracts that
smooth and sliding sensation in sailing which affects the stomach.'
Long before Rowland Hill decided to take an abiding interest in
postal reform, he went to Ireland in the summer of 1821, crossing
on a sailing packet and returning on one of the regular steam vessels.
The captain of the steamboat told him that the Company intended
to run throughout the next winter, and added that 'in a storm a
steamer might even have some advantages over a sailing vessel'.[1]

---

[1] ibid., 4, 110, 114-18. Rowland Hill first saw a steamboat at Margate in 1818. The
vessel ran between London and Margate three times a week. When it entered the
harbour, according to Mr Hill, 'there was a great crowd and much enthusiasm, though
carpers predicted failure and sneered at smoke-jacks'. *Life of Rowland Hill* (1880), 1,
136, 160, 168.

When the Post Office decided to introduce steam mail-packets in 1820 it could hire the *Talbot* and the *Ivanhoe*, or build vessels for the service. The agent at Holyhead favoured the hiring of the competing steam vessels. This was in line with the policy that had long been in use—ever since the recommendations of the Commissioners in 1788. But at headquarters in London there was no desire to hire the packets that had been running in direct opposition to the official service. Moreover, the Post Office had seven sailing packets on its hands, which would, of course, have to be purchased if they were not kept in the service. It decided to keep the sailing packets until satisfied of the value of steam.

The vessels were built on the Thames, and equipped with Boulton & Watt engines. The two new steam packets were hopefully named the *Lightning* and the *Meteor*, the former of 205 tons and 80 horsepower, and the *Meteor* of 189 tons and 60 horsepower. When ready in May 1821 they were manned by crews sent from Holyhead to bring the vessels round, to give the men some experience of engines with which they were unfamiliar. When they left the Thames, the pilot was astonished at finding himself for the first time in his life going at such a rate with the wind against him. The steam service began in June 1821. On her first trip the *Meteor* proved faster than the *Talbot*. The *Lightning*, which went out some distance to race the *Ivanhoe* into port, reached the harbour half an hour earlier. The acceptance of the new steam packets was assured when King George IV used the *Lightning* for crossing to Ireland in 1821; the King chose Captain Skinner's *Lightning* because of his long acquaintance with, and high regard, for the Captain. After this trip Captain Skinner's vessel was renamed the *Royal Sovereign* by permission of the King. Before the end of the year, the private steam packets were withdrawn.[1]

The next station to use steam packets was Dover where the *Arrow* and the *Dasher* were crossing to Calais before the end of 1821; they were later replaced by the *Spitfire* and the *Fury* when the *Arrow* and the *Dasher* were sent to Port Patrick to meet the competition of the passenger vessels crossing between Glasgow and Belfast. The competition of passenger steamers had forced the Post Office to introduce steam packets on the Channel crossing to

[1] *22nd Rep. Commrs. of Rev.* (1830), 11-13, 114-16; *Pkt. Rep. Bks.*, 1820-4, 111, 116, 212-22. When a third steam packet was found necessary to keep to schedule, the *Ivanhoe* was added; it was not hired but purchased. Captain Skinner continued on the Holyhead station until his death in a violent storm; he was swept overboard when leaving Ireland in 1832. He had served as a mail-packet captain for nearly forty years.

Calais, on the Weymouth station and on the routes out of Holyhead and Port Patrick. Sailing packets, however, continued to carry mails between Calais and Ostend and from Harwich to Helvoetsluis because steamers offered no serious competition.

The Milford station was converted to steam in 1824, though the receipts from mail and passengers were slight. This was done even after the Bristol Chamber of Commerce had bombarded the Post Office with reasons for transferring the Milford packets to the port of Bristol. The businessmen of Bristol held quite rightly that it could easily be made a commodious and busy packet station, and that the demands of a large commercial city were certain to make the regular mail-packet services more and more valuable. The Chamber of Commerce prophesied that the traffic would soon be so extensive that it would free the Government from any expense other than a comparatively nominal sum for the transport of the mails.[1]

As a result of the change to steam, a new packet port was added at this time. Bristol's desire for a mail-packet service might be ignored, so it would seem, but Liverpool's case was so compelling that a Government steam service began running from Liverpool to Dublin in 1826. Competition, again, was the telling argument. Previously Liverpool's Irish letters had gone to Chester to join the London mails on their way to Holyhead. This was inconvenient because the mail by way of Holyhead had to leave Liverpool before the day's business was over, and the Liverpool letters were twenty-four hours on the way. But direct steam passenger traffic between Liverpool and Dublin was being done regularly in twelve to fourteen hours. This direct service meant, of course, that much of the mail between the two islands was carried by private steamers of the St George and St Patrick Steam-Boat Companies, as well as by an Irish Line named the City of Dublin Steam Packet Company.

Liverpool already had a steam postal service that carried mail between Liverpool and the Isle of Man. When private steam vessels began regular voyages between Liverpool and Glasgow, they passed by the Isle of Man. It seemed obvious that they could give a service to the Isle of Man superior to that furnished for many years by sailing packets from Whitehaven. The new steam service by private vessels began in 1822; mail was left at Douglas twice a week in summer and once a week in winter.

A contract service between Liverpool and Dublin, similar to that for the Isle of Man, might well have been chosen. Already powerful

[1] *22nd Rep. Commrs. of Rev.* (1830), 326-7, 331, 396, etc.

steam vessels were in use on this route, and the private companies were eager to carry the mails on advantageous terms, since there were several lines that wanted the business. But the Post Office ignored the private services, and built competing post-office steam packets instead. The Revenue Commissioners of 1830 condemned the step as contrary to long-time precedent and unnecessarily expensive.[1]

The changes from sail to steam on five mail-packet toures had meant the replacement of twenty-one sailing packets by twenty steam vessels, and six more were added when Liverpool was made a mail-packet port for Irish mails. The Commissioners of Revenue, who were busy in the twenties examining the various public departments, criticized the Post Office severely for the sudden increase in expense and for the departure from the established practice that had been recommended in 1788. The Post Office felt that it had been forced to abandon the older policy because of the special conditions faced at Holyhead and Dover. Once having taken the stand for government ownership, it was naturally extended to the other stations. Sir Francis Freeling argued rather speciously that private owners would have no inducement to avoid delay and irregularity, and that the safety of the mails was so important that it could not be left in private hands. An annual expense for these services, which had been about £78,000 in 1817, had more than doubled in ten years.[2]

The Report of the Commissioners of 1830 was followed, six years later, by another examination and report on the home stations by another group of Commissioners 'on the Management of the Post Office Department'. Their Report of 1836 was even more damaging, for it came at a time when the Post Office was under

---

[1] ibid., 27-31, 196-9, 444, 717. The new steam packets did not use Howth as their Irish port because of their greater draught, but the harbour of Kingstown (now Dun Laoghaire). This harbour was under reconstruction at the time, and soon succeeded Howth as the packet station for both Holyhead and Liverpool. The tidy little harbour of Howth had been rebuilt at great expense during the Napoleonic war. It is now principally the resort of fishing vessels.

[2] ibid., 4-6, 36, 47, 58. The Report of 1830 furnished the expenses and the receipts for the eight years since the introduction of steam mail-packets.

Station	Expenses £	Receipts £
Holyhead	231,000	140,000
Liverpool	170,000	64,130
Milford	160,000	19,150
Port Patrick	35,370	9,630
Weymouth	24,850	9,960

An expense of nearly £350,000 in eight years was more than twice as large as the postal income.

heavy attack for its high postage rates, an attack that was to lead to internal uniform penny postage four years later. The Commissioners of 1836 recommended that the packet services still remaining under the Post Office be transferred to the Admiralty; that they should join the Falmouth station which had been under Admiralty control since 1823. At the time, there were five home stations, in addition to the Dover and Harwich services to the Continent.

Harwich, as we have pointed out earlier, had never been converted to steam. It was comparatively inaccessible, as it had not yet received a railway connection with London. And when steam vessels began making regular trips across the North Sea from London, they could reach Holland and Hamburg much sooner than the mails that went by horsed coach to Harwich and from there across the North Sea in sailing packets. This was so evident by the early thirties that the route via Harwich—in use for 170 years—was given up. Instead the mails for Holland and Germany were carried by the General Steam Navigation Company. This Line, founded in 1824— and still going strong—received its first postal contract in 1831. The Company proudly announced that its 'powerful steam packets' would depart regularly from London for Rotterdam and Hamburg, reaching Rotterdam in twenty-eight hours and Hamburg in fifty-four. By the mid-thirties steam mail-packets were leaving the Thames twice a week. About the same time the mails that had been going to Sweden via Harwich were sent north to Hull and from there across the North Sea.[1]

STEAMSHIPS CROSS THE ATLANTIC

By 1837 when the Admiralty took over the remaining packet stations, it had already done much to enlarge and improve the Falmouth foreign services. Since 1823 ten-gun brigs under naval lieutenants had been used along with such of the established packets, privately owned, as were still under contract. In 1835, thirty-seven Admiralty packets carried the mails that went out of Falmouth. Of these, thirty were sailing vessels and seven steam driven. No attempt had yet been made to use steam packets for the transatlantic routes, and even the Lisbon mails were still carried by sailing vessels. Of the seven steam vessels used by the Admiralty for

[1] For the General Steam Navigation Company, see L. Cope Cornford, *A Century of Sea Trading, 1824-1924* (1924).

carrying mails, three were on the route between Falmouth and Malta, and two were employed in the Mediterranean between Malta, Alexandria and Corfu. Two others, the *Spitfire* and the *Flamer*, conveyed mails between Barbados, Jamaica and St Thomas. This use of steam mail-boats in the West Indies, a service that Mr Freeling had earlier rejected as 'hazardous', was a distinct advance. The Admiralty steam packets ranged from 300 to 550 tons.

The routes with which we are familiar had also seen some changes. The steam packets for Malta left once a month, and their expected absence was just over seven weeks. The Brazil sailing packets plied by way of Madeira and Santa Cruz (in the Canaries), and they were expected back in twenty weeks. A new monthly service to Mexico was routed by way of Crooked Island in the Bahamas, Havana, Belize in British Honduras, Vera Cruz and Tampico. It was a monthly service, the round trip taking about eighteen weeks. The British West Indies were served twice a month, the round trip being twelve weeks in length. Barbados was still the first port for the West Indian packets; their last before the homeward voyage was St Thomas, where they awaited the mail-boats from the Leewards, and also the mails brought by steamer from Jamaica and Jacmal, a port on the south coast of Haiti.

The only Admiralty service to North America was a direct monthly service to Halifax. Since early in the twenties the Bermuda mail had been taken by a branch packet from Halifax, the contractor for this service being Samuel Cunard of Halifax. Newfoundland was also served from Halifax. Another branch service from Halifax to Boston carried American mails that had come on the Government packets. The Falmouth packets had not called at New York since 1828, for reasons already made clear in the previous chapter.[1]

The Admiralty arrangements for mails to and from the United States were hopelessly inadequate. The explanation, of course, was the use of the fast American liners for ship-letter mail. The *Edinburgh Review* for April 1837 lauded these liners as the 'best sailing vessels between this country and New York'. During the previous year their average for the westward voyage was 35 days and 17 hours; eastward, it was 19 days and 7 hours.[2]

Could an Atlantic more than 3,000 miles wide be crossed by

[1] Albion, op. cit., 17; *Br. Almanac* for 1838, 83; for 1851, Comp. 69.
[2] *Edinburgh Review*, LXV, 136; *Br. Almanac* for 1838, 82; F. Lawrence Babcock, *Spanning the Atlantic* (N.Y., 1931), 33.

steam vessels on a regular schedule? The question was arousing great interest in the mid-thirties. Several sailing vessels with supplementary steam engines had already made long sea voyages before 1838, three even crossing the Atlantic. Back in 1819, the *Savannah*, an American vessel, had come all the way from Savannah, Georgia, to Liverpool. Built in New York, she was a full rigged three-master, of some 300 tons burthen. Engines were added to drive paddle wheels that were so constructed that they could be folded up like a fan and laid on deck when not in use. Although the vessel's owners advertised in the local newspaper for passengers, none cared to make the voyage, and she left Savannah in ballast. The engines were worked 18 days of the 26 required for the crossing. The sight of a vessel on the high seas belching forth smoke aroused concern as she neared the British Isles. *The Times* of June 30, 1819 reported that the '*Savannah*, steam vessel, recently arrived at Liverpool from America—the first steam vessel of the kind that ever crossed the Atlantic. She was chased a whole day off the coast of Ireland by the *Kite*, a revenue cruiser, which mistook her for a ship on fire.'[1]

The next steam vessel to cross the Atlantic was the *Curaçoa*, 350 tons and 100 horsepower. Built on the Clyde and sold to the Netherlands, she made her first transatlantic voyage to the Dutch West Indies. She left Helvoetsluis in April 1827, and reached Surinam in twenty-eight days. The *Curaçoa* was under steam about half the time. She was later added to the Navy of the Netherlands.

The third crossing by a vessel equipped with a steam engine began in British North America. The *Royal William* was built at Quebec. When launched in 1831 she was christened by the wife of the Governor with the name of the reigning British sovereign. The vessel was a large three-masted schooner, described as of 'a magnificent appearance . . . the underdeck fitted out with taste and elegance, and containing some fifty berths, besides a splendidly furnished parlour'. The *Royal William* made several trips as a passenger vessel from Canada to Nova Scotia, and on one voyage even went to Boston. She was then sent to England for sale or charter. After taking on 330 tons of coal but only seven passengers, she left in August 1833. The voyage was a difficult one because of

---

[1] The *Savannah* went on to the Baltic where the owners hoped to sell her to the steam-minded Czar of Russia. Failing, they brought the ship back to the United States where she was re-converted to sail. See G. H. Preble, *A Chronological History of Steam Navigation* (1883) 197-202. The best source for details of ships used on the North Atlantic is N. R. P. Bonsor, *North Atlantic Seaway* (Prescot, Lancs., 1955).

rough weather that damaged both her rigging and engine. But the
Royal William limped into London. The trip had taken twenty-five
days and the vessel, apparently, had been under steam all the way.
The Canadians were so proud of the achievement that a tablet in
the Houses of Parliament at Ottawa praises the *Royal William* as
'the first vessel to cross the Atlantic by steam power . . . The
pioneer of those mightly fleets of Ocean Steamers . . . now [1894]
on every sea throughout the World.' On the centenary of the
voyage, the Canadian Post Office issued a beautiful stamp picturing
the *Royal William*.[1]

Keen interest was aroused in Britain in the thirties as to the
possibility of making a transatlantic voyage westward in a steam-
driven vessel—a much more difficult feat than an eastward crossing,
because of the prevailing westerlies. At a meeting of the British
Association in Bristol in September 1836, there was much discussion of its practicability. Dr Dionysius Lardner, a writer on
scientific subjects and the editor of the *Cabinet Encyclopaedia*, had
declared at the meeting that 'in the present state of the steam
engine', a voyage across the Atlantic was in a high degree 'improbable', because of nautical and mechanical difficulties. He was
even quoted as saying that 'it is as easy to go to the moon as to go
direct from a port in England to New York'. An article in the
Edinburgh Review of April 1837, attributed to Dr Lardner, discussed these difficulties at some length; the boiler, it was asserted,
would become completely clogged by using sea water for so long a
time, the vessel could not carry enough coal for a trip of over 3,000
miles and leave any room for passengers, crew, freight and stores,
and the necessary fuel, when loaded, would destroy the trim of the
vessel. It might be done, the article concluded, if the shortest
possible distance between the two continents was used—from the
west coast of Ireland to Halifax. The article warned against the
attempt by 'projectors much more highly supplied with zeal than
with knowledge'.[2]

Several 'projectors', notwithstanding, determined to make the
attempt. In the eagerness to win the credit for the first steam

---

[1] Another long voyage of the time was that of the *Enterprize*, which made the first
trip by a steam vessel to India. This voyage in 1826 took 113 days, of which only
sixty-two were under steam. See below, ch. XV. The *Br. Almanac* for 1839, Comp. p.
99, in a summary of steam voyages to that time, mentions the *Savannah*, the *Curaçoa*
and the *Enterprize*, but not the *Royal William*—a strange omission. The Canadian
vessel did not continue in the transatlantic service; she became a part of the Spanish
Navy as the *Isabella II*.

[2] *Edinburgh Review*, LXV.

voyage from east to west, two vessels set out for New York in April 1838. The newly founded British and American Steam Navigation Company chartered the *Sirius* from the St George Steam Packet Company, a vessel that had been used in the Irish Sea and on the run between Cork and London. The *Sirius* left Cork on April 4th. The other vessel was the *Great Western*, built by the Great Western Railway Company as an extension, so to speak, of the railway line that was soon to connect London with Bristol. As the engineer of the Line, Mr Brunel, put it: 'Why not make it longer and have a steamboat to go from Bristol to New York and call it the Great Western?' The vessel left for New York on April 8th, four days after the *Sirius* had departed from Cork.

The two pioneers were not of equal size and power. The *Sirius* was hastily hired by the British and American Steam Navigation Company, and hurried off to obtain the credit for the first crossing from east to west. She had been hired because their *British Queen* was not yet ready to meet the *Great Western*'s challenge. The *Sirius* was of 700 tons and 320 horsepower, and was loaded with 453 tons of coal and 43 barrels of resin. She steamed into New York Harbour on April 23rd, with only 20 tons of her load of coal still in the bunkers.

The *Great Western*, built at Bristol and intended to open a regular line between Bristol and New York, was of 1,340 tons burthen and equipped with two engines totalling 450 horsepower. She carried 600 tons of coal in addition to passengers and mail. Although the *Great Western* had a much longer voyage than the *Sirius* and had started four days later, she reached New York only a few hours *after* her rival. The *Great Western* had used 452 tons of her load of coal. Great was the excitement in New York with the arrival of two steam vessels on the same day from Great Britain. The *Sirius* had crossed in eighteen days, the *Great Western* in fifteen. A New York newspaper of the time applauded the double accomplishment 'as bringing England nearer to us than many parts of our own country . . . Steam navigation across the Atlantic is no longer an experiment but a plain matter of fact.'

On her return voyage the *Sirius* had difficulties. When within two days of the British Isles her engines were run at half speed so as not to exhaust her supply of fuel; as it was, she had to burn everything about the ship that could be spared. She stopped at Falmouth to obtain coal before going on to her destination in the Thames. The *Sirius* was not long continued on the Atlantic run, but did coastwise service from Dublin until she was wrecked some years later.

The *Great Western* made the return trip in less than twelve days, bringing back 68 passengers and 20,000 letters. It was the beginning of a regular mail and passenger service between Bristol and New York. The prophecies of Dr Lardner had been proved false. As a mail carrier the *Great Western* took letters westward at ship-letter rates. The charge for letters from New York to England was the same as on the New York sailing liners—25 cents or 1s each, and her captain received 2d from the British Post Office for every letter he landed at Bristol.

The most severe test yet given steam on the open ocean had been met successfully. The *British Almanac* gloried in the victory. 'Transatlantic voyages', it declared, 'may now be said to be as easy of accomplishment by means of ships of adequate size and power, as the passage between London and Margate.' Despite this obvious overstatement, it was clear that the continuous improvement of steam vessels and of their engines was soon to revolutionize the mail service of Great Britain to all lands beyond the seas.[1]

---

[1] *Rep. S.C. on Halifax and Boston Mails* (1846), Evidence p. 7; *Br. Almanac* for 1839, Comp. 101-2; Bonsor, op. cit., 4-6.

Three Falmouth sailing packets of the 1830s in Falmouth Harbour, showing Pennis Castle near the entrance. The *Sphynx* (foreground) and the *Eclipse* were Admiralty ten-gun brigs; the *Sandwich* (background) was a post-office packet continued in the service. Oil painting by Goudy in the National Maritime Museum, Greenwich.

The American *Savannah*, the first steamship to cross the Atlantic, 1819. The primitive paddle wheels could be laid on deck when not in use. *Source: Gleason's Pictorial Drawing Room Companion*, VI, 308 (1854).

Two letters without envelopes that crossed the Atlantic in the mid-1850s. The one for Philadelphia left Liverpool for New York in the Collins liner *Baltic* in March 1855; the charge of three cents was for the internal postage from New York to Philadelphia. The other was mailed in Hong Kong and reached

Two letters without envelopes carried to the United States. The one on the *Great Western* was a ship letter mailed on July 5, 1839; it reached New York twenty days later. It was carried across for a shilling. The other left

13

MAILS ON THE NORTH ATLANTIC SEAWAY

THE exploits of the *Great Western* and the *Sirius* aroused the hope that British steamships might capture the business of the American sailing liners out of New York and Boston. If regular and faster crossings were possible, the steamers would carry both the mails and the passengers. During 1835 British steamers had made ten round voyages to New York. Although the *Sirius* dropped out after the second trip, the *Great Western* crossed five times in 1838 and six times in 1839, using Bristol, of course, as its home port.

Liverpool, on the other hand, was favoured by the American sailing liners because it was the chief port of the industrial Midlands. In 1838 a Liverpool Line sent two steamships across the Atlantic. The *Royal William*, 617 tons and 275 horsepower—not to be confused with the Canadian *Royal William*—crossed in July with thirty passengers and some 10,000 letters. This diminutive vessel was advertised as providing every comfort; it was to remain in New York ten days so that the passengers could view the 'celebrated falls of Niagara'. Later she was joined by the *Liverpool* of 1,100 tons. But their owners soon retired from the transatlantic business.[1]

The British and American Steam Packet Company planned another regular service with London as the home port and a stop at Spithead for mails. Its *British Queen*, 1,300 tons, made the first voyage in the summer of 1839. Later the *President* was added as a consort to the *British Queen* in the hope of giving regular monthly departures. The *President*, 2,366 tons and 540 horsepower, was the largest steamer then afloat, but not for long. The *President* left New York in the spring of 1841 with 136 persons on board in addition to the mails. but she was never heard of again and no wreckage was

[1] Albion, op. cit., 257; Bowen, *A Century of Atlantic Travel* (1930) 25ff.; Capt. H. Parker and F. C. Bowen, *Mail and Passenger Steamships of the Nineteenth Century* (1928), 179.

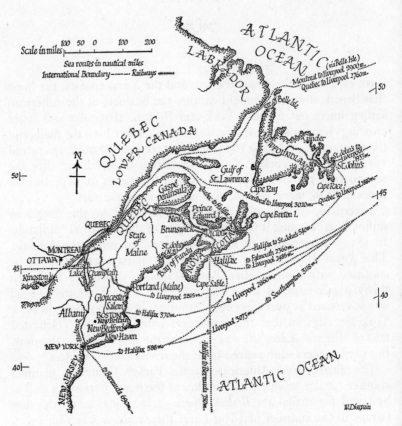

MAP 4. The American End of the Atlantic Ferry.

ever found. One of her passengers was the Irish actor, Tyrone Powers. Had monsters like the *President* exceeded the margin of safety for long oceanic boyages?

No steamship line had yet attempted a year-round regular service across the Atlantic. Even the owners of the *Great Western* did not keep her on the route to New York during the winter months. Yet the sailing liners shuttled back and forth between New York and Liverpool, and Admiralty brigs left once a month for Halifax. These ten-gun brigs, however, did not have a good reputation as sailers. Samuel Cunard called them 'coffins' because of their alleged unseaworthiness in an Atlantic gale, but he maligned them when he was seeking a mail contract with steam vessels.[1]

In 1839 the Admiralty mail brig *Tyrian* was returning from Halifax just as the *Sirius* was steaming home from her first voyage to New York. The *Tyrian* carried a distinguished Nova Scotian, Joseph Howe on his first visit to England. Howe had just made his name as a vigorous advocate of responsible government for Britain's North American colonies. He was the son of a Loyalist, who had left Massachusetts at the time of the Revolution to settle in Halifax. The elder Howe had been rewarded for his loyalty with the office of King's Printer and also that of Postmaster-General of the Maritime Provinces *and* Bermuda. The son might well be interested in better communications.

As the *Tyrian* lay rolling in a 'flat calm' several hundred miles from its home port, it was surprised by the approach of a steamer from the west; it was the *Sirius*. The Captain of the *Tyrian* decided to send his mail by the steamer, and while it was being transferred Joseph Howe visited the *Sirius*, where he heard first-hand accounts of its victorious voyage while he was enjoying a glass of champagne with the officers. When the *Sirius* steamed off, the *Tyrian* was still 'whistling for a breeze'.

That meeting in the Atlantic made a deep impression on Joseph Howe. On reaching England, he was responsible for an address to the Colonial Secretary on the imperative need for steam communication with British North America. Why should not the line of packets between the mother country and the provinces in North

---

[1] A famous ten-gun brig that performed well was H.M.S. *Beagle;* in 1831 she began a memorable voyage that carried Charles Darwin around the world on one of the most famous expeditions ever made by a naturalist. Darwin recorded a speed of 9 knots when the *Beagle* was off the coast of South America; on another occasion she made 160 miles a day before the steady trade wind. This 'good little vessel' as Darwin called her, landed him back at Falmouth in 1836. See his *A Naturalist's Voyage . . . Round the World* (2nd ed., 1869), 1, 39, 402, 501.

America be put on a more efficient footing? He recalled the necessity, during the recent Canadian Rebellion, of sending dispatches to England by way of New York. Howe believed that Great Britain 'must, even at an increased expenditure for a time, establish a line of rapid communication by steam . . . through channels exclusively British'. New Brunswick and Lower Canada (Quebec) joined with Nova Scotia in asking for 'communication twice a month with British North America'.[1]

The outcome was an advertisement by the Admiralty in November 1839 asking for tenders for a service between England and Halifax and also between Halifax and New York; the service was to be performed by steam vessels of not less than 300 horsepower. Voyages were to be monthly, the home port to be any one of five—Liverpool, Bristol, Plymouth, Falmouth or Southampton.

Two tenders resulted. The St George Steam Packet Company, owner of the *Sirius*, offered a service from Cork in Ireland, which was to be connected with Liverpool by a smaller vessel than those used on the Atlantic. Smaller craft would also be used at the other end for the run between Halifax and New York. A second tender came from the Great Western Steamship Company. This Company believed that steamships of 1,000 tons, if made of iron, or of 1,500 tons if made of wood, would be needed for a monthly service between Bristol and Halifax. The Company offered to build two additional vessels, and to begin the voyages in two years' time. The proposal was limited to a service to Halifax only. Neither of these offers fitted the conditions, and they were declined.[2]

Just about this time another Nova Scotian, Samuel Cunard, came across the Atlantic to seek a contract for the transatlantic service. Cunard, who was already in his early fifties, had been active for many years in the colonial life of Nova Scotia where he owned and operated sea-going vessels. After the Napoleonic war Cunard had the contract for carrying mails between Halifax and Bermuda, and another for mails to Newfoundland. He had been a shareholder in the *Royal William* before she crossed the Atlantic in 1833. Samuel Cunard was a keen man of business, of strong will, with great energy and a tenacity so stubborn that it prevented him form seeing fairly viewpoints other than his own. He needed all this equipment,

[1] Babcock, op. cit., 33-35; W. L. Grant. *The First Tribune of Nova Scotia* (Toronto, 1920), 93-94; J. W. Longley, *Joseph Howe* (Makers of Canada, 1926), 232. The *Tyrian* and the *Beagle* were similar to the *Sphynx*. See illustration, above, p. 128.

[2] *Parl. Ret.*, 464/1846; *Rep. S.C. Contract Pkt. Service* (1849), 122; *Rep. S.C. Halifax and Boston Mails* (1846), 8-9.

as he came to England without having ships for such a service, nor adequate financial resources for so elaborate a project.[1]

Of his visit in 1839, Samuel Cunard later declared: 'I came to England for the express purpose of submitting a plan of my own. Although I am a colonist, I have many friends in this country. I arrived just about the time the Government was perplexed about the Tenders that had been made.' His friends were of great help. James G. Melvill, Secretary of the East India Company, introduced him to the firm of Wood & Napier in Glasgow. Robert Napier, an eminent marine engineer, agreed to build the vessels. After this was arranged, Cunard then approached the Admiralty, where, of course, he was well known. The outcome was the first of a long series of contracts.[2]

BEGINNINGS OF THE CUNARD LINE

The agreement made with the Admiralty on May 4, 1839 provided for carrying the mail with all possible speed from Liverpool to Halifax and on to Boston (not New York)—a variation from the original Admiralty terms. He was required also to serve Quebec 'when the River St Lawrence is unobstructed by ice', the mail steamer to start from Pictou on the north coast of Nova Scotia. The vessels for the Boston and Quebec branches were to be of 150 horsepower, half the power of those crossing the Atlantic. A significant clause required the contractor to make such changes in construction and machinery 'as the advanced state of science may suggest and the Commissioners may direct'. The contract was for seven years at £55,000 per annum.

With a mail contract in hand, the astute Nova Scotian next sought further financial aid to make possible the building of larger ships than he had on order. The result was a partnership with George Burns and David McIver as the principal other stockholders; Burns to have charge of the Glasgow end of the business, McIver

[1] The original Cunard family had migrated from the Rhine country to Pennsylvania when William Penn was setting up his Quaker colony in America. The family name was originally Kunders, but later descendants changed it, some to Cunrads, others to Conrad, and still others to Cunard. The father of Samuel Cunard remained loyal to the British cause during the American Revolution and, like Joseph Howe's father, removed to Halifax. There his son Samuel was born in 1787. Samuel Cunard had numerous other business interests in addition to his mail contracts, including an agency of the East India Company. See Babcock, op. cit., 5-14; Bowen, op. cit., 31, where he is made the descendant of a Welsh family.

[2] For the quotation, see *P.O. Records*, ep. to the P.M.G., Viscount Canning, March 11, 1853.

the Liverpool agency and Cunard the American end of the service.[1]

Several changes were made in the original contract before it settled down, so to speak. By August 1841 the annual payment had risen to £80,000, when it seemed necessary to have five ocean-going vessels. That the Admiralty was making the contract is evident when it required the vessels to carry officers and men in military service at special rates, and the vessels to be of sufficient strength to 'carry guns of the largest calibre'. The ships must be built of wood and not of iron.

The Post Office viewed with the 'gravest concern' the use of postal contracts for other than postal purposes. When the Admiralty had taken over the Falmouth services in 1823, the purpose was to save expense by the use of Admiralty brigs. The Admiralty, by the policy started in the late thirties, had reverted to contracts for privately owned vessels, and on a scale never dreamed of in 1823.[2]

The first four ships of the Line, built on the Clyde and fitted with Napier engines, were named the *Britannia*, *Acadia*, *Caledonia* and *Columbia*. They had brig lines, three masts and one funnel, were under 1,200 tons with paddle wheels driven by engines of 750 horsepower; each could accommodate about 100 passengers. A great deal of space was needed for coal, as the early engines were far from economical, and sufficient fuel was carried to go twice the required distance. A smaller vessel, the *Unicorn*, was sent ahead of the regular packets to make the necessary dockage arrangements in Boston; later it was put on the Pictou-Quebec branch. The Line never adopted the use of a smaller vessel for the so-called Boston branch, because the freight and passengers and mail for the United States were too important to be transferred at Halifax.[3]

Nova Scotians were naturally proud of the new steamship arrangements that made Halifax the first port of call for the pioneer official steamship line for carrying mail across the Atlantic. Their elation was well expressed by T. C. Haliburton, a distinguished judge in Nova Scotia, but better known as a brilliant humorist

[1] Babcock, op. cit., 44-48. The original name of the Line was the British and North American Royal Mail Steam Packet Company.
[2] *Parl. Ret.*, 464/1846; Babcock, op. cit., 44-48.
[3] The *Unicorn*, according to Bowen, op. cit., 41, was wrecked at the mouth of the St Lawrence in 1844, and he seems to infer that her life ended at that time. J. H. Kemble, *The Panama Route* (Berkeley, Calif., 1943) has her on the Quebec branch until 1846 when she was sent to California. See below, p. 155.

writing under the name of Sam Slick. He visited England in the year that Samuel Cunard arranged for the transatlantic service, and published an amusing volume of imaginary letters written by supposed passengers on a voyage to America in the *Great Western*. *The Letter Bag of the Great Western* contains letters of the various passengers as they were supposed to react to the novel experience of a transatlantic voyage—the butcher, who had charge of 2 cows, 10 pigs and some fowl; one of the stokers; a Quakeress; a Colonist writing back to his brother; a coachman who lost his job when railways replaced coaches, and who was now on his way to Nova Scotia to find work as a coachman.

The last letter from the author was a serious appeal to Nova Scotians, as the new service was about to begin. 'I am desirous', wrote Sam Slick, 'of calling the attention of my countrymen to the importance of steam' and to seek internal improvements and not like the Canadians of Upper and Lower Canada who were preoccupied with infectious political agitation. The author saw a golden future for Nova Scotia: 'Since the discovery of America by Columbus, nothing has occurred of so much importance to the New World as navigating the Atlantic by steamers, and no part of the continent is likely to be benefited by it in an equal degree with Nova Scotia, which is the nearest point of land to Europe.' The author urged the building of a railway to the Bay of Fundy 'to give full effect to the noble scheme of Atlantic steam navigation—we owe it to New Brunswick and Canada to complete our portion of the great inter-colonial line'.[1]

The regular Cunard service began with the sailing of the *Britannia* on July 4, 1840. She reached Halifax on the 17th and was off Boston Light the next day. Samuel Cunard was one of the sixty-three passengers on this first voyage. The reception in Boston was enthusiastic. He received over 1,800 invitations for dinner from Bostonians who were overjoyed at the selection of Boston rather than New York as the terminus of the Line. At a banquet honouring Mr Cunard, a prominent Bostonian proposed a toast 'To the memory of Time and Space, famous in their day and generation, but now annihilated by the Steam Engine.'

The *Acadia* made the second crossing in August, reaching Boston one day sooner than the time taken by the *Britannia*. By

[1] [T. C. Haliburton], *The Letter Bag of the Great Western ... by Samuel Slick* (1840). Judge Haliburton had recently visited Bristol to urge the Great Western Steamship Company to establish steam communication with Nova Scotia. As we know, their bid had been rejected.

March 1841 the voyages were twice a month from April to November, and once a month in winter.

Charles Dickens crossed on the *Britannia* in 1842 to make a lecture tour. His *American Notes* furnish a lively description of a crossing that few would care to make under the same conditions nowadays. It was a winter crossing, in January. After boarding, Mr and Mrs Dickens saw the 'taking on of the milk, in other words, getting the cow on board', watched the ice-houses being filled with provisions, and last of all the bringing on of the 'latest mail-bags, which were thrown down for the moment anywhere'. The ship finally moved out under the direction of the Captain, who took his stand with a speaking trumpet on one of the paddle boxes. As the 'noble ship' moved down the Mersey, Dickens noticed that she was 'pretty deep in the water, with all her coals on board and so many passengers'—eighty-six in all. It was an adventure, this 'going across as if it were a ferry, especially in winter, and there was talk of how long it was since the poor *President* went down'.

The weather was bad, 'as it is likely to be in January on the north Atlantic'. In a gale 'of last night the life boat had been crushed by one blow of the sea, like a walnut shell' and all the planking of the paddle boxes had been torn away. Despite the weather, the *Britannia* reached Halifax on the fifteenth night. She stayed seven hours to 'deliver and exchange the mails,' and entered Boston Harbour on January 22nd. The journey ended when an 'American pilot-boat came alongside, and soon afterwards the *Britannia*, steam packet from Liverpool, eighteen days out, was telegraphed to Boston'.

Charles Dickens returned to England after four months of travel in the United States and Canada, but not on a Cunarder from Boston. He re-crossed the Atlantic on a sailing packet of the Swallowtail Line from New York. The return voyage in the *George Washington* seems to have been more pleasant than the winter crossing to America. Dickens admired 'the gallant ship, her tall masts pointing up in graceful lines against the sky'. There were but 18 passengers in 'first class'; 100 were below in the steerage. When five or six days out there was talk of icebergs—a double look-out was kept and 'many dismal tales were whispered'. But all went well save for a stretch of calm weather, and 'there was talk as to where the *Great Western* (which left New York a week after us) was now . . . and what was thought of sailing vessels as compared with steamships'. Twenty days out of New York they sighted Cape Clear. A pilot was taken on at Holyhead, and the packet safely reached Liverpool.[1]

The Cunard Line kept to its schedule remarkably well. In February 1844 the *Britannia* was frozen fast in Boston Harbour, but was freed by the Bostonians, who cut a seven-mile channel through the ice. The only serious loss in the forties was the *Columbia* on a homeward voyage in 1843; she was wrecked off Cape Sable. Although the vessel had to be abandoned, no lives were lost and the mail was saved.

The branch service to Quebec was dropped in 1845, much to the disgust of the Canadians. They felt quite rightly that the mail service on which they had counted was disregarded in favour of the 'fleshpots' of their non-colonial neighbour to the south. Other branch services, however, were added. Two monthly steamers went out of Halifax shortly after the arrival of the transatlantic liner from Liverpool; one carried mail to Bermuda, and the other went to Newfoundland. In 1851 the Cunard Line even started a branch between Bermuda and St Thomas in the West Indies.

Other British shipping lines, especially the Great Western Company, bitterly objected to the Cunard monopoly, assisted by an exceedingly liberal subsidy. In 1845 the Great Western Company had added a remarkable and expensive vessel to share with the *Great Western* a regular service between Bristol and New York. Mr Brunel was responsible for several improvements built into the *Great Britain*. Her hull was of iron instead of wood, and she was fitted with a screw propeller instead of paddle wheels. There was some thought of naming her the 'Mammoth', as she was larger than any ship built up to that time. The *Great Britain* was some 300 feet long, of 3,200 tons—nearly three times the size of the *Britannia*. The new mammoth was launched at Bristol in 1843 in the presence of the Prince Consort, who had been invited to grace the occasion.

A director of the Great Western Steamship Company testified before the Committee on the Halifax and Boston Mails (1846) that his Company had been alarmed by a report 'a few months back' that New York was to be made the terminus of the Cunard Line.

---

[1] *American Notes*, I and XVI. The sailing packet still found much favour in the forties. Ralph Waldo Emerson used one in crossing the Atlantic in October 1847, also to give a series of lectures. He left from Boston in the *Washington Irving*, describing her as of 750 tons, with a deck of 155 feet, and with cabins that were not well lighted. Emerson did not enjoy life at sea—'an acquired taste', wrote Emerson, 'like that for tomatoes and olives'. He believed the risk on a steamboat greater, though the time at sea might be shorter. The *Washington Irving* reached Liverpool in the excellent time of sixteen days. See *English Traits*, II, 'Voyage to England.'

E*

He pointed out that for eight years the *Great Western* had gone back and forth between Bristol and New York without the slightest aid from government, and always carrying mail. Various memorials to the Committee supported the desire of the Great Western Company for at least a share of the mails. One signed by fifty-four Birmingham merchants stated that the proposed Cunard service to New York would be the ruin of the Great Western Company, 'which Company really led the way and by its successful example was the founder of successful transatlantic steam navigation'. This memorial also pointed out the obvious desire of the Cunard Line to kill competition by lowering their fares when the *Great Western* was about to sail at the same time as a Cunarder. The Committee was asked for some plan by which the Bristol Line might participate in the contract, which should in 'common justice be open to competition'.

Samuel Cunard, in rebuttal, told the Committee that he came to England in the winter of 1839 to make arrangements for improving the communication, and that he knew nothing of anybody else's plan. It was true, he said, that fares were altered when the *Great Western* sailed at nearly the same time as a Cunarder, but it was not with his concurrence: 'I regretted it—it looked like an opposition.' Mr Cunard insisted that he 'always had it in view to go to New York'. He had decided to add this route because 'I saw the American Government was giving encouragement to a mail line that would interfere very much with me—it would deprive the British Government of half the postage and me of half the passengers.' A member of the Select Committee proposed that the contract for the New York mails be opened to public tender, but a public tender was not acceptable to a majority of the Committee.[1]

The new contract that gave Cunard a direct service to New York was signed in July before the Select Committee had reported. The contract provided for two routes, one to New York, the other to Halifax and Boston. The service was to be on alternate Saturdays for eight months, April through November, and monthly during the winter. The New York service actually began in 1848, although a Cunarder, the *Hibernia*, had gone to New York from Boston in December 1847. By 1852 the service was made weekly throughout

---

[1] *Parl., Ret.*, 464/1846, 37; *Rep. S. C. Halifax and Boston Mails* (1849) 1–5; and the Cunard contract of July 1, 1846. The Great Western Steamship Company soon gave up the unequal struggle, selling the *Great Western* to the Royal Mail Line serving the West Indies, and the *Great Britain* to a shipping line in the Australian trade. For her use on the Australian run, see below, pp. 151, 194 and illustration, facing p. 160.

the year, the vessels leaving Liverpool on Saturday of each week alternately for the two American ports. Within a dozen years from the first voyage, various contracts won from the Admiralty had increased the Cunard subsidy from £55,000 to £173,340 a year, or if the branches be included, to £188,040.

The packets used by the Line had also grown in size and power. The 'advanced state of science' had been partly responsible, though the bitter competition faced by the Cunarders had more to do with the continuous improvements. The *Hibernia* and *Cambria*, added in the mid-forties, were of over 1,400 tons. By the mid-century the fleet included the *Asia* and the *Africa* of 2,227 tons each. They had a speed of about 12 knots, but to attain it had to burn some 75 tons of coal a day. The Atlantic horsepower race had begun.[1]

CUNARD LINERS FACE AMERICAN COMPETITION

By 1845 American shipping interests determined to win back the prestige that their sailing liners had held before the advent of steam. The first attempt was made by two large ships for a New York–Bremen service, with a stop at the Isle of Wight for British mail and passengers. The *Washington* began its voyages in 1847, and the *Hermann* was later added as her consort. They proved disappointing, as they were slow and 'rolled' across the Atlantic. They ran on this route until 1857 with the aid of a subsidy from Congress. A second transatlantic line out of New York began in 1849: the New York and Havre Steam Navigation Company, also aided by a subsidy, used the *Franklin* and the *Humboldt*, and they also stopped at the Isle of Wight to accommodate British mail and passengers.[2]

The most ambitious American to enter the transatlantic service was Edward K. Collins. He had founded the Dramatic Line of sailing liners, but was now firmly convinced of the virtues of steam. In November 1847 Congress promised him a subsidy of $385,000 annually, if he would provide a steamship service between New York and Liverpool that would be at least as fast as that of the Cunard Line.

A spirited contest followed between Cunard and Collins. The American promoter built vessels that were in size and appointments

---

[1] The older ships were sold as they became outdated. The Cunarders continued to be built of wood and driven by paddle wheels. They were comfortable and well run, according to the standards of the time. For Anthony Trollope's pleasant voyage in the *Africa*, see below, p. 157.

[2] Bowen, op. cit., 49, 82; Bonsor, op. cit., 59–61.

the best of their day. They were so costly, however, that Mr
Collins asked for and received a larger subsidy—in 1852 it became
$858,000 (£178,750) per annum for twenty-six round voyages.
This, in turn, was justification for Mr Cunard building larger ships.
He wrote Viscount Canning, Postmaster-General at the time:

'If we were to relax now in the power and size of our vessels, the
whole service would fall into the hands of the Americans which are
well sustained by their Government. We can only retain our
position on the Atlantic by continuing to build powerful ships.
The risk of doing so is very great, as at the termination of a contract
the ships would be valueless, being too expensive to use for any
other purpose . . . These risks we have to meet at fearful cost.'

Clearly the subsidy for postal purposes had become subordinated to
combat for the supremacy of the north Atlantic. A ruinous subsidy
war was on.[1]

The Collins Line built four liners for this service, the *Arctic*,
Baltic, *Atlantic* and *Pacific*. Each had a tonnage of 2,856 and engines
of 2,000 horsepower. The vessels were two-masted, built of wood
and paddle driven, and with straight stems in contrast to the clipper
bows then in general use. It was to meet this competition that the
Cunard Company built such vessels as the *Arabia* and the *Persia*.
The *Arabia* (1852) had a tonnage of 2,400 and the *Persia*, ready in
1856, was a 'leviathan' of 3,400 tons. The *Persia* was the first
Cunarder to be built of iron, but like all her predecessors in the
fleet she was propelled by paddle wheels.

The Collins Line voyages, which began in 1850, proved at first
faster than those of their British rivals. The *Pacific* did an eastern
crossing in 1852 in 9 days and 17 hours, and a westward run in
9 days and 18 hours. The Collins Line kept the record—it became
known as the Blue Riband—from 1851 to 1856, when it was taken
over by the *Persia* with a crossing of 9 days and 5 hours. This
record held until 1863.

Striving for the blue riband meant a dangerous overtaxing of
engines and hulls, and a disregard of precautions in days when there
was no adequate warning against possible collisions. The rather
childish encouragement of speed and size by heavy so-called postal
subsidies was a dangerous as well as a foolish policy. The Cunard
Line at least kept up its reputation for safety. In 1846 it adopted the

1 *P.O. Records*, ep., Samuel Cunard to Viscount Canning, May 21, 1853.

now familiar ship's lights—white at the masthead, green on the starboard and red on the larboard (port) bow. As the steam whistle was not yet in use, a tin horn was blown in foggy weather.

Just at this time a series of marine disasters pointed to the need for even more attention to the safeguarding of life and mails at sea. The Collins Line came in for more than its share of ill luck. The first disaster was the loss of the *Arctic* in September 1854 just after her engines had been refitted at great expense. She was rammed by a small French steamship in a dense fog off Cape Race. Of 371 on board, 322 lost their lives, including the wife, son and daughter of Mr Collins. As if this were not enough, the *Pacific* disappeared in January 1856 on a westward crossing, without leaving a trace. The Cunard *Persia* had left Liverpool about the same time—an exciting race was in prospect. The *Persia* finally limped into New York overdue, having hit an iceberg that buckled her bow. An iceberg was probably responsible for the disappearance of the *Pacific*, as her straight stem offered little protection to a vessel built without bulkheads.[1]

The Collins Line, mortally injured by the loss of half its fleet, fought on for a time. The largest of the fleet, the *Adriatic*, 3,670 tons, was launched in April 1856 to replace the *Arctic*, but she made only one voyage for the Collins Line. By that time Congress was becoming much less interested in heavy subsidies for the merchant marine. In 1857 the Collins subsidy was sharply reduced from $858,000 per annum to $346,500. The Line finally gave up the contract after the *Baltis* made the last westward crossing early in 1858. The Line had never paid a dividend. The vessels were seized by creditors and sold at auction. In the same year Congress decided to discontinue subsidies altogether for the carriage of mails. An Act of 1858 provided that foreign overseas mails should be carried for the postage: if in an American ship, for both the inland and sea postage; if in a foreign ship, for the sea postage only.[2]

The decision of the American Government to abandon expensive so-called mail contracts had no parallel in Britain. Her ever growing trade had expanded with even greater speed after the adoption of a free-trade policy in the early forties. In the ten years before 1850

[1] One result of these disasters was the general adoption of lights on ships such as those used by the Cunard Line, and the arrangement of different sea lanes for vessels bound eastward and westward. Steam whistles soon came into use to give the whereabouts of ships in foggy weather.

[2] *35th Congress, Sess. I, ch. 164;* Bowen, op. cit., 83-93. The *Adriatic* was bought in 1861 by the Lever Line, and was soon carrying transatlantic mail under a British contract. See below, p. 244.

British exports had grown by more than 50 per cent. In 1851, the first great International Exhibition of the Works of Industry was held in the Crystal Palace. Great Britain had become the leading industrial nation and the greatest trading and financial centre in the world. Communication, even by expensive subsidies, seemed essential.[1]

The Post Office, of course, was not opposed to commercial expansion, but it objected strongly to Mr Cunard's oft repeated statement that his large subsidy was completely covered by the postage of the mails that he carried. To the Post Office, such an assertion was in error, and Mr Cunard should have admitted it. An important inquiry into packet contracts was made in 1853 by a Committee headed by Viscount Canning, the Postmaster-General. In anticipation of the inquiry Samuel Cunard sent a long letter to Viscount Canning, in which he attempted to justify the large subsidy. He wrote in part:

'I have good reason to believe that the postage received has exceeded the amount paid to me besides saving £40,000, the cost of the old sailing ships, and furnishing a regular weekly communication instead of the uncertain monthly one . . . I am now bound by a contract to have eight Ships of 400 Horse power which cost £50,000 each, instead of which our Ships are from 700 to 1,000 Horse power, costing from £90,000 to £110,000 each. If we had confined the power of our Ships to 400 Horse, the Americans would have carried all the letters, it is true they would also have carried the passengers, but the Government receive the advantage of our vast outlay by having the carriage of the letters secured without any additional advance on the part of the Government . . . The Merchants in this country hesitated to run the risk of performing this service [?], while I, a Colonist, undertook it upon my own responsibility and risk; these are the circumstances which together with the manner in which this service has been performed for thirteen years that will, I trust, entitle me to the continuation of this Contract.'[2]

The Canning Committee did not hesitate to commend the Cunard Line for the great regularity of the voyages. But Mr Cunard's claim

[1] See A. H. Imlah, *Economic Elements in the Pax Britannica* (Cambridge, Mass., 1958) for a careful statistical examination of the long period of peace following Waterloo.
[2] *P.O. Records*, ep. of March 11, 1853. Frank Staff, op. cit., 140-2, has reprinted this letter in full.

that the postage equalled the subsidy was denied by the Committee. The service actually cost the Government £188,000 annually, and the sea postage only amounted in the last year to £121,000. Nor was the Committee willing to concede the need for large and continuous subsidies. When a shipping line was doing well, with a good freight and passenger business, the Government had a right to expect the postal service to be done 'for a payment that will cover the freight of the mail-bags'.[1]

Much more outspoken than the Canning Committee was a merchant and shipowner of London, Robert McCalmont by name. His *Remarks* appeared in print in 1851. McCalmont sharply attacked the system of subsidies by which 'monstrous and intolerable monopolists' were being reared up, as the 'seas are being parcelled out . . . to intriguing companies'. He ridiculed the idea that vessels carrying mails should be regarded as a naval reserve: 'A steam packet and a steam man-of-war have little in common except their chimneys, if even that.' He was especially opposed to Atlantic subsidies. He thought a subsidy for vessels plying the great commercial thoroughfare between New York and Liverpool 'perfectly preposterous'. To McCalmont, the contract system was a new Navigation Law, and most unjust.[2]

The Post Office strongly opposed the renewal of the Cunard contract in 1857, especially as it had four more years to run. At that time the American Government was withdrawing subsidies. When Mr Cunard was asked later why he was so insistent, he restated views that he must have been aware were contrary to fact: 'I had no particular ground except that I wanted it renewed . . . We had brought in the whole [?] of the postage, and the Government had this Line in beautiful operation without any cost, and therefore we were entitled to renewal.' Nor did the Post Office's objection to renewal have any effect on the Admiralty or the Treasury: the Secretary of the Admiralty wrote that 'the best course for insuring a satisfactory performance will be to prolong the contract. Keeping the superiority of the British Line appears to my Lords to be of

---

[1] *Rep. Com. on Contract Pkts.* (1853), 2, 30, 77. A contemporary American judgement on this subsidy matter was that of Thomas Rainey in his *Ocean Steam Navigation and the Ocean Post* (New York, 1857). He particularly lamented America's slavish dependence on Britain by allowing 'half our letters to Europe to go by the Cunard Line'. Rainey favoured subsidies, but thought it unfair, as did Canning, to charge such subsidies against the Post Office. They should be paid directly by the Treasury.

[2] Robert McCalmont, *Some Remarks on the Contract Packet System and on Ocean Penny Postage* (1851); it was addressed to the President of the Board of Trade. The title indicates that he thought high subsidies were hindering cheaper ocean postage.

national importance.' The Admiralty regarded the 'pecuniary question of postage is of minor importance in regard to this service'. When the Admiralty renewed the contract, the Collins Line was already bankrupt.

Samuel Cunard was fortunate that renewal came when it did. Three years later, a Committee on Packet Contracts, saw so little need for extravagant arrangements by the Admiralty that it recommended the return to the Post Office of the power to contract for sea-going mail services. This power was returned in 1860 by Act of Parliament.[1]

[1] *1st Rep. S.C. on Packet and Telegraph Contracts* (1860), pp. xxvi, 8-11, 18, 252; Act of 23rd Victoria, ch. 6. Samuel Cunard was created a baron in 1860. He died four years later, leaving a personalty of £350,000, according to the *D.N.B.*

14

TRANSATLANTIC MAILS— CANADA, THE WEST INDIES, SOUTH AMERICA

THE colonies that remained loyal to the mother country during the American Revolution were known collectively as British North America, but at the time that steamships began crossing the Atlantic they were still seven separate colonies. Newfoundland was an isolated island to the east; the maritime colonies were Nova Scotia, New Brunswick and Prince Edward Island; up the St Lawrence were the two provinces of Lower and Upper Canada, later to be known as Quebec and Ontario. The two Canadas were united in 1840 after the Canadian Rebellion and the mission of Lord Durham. All the colonies in British North America were granted internal self-government either before or shortly after 1860, and all became a part of the Dominion of Canada in 1867, save Newfoundland.

Just as they were obtaining self-government, these colonies were acquiring control of their postal administrations—actually in 1851. This was followed by the lowering of internal postal rates, and by a strong desire for lower postage on their overseas letters to and from the mother country.

The overseas postal services, however, presented peculiarly difficult problems for the widely scattered colonies to the north of the United States. The British colony with the best transatlantic connection was, of course, Nova Scotia, since Halifax had long been a port of call for the Falmouth sailing packets, and was the first American port to receive the Cunard services. This port of call, however, was of little use to the two inland Canadian provinces, especially after the Cunard Line discontinued its steam service on the St Lawrence from Pictou to Quebec after it had been in use for only five years.

The two Canadas, as a result, were left to fare as best they could.

A land route from Halifax to Quebec, 700 miles long, was used occasionally about this time; the Canadian Post Office reported that a 'special courier, generally an Indian, was sent now and then through the wilderness' to carry dispatches between the two cities.

A CANADIAN MAIL LINE

The only alternatives for transatlantic Canadian mails were by chance vessels using the St Lawrence, or by way of the Atlantic ports along the northern coast of the United States. Mails by way of the United States involved an overland journey, but the routes were shorter and less difficult than the one between Quebec and Halifax. The Canadians naturally resented receiving their mails by a British mail line to the United States, the mails then going on to Canada overland. It was only too clear to Canadians that the Cunard Company was less interested in the Canadian mails than in cultivating business relations with the United States. The Canadian view was well put by John Rose, Commissioner of Public Works in Canada in speaking to a British Select Committee on Packet Contracts. He said in 1860 that the large Cunard subsidy was a direct bounty to American ports, American railways and the American canals. The Canadians resented paying an addition to the sea postage on letters that crossed the Atlantic. 'It would certainly seem', said Mr Rose, 'that Canada is placed in a much less favourable position than the other English colonies.' By other British colonies, he meant, not only the Maritimes and Newfoundland, but New South Wales, South Africa and the West Indies. In 1848 the Canadian Post Office had made a convention with the United States by which the letters on this overland route were taxed with the combined postage of the two countries, in addition to the sea postage. Canadians naturally objected to a higher postage for their British mail then was charged on British mail to Jamaica or Newfoundland or Bermuda.[1]

Canada's only recourse, in view of the unwillingness of the Cunard Line to continue the branch service to Quebec City, was a steamship line of her own that would use the St Lawrence seaway. In 1852 the Canadian Government sought tenders for such a service, and accepted the offer of Hugh Allan of Montreal. He was

[1] *1st Rep. P.M.G.* (G.B., 1855), 36; William Smith, *A History of the British Post Office in North America*, 1639-1870 (1920), 284; *Life of Rowland Hill*, II, 241-4. See below, ch. XXI, for the general lowering of colonial rates at the mid-century.

the son of Captain Alexander Allan, a Glasgow shipmaster, who began sending vessels to Canada as early as 1819. Hugh Allan had migrated to Canada in 1826. His tender resulted in a Canadian steam mail line called the Montreal Ocean Steamship Company, but usually known in later years as the Allan Line. The contract, drawn up in 1853, called for a regular steam service fortnightly in summer, and once a month during the winter, at a cost of £45,000 per annum. Later when it became a weekly service the subsidy was raised to £55,000. Montreal was to be used as a terminus for seven months of the year, and Portland in the State of Maine during the winter. The land route between Portland and Montreal, via the Grand Trunk Railway, was much the shortest route from Canada to any Atlantic port that was open throughout the winter. Montreal is less than 300 miles from Portland—much nearer than to Boston or New York, and only a third of the distance overland between Montreal and Halifax. The Allan Line used Glasgow and Liverpool as eastern termini, and stopped at Londonderry for Irish mail and passengers.[1]

The Allan Line mail services began in 1856. From the beginning the vessels of the Line were screw propelled and compared favourably with other transatlantic mail steamers as to horsepower and tonnage. The time taken by the Allan Line in the fifties averaged under eleven days eastward and less than twelve days westward, somewhat better than the record of those Cunarders using Boston as their final port. The Allan Line was so well regarded that the United States Post Office, after the collapse of the Collins Line in 1858, arranged for the Allan Line ships to bring to Portland during the winter the mail that had previously been carried by the Collins Line. Canada had succeeded in making arrangements for her needs for an ocean mail service by establishing and financing her own Line.[2]

When the British Post Office proposed to Canada in 1856 that the colony share the cost of the British transatlantic services, the Canadian Postmaster-General Robert Spence, thought the suggestion presumptuous. 'Why should Canada support a line of

---

[1] The Intercolonial Railway between Halifax and Montreal was not completed until 1876. In speaking before the Committee on Postal Contracts in 1860, Mr Cunard asserted that he could have had the Canadian contract: 'They offered it to me.' If so, he found it no more attractive than the arrangement of 1840.

[2] *1st Rep. S.C. on Packet and Telegraph Contracts* (1860), 33-36, 256; *Instructions to Postmasters*, No. 55 of 1858. The Allan Line was maintained as a passenger and mail service under that name until it was acquired by the Canadian Pacific Company during the First World War. For an account of the Line, see Bonsor, op. cit., 83-103.

steamers to New York and Boston'? And he added: 'It may be that the Imperial Government has other views than merely the transmission of mail.'

The British Post Office next proposed that Canada should divide with the British Post Office the returns of the Allan Line mails. This was, of course, declined on the ground that the service was wholly supported by Canada. In that year the two Canadian Houses of Parliament sent a joint statement to the Queen—it was signed by the two Speakers—that the continued large subsidy to the Cunard Line is 'exceedingly detrimental to Canada'. The Memorial stated that they had learned with regret that Great Britain had renewed the contract with the Cunard Company in 1858 'without any opportunity being offered to the Government of Canada to urge such arrangements as would be conducive to the prosperity of Canada'. And there the matter ended for the time being.[1]

THE WEST INDIES

The West Indian route furnished the greatest test for a transatlantic mail service. A long ocean voyage was followed by complicated journeys among the islands and to the mainland of South America. Now that steam was in use, the older Admiralty arrangements were outmoded in the opinion of James Macqueen, who was largely responsible for the changes when steam mailpackets were introduced.

Macqueen was a Scot who had gone to Grenada in 1798 to manage a sugar plantation. Being fond of travel, he became well acquainted with the West Indies and wrote about them at great length. His *General Plan for a Mail Communication by Steam between Great Britain and the Eastern and Western Parts of the World* appeared in 1837. In it, Macqueen expressed the hope that there would be 'no narrow or parsimonious views on the part of this great country' in the use of steamships for sending mails overseas. In the same year the Treasury asked Macqueen to prepare a plan for steam communication between England and the Caribbean.[2]

In 1839 merchants interested in the West Indies organized a company to furnish a steam service such as Macqueen had recommended, and in the next year the Royal Mail Steam Packet Company

[1] *Parl. Ret.*, 84/1857, 2nd sess., p.3; 241/1859; William Smith, op. cit., 284, declares that the British Post Office persisted in regarding the Allan Line as a foreign service, making the same charge for its mail as for that of foreign lines.

[2] *Br. Almanac* for 1851, Comp., pp. 51, 67; T. A. Bushell, '*Royal Mail*', *A Centenary History of the Royal Mail* (1939), 213.

obtained a contract for the service. Macqueen was chiefly responsible for the arrangement of the routes; during the next nine months he travelled over 18,000 miles to prepare for the new service.

The contract of the Royal Mail called for 15 steam vessels of 450 horsepower, and 4 additional sailing vessels that were to be used on some of the less important routes. Various Admiralty provisions included the use of Admiralty agents on the boats carrying the mails, the transport of military personnel at reduced rates, the requirement that the vessels be of wood and capable of carrying guns of the highest calibre. The subsidy was to be £240,000 a year. Macqueen's hopes that 'no narrow or parsimonious views' should accompany the use of steam packets was abundantly realized in the lavish provisions for the West Indian mail service by steamships.[1]

The routes made a complicated network, requiring travel during the year of nearly 550,000 miles, with stops at some sixty ports among the islands and on the mainland. The transatlantic packets left the English Channel twice a month. Barbados was the chief base for the branch lines to the other islands and to the Spanish Main. Havana was included, and a route originally connected New Orleans at the mouth of the Mississippi with the main-line steamers. One route proposed by Macqueen connected the islands with Savannah, Charleston and New York. Macqueen's arrangements proved altogether too elaborate. As a result the itineraries were cut down and simplified—and the ports of call to the United States were later omitted. Three weeks was allowed the ocean packets for crossing the Atlantic. As the arrangements finally settled down they provided for some eleven routes in the Caribbean, with some thirty ports of call, including places outside British territory, such as Cuba, Curaçao, La Guaira and Vera Cruz. By the contract of 1846 an important addition was made—Chagres became a port of call. This port on the Isthmus of Panama was valuable because it was at the Atlantic end of the shortest crossing to the Pacific.[2]

The contract of 1850 with the Royal Mail also included the old packet route down the east coast of South America. However, the

[1] Bushell, op. cit., 4-6; Macqueen's *Reply* to the Directors of the Royal Mail (1844) with whom he disagreed by this time. Like the Cunard contracts, those of the Royal Mail, in the early years, were not open to competitive bidding. For the Admiralty agents aboard mail steamers, see below, ch. 19.

[2] The contract of July 5, 1850, next after that of 1846, made St Thomas the starting point of most of the branches. The through packet from Southampton was to reach St Thomas within twenty-four days. See *Parl. Ret.*, 318/1852 and the contract.

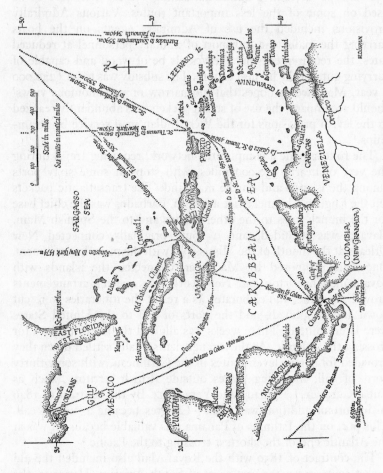

MAP 5. Packet Routes—the West Indies and Panama.

Royal Mail packets for Rio de Janeiro did not go by way of the West Indies but by the route formerly used by the sailing packets—via Madeira and Tenerife. For this addition to its services, the Royal Mail received £30,000 annually, making the total subsidy £270,000, and providing for the continuance of both transatlantic routes to the end of 1862.

The steam service to the West Indies began in 1842, with the departure of the *Thames*. She sailed from Southampton with her passengers, and stopped at Falmouth to take on the mails. The vessels of the Line bore names, for the most part, of rivers and estuaries in Great Britain, such names as *Medway*, *Trent*, *Solway*, *Tay*, *Severn*, *Teviot*. Owing to some early losses, purchases had to be made to keep up the contract requirements. One vessel that was added in 1847 was the *Great Western*, already familiar to the reader. The *Esk* that began its service in 1849 was screw propelled— the first screw steamer used by any British mail company.

When the *Thames* returned from her first voyage, she did not stop at Falmouth but went directly to Southampton, and Southampton has been the terminus of the Royal Mail Line ever since. Even before the first voyage of the *Thames* a Committee of the Admiralty had made elaborate inquiries as to the best Channel port for the steam services that were fast replacing the sailing packets out of Falmouth. The original Royal Mail contract had not named a particular port. Falmouth, naturally, made strong claims for its continued use. Memorials and testimony from that port held that Falmouth was the best port of refuge in the Channel—in only thirteen out of the last 1,740 voyages had the mail-packets found it necessary to use a port to the east.

The various south coast ports made claims that were numerous, conflicting and highly competitive. When Plymouth proposed the use of its harbour, Falmouth retorted that Plymouth was a naval base and did not have a harbour, only an open roadstead, making difficult the landing of passengers and mails. The Admiralty favoured Dartmouth, which was still farther east. In general, the Committee preferred a western port, if there was a railway connection, since rail travel was already much faster than that of steamers. The lack of a railway to Falmouth was the great objection to that port; at that time the mails were taking twenty-eight hours between London and Falmouth. In fact, the railway did not reach Falmouth until 1863.[1]

[1] *2nd Rep. Commrs. on Channel Port* (1841), 1-5; *3rd Rep.*, 48-55, etc.

The Royal Mail, considered Falmouth as 'utterly ineligible' and disliked Plymouth and Portsmouth because of their great naval stations. Southampton was regarded—strange as it may seem to the modern traveller—as a 'quiet port' far from the bustle of the great naval stations. Its harbour could take the newest steamships, an approach was possible from either side of the Isle of Wight, and the double tides were a distinct advantage to ocean vessels. Elaborate plans had been started in 1838 for a dock area that would enclose a space of 16 acres. What made Southampton a particularly attractive port was its nearness to London, only 75 miles away. The railway connection had been completed in May 1840. Soon frequent trains— six a day even in the forties—were taking only three hours to make the journey. Superlative natural advantages had brought South-ampton a pre-eminence it has held ever since.[1]

The Peninsular Navigation Company, whose beginnings are to be considered in the next chapter, felt much the same as the Royal Mail. The preference of these two great companies for Southampton proved decisive. Falmouth, which had been a packet port for ocean mails since 1689, lost out to Liverpool and Southampton where the harbours were more useful and better adapted to rapid inland communication. The marine engine and the building of the railways had brought the change. The Royal Mail packets began to use Southampton in 1843 for its route to the West Indies, but the packets serving Brazil received and delivered the mails at Falmouth until 1850.[2]

The Committee on Contract Packets of 1853, headed by Lord Canning, sharply criticized the service of the Royal Mail. It was reported as 'very irregular'. During the previous two years, for example, the packets had arrived at Southampton on schedule in only three instances, and had been as much as two weeks late on occasion. As to the slowness of the service—the Committee found that duplicate letters from Chagres on the Isthmus of Panama that went to New York and by Cunard or Collins Line steamers to Liverpool commonly arrived in England sooner than the originals by the Royal Mail. The Admiralty agents on the vessels of the Royal Mail also reported that the steamers occasionally took too much time in coaling with the apparent purpose of obtaining more cargo.

---

[1] *Parl. Gaz. of England and Wales* (4v., 1843), IV, 1612.
[2] *3rd Rep. Commrs. on Channel Port* (1841), 33, 43; *Parl. Ret.* 315/1867 for a revival of Falmouth's efforts to be made a packet port.

The Company replied that the delays were frequently caused by waiting for inter-colonial mails. The Royal Mail was hard hit by serious losses in the first decade of the Line's activity. In ten years six ships had to be replaced. There had been laxity in other ways as to the terms of the contract, partly because the Royal Mail was without competition in the Caribbean region. The Cunard Line, on the other hand, had a splendid record for punctuality, for which her competitors may take some credit. The Admiralty had been unusually lenient in not fining the Royal Mail ships for delays. The Canning Committee noted that other companies were willing to carry the mail into the Caribbean at more reasonable rates. Worst of all, the amount paid to the Royal Mail was out of all proportion to the postage received. By 1853 the West Indian service had an annual deficiency of over 75 per cent. The Brazil Line, on the contrary, brought in more postage than the cost of the contract.[1]

THE PACIFIC STEAM NAVIGATION COMPANY

A British 'mail' down the Pacific side of South America should be included here, since its mail were received and dispatched by way of the Isthmus of Panama and the Royal Mail Line. As early as 1836 the British Government had become interested in better communications up and down this coast where independent republics had replaced the older Spanish colonies, and where trade was likely to increase. The actual promoter of this line was the American-born William Wheelwright, for a time the American consul at Guayaquil. After moving down the coast to Valparaiso, Wheelwright became obsessed with the idea of steam communication along this coast. When he failed to obtain financial assistance in the United States, he went to London where he was favourably received. The Pacific Steam Navigation Company, chartered in 1840, was the outcome. Before the end of the year it had sent out by way of Cape Horn two steamboats of about 700 tons each. These paddle wheelers worked up and down the coast between Valparaiso and Panama.

From 1841 to 1845 the struggling Company, unassisted by a

---

[1] *Rep. Com. on Contract Pkts.* (1853), 24-26, 57, 70; *Rep. S.C. Contract Pkt. Service* (1849), 181; *Parl. Ret.* 270/1853. A comparison of the size of the various contracts and the postage received on other postal lines in the year 1853 shows some deficiency in every case. On the Pacific Steam it was nearly 80 per cent; on the Cunard Line 32 per cent. With regard to the Peninsular and Oriental services—discussed in the next chapter—the deficiency was 23 per cent.

British mail subsidy, nearly went bankrupt. But its obvious commercial value led to a so-called mail contract in 1846 that considerably improved its fortunes at the expense of the Post Office. The contract required a monthly service by vessels of 170 horsepower. The contract differed from all others made by the Admiralty in that the vessels did not touch at any British port. The mail value of the Line was so slight that the postal receipts were only about a fifth of the subsidy. As the Report of the Canning Committee put it: 'The extension of British influence and British commerce appears to have been the chief inducement for supporting this communication between the republics of New Grenada [Colombia], Bolivia, Peru and Chile.'[1]

Because of the primitive means of crossing the Isthmus, the Pacific Mail's steamships could be held for as much as 120 hours beyond the time they were scheduled to leave Panama, if the Atlantic mail had not arrived. The crossing of the Isthmus was just under 50 miles. At that time, no road connected Chagres on the Gulf of Mexico with Panama, nothing by a mule track where river courses were not available. Mails, goods, and travellers used dug-out canoes on the waterways, and mules where water courses were not available.[2]

The contract of 1850, which made the service fortnightly instead of monthly, was partly the result of the growing attraction of the Isthmian route. It had become of prime value to the United States because of its territories on the Pacific coast. The Oregon boundary dispute with Canada had been settled in 1846, and in that year the United States declared war on Mexico, with the result that the west coast of North America from Oregon to Lower California became a part of the United States. Hardly had the cession taken place before gold was discovered not far from San Francisco. The gold rush began in 1849. The vast expanse of the Great Plains and the mountain barrier to the west made land travel difficult, as a transcontinental railway had not yet been built. It was much easier to go from the eastern United States to California by the two water

[1] *Rep. Com. Contract Pkts.* (1853), 32. Panama was, at that time, a part of New Grenada.
[2] *Rep. S.C. Contract Pkt. Service* (1849), 204-6; W. Wheelwright, *Statement and Documents Relative to the Establishment of Steam Navigation in the Pacific* (1838). Kemble, op. cit., ch. VI, has an interesting account of the 'Isthmian Link'. Bushell, op. cit., 87-88 gives the Royal Mail credit for keeping up the land route before the railway was ready in 1855. Bushell claims, without giving his source, that a loan from the Royal Mail in 1850 to the American Railway Company made possible the completion of the line. The Isthmian link was much more than a Royal Mail connection with the Pacific Steam, even before the gold rush to California in 1849.

routes that were connected by the Isthmian link at Panama. Even before the gold rush an American steamship line was running between New York and Chagres. Another United States Line, the Pacific Mail Steamship Company, ran between Panama and California. The traffic across the Isthmus had increased so much by 1850 that a group of New York capitalists began the construction of a railway from Chagres to Panama City. It was completed in 1855. Chagres was replaced by a more modern port slightly to the east, known as Colon, or Aspinwall as it was usually called by the Company that built it. The fear of the British that the Americans might wish to extend their activities down the west coast of South America in competition with the British Pacific Mail Line was unfounded. The gold of California and the peopling of the west coast of the United States were much too attractive.[1]

The route via Panama even caught the attention of Samuel Cunard. He wrote Viscount Canning in 1853 about a possible Cunard service from New York to the Isthmus. According to Cunard, this branch might be able to bring letters and specie from the Isthmus to England in about three months. He insisted that this proposed extension was not intended to interfere with the West Indian Royal Mail Line, although one is at a loss to know how interference could have been avoided. Samuel Cunard declared that his primary concern was carrying letters and specie 'now brought by American steamers'. He also dreamed of a link from Panama to Australia, and a vast increase in the size of the mails, and 'to get our steamers on the Line before the Americans occupy it'. Back of these plans, according to Mr Cunard was the desire 'to assist our present contract and enable us to hold out against the Americans'. Nothing came of these proposed extensions, much to the great relief of the Royal Mail Company, who were very suspicious of the Cunard schemes.[2]

TROLLOPE INSPECTS THE WEST INDIES

The experience of a Post Office surveyor, may give an idea of the

[1] Kemble, op. cit., 6ff., 153.

[2] Samuel Cunard to Viscount Canning, April 16, 1853. Thomas Rainey, op. cit., 130, had heard of the Cunard designs for another line to Aspinwall, and of one from Panama to the East Indies. The *Unicorn* that had made the first Cunard crossing to Boston in 1840, was sent to California in 1849 with a load of gold seekers. The journey around Cape Horn took over three months. The *Unicorn* was later sold to an American company, used by them until 1853, then sold again, and she finally returned to England via Australia. This most adventurous of early Cunarders ended her active life in the Portuguese Navy. See Kemble, op. cit., 39, 249.

conditions faced by the packets of the Royal Mail. The Post Office
sent Anthony Trollope to the West Indies in 1858 'to cleanse the
Augean stables of our Post Office there', to use his own words. He
also visited Cuba and Panama for the purpose of making postal
treaties. Trollope travelled by Royal Mail to the West Indies and
within the Caribbean area. In making the journey between Southampton and St Thomas, the *Atrato* took only fifteen days. Trollope
was not at all impressed with St Thomas; he believed that Kingston
Jamaica, would serve as a better headquarters for the complicated
service, and so recommended on his return. After doing his assigned
task in Cuba, he visited the Windward Islands and went on to
Trinidad and then to British Guiana on the mainland, and back
again to St Thomas 'which is the starting point for all places in that
part of the globe'. He then returned to the Spanish Main, with a
stop at the 'wretched' village of Santa Marta, where 'with intense
cruelty we maintain a British consul and a British post-office'.
From Santa Marta he moved on to Cartagena and the Isthmus.

Anthony Trollope found Colon (Aspinwall) a thriving 'little
American town created by and for the railway and passenger
traffic which comes here both from Southampton and New York'.
He crossed to the Pacific on the recently completed railway to
Panama. Just off the mainland from Panama City lay several
picturesque islands, one of which was the depot of the American
steam packet company carrying on a service with California. On
another of the islands, Tobago by name, were the headquarters of
the 'English Company whose vessels run down the Pacific to Peru
and Chili'. When Trollope visited Tobago he found a small English
maritime colony. This, he assumed, would become the headquarters
of another large ship company, if the route from Panama became
one of the 'high roads to Australia.'

Anthony Trollope returned to St Thomas after a visit to Nica-
ragua and Costa Rica, and the Mosquito Coast 'of all places in
which I have ever put my foot the most wretched'. He returned to
St Thomas on the *Trent*. He finally left St Thomas for Bermuda on
the Cunard Company's *Delta*, a screw steamer that 'rolled horribly'.
It gave Trollope a strong aversion to the propeller: 'Screws have
been invented with the view of making sea-passages more disa-
greeable than they were.' Since Trollope wished to go to New York
and the *Delta* did not go to New York, he completed the journey on
a sailing vessel, 'the only way of getting from Bermuda to New
York or of going anywhere from Bermuda except to Halifax and

St Thomas, to which places a steamer runs once a month'. After visiting Niagara and Montreal, Trollope returned to New York to go on the Cunarder *Africa* to Liverpool. Of this paddle-wheel steamer he wrote: 'I have sailed in many vessels, but never in one that was more comfortable.' It was on this return journey that he finished his volume on *The West Indies and the Spanish Main*.

Anthony Trollope's recommendations to the Post Office included a transfer of headquarters in the West Indies from St Thomas to Jamaica, and a more economical scheme of routes. As the contract with the Royal Mail had recently been renewed by the Admiralty without the assistance of the Postmaster-General, the new scheme of routes had to wait until the contract ran out in 1864. Rowland Hill, then Secretary of the Post Office, summarized the Department's views on the Royal Mail by asserting that the Line was established, not for postal, but for political purposes.[1]

---

[1] *Life of Rowland Hill* (1880), II, 288-9. Trollopians may not be aware that Trollope, according to his *Autobiography*, regarded his work on the West Indies as the 'best book that has ever come from my pen'.

15

MAILS BY STEAM FOR INDIA
AND THE EAST

A REGULAR service for the lands east of Suez was not of importance
before the fall of Napoleon. Only in 1813 was the trade with India
opened to private British commercial interests—a welcome outlet
for a Britain that was being rapidly industrialized by the steam
engine. When the Charter of the East India Company came up for
review twenty years later (1833) the pressure for new markets
opened the Far East to trade, that is, the area beyond India where
the East India Company had a monopoly so far as British traders
were concerned. Also in 1833 the Company ceased its commercial
activities, and became the governing representative for Britain's
Indian Empire.

Shortly after the opening of India to private commerce, the Post
Office started a mail service by sailing packets to India. The new
postal route was soon abandoned, however, owing largely to the
opposition of the still powerful East India Company.[1]

The lumbering trading vessels of the Company continued to be
the usual means of travel and communication. When its Charter
was revised in 1833, Lord Macaulay was sent out to India to review
the Penal Code. He left Falmouth in 1834 aboard an East Indiaman.
As Macaulay was an insatiable reader, he broke the monotony of
what he called 'an easy and rapid voyage' by several months of
reading. During the twelve weeks at sea he read all seventy volumes
of the works of Voltaire, Gibbon's *Decline and Fall*, the seven
'thick folios' of the *Biographia Britannica* as well as numerous
Greek and Latin classics.

When Macaulay returned in 1838, it was on another East Indiaman, the *Lord Hungerford*, described by him as the 'most celebrated
of the huge floating hotels which run between London and Calcutta'.
'I intend', he added, 'to make myself a good German scholar by the

[1] See above, pp. 108–9.

time of my arrival in England.' It was entirely possible, for the
Lord Hungerford was six months on the way. By that time the
carrying of the mails and dispatches in as short a time as possible
was much more important than the learning of a new language *en
route*.[1]

The passage to India was not easy, however, for vessels driven
by the early marine engines, both on account of the distance—some
11,000 miles—and because of the absence of well-spaced coaling
stations along the route. The first attempt occurred in 1825. A
'Steam Committee' of Calcutta had offered a liberal award to anyone whose steam-driven vessel could make the long voyage in no
more than seventy days. Captain Henry Johnston, a naval officer,
hastened back from Calcutta to arrange for a ship that would win
the award. The result was the happily named *Enterprize*, a small
paddle steamer of 500 tons and about 60 horsepower. She left
Falmouth in August 1826 with passengers, dispatches and mail. The
voyage from Falmouth to Calcutta took, not seventy, but 113 days.
The engines were in use only about half the time; as one of her
passengers put it: 'They put out her fires pretty often.' The *Enterprize* was capable of only 6 to 7 knots under steam, and had to use
at least 10 tons of coal a day to do so. Yet it is to the credit of
Captain Johnston that his vessel had made the longest voyage ever
undertaken by a vessel equipped with a marine engine. More rapid
voyages were to take place not many decades later.

An energetic Englishman with the curious name of Waghorn had
been inspired by this first steamship voyage from Britain to India
to advocate the development of a steam service. Thomas Waghorn,
who was born in 1800, had gone to India after some service in the
Royal Navy. After reaching Calcutta in 1819, he joined the pilot
service of the Bengal Marine, and it so happened that he was the
pilot who brought the *Enterprize* up the Hooghly in 1825.[2]

When Thomas Waghorn returned to England in 1827 he proposed an express service by way of the Cape of Good Hope in
vessels with engines of fifty horsepower. Mr Freeling the Secretary
of the Post Office, rejected Waghorn's 'wild scheme' for using

[1] G. O. Trevelyan, *Life and Letters of Lord Macaulay* (1876), I, 360-2, 464; II, 1.
[2] Boyd Cable (Ernest Andrew Ewart), *A Hundred Years of the P. & O.* (1937),
pp. 58-60; it is a Company history. Halford Hoskins, *British Routes to India* (N.Y.,
1928), pp. 110, 121, 127; it is an excellent treatment. J. K. Sidebotham, *The Overland
Mail* (1946) is a vivid account of Waghorn's career, but it lacks an adequate bibliography;
references to letters as 'preserved' or to G.P.O. Records should be more precise.
Waghorn's claim that he was intent, from 1826, on a steam service via the Red Sea is
contradicted by documents in this volume; see pp. 9, 16-20, 41.

vessels by way of the Cape that were no more powerful 'than those we use upon the voyage between Dover and Calais'.

THE OVERLAND ROUTE

Attention soon became centred on a shorter route. If the journey could be made by the Mediterranean and across Egypt, it would mean a route 6,000 miles long, only about half the length of the journey around Africa. The route by way of Egypt was made up of three distinct sections. From the viewpoint of the British resident in India—it was there that the early enthusiasm for this route was most evident—the first section was from Bombay on the west coast of India to the Red Sea and thence north to the port of Suez where mail and passengers would be landed. The second section of this shorter route—through Egypt—was far from easy. It meant some 80 miles of desert to the Nile and thence down to the port of Alexandria on the Mediterranean. The third section of this 'overland' route was another journey by sea to England by way of Malta and Gibraltar. This western section had been used by packet-boats for some years, but only as far as Malta.

The first steamer to complete the eastern sea-section of the journey was the *Hugh Lindsay*. The vessel left Bombay in March 1830 on a voyage to Suez that took thirty-three days, of which twelve had been taken up with coaling on the way. It was a real accomplishment, for the route was nearly 3,000 miles long—about as far as New York is from Liverpool. The mail carried by the *Hugh Lindsay* reached England in half the time it would have taken by the all-sea route around Africa. It was a significant journey, for the East India Company had definitely turned to steam and to the overland route for its mail and dispatches.[1]

The *Hugh Lindsay* made occasional voyages from this time on, and in the late thirties was joined by the more powerful *Atlanta* and *Berenice*. After the vessels had crossed the Indian Ocean from Bombay, their main coaling station was at Mocha, a port just inside the entrance to the Red Sea. Mocha, however, had such limitations as a coaling station that the Company replaced it in the mid-thirties. In 1837 a richly laden vessel flying British colours was wrecked and plundered at Aden, and an inquiry followed. Captain Haines of the East India Company, who was sent to investigate, was so impressed with the value of Aden as a supply depot for coal that the Company

[1] Sir Evan Cotton, op. cit., 123; Hoskins, op. cit., 108; Cable, op. cit., 49-51.

The launching of the *Great Britain*, 3,200 tons, in 1843 in Bristol, the Prince Consort attending. The *Great Britain* was the largest vessel built up to that time and the first screw-driven steamship built of iron. Coloured lithograph by Pieken after J. Walter, National Maritime Museum, Greenwich.

The *Hindostan*, paddle wheeler, 2,000 tons, leaving Southampton in 1842 for Suez by way of Cape Town to open the P & O mail service east of Suez. *Source:* G.P.O.

Anthony Trollope, novelist and Post Office surveyor. He was sent on several important postal inspections overseas. Painting by Samuel Lawrence in the National Portrait Gallery.

attempted to purchase the port from the local sultan. After the sultan had agreed to the cession he repudiated it, whereupon an expeditionary force from India occupied Aden in 1839. The village of miserable adobe huts was very soon a centre of maritime activity; it became a regular port of call, and has remained so ever since. Aden was of the first importance in making possible the regular use of the overland route.[1]

The enthusiasm in India for a steam service by way of Egypt was not matched by an equal interest in Great Britain. The Admiralty had not seen fit to extend the Mediterranean mail route to Alexandria. Time and again, travellers and dispatches, having crossed Egypt from Suez, found no convenient conveyance westward from Alexandria. In one instance, the mail and passengers of the *Hugh Lindsay* were kept waiting a month at Alexandria before obtaining passage. This gap was finally closed in 1835 when the Admiralty packets began a monthly service from Malta to Alexandria. At last a steam service had reached Egypt from the west as well as from the east.

The increasing desire for steam communication led to the appointment, in 1837, of a Select Committee to report to the House of Commons on 'Steam Communication with India'. The chairman was Lord William Bentinck, who had recently returned from India where he had been a distinguished Governor-General. The testimony and the report made only too clear the desire of Calcutta and Madras, on the eastern side of the Indian Peninsula, for communications that would not be routed via Bombay on the west coast. At the time, dispatches from Calcutta to Bombay were carried across India by native runners. Their journeys took eleven days on the average—three more during the wet season. But the *dawk*, as this service was called, did not provide for passengers and goods.

The conditions on the Egyptian section of the overland route were given much attention by this Select Committee of 1837. They badly needed attention. A canal of sorts, the Mahmoudie Canal, had been built by the Pasha to join Alexandria and the Nile, the junction being at Afteh, some miles above the dangerous bars at the mouth of the river. The voyage up the Nile between Afteh and

---

[1] Hoskins, op. cit., 198-207; *Rep. S.C. on Communication with India* (1837), I, 58. An alternative overland route was by way of the Persian Gulf, up the Euphrates and across to the Mediterranean over the intervening desert. This route had been examined and enthusiastically advocated in the early thirties by Captain Francis R. Chesney. The British Government was so impressed that it spent £40,000 on a trial of this route before it was abandoned. Hoskins treats this route fully; and see *Br. Almanac* for 1851, 52-54.

Cairo was not difficult, but between Cairo and Suez stretched 80 miles of shifting sand. One witness before the Committee, a barrister of Calcutta, reported that his family carried their own drinking water across the desert. Camels were in use for conveying goods, but the motion of a camel was so 'laborious' that travellers preferred to ride on donkeys, horses, or 'asses of a superior breed'. The journey between Cairo and Suez took at least three days. The fresh water that was carried by travellers going to India was often taken from the Nile; this water was reported to be very 'sweet' and good for a long time. To the modern traveller, the praise of the desert route as 'without inconvenience' would seem a considerable understatement.[1]

Private messengers, either belonging to the Bombay Government or to the great business houses carried mail and dispatches. Long before the Post Office was willing to provide official arrangements, private expresses were in common use. The most widely known of the express agents was Waghorn. A restless traveller and ceaseless promoter, Waghorn was at this time a vigorous advocate of the postal route by way of the Red Sea, having long ago given up his idea of employing steam vessels by the all-water route around Africa. In fact, the first evidence in the *Report* of 1837 was a letter from Waghorn. He wrote that he was unable to attend the Committee hearings, as he was leaving 'tomorrow' via Marseilles, charged by the East India Company with improving communications by way of the Red Sea.

One device that he used at the end of the twenties to popularize the overland journey was to make the journey himself and to prove that dispatches could be carried from England to India by way of the Red Sea within fifty days. Mr Waghorn left London on this trial run in October 1829. He travelled by way of France to Alexandria, and on to Suez where he expected to find the *Enterprize*. It was not there. After using various sailing vessels, Waghorn finally reached India late in March after having been nearly five months on the way. Mr Freeling was more than ever convinced that this 'extremely persevering' individual was not a man of good judgement. In 1835, the year that the Admiralty extended its Mediterranean packet service to Alexandria, Thomas Waghorn set up an express service for the fast carriage of letters and parcels entrusted to his care.

[1] *Parl. Ret.*, 250/1838; *Br. Almanac* for 1838, 74; *Rep. S.C. on Communication with India* (1837), 69, 83, 125, 157, 178. Kipling, in his poem on 'The Overland Mail' refers to the messenger service across India by native runners.

Two other Englishmen, Hill and Raven, were intent on giving a like service. A spirited contest ensued between the rival agencies. Both the agencies built hotels at Suez. A rivalry that may have improved the overland passage was ended in 1841 when Waghorn joined his opponents to form J. R. Hill & Company. In 1845 J. R. Hill & Company were bought out by the Egyptian Transit Administration of the Pasha's government. By that time Waghorn was off on a new venture, the endeavour to prove that a route through Europe via Trieste would be better than one across France to Marseilles. Waghorn died in 1850.[1]

It is clear that the eastern water section as well as the land part of the route through Egypt was much more eagerly sought by British residents in India than by those living in England. It was the concern of Britons away from home that had much to do in making feasible the complicated journey by way of the Red Sea, just as the beginning of the Cunard Line found its stimulus in Nova Scotia.

THE RISE OF THE P & O

A much improved mail service soon developed on the western water section of the overland route—the stretch between England and Alexandria by way of Gibraltar and Malta. The Peninsular Steam Navigation Company did for this mail route what the Cunard Company was doing so effectively for the mail service in British ships across the north Atlantic.

The P & O, the usual name for the Peninsular and Oriental Steam Navigation Company, started in a very small way. After the fall of Napoleon, Brodie McGhee Willcox set up as a ship broker in London, employing as his clerk a young Shetlander by the name of Arthur Anderson. Anderson, who had come to London in 1815 after serving in the Navy during the recent war, proved so valuable that the firm by 1822 became known as Willcox & Anderson. They ran a service of small vessels in the Peninsular trade, that is, to Spain

---

[1] Hoskins, op. cit., 226-30; Cable, op. cit., 80-1; Robson Lowe, *Encyclopaedia of British Postage Stamps* (1949), II, 265-6. Waghorn's express service has caught the attention of postal historians and collectors because the letters he handled were stamped 'Care of Mr Waghorn'. Such letters are known for the years 1836 to 1841. Waghorn's hustle and bustle became legendary. Thackeray satirized it in his *Journey from Cornhill to Cairo* (1844). He wrote of Waghorn at Cairo bounding 'in and out of the courtyard, full of business. He left Bombay only yesterday morning, was seen in the Red Sea on Tuesday . . . and I make no doubt that he is at this time in Alexandria or Malta, perhaps both.' Waghorn was not the 'Pioneer and Founder of the Overland Route' as a monument in his birthplace (Chatham) declares. Others had preceded him in the use of the Red Sea route. See the *D.N.B.*, 'Waghorn'.

and Portugal. At first the vessels were chartered from Bourne & Company, whose Line in the Irish Sea is already familiar under the name of the City of Dublin Steam Packet Company. The efforts of Willcox and Anderson to set up a commercial service to the Iberian Peninsula was touch-and-go for some time. The trade to post-war Portugal and Spain was seriously affected by the unrest following the long Napoleonic War. But they persevered, and by the mid-thirties had established a service of sorts to the Iberian ports.[1]

By 1837 Willcox and Anderson had a regular connection with some half-dozen steamships plying between England and Oporto, Lisbon, Gibraltar and Malaga. Their vessels ranged from the *Iberia* of 300 tons to the *Don Juan* of 485 tons. Thackeray made his journey 'from Cornhill to Cairo' in the *Iberia*, a vessel he praised very highly.

Just at this time the Admiralty decided to ask for tenders for a mail service to Malta and Portugal, as they were unwilling to provide steam vessels of their own for a route that seemed comparatively unimportant. Willcox and Anderson were eager to obtain the assistance of a mail subsidy for a business venture that had not, as yet, been a conspicuous success. A mail contract might well be the 'saving of the Line'. According to the tender that was acceptable to the Admiralty, the vessels were to have at least 140 horsepower, to depart from a Channel port once a week, and to carry mails as far as Gibraltar by way of Vigo, Oporto, Lisbon and Cadiz. The voyage to Gibraltar was to take nine days. The career of the P & O as a mail carrier had begun.

The service opened in September 1837. Several changes occurred in the next few years; the home port was changed from Falmouth to Southampton, and the voyages were cut from four to three a month because of the continued 'unsettled state' of the Iberian Peninsula. The greatest change was the expansion of the mail service into the Mediterranean, for the vessels had been so regular that the Admiralty asked the Company for suggestions as to a longer route.

In the meantime, the Post Office had developed a variant for the Alexandrian and Indian mails. The British Postmaster-General had suggested in 1838 that the route overland through France might well be used if the dispatches of the East India Company from India were too late for the monthly Malta packet. Waghorn had

---

[1] Boyd Cable's volume is a lavish account of the P & O from the Company's viewpoint. The account of the Packet Service (ch. VI) is superficial and biased. The date when the Admiralty took over the Falmouth services needs correction—it was not 1818 but 1823.

used this route, and had found that the journey between London and Alexandria would take only eighteen days.

A postal convention of 1839 legalized this carriage through France. It was regarded only as an express service that would not seriously interfere with the all-water route by way of Gibraltar, in which Willcox and Anderson were so much interested. The Post Office wrote the Treasury: 'Because of the high rate of postage through France, only such correspondence as demands a speedy communication will be sent via Marseilles.' By way of Gibraltar the rate was 1s the half ounce; by way of France it was 2s 8d the quarter ounce—so great a difference that only the wealthy would send letters via Marseilles. Agencies like J. R. Hill, Thomas Waghorn and Grindley & Company were prepared to handle this correspondence—at an additional fee.[1]

To return to the route via Gibraltar. In 1840 the Admiralty advertised for bids on the sea route between England and Alexandria. Four were received, and that of Willcox and Anderson was accepted, as it was considerably lower than the others. The Peninsular Company, anticipating this outcome, had been renamed the Peninsular and Oriental Steam Navigation Company. So ambitious a programme required more financial backing, with the result that the new P & O was much more than a renamed shipping line. Captain Bourne of the Dublin Company was included, and the P & O was further strengthened by the addition of the Transatlantic Steam Ship Company with its *Liverpool*. This Line was represented on the Board by Joseph C. Ewart. Indian financial interests were included as well. As a climax to this momentous year, the P & O was incorporated as a joint-stock concern in December 1840. The enlarged Company was already planning to expand beyond Egypt, for the Charter included an agreement to establish a mail service between Suez and India within two years.[2]

The contract of 1840, which cost the Post Office £35,000 annually, required vessels of at least 400 horsepower between England and Alexandria. The service which was monthly, was to reach Gibraltar from Southampton in five days, take another five days to Malta, and to reach Alexandria on the 15th day out. An Admiralty agent was

[1] *T.L.B.*, XXXIV, 377; XXXIX, 184, 194; XL, 274; XLII, 401; *2nd Rep. on Steam Communication with India* (1851), 8.

[2] The armorial bearings included the significant motto *Quis nos separabit* (Who will separate us), and the four animals that appeared on the quarterings were a British lion, the Chinese dragon, a kangaroo and an elephant with his 'castle'. Joseph C. Ewart was the son of a Liverpool merchant, William Ewart after whom John Gladstone named his well-known son.

aboard every vessel, and he was to take the mails on and off at each port in a suitable boat of not less than four oars. The P & O announced that 'swift and commodious steam vessels' were to be placed on the Nile, and that a 'powerful Steam Ship will shortly be started to run between Suez, Calcutta, Madras and Ceylon'.[1]

THE P & O EAST OF SUEZ

The extension of the P & O into eastern seas presented difficulties. Coal depots had to be made ready, and coal sent out from Britain. The Company had to mollify opinion in India where both the East India Company and various steam committees were jealous of their rights. The East India Company in particular, was very reluctant to give up its steam service between Bombay and Suez via Aden, where the Company had established a port of call entirely at its own expense. The East India Company had done much to improve the carriage of mails across Egypt, and continued to pay for the overland carriage through Egypt as far as Alexandria. It had its own Navy and desired to use its own vessel for the Indian mail route east of Suez. But the East India Company could not give a general service, as it was forbidden by the Charter of 1833 to carry on trade. Their war vessels were confined to the carriage of mails, specie and a few passengers. Yet the East India Company continued to carry on the Bombay mail service until 1854.

The P & O services, therefore, did not include a line to Bombay. Instead, they served Ceylon, Madras and Calcutta, as well as Singapore and Hong Kong, which had been opened to general British trade by this time. The first vessel sent out for the route beyond Suez was the *Hindostan*, a paddle steamer of 2,000 tons. The contract of 1844, for £160,000 a year, provided for a stop at Point de Galle on the south-west coast of Ceylon. There she dropped the mail for the Far East, and went on to Madras and Calcutta. The vessel taking the Hong Kong mail called at Penang and Singapore on the way. The journey between Suez and Calcutta was to take a month, and the time between Suez and Hong Kong was set at thirty-five days.

Following the recommendations of the Select Committee of 1851,

---

[1] Cable, op. cit., 42-46, 65-67, regarded the public advertisement for tenders as a 'shabby trick' on the part of the Admiralty. He had in mind the grant of contracts to Cunard and the Royal mail without competition. The unsuccessful bidders were J. P. Robinson, G. H. Jackson and Macgregor Laird. Mr Laird proposed to use the *British Queen* and the *President*. See above, p. 129.

a new contract with the P & O, that of 1853, required the Company
to have fifteen steamships of 1,100 tons each, veritable 'floating
taverns' as they were named by an unfriendly witness. The vessels
were to have a speed of at least 10 knots on the Line to Calcutta.
The Canning Committee of 1853 found that the postal earnings of
the P & O in the previous year had been over £150,000, which
meant that the service actually cost the Post Office about £47,000
annually, the difference between the postal income and the subsidy
of nearly £200,000.[1]

At last the three sections of the overland route were in operation.
It remains to note some further improvements in the overland part
of the route.

THE JOURNEY ACROSS EGYPT

The most difficult part of this great 'arterial line' was the land
crossing between Alexandria and Suez. By 1840 the transit was in
three distinct parts. From Alexandria to Afteh on the Nile, 'track
boats' carried mail and passengers on the Pasha's Mahmoudie
Canal, the boats being towed by horses or small steam tugs. The
section of 120 miles up the Nile to Cairo was by steamship. From
Cairo to Suez, about 80 miles, camels were used for goods and
mails, but mules and horses for passengers, although they were
being replaced by carriages at this time, and various stations along
the way allowed for stops to break the tedious journey across the
desert.

In 1841 Arthur Anderson visited Egypt in the hope of smoothing
the journey between Alexandria and Suez. The Pacha, Mehemet
Ali, promised protection for goods and passengers in transit. The
P & O put their own steamers, flying the British flag, on both the
Canal and the Nile. A code of 1843 standardized the charges for the
crossing. Improvements were very noticeable by 1850. Stages 5
miles apart along the desert section had ample relays of horses to
speed on the mail and the passengers. At this time some 500 horses
were stationed along the desert road. The journey by the mid-
century could be made in some fifteen hours, instead of the two and
a half days it formerly took to cross the desert.[2]

[1] *Rep. Com. on Contract Pkts.* (1853), 13-17, 39, 57; *Further Statement of Facts
Relative to the Contract Packet Service* (c. 1866), an undated pamphlet of 11 pp.,
published in defence of the P & O; it summarized the changes.

[2] *Rep. S.C. Contract Pkt. Service* (1849), 127; *Rep. S.C. on Steam Communication
with India* (1851), 63, 377-9. John Wood, one of the witnesses before the latter Committee, insisted on calling the overland route the 'sea and desert route'.

What was really needed to connect the Mediterranean and the Red Sea was a railway or a canal or both. Mehemet Ali seemed willing to consider the building of a railway, but it was slow business to obtain Egyptian approval for such an innovation. The Pasha was fearful that a foreign company might obtain too much power, and he wanted to be certain that his Government would profit from the rapidly increasing traffic. One way of doing this had been to create an Egyptian Transit Company.

Political bickerings slowed down any real advance. The French were at least as much concerned in Egyptian affairs as the British—had been ever since the days when Napoleon invaded Egypt half a century earlier. The French wanted at this time to strengthen their hold in Egypt, and do this by building a canal. The canal idea had even appealed to Napoleon, whose surveyors in 1798 had actually made some study of a canal route. The survey was so badly done, however, that it had set back indefinitely the building of a canal because of the belief that the Red Sea was some thirty feet higher than the Mediterranean! It was only in the mid-forties that the French engineers of the Pasha restudied the levels and found after all that there was no difference in the height of the two seas.[1]

When the pro-French Mehemet Ali died in 1849, his successor, Abba Pasha, saw matters more from the English point of view. As he was not opposed to a railway, its construction was actually begun under the direction of the well-known English engineer, Robert Stephenson. By 1853 the section from Alexandria to the Nile was ready. Shortly afterwards, Abba Pasha died, only to be succeeded by the pro-French Saïd Pasha. As a result, the canal project again came to the fore under the direction of Ferdinand de Lesseps. After delays that would have dampened the enthusiasm of anyone but De Lesseps the digging of the canal was actually begun.

The British did not like the idea of a canal under French control. Lord Palmerston, in presenting the Government's views, told De Lesseps in 1855: 'I must tell you frankly that what we are afraid of is our commercial and maritime pre-eminence . . . We are not quite easy on the score of the designs of the French.' Lord Clarendon phrased it differently: 'All that the British Government wants in Egypt is an easy and rapid route to India for travellers, light goods, letters and dispatches . . . The continuation [completion] of the railway would give them that thoroughfare.'[2]

[1] Hoskins, op. cit., 237-8, 291, 293, 300.
[2] ibid., 312-14.

The laying of a railway line was much easier than excavating a channel for sea-going ships. As a result, the Suez Railway was nearing completion, and was likely to be finished in 1858. But at least another decade would elapse before the Suez Canal was ready to receive the shipping of the world. The need for a rapid thoroughfare to India was made the keener just at this time by the Sepoy Mutiny in India.

In order to obtain a satisfactory agreement for the transport of the mails by railway, the Post Office sent out a special representative to make arrangements with the Government of Saïd Pasha. Anthony Trollope, the choice of the General Post Office in London, reached Alexandria in February 1858. It was the sort of experience that he as a surveyor relished, Trollope was eager to see more of the Near East, and he would have leisure to complete the writing of his current novel, *Doctor Thorne*.[1]

Anthony Trollope found railway construction in Egypt almost at a standstill. Twenty miles of the line remained to be built across the desert in order to reach the southern terminus at Suez, with construction going at a snail's pace. Trollope soon realized that one cause of this 'sickening delay' was the P & O itself. John Green, the consul and postal agent at Alexandria, wrote in January 1858 that 'the Peninsular and Oriental Company's agent is doing all he can to prevent the Transit Administration agreeing to carry the mail rapidly'. As Green put it in another letter: 'I am not entirely convinced that the Peninsular and Oriental Steam Company is anxious to see the completion of a railway of which one of the first fruits would certainly be a great increase of steamers of all descriptions in Seas where the Company has hitherto enjoyed a monopoly.'[2]

The P & O was interested in keeping down the speed of the mail transit across Egypt so that the P & O freight might cross at the same time as the mails, and depart on the same ship. The Company even had an agreement with the Transit Administration by which it was bound to carry goods at the same rate of speed as the mails. One mail for India, in 1857, to take a random example, was seventy-five hours in crossing Egypt. Trollope and the postal administration he represented saw no reason why the mail should not cross Egypt— a distance of 200 miles—in twenty-four hours on the completion of the railway. Nubar Bey, in charge of the Egyptian Transit

---

[1] It was after Trollope had returned from his successful negotiations in Egypt, that he was sent to the West Indies as a surveyor for the Post Office.

[2] These quotations and other material on Trollope's negotiations are in *P.O. Records*, Pkt. 1004/1858.

Administration, was certain that it would take twice that time. He
was in agreement with the agent of the P & O, who 'laughed' at the
idea of the mail being carried across Egypt from ship to ship in
twenty-four hours.

Anthony Trollope soon found out the reason for the delay in the
completion of the railway, and for the opposition to a crossing in
twenty-four hours. In June 1858 he wrote to Frederic Hill, assistant
Secretary to his brother Rowland Hill at the General Post Office in
London: 'I must observe that Nubar Bey's objection to the twenty-
four hour clause—namely that of sea risk—is moonshine . . . His
real objection is that afterwards named by Mr Green, viz. that "the
agent of a Company to whom the Viceroy [Pasha] owes from
seventy to eighty thousands, and who is always ready with cash, is
very likely to have influence!" '

Negotiations with Nubar Bey dragged on and on, and Anthony
Trollope remained firm in his determination that the mails should
cross in twenty-four hours by the railway. His *Autobiography*
furnishes an amusing account of the negotiations:

'I found on my arrival that I was to communicate with an officer
of the Pasha, Nubar Bey . . . I never went to his office nor do I
know that he had an office. Every day he would come to me at my
hotel, and bring with him servants and pipes and coffee. I enjoyed
his coffee greatly, but there was one point on which we could not
agree . . . I was desirous that the mails should be carried through
Egypt in twenty-four hours, and he thought that forty-eight should
be allowed. I was obstinate and he was obstinate, and for a long time
we could come to no agreement.'

At last Nubar Bey's tranquillity gave way, and he assured Trollope
'with almost more than British energy that if I insisted on the quick
transit, a terrible responsibility would rest on my head'. If a shorter
transit were insisted on, Nubar Bey declared that he would at once
retire into obscurity. 'He would be ruined, but the loss of life and
bloodshed would not be on his head.'

Still the negotiations dragged on. 'I smoked my pipe, or rather
his, and drank his coffee with oriental quiescense but British
firmness . . . At last he gave way, and astounded me by the cordiality of his greeting. There was no longer any question of resignation from office.'

Trollope's persistence and success in his dealings with Nubar

Bey resulted from information 'whispered to me that the Peninsular and Oriental Steam Company had conceived that forty-eight
hours would suit the purpose of their traffic better than twenty-
four . . . I often wondered who originated that frightful picture
of blood and desolation. That it came from an English heart and
an English hand I was always sure.'

Trollope's arrangement with the Egyptian Government provided
that the transit, as soon as the railway was completed, was not to
exceed twenty-four hours from the time the mails left one ship until
they were on board the corresponding packet at the other end of the
railway. The Post Office was to send their messengers with the
mails, which were to be in 'closed trucks'. The British Post Office
agreed to pay the Egyptian Government £12,000 a year for the use
of the railway. The agreement signed at Alexandria in June 1858
came just as the mails were increasing far beyond expectation. In
one month of that year the mail totalled over 200 boxes, weighing
nearly 14,000 lb. The boxes seem to have been made originally so
that they would weigh about 100 lb. each so that four boxes could
be carried by a camel, two on each side of that patient and plodding
animal.

On leaving Egypt, Anthony Trollope visited Jerusalem, and also
inspected the post offices in Malta and Gibraltar. When he again
set foot on English soil, Trollope had ready the manuscript of
Doctor Thorne. Strange that this delightful story of the village of
Greshambury in East Barsetshire should have been completed at a
time when Trollope was engaged in smoking the tobacco and
drinking the coffee of Nubar Bey in a Cairo hotel.

The startling changes that have been reviewed had occurred in
three decades. The magic of steam on land and sea had so improved
communication that India was now but a month away from Britain.
In time, the Canal was to share in a further easing of the difficulties
of a route that was to be of ever greater use.

During this time the P & O had grown from an Iberian service to
mail routes on both sides of Egypt. A fleet that had included but
half a dozen paddle-wheel steamers in 1835 numbered fifty-five
liners by 1860. Some of these were over 2,000 tons, and well over
half were screw propelled. Willcox and Anderson deserve great
credit for this transformation. A difficult route, partly overland with
extensive sea sections, had become a mail and passenger highway—
the longest postal route out of England.

16

MAILS TO AFRICA—WEST,
SOUTH AND EAST

THE colonies south of the Equator were as much in need of regular mails as Canada and the West Indies. Yet an adequate service to the south Atlantic was more slowly developed because of the greater distance and the comparatively small number of British settlers that had gone to the African colonies.

Cape Town was already a regular port of call for the vessels of the East India Company on the long all-sea route around Africa. As the India Empire grew more and more attractive, the highway was made easier for vessels and passengers by various stopping places along the route. In the south Atlantic lay Ascension Island, and 700 miles farther to the south-east the more important St Helena. From St Helena it was 1,700 miles to the Cape of Good Hope. St Helena had become a possession of the East India Company in the seventeenth century because, as an early Charter put it, it was 'very necessary for refreshing their servants and people'. The only other island near this route in the vast expanse of the south Atlantic is Tristan da Cunha, some 4,000 miles due west of the Cape of Good Hope. This small volcanic group had been annexed in 1816 at the suggestion of the Governor of Cape Colony. Tristan da Cunha was only occasionally sighted by sailing vessels bound for India, Australia or New Zealand, as they sought favourable winds for their 'easting' well below the Cape of Good Hope.

Cape Town itself was first taken from the Dutch in 1795, returned in 1802 but recaptured and held as a result of the Napoleonic War. Its value as a victualling station on the route to India was the chief reason for retaining it after 1815. The long journey around Africa to the Indian holdings was safe so long as Britain kept command of the seas and of the necessary victualling stations and outposts on the way.

The route to India by way of Egypt had come into greater

favour, as we have learned, when it shortened the route for the passage to India. By the mid-nineteenth century, however, the marine engine had so improved that steam communication over long distances became feasible. One advocate of the Cape Route wrote prophetically in 1848: 'We are not masters in Egypt; in case of war, the Mediterranean and the Red Sea route would be hazardous.'[1]

After the final recapture of Cape Town in 1806 British settlers began to move into the farm lands east of Cape Town, and large numbers of Dutch farmers (the Boers) trekked into the back country. Soon Cape Town was the capital of a colony that spread north and east. Beyond lay Natal with its port of Durban, and in the interior to the north the Boer settlements grew into 'free states', whose only convenient outlet was through the British colonies. Natal became a British colony in 1844.

The first regular steam line to Cape Colony began its runs in 1850. The General Screw Steam Shipping Company, as its name indicates, had adopted the screw propeller from the beginning, in preference to the paddle wheel.

The superiority of the screw was becoming clear by 1845 when this steamship company was organized. The greater symmetry of a screw-driven vessel made it possible for the vessel 'to glide more freely through the water under the momentum of wind and sail'. The early use of the screw was largely with full-rigged ships. The actual superiority of the screw to the cumbersome paddle wheels was first clearly demonstrated as early as 1846 when the two forms of power were tried against each other. The screw-driven *Rattler*— the first screw vessel in the British Navy—and the paddle-driven *Alecto* were fastened stern to stern, and both pulled with their maximum power; in the test the *Rattler* towed the *Alecto* at 2 miles an hour.[2]

In 1850 the General Screw began sending ships to South Africa under a mail contract that called for stops at Freetown. But the attempt to combine a mail and passenger service to South Africa with a call along the West African coast did not attract passengers *en route* to Cape Town. The Company, of course, depended on the carriage of passengers and goods to make the contract a success.

The General Screw, in consequence, sought and obtained in 1852 an even more ambitious mail contract. A stop at Ascension

---

[1] Frederick Jerningham, *Steam Communication with the Cape of Good Hope, Australia and New Zealand*, p. 40. The danger of interference has been abundantly illustrated in the twentieth century.
[2] Preble, op. cit., 186.

Island was substituted for the call at Sierra Leone. This was agreeable to the Admiralty, since Ascension was the base at this time for the West African squadron. The contract provided not only for a service to Cape Town but included an extension of the route across the Indian Ocean to Calcutta by way of Mauritius.

A West African service was continued even though the General Screw had ceased to make calls at Sierra Leone. The interest in West Africa was partly commercial and partly philanthropic, for strong measures were being taken at the time to suppress the slave trade on both the west and east coasts of the African continent. When the Admiralty called for tenders for a general West African service, the so-called postal contract went to a shipping Company headed by Macgregor Laird, son of the founder of the well-known shipbuilding firm at Birkenhead. Macgregor Laird had been a pioneer in opening up the Niger River basin to trade, and was so idealistic that he firmly believed that regular trade and communication would discourage the traffic in negro slaves. When the contract was renewed in 1858 the Line was known as the African Steamship Company. This was not a postal contract, but rather one for economic and political ends, and should not have been charged against the Post Office. There was, of course, a heavy postal loss on the contract.[1]

The agreement with the General Screw—to return to the South African mail contract—was for ships of 1,400 tons and of at least 250 horsepower with an average speed of 8 knots. The contract was to run for seven years, and to cost the Post Office about £42,000 a year. So impressive was the outlook for the General Screw's up-to-date fleet that one writer prophesied that the Company 'bids fair at no distant date to appropriate a large share of the oceanic traffic of the world'. The *Queen of the South* did $10\frac{1}{2}$ knots in her test 'and she is, we can testify, perfectly free from that tremulous motion which sometimes makes itself so unpleasantly felt in paddle steamers'. The General Screw appeared to have a bright future.[2]

The General Screw met fairly well the terms of its contract, although it found that an average of 8 knots for the long journey to India was difficult to maintain. The Company soon realized as well that the cost of the service was far beyond the subsidy they were receiving. The chairman reported to the Canning Committee of

---

[1] *Parl. Ret.*, 284/1852. The service was monthly by screw steamers.
[2] The quotation is from an Auckland newspaper, the *New Zealander*, of October, 2, 1852.

1853 that the annual loss was no less than £40,000, and asked for an increase in the subsidy. The Committee regarded what would amount to a doubling of the subsidy as out of the question. The General Screw finally surrendered the contract, as its business did not improve. A successor, the W. S. Lindsay Company, then took over the route, but gave in after a year's trial. One cause for the failure of these lines to obtain sufficient Indian business was the development of the overland route to India. The P & O was already serving Calcutta.[1]

THE UNION STEAM SHIP COMPANY

South Africa finally obtained a permanent mail service by an agreement with the Union Steam Ship Company in 1857. Curiously enough, this Line which has been connected with the South African colonies for more than a century, began with no thought of making this route its own. It was organized in 1853 as the Union Steam Colliery Company, the chairman being no less a person than Arthur Anderson of the P & O. The need, at the time, for coal at Southampton was so critical that the steamship companies using the port—the P & O, the Royal Mail and the General Screw—required better supplies of fuel than were being brought by the small sailing colliers. Steam colliers would better meet the need.[2]

The Union Steam Colliery Company ceased to be a coal-carrying Line with the onset of the Crimean War in the mid-fifties, as its ships were used in the Mediterranean, partly to replace the P & O service to the Near East, and partly for carrying supplies to the Crimea. After the close of the war when the Admiralty was asking for tenders for a mail service to Cape Town to replace the Lindsay Line, the Union Company submitted an offer and won the contract. As Marischal Murray put it: 'Almost as if by accident, the Union Line, which had begun its operation with a modest fleet of little carriers, now found itself among the select fraternity of the world's great Mail Steam Packet Companies.'

The contract of 1867 called for a monthly service by vessels of at least 530 tons. Each voyage in or out was not to take more than forty-two days—a requirement that was easy to meet since it meant an average running time of but 6 knots. The vessels were to

[1] *Rep. Com. on Contract Pkts.* (1853), 32-34, 51-53, 71-72. Marischal Murray, *Union-Castle Chronicle*, 1853-1953 (1953), 12. This is a satisfactory Company history.
[2] The first vessel of the Line was called the *Union*, 350 tons and 40 horsepower.

take on the mails at Plymouth, go directly to Cape Town, and call at St Helena and Ascension on the homeward trips. The subsidy was £33,000, the contract for five years.

The first vessel to make the long journey was the *Dane*. She left in September 1857 and reached Cape Town at the end of October. The renewal of a regular service was hailed by the residents of Cape Town as evidence that the 'Old country has not yet begun to forget the interests of her dependancies, at a time when all of her attention might well have been absorbed in providing for the ominous struggle now proceeding in the Indian Empire [the Sepoy Mutiny].' The *Celt*, making the second voyage, carried 11,000 letters and 3,600 newspapers to keep fresh the memory of the homeland. The Company soon added larger and faster vessels. The *Cambrian* was the first mail liner especially designed for the South African route, and the first of the Line of over 1,000 tons; it was launched in 1860. But even the smaller and older vessels generally made better time than called for by the contract. The *Report* of the Postmaster-General for 1860 declared the voyages of the Union Line ships were more frequently under contract time than any others, 'the next being those of the Cunard Line'.

One reason for the excellent record of the Union Line was an additional incentive proposed by the Legislative Assembly in Cape Town. In 1859 it offered a bonus of £250 per day for every time a Union packet made the voyage from Plymouth in less than thirty-five days, with the result that the bonus was won time and again. The schedule, it appears, was not well arranged; an outward voyage taking thirty-five days or less was necessary to give the residents of Cape Town time to answer the letters of the last in-coming packet so that the replies could go north by the packet then about to leave. A vessel remained about a month in South Africa before making the return voyage. Mail day was all important. 'The *Celt* has gone,' wrote the *Cape Argus*, 'and the City, overworked for the last week past, may now find time for a little leisure . . . England was so far off that we had ceased to call it Home, until the Union Company came and reduced the distance.' Another reason for the faster service was the desire of the urban ports to the east, particularly Port Elizabeth and Durban, that they receive mail in the shortest possible time. With the renewed contract in 1862, the Company began a so-called inter-colonial service along the southern coast as far as Durban.[1]

[1] Murray, op. cit., 14, 25-26, 37; *Rep. P.M.G.* (1859), 53-55; (1860), 34-36, 53-55.

The contract of 1862 brought other less desirable changes. Two years before an Act of the British Parliament had returned to the Post Office from the Admiralty the business of negotiating the ocean mail contracts. The Post Office, which had long objected to the large subsidies, was determined to cut down the cost of the contracts as they came up for renewal. As a result, in 1862, the Union contract was cut over a third—from £35,000 to less than £20,000 a year. At the same time the vessels were required to make the voyage in no more than thirty-eight days. The Company accepted the change, since it had been prospering, and could without difficulty meet the time set out in the new contract. In 1863 the new *Saxon*, 1,142 tons, made the run in the record time of thirty-one days at the rate of 8 knots. In 1864 the Company extended its service eastward by sending mail steamers from Cape Town beyond Durban to Mauritius, so that they could connect with a branch of the P & O that was making Mauritius a port of call between Suez and Australia. Other changes in the sixties included the renewal of the contract in 1868 for eight years (to 1878) with the service to be fortnightly, and the stated time of the voyages to and from Cape Town to take no more than thirty-seven days. In 1870 the Union Line began taking on and disembarking passengers and mails at Southampton instead of Plymouth. Southampton, in fact, had been from the beginning the home port of the Company. The chairman of the Union Line during these years was Arthur Anderson of the P & O. His death in 1868 removed a vigorous and wise leader, who was sadly missed in the contentions that were growing more tense just at this time.

The Post Office took a decidedly backward step in 1863 when it announced that the postage on letters, sent by the contract steamers to South Africa and to the West Indies as well, was to be raised from 6d to 1s the half ounce. This was done in the hope of removing the large deficits on these services. This increase in the postage rate was made at the same time that the Company's subsidy was slightly lowered. The Treasury, of course, was gratified. In writing to the Duke of Newcastle, then Secretary of State for the Colonies, it expressed satisfaction at the change since the heavy loss on the 'West Indian mails has been greatly reduced and the Cape service is now self supporting.'[1]

Just as these changes were being made in the contract mail service the whole outlook in South Africa was dramatically changed

[1] Murray, op. cit., 33-34. 37; *Rep. S.C. on Cape of Good Hope and Zanzibar Contracts* (1873), 6-24, 30. For the P & O service via Mauritius, see the next chapter.

by the discovery of diamonds in the western part of the Orange Free State. After their discovery in 1867 near Kimberley, it became the greatest of the diamond-mining centres. So valuable had Kimberley and its district become that they were annexed by the British in 1871, much to the dissatisfaction of the Boers in the Orange Free State. Diamonds not only revolutionized South African conditions and intensified political feeling; they made postal connections with the region of much greater importance.

Even before this sudden increase of interest in South Africa, the general growth of trade and population had led other shipping companies to seek a share of the business. The first serious rival of the Union Company was the Diamond Line, which had unsuccessfully tendered in 1862 for the contract. The name of the Company, strangely enough, had nothing to do with the diamond fever of the late sixties, for the Diamond Line actually ceased its operations in 1868, just as the discovery of diamonds was beginning to attract diggers from beyond the seas. A short time afterwards a shipping Line called the Cape and Natal Company struggled for a share of the business but gave up in 1872.[1]

CURRIE'S CASTLES

Much more serious competition came from a Line established by Donald Currie in the early seventies. Currie, who was born in Greenock, Scotland, moved to Liverpool in 1842 to work for the recently organized Cunard Line. Donald Currie rose gradually to be an important member of the Cunard staff, but he was ambitious to have a shipping business of his own. In 1862, therefore, he ended his connection with the Cunard Company and formed the shipping firm of Donald Currie & Company. The Company began its activities with the sending of fast sailing vessels to India—there was as yet no Suez Canal. He chose as names for his ships the names of well-known castles in the British Isles, such familiar names as Stirling Castle, Windsor Castle and Caernarvon Castle. Currie's Calcutta Castles, as they were called, were noted for their beautiful lines and for their speed. When the Suez Canal was finally opened in 1869, sailing vessels were no longer profitable for the India route by way of the Cape. Consequently Donald Currie changed to steam, using his steamships at first in the Baltic and North Sea trade. Currie's interest in the South African route came by way of the

[1] ibid., 42; Murray, op. cit., 32-35.

Cape and Natal Company, which had failed, as we have found, in 1872. In that year the Cape and Natal Company had chartered two of Donald Currie's vessels. When the Cape and Natal Company was unable to meet the cost of the charters, they urged Donald Currie to put his ships on the South African route. Currie decided to make the venture, and started a service to South Africa that has been continuous ever since.

Currie's Castles gave the Union Company the most severe competition it had encountered in its fifteen years as the mail line to South Africa. His vessels went from their home port of Dartmouth to the Cape, and were soon continuing the voyage to Natal to add to the competition. They made trips to South Africa that were as regular as those of the Union Line. Currie testified before the Select Committee of 1873 that was considering the Cape contract: 'Our steamers leave with undeviating regularity, and, as you may not be aware, the fastest passages on record to the Cape have been made by steamers of our Line.' In May 1873, for example, the *Windsor Castle*, 2,672 tons, made the voyage from Dartmouth to Cape Town in the fastest time to date—twenty-three days at a speed of nearly 11 knots. The only payment to Currie's Line for carrying mail was 1d out of 4d for a half-ounce letter. This ship-letter rate was one third the cost of a similar letter by the contract service. When Donald Currie sought postal recognition of his Line, the British Post Office was anything but cordial, as any mail sent by ships other than those of the Union Line would naturally lessen the income under the postal contract. Letters for Currie's Line had to be especially directed on the envelope 'By private ship via Dartmouth'. Donald Currie printed bills announcing the unsubsidized Line but the Post Office did not permit him to put up his bills in the provincial post offices, and the *Postal Guide* refused to carry information about the Dartmouth service.

The shilling rate under the mail contract may have lessened the postal deficit, but it certainly exasperated the public. Protest meetings were held in Cape Town in 1873 when the Government was preparing to renew the contract with the Union Company, and to continue the shilling rate. The colonial merchants stated that the Currie steamers were as punctual and regular as the subsidized Line, and also running twice a month. The shilling rate might have been fair earlier, but when 400,000 letters were carried each year, it was unreasonably high. A London merchant trading with the Cape told the Committee of 1873 that instructions from his Cape Town correspondents were 'to send all our originals and important documents by the opposition post and the duplicates by the Royal Mail [the Union Line]'. In 1872 the Governor of Cape Colony, Sir Henry Barkley, wrote to Lord Kimberley, Secretary of State for the Colonies, that there was 'universal dissatisfaction out here' with the heavy postal rate of 1s, and that a rate of 6d would meet the criticism. Sixpence, in fact, was the charge for letters between Australia and the mother country, although Australia was twice as far away as Cape Town.[1]

The whole matter came to a head in 1873 when the Union Line used a possible East African route to Zanzibar as a means of extending their Atlantic contract in order the better to compete against Currie's Castles.

The desire for a regular route on the east coast of Africa grew out of an interest in trade along that coast, and also from the desire to suppress the large traffic in slaves. The conditions in East Africa, both with regard to the possibilities of trade and to the extent of the slave traffic had been revealed by Livingstone's remarkable expeditions into the interior of central Africa. He believed that it was Britain's principal duty to end the slave trade in East Africa. The Arab dhows carried on a large traffic in negro slaves. The principal market was at Zanzibar, just off the coast of the present-day Tanganyika. The slave trade, however, was difficult to regulate, and almost impossible to suppress. A Treaty of 1846 with the Sultan of Zanzibar had forbidden the export of slaves, but it was systematically violated. The master of an Arab dhow might take on slaves as part of the freight, but it was difficult for British naval officers to tell who on the Arab dhows were slaves and who were regular members of the crew. Sir Bartle Frere was sent by the British Government to Zanzibar to further the suppression of the trade; he reported in 1873 that the suggested regulations were ineffective. Finally a new treaty was concluded with the Sultan in 1873 by which all the public slave markets were closed.

The hope that the opening up of the East African coast to trade would bring more humane conditions soon brought results. Edgar Layard, who represented Great Britain on the Mixed Commission for Suppressing the Slave Trade believed that 'regular communication would extend commerce and do more to suppress slavery than the presence of our squadron.' To bring this about, apparently, the

[1] Murray, op. cit., ch. VI, and p. 73; *Rep. S.C. on Cape of Good Hope and Zanzibar Contracts* (1873), 45, 60, 65-71, 157.

British Government formed a plan by which the Union Line would send a steamer regularly up the east coast of Africa to Zanzibar, where they would connect with vessels of the British India Line that came down the coast from Aden. Whether or not this would really affect the slave traffic, it certainly opened the region to commerce, and gave Cape Town another route for the mails going north from South Africa. Although the east-coast route was slower as a postal route than that by way of the Atlantic, it had some value for telegraphic communication between South Africa and England. The telegraph had already been extended to Aden. If a letter from South Africa went up the east coast to Aden, it would take about seventeen days, and at Aden telegraphic communication with Britain could be used for letters and dispatches of importance. At the time a letter sent by steamer on the Atlantic route took about three weeks to a month.[1]

The Union Line was eager to add an East African route to its services, not primarily for philanthropic purposes, but as a possible means of strengthening its hold on the very profitable Atlantic contract. It proposed, therefore, that the Admiralty and the Port Office grant a contract for a monthly service from the Cape to Zanzibar at £29,000 annually, the contract to run for seven years. Tied to this offer was the condition that, at the same time, the Atlantic contract should be extended for eight years from the time when it was to run out. This meant that the Atlantic contract—it had four and a half years to go—would be renewed for over twelve years. Along with this proposal the Union Company wanted the option of making a third voyage each month between Cape Town and England. Clearly these arrangements were intended to embarrass its competitor and his Castles on the Atlantic.

Although the British Post Office was agreeable to the extension of the Atlantic contract, the Treasury was not, on the ground that the Post Office should be able to make better terms when the present contract ended, instead of having it run for twelve more years. There was a rumour going around at the time that 'another Company [the name is not hard to guess] was willing to carry the mail on the basis of 6d the half ounce', if the Post Office asked for tenders.[2]

The negotiations with the Union Line for the prolonged western contract were kept a secret, but like so many secrets it leaked out.

[1] ibid., 176-7, for the prediction by Edgar Layard.
[2] ibid., pp. iii-iv, 94, 157, 176-7. The Union Line was willing to carry the mail for 6d *if* the contract was extended for twelve years.

In consequence, a Parliamentary Select Committee was appointed in 1873 'to inquire into the circumstances under which articles of agreement were made on June 8, 1873 between the Union Steam Ship Company and the Postmaster-General'. The result was a thorough airing of the unsavoury business by which the Union Line hoped to keep a sure grip on the South African contract for years to come and weaken the effectiveness of a troublesome competitor.

The colonial government in Cape Town, which had not even been consulted, felt the affront very keenly, especially as it had just been granted responsible government. When the Select Committee considered the business, the contracts had already been ratified. But the objections were so vehement against the extension of the western contract that it was abandoned.[1]

Before the contract with the Union Line came to an end in 1876, the Molteno Ministry of Cape Colony was negotiating with Donald Currie about a service to supplement the mail contract that was soon to expire. The Cape Government wanted cheaper postage, more frequent mails, and no combination of the Union and Currie Lines that might hinder the colonial interest in a cheaper service. Mr Molteno went to London in 1876 for discussions with the home authorities on various colonial matters, including the mail service. Largely through his efforts a solution was reached, to which even the Union Line agreed. Parallel contracts were made with the Castle Packets Company and the Union Steam Ship Company, not by the British Post Office, but by the Government of the Cape of Good Hope through the Crown Agents for the colonies. The two Lines were to make alternate sailings, thereby giving a weekly service. The trips were to take no more than twenty-six days, or twenty-seven when calls were made at Ascension Island and St Helena. No subsidy was to be paid, but the companies received the whole of the inland postage of both countries and the sea postage. Best of all, the postage was lowered from 1s to 6d the half ounce. The value of competition seemed so obvious that the two companies were forbidden to unite under the terms of the agreement—from 1876 to 1883.

It was a great victory for Sir John Molteno, the first Prime Minister of the self-governing Cape Colony—a lower sea-postage, a weekly service to Europe, and by voyages that were to take less than four weeks. In 1857 the time allowed had been six weeks. The

[1] ibid., pp. iii-xi; Murray, op cit., 60-70.

cutting of the time by a third was vivid evidence of the improvement of the marine engine, of the need for better and cheaper mails, and of the virtues of competition. The two South African official mail lines continued to use different ports in the Channel until 1891, when the Castle Packets Company joined the other mail lines by moving its terminus from Dartmough to Southampton.[1]

[1] For the later changes, see below, ch. 20.

17

AUSTRALIAN MAILS BEFORE 1870

THE colonies on the vast Australian Continent and in New Zealand islands were the last settlements to receive regular mails from Great Britain. It is understandable, for the Australian colonies were so remote that it took tedious months of sailing to reach the south Pacific. Cape Town is about 6,000 miles from England, and Fremantle on the near side of Australia is 5,000 miles farther on. To make regular communication more difficult, the chief Australian settlements in the early nineteenth century were on the south-east coast of the Continent, a coast made familiar by Captain Cook's famous expedition of 1766-71. Sydney lies about 2,000 miles beyond Fremantle. This meant that emigrants and mails from the British Isles for Sydney or Melbourne or Tasmania had a journey of over 12,000 miles—four times as far as from Liverpool to Halifax.

The first knowledge of the south Pacific had come from Dutch voyagers in the early seventeenth century. Their explorations are preserved for us by such geographical names as Cape Leeuwin at the south-west tip of Australia, and the name of the large island off the south-east coast, known at first as Van Diemen's Land from the Dutch Governor of Batavia, who sent Abel Tasman on an exploring voyage. Abel Tasman also discovered and named the New Zealand archipelago.

The initial British settlement in Australia, as is well known, was started by a fleet transporting convicts from England to Botany Bay. It was named in 1770 when Captain Cook's expedition visited the Bay where the variety of flora along its shores impressed Joseph Banks, the botanist of the expedition. In January 1788 the first convict fleet in charge of Captain Phillip reached Botany Bay after an eight months' voyage. Botany Bay was soon found to be less fit for a permanent settlement than the magnificent harbour of Port Jackson a few miles to the north. Captain Phillip soon transferred his ships to Port Jackson, calling the new settlement Sydney after the Colonial Secretary of the time.

It thus happened that the first, and for some time the only important centre of settlement, was on the south-east coast of the Continent. The customary route to Sydney was around Africa, as sailing vessels were aided in the south Atlantic by the prevailing westerlies. They blew so consistently in the southern latitudes that sailing vessels usually returned to England from Sydney or Tasmania by continuing eastward and rounding South America.

Gradually free settlers came in greater and greater numbers to establish important colonies. The transportation of convicts was discontinued to eastern Australia in 1840. Van Dieman's Land was renamed Tasmania in 1853 when the transportation of convicts to the island ended, and self-government began. Settlements were also made north of Sydney where Brisbane later became the capital of Queensland, and south of Sydney in what is now the State of Victoria at the south-east tip of the Continent. Melbourne on the shores of Port Phillip became the capital of a colony named Victoria when this area separated from New South Wales in 1851. Melbourne had the advantage over Sydney of being nearly 600 miles nearer England by the usual outward sailing route.

Two other settlements were to add to the complexity of the mail services. Western Australia received its first colonists in 1829, where Perth as the capital was laid out on the Swan River a few miles back of the port of Fremantle. The colony was so small for some years, and the harbour of Fremantle so dangerous—it was an open roadstead at the time—that mail vessels bound for Sydney usually stopped at King George's Sound on the south coast to the east of Cape Leeuwin. From there the mail for Perth was carried overland by horse-post. It was a journey of 300 miles, and in the early days usually took a week.

A settlement at Adelaide in what is now the State of South Australia began in 1836. Adelaide is 1,000 miles east of King George's Sound, and 500 miles west of Melbourne. New Zealand where systematic settlement began in 1840 is 1,200 miles to the south-east of Sydney across the tempestuous Tasman Sea.

EARLY MAILS

For half a century after the first fleet went to Sydney, letters came and went by private ships. A chance merchant vessel or an emigrant ship or a whaler might be used to carry the mails. Western Australia, which was the first colony to be reached by vessels rounding Africa, did not learn of the accession of Queen Victoria until five months after it had happened. The service to Sydney was usually quicker than that to Van Diemen's Land or Melbourne or Brisbane, as all the Australian mail was often dispatched directly to Sydney to be forwarded to the other settlements by the first opportunity.

This is brought out vividly by a letter sent to London from Van Diemen's Land in 1815. Robert Mitchell, the newly appointed postmaster of the island, wrote Francis Freeling, the Secretary of the Post Office in London, on September 23, 1815. The letter, sent from the capital of the colony 'Hobart Town Island of Van Diemen South Pacific Ocean', accompanied the 'first mail by public Conveyance from this island to England'. It went by the ship *Jefferson*, a South Sea whaler out of London that was proceeding direct to England. The faith in Robert Barnes, the master of the *Jefferson*, was justified, for Francis Freeling finally received Mitchell's letter and the accompanying mail. Robert Barnes, however, must have done more whaling on the way, for the consignment did not reach London until May 6, 1816, 225 days after it had left Van Diemen's Land. Mitchell asked that mails be sent direct to him rather than by way of Sydney as they 'often remain at Port Jackson for months'.

An added difficulty for these remote colonies was the occasional reluctance of masters of vessels to take letters for England. Ship-letters, as we know, were regularly carried from England to the colonies, but British regulations were not binding on ships leaving a colonial port, though a captain would receive the customary gratuity for the letters when he reached England. Colonel Maberly, who had succeeded Francis Freeling in 1836 as the Secretary of the Post Office in Britain, wrote the Governor of New South Wales in the forties that the British Post Office could not compel the commanders of private ships 'to take on board ship-letters for England at any place where the Post Office is not under the control of this Department'.[1]

Two measures were taken at the time to improve the mail services. An Act of the British Parliament authorized the Post Office in Great Britain to take under its control the postal arrangements of the Australian colonies and of New Zealand 'in order to remedy the inconvenience which has so frequently of late been complained of, arising from the irregular receipt of correspondence to and from these colonies'. The second measure for the better regulation of these

[1] MS. *Despatches* to the Governor of New South Wales (in the Mitchell Library, Sydney), pp. 365, 369, 376.

colonial posts was the sending of two commissioners to make a careful survey of the colonial postal services, pending their possible control from London. The two Commissioners, E. D. James of the Inland Office and R. R. Smith of the Surveyor's Department, journeyed to the south Pacific late in 1844. They thoroughly investigated communications within the five colonies—then under separate colonial governments—and made full returns of their findings. The first report, on New South Wales, was signed in March 1845.[1]

The permissive Act of 1844 and the investigations of the commissioners did not result in the direct British control of the Australian post offices. It would have been a decidedly backward step to subordinate these colonial post offices to St Martin's-le-Grand, just as the other colonies of settlement were rapidly moving towards internal self-government. As we have already found, the Canadian colonies obtained control of their own post offices in 1851.

The British Post Office had already arranged for regular mails to Australia before James and Smith were sent out. The Admiralty had entered into an agreement with Henry and Calvert Toulmin, of Grape Yard, Lombard Street, London on October 10, 1843. The service, to begin early in the next year, provided for a sailing vessel to leave Gravesend or Liverpool for Sydney the first of each month. The contractors for this sailing packet service were to receive £100 for carrying each monthly mail outward. A return service was to be arranged later. The Toulmins were expected to supplement the subsidy by the carrying of freight.

The English Commissioners reported in July 1845 that the Toulmin service homeward had not yet been arranged, but that it would probably start early in the next year. The delay was caused by the difficulty in collecting enough freight for a voyage that could not be indefinitely delayed. The colonial merchants, it seems, would not guarantee a freight homeward, as 'each looks to the load of his own ship'. Freight was not easily come by, as the colony of New South Wales was in a 'depressed and almost bankrupt state', according to the Toulmins.

The Toulmin service began with the voyage of the *Mary Sharpe;*

---

[1] Act of 7 and 8 Vict., ch. 49; *Hist. Records of Australia*, 'Governor's Despatches to and from England', XXIV (1925), 195-6. The Reports of the two Commissioners will be referred to as *Rep. James and Smith*. The original and a duplicate copy of the Reports were sent home, each signed by the Postmaster-General of the colony concerned, and by the two Commissioners. The original of the Report on N.S.W. was sent by the *Ganges* and the duplicate by the *Royal Tar*.

she left at the beginning of February 1844, and reached Sydney 131 days later—June 11th. The *Georgetown*, departing in March, took 113 days: the *Ceylon* with the April mail was 134 days on the way. The Commissioners reported general dissatisfaction with the Toulmin voyages, as their vessels took longer than many other merchantmen. The *Abel Gower*—the packet for February 1846— was so slow that she was judged to be 'anything but an *able goer* or she would have been in port long ago'. The Postmaster-General of New South Wales reported in 1846 that the average time taken by the post-office packets on their trips to Sydney was 124 days; higher by twelve days than the average for private ships. The return journey by way of Cape Horn averaged 138 days.[1]

The colonials in Melbourne and Van Diemen's Land were even more dissatisfied with the Toulmin packets because they went to Sydney only. The ships carried Melbourne mail to Sydney, to be returned to Melbourne by boat or by the recently established overland mail. The British Commissioners believed that Melbourne had a real grievance. Although Melbourne was five or six days nearer England than Sydney, its residents had to wait an additional two weeks or more for mail that had reached Sydney by the official packet-boats. The overland postage rate between Sydney and Melbourne was 1s 3d the half ounce, which with the 3d for the sea postage made a total tax on a half-ounce letter of 1s 6d. The Melbourne *Argus* strongly condemned the 'monstrous practice' of having 'our letters taken past our doors and sent back to us after a delay of three to six weeks with a six-fold postage'. In March 1846 the Melbourne Town Council had petitioned the Queen to cause 'the mails from London to Port Phillip to be landed direct'. The request was denied by the Post Office in London, as the Toulmins would require 'additional mail money'. If they stopped at Melbourne, the Sydney merchants would not ship by their packets; if they depended on shipments from Melbourne, there would not be sufficient for more than a third of a ship's load.[2]

[1] *Hist. Records of Australia*, XXIV, 319; *Rep. James and Smith* (N.S.W., 1845), 147; *Votes and Proceedings* (N.S.W.) 1844, I, 362; 1846) II, 5; Melbourne *Argus*, July 7, 1846.
[2] *Hist. Records of Australia*, XXIV, 651; Melbourne *Argus*, July 7, August 4 and 14, 1846; *Rep. James and Smith* (N.S.W., 1845), Return No. 19, and for the amount of mail, p. 145. Sydney and Melbourne received the following mail in 1844. During the first half of 1844 before the Toulmin service began:

	Letters	Newspapers
Sydney received	28,839	41,189
Melbourne received direct	7,586	14,501

THE DEMAND FOR STEAM COMMUNICATION

The Toulmin contract was not renewed in 1848, for it was clear by that time that nothing but a steam service would satisfy the colonists. The agitation for steam had begun in New South Wales, where a petition with numerous signers was presented to Governor Sir Charles Fitzroy in November 1846. The petitioners favoured a junction with the new P & O service to the Far East. Shortly afterwards a Select Committee of the colonial legislature made specific recommendations, that steam packets connect Sydney and the P & O by a route through Torres Strait. This meant a route directly north from Sydney, the packets calling at Brisbane and Batavia with the northern junction made at Singapore. The Committee preferred this route rather than the one by Cape Leeuwin and Melbourne because the Torres Strait route was through comparatively smooth water where vessels of smaller power and tonnage could be used. The real reason for the choice of this route, though it was unstated, was that it would favour Sydney over Melbourne and Adelaide—by the way of Torres Strait, Sydney would receive its mail first. The Sydney Committee recommended a colonial grant of £6,000 a year, and hoped that the home government, 'which has not hesitated to spend large sums for other colonies', would be liberal here as well.[1]

What might well be called a Battle of the Routes followed. One possibility was a trans-Pacific route by way of Panama and the Royal Mail to England. But the Panama route was not seriously considered, largely because no railway had yet been built across the Isthmus of Panama.

The all-sea route around Africa received much attention, for this course was used by the sailing vessels, emigrant ships and the Toulmin packets. Another possible route, also by way of Cape Leeuwin, would diverge from the P & O Line at Ceylon or Singapore, and come down the western side of the Australian Continent. To some it seemed preferable to the rather devious route by way of

---

During the second half of 1844 after the Toulmin service began:

	Letters	Newspapers
Sydney received by private ship	11,156	5,661
Sydney received by the packets	24,307	58,071
Melbourne received by private ship direct	3,060	2,557

[1] *Votes and Proceedings* (N.S.W., 1846), II, Fitzroy Message No. 4; *Rep. S.C.* (N.S.W.) *on Steam Communication with England* (1846, 27 pp.).

Torres Strait. As a matter of fact, Ceylon and even Singapore lie considerably west of the meridian passing through Cape Leeuwin.

Thomas Waghorn, so much interested in the overland route, favoured Torres Strait. Another advocate of this route was Adam Bogue, whose *Steam to Australia* (1846) was published in Sydney. He quoted a Captain Beaufort, who was sure that the quiet seas of the East Indies were preferable to the Indian Ocean 'where the heavy western swell is notorious and particularly unsuitable to steam navigation'. Captain Beaufort was candid enough to add that 'Sydney, the seat of government, would be the last place to receive Her Majesty's Mails', if they came by way of Cape Leeuwin. A meeting held at the London Tavern (in London) in April 1846 highly approved of steam communication, but those present would recommend no particular route, even though Waghorn spoke vehemently for the route by Torres Strait.

The all-water route around Africa had strong supporters. C. D. Hays in his *Remarks* 'upon the Proposed Establishment of Steam Communication with the Australian Colonies' (1847) was sure that passengers would much prefer the all-sea route. Nor would the vessels have to encounter the dangerous navigation through the Torres Strait and along the Great Barrier Reef. Jerningham wrote in 1848 that 'steam communication has now been established to most parts of the world except to the Cape of Good Hope, Australia and New Zealand' and added: 'Only yesterday I received a letter from New Zealand and one from Australia, the former was seven and the latter six months old.'[1]

TRIAL AND ERROR

The home government finally asked for tenders in 1847. The P & O made an offer that was a counter suggestion rather than a tender. The Company was so eager to take over the Aden-Bombay route from the East India Company that the P & O offered a monthly service from Singapore to Sydney, if the Aden-Bombay Line was released to them by the East India Company. The P & O agreed to do both the Bombay and Sydney services for £50,000 annually,

[1] Jerningham, op. cit., 9. An anonymous pamphlet, *Steam to Australia, the Rival Routes by XXX*, favoured the use of the P & O Line to Singapore. C. D. Hays also wrote *Steam to Australia . . . with a Comparison of the Different Routes* (1849). All the writers in this pamphlet war reckoned the distances and there was little agreement. The *Br. Almanac* for 1851, Comp., 58-61, gave the distances as follows: to Sydney via South Africa, 13,800 miles; by way of Suez and Torres Strait, 13,200 miles; via Panama, 12,690 miles.

which was the total subsidy being paid for the Aden-Bombay run at the time. The offer was rejected partly because of a growing fear of the monopoly then being built up by the P & O in the eastern seas, and partly because the East India Company was unwilling to surrender the Bombay Line.

By 1851 it was clear that some decision must be made. The gold rush to Australia was then in full swing, as rich gold deposits had been discovered back of Sydney and not far from Melbourne, and Melbourne was now the capital of the separate colony of Victoria. Regular mail service was imperative because numerous emigrant ships were rapidly increasing the population of the two colonies. A Select Committee of the British Parliament, headed by Lord Jocelyn, was appointed in 1851 to look into the best ways of establishing communication 'between England and India, China, Australia and New Zealand'. The urgency for deciding on an Australian service led the Committee to report first on Australia 'in order to come, at as early a period as possible, to some definite conclusion'. The Jocelyn Committee decided that the Cape route had the greatest advantages with the smallest cost to the public.[1]

The Admiralty did not confine its arrangements to the recommendation of the Jocelyn Committee. Instead, it sought tenders for voyages by way of the Cape of Good Hope, and also via Egypt and Singapore, in the belief that the trial of both at the same time might determine the better route. The P & O was the successful bidder for the extension of its mail line to Australia from Singapore. The Company agreed to run a steamship every alternate month, the time between Singapore and Sydney to be twenty-eight days, and the total time for mails from London not to exceed seventy days. The P & O service went by way of the west coast of Australia, past Cape Leeuwin to King George's Sound, Melbourne and Sydney.[2]

As additional vessels were needed for the Australian branch of this widespread service out of Suez, the Company sent out the newly built iron steamer *Chusan* to make the first run from Sydney to Singapore. It left Southampton in mid-May 1852.

At the same time another steam line began a service by way of the Cape of Good Hope. The Australian Royal Mail Steam Navigation

[1] *Votes and Proceedings* (N.S.W., 1850) for the Report of the N.S.W. Committee: *1st Rep. S.C. on Steam Communication with India* (1851), pp. iii–xiii (the Jocelyn Committee).

[2] The total subsidy of the P & O by a new general contract of 1853 was £196,000 annually. In the next year the P & O finally obtained the Bombay-Aden route from a reluctant East India Company, by a contract of July 7, 1854. By that time the subsidy of the P & O had risen to £224,300 per year.

Company, by a contract of June 1852, agreed to run its steamers every other month so as to alternate with the vessels of the P & O. The steamers of the Royal Mail were screw propelled, each of about 1,500 tons and 300 horsepower. The company used Plymouth as its home port. The long voyage around Africa was set at ninety days. The first vessel to leave was the *Australian*, departing exactly three months after the *Chusan* had departed from Southampton. The Melbourne *Argus* in a letter of March 17, 1852 was cautiously optimistic: 'At last there is some hope of a competent and regular service . . . The news of the gold discoveries has shamed the [home] government into a show of action.'[1]

The *Chusan*, which had left on May 15th, reached Melbourne at the end of July. This small barque-rigged vessel of only 700 tons and 80 horsepower was deliriously welcomed as she opened 'an important epoch in the history of Victoria'. She was praised to the skies: 'Her extreme length gives her a very majestic appearance in the water, and her internal arrangements are positively luxurious. Her saloon is fitted up with almost oriental splendour, while the sleeping cabins on each side are large, roomy and elegant.' The *Chusan*'s mail consisted of fourteen 'leviathan bags'. When the *Chusan* arrived at Sydney on August 3rd, eighty-four days out of Southampton, she was greeted with equal enthusiasm. A Ball was held at the Museum, someone composing a 'Chusan' Waltz for the occasion.

When the *Chusan* left Sydney for the voyage to Singapore, the *Sydney Morning Herald* carried a poetic effusion, the first quatrain of which reads:

'Swiftly she glides o'er the ocean wide,
This stately vessel which we hailed with pride;
She smiles at space and stern old Time defies,
While gladly o'er the foaming wave she flies.'

The enthusiastic versifier found the small barque 'stately' and she flew over the ocean wave at a speed of 8 knots![2]

When the *Chusan* reached Melbourne on the return voyage, Captain Down and the crew were entertained at another 'Chusan'

---

[1] See *Rep. Com. in Contract Pkts.* (1853), 34, 51, 75. The subsidy of the Australian Royal Mail was £26,000 a year for service every other month. It was to become monthly when the traffic justified the increased sailings.

[2] The *Morning Herald* (Melbourne) for July 31, 1852 for the mail load; The *Sydney Morning Herald* of September 1st.

Envelopes of two letters sent from Glasgow to Dunedin in New Zealand. The date stamps on the back show that the letter sent overland through France for 1s 2d took 77 days; the other by way of Panama cost 6d and took but 54 days. *Source:* Mr. Clive Shelton, Upper Hutt, New Zealand.

The *Mataura*, 1,700 tons, largest liner of the New Zealand Line to Panama in the 1860s. The tonnage given on the caption is an error. *Source:* Alexander Turnbull Library, Wellington, N. Z.

The *Arabia* of the Cunard Line, a paddle-wheel liner of 2,400 tons, was the first Cunarder to have but two masts. The absence of the mainmast made possible a 'cupola' with stained glass over the saloon, which was capable of seating 160 diners. The *Arabia* had the 'latest and most powerful engines ever put into a ship'. *Source: Gleason's Pictorial Drawing Room Companion*, IV, 224 (1853).

The *Adriatic*, built in 1856, 3,670 tons. A Collins liner later used in the British Galway mail service. She was one of the last paddle-wheel steamers used for the Atlantic crossing. *Source: Frank Leslie's Illustrated Newspaper*, Nov. 28, 1857.

Ball, and the Captain was presented with a medal 'manufactured from our native gold', bearing the inscription 'To commemorate the arrival of the first ocean steamer from England . . . *Quis separabit.*' On the return journey the *Chusan* carried passengers and mail, but no freight apart from gold dust. The regular outward service began early in the next year. The long association of the P & O with Australia had begun.

And what of the *Australian*, twice the size of the *Chusan* and with engines four times as powerful. Although she was scheduled to reach Melbourne in seventy-five days, the *Australian* arrived just as the *Chusan* was departing. The *Australian* had left Plymouth on June 5th. She ran out of fuel in the mid-Atlantic and had to make for St Helena. She was again short of coal on the way to Cape Town, which was only reached under canvas. The tardy *Australian* finally docked at Melbourne after a voyage of ninety-one days; Sydney was reached four days later. Her return trip was even more disappointing, it took 113 days.[1]

The first voyage of an Australian Royal Mail steamship was a warning of things to come. The much touted steamers were almost uniformly behind schedule. Accidents to the machinery, insufficient arrangements for fuel, and poor management in general were to blame. The *Melbourne*, which left in mid-October two weeks behind schedule, was 118 days reaching Melbourne. The *Adelaide*, set for the December departure, weighed anchor on the 16th, but had to return in a leaky condition, and finally departed on January 2, 1853. Because of various difficulties she was still at St Helena seventy-seven days later. The *Australian*'s second voyage was even worse than her first; she had to return to Plymouth twice with mails that were badly damaged by water. The mails for South Africa were finally sent by the General Screw, and the Australian bags went out by the P & O Line. Little wonder that the Australian Mail Line gave up after less than a year.

The collapse of the Line was a great disappointment to the colonists in Australia; they condemned the disgraceful failure and the wretched management that had made it possible. The *Argus* even suggested that the *Australian* and her consorts be made ferry boats on the Styx to delay 'to the latest possible instant of time, the entrance of departed spirits into the region of the manded'.[2]

[1] Melbourne *Argus*, August 7, September 2, 1852.
[2] ibid., February 5, 15; April 22; July 13, August 19, 1853; *Rep. Com. on Contract Pkts.*, (1853), 34-36, 73-76.

G

In October 1853, a Melbourne petition asked for the immediate restoration of the steam postal service by the Cape, for which the General Screw Steam Shipping Company was available. As we already know, this Line had been sending its ships to the Cape and India. They had also made excellent runs to Australia in 1853, whence they had carried mail homewards by the route around South America. In July the *Argo* reached Melbourne in sixty-five days, running the whole of the way from St Vincent to Victoria without having to touch at any coaling station. It was a striking contrast, according to the Melbourne *Argus* 'with the piddling and miserable doings . . . of another Company now, we trust, happily defunct'. The *Argo*'s voyage had been the fastest up to that time. Early in 1854 the General Screw completed arrangements for a service to replace that of the expensive contract with the Royal Mail. The time of the voyage out or home was to be sixty-seven days, out by the Cape of Good Hope, home by Cape Horn. The Company was to be paid 6d for each half-ounce-letter, and to have a monopoly of letter carrying by the two Capes.

The outlook seemed bright, for the General Screw was efficient. Australia had become very promising for shipping with the opening of rich gold fields in both Victoria and New South Wales. Even that 'monarch of the waters', the *Great Britain* (3,200 tons) had arrived in October 1853 after a voyage of sixty-five days. An adequate mail service by the P & O and the General Screw seemed assured.[1]

Misfortune again upset the 'best laid plans'. It was not the fault of the General Screw that its service to and from Australia ended the year it began. The Line was unable to furnish a ship for the December sailing because of the demand for transports to carry troops to the Black Sea for the war against Russia. The Crimean War also put a stop to the service of the P & O via Singapore. The Company took its vessels off the branch to Australia, giving as the reason 'the need of ships for military transport'. The Australians were bitter over the treatment they received, for the P & O did not find it necessary to discontinue the Hong Kong service. What nettled the Australians more than ever was the stopping of the

---

[1] *Tr. Min.*, November 27, 1855; *Report* of the General Screw's annual meeting, March 6, 1854; Melbourne *Argus*, June 15, 16; August 13, 14; November 26, 1853. The *Great Britain*, which made regular runs to Australia for a number of years, but not as a mail-packet, lowered the time between Melbourne and Liverpool, in 1860, to fifty-six days. See the *Letters of Rachel Henning* (Sydney, 1952) for an account of a voyage in the *Great Britain*, and see above, p. 137-8.

Singapore-Sydney service without giving notice. Comparisons were natural: 'If the service between Liverpool and New York were interrupted, a week would not pass without arranging for its resumption.' The Cunard, it might be added, also furnished transports, but without any serious effect on the New York run.[1]

The home government expressed deep regret in a Treasury note of November 1855 at the interruption of this 'important service'. It was resumed, shortly after, by the revival of sailing packets. The Admiralty contracted with two Liverpool shipping firms in the emigration trade, the Black Ball Line of James Baines and the White Star of Pilkington and Wilson. The sailings of their ships were to alternate on the 5th and 20th of each month. These fast sailing vessels often made excellent time, especially such clippers as the *James Baines*, the *Lightning* and the *Donald McKay*. In 1856 the average outward voyage of these sailing packets was eighty-four days, the average homeward voyage by way of Cape Horn ninety-three days. The *James Baines* made one voyage out in sixty-five days. On a trip to Melbourne in 1857, the *Lightning* while running her 'easting' south of Africa made 430 miles in one day.[2]

THE RETURN TO STEAM SERVICES

Shortly after the end of the Crimean War, the Treasury issued a long minute. They regarded the speedy restoration of a monthly postal communication by steam with Australia as imperative. The Treasury also believed that the home government should take the initiative, since the various colonies could not agree on the routes or the terms, and they also announced that each colony should pay its proportionate share in meeting the expense of a mail route that was not bringing in enough postage to pay for the service. The previous financial offers by the colonies had been noteworthy for their disagreement. New South Wales was willing to grant £6,000 per year for a route via Torres Strait. Western Australia pledged £1,000 a year if the vessels stopped at Fremantle. South Australia would assist if there was direct delivery to that colony. Victoria agreed to give financial assistance if the mails reached Melbourne in sixty-five days by way of Cape Leeuwin.

The Admiralty sought and received several tenders in 1856. One

---

[1] *Rep. P.M.G.* (1856), 24; Cable, op. cit., 192.
[2] *Votes and Proceedings* (N.S.W., 1856-7), III, 108, 127; *Lloyd's Calendar 1950*, 393-401 for records of fast sailing voyages.

of them, from James MacQueen, was by paddle-wheel steamers around Africa. It was rejected because it would be some time before the ships would be ready. Nor was an offer from the P & O acceptable; it offered a monthly service to Sydney for £140,000 a year, the mails to leave the main line at Point de Galle in Ceylon, and go by way of Cape Leeuwin and King George's Sound. It was unacceptable because the P & O was unwilling to stop at Fremantle or Adelaide whose ports were not regarded as fit to receive their large vessels. Nor would the P & O submit to a system of penalties if their mail-packets ran behind schedule. The Treasury felt that the P & O was trying to impose its own conditions rather than offer a tender.[1]

The successful tender was by the European and Australian Steam Navigation Company. The Line had three large ships ready, the *European*, the *Columbian* and the *Oneida*, vessels recently built for carrying mails across the Atlantic, but during the recent war they had been used as transports. Additional packets were to be added as fast as possible. The Company's offer was much higher than the tender of the P & O, £185,000 per year. The mails were to go by way of Suez monthly; the vessels were to be of 1,600 tons between England and Alexandria, and of 2,300 tons between Suez and Sydney. At long last it was hoped that the colonists would be satisfied with this expensive contract of October 1856.

But once again the Australians were let down; as one of the colonials put it: 'A fatality seems attached to this service.' The vessels sent around Africa for the run to Sydney had great difficulty in keeping to time. During 1857 no ships were ready to take home the April and December mails, and in 1858 the mail steamers arrived on schedule only once. Little wonder that the annual Report of the Postmaster-General of New South Wales declared the Line less satisfactory than the sailing clippers during the recent war. When the European and Australian Company gave up after a year it had lost £700,000 on its disastrous excursion into mail carrying, an excursion that ended in the court of bankruptcy.[2]

The next turn of events was the acceptance of a tender by the P & O. The West Indian Royal Mail wanted £250,000 for a monthly

[1] *Parl. Rets.*, 259/1856, 84/1857, and 10/1856, being the Treasury Minute of November 27, 1855.
[2] Ibid., 19/1857 for the contract; *Rep. P.M.G.* (N.S.W.) for tables of arrivals and departures. South Australia refused to contribute to the service, since the ships did not stop at Adelaide. The West Indian Royal Mail, which had been allied somewhat loosely with the European and Australian Line, carried on the service for a time at the request of the Admiralty. Its price was high—£185,000 for the next eight months.

service by way of Egypt. The P & O, which certainly did not relish such competition, offered a monthly service by way of Mauritius. The P & O, which had recently opened a mail route between Aden and Mauritius, now proposed to extend the line to Australia. The Company agreed to stop at King George's Sound with the mail for Western Australia, and at Kangaroo Island to discharge the mails for South Australia. In 1860, not long after the new contract was started, the P & O abandoned the Mauritius route, and sent its mail steamers to Australia via Point de Galle in Ceylon, which was already the junction for routes to Bombay, Calcutta and Hong Kong. And Ceylon has remained ever since as the hub for the diverging services of the Company. With this change, the subsidy for the Australian branch cost £143,672, one half of which was paid by the Australian colonies.[1]

THE SUEZ CANAL

By 1860 the Australian mails were in the care of the P & O after the trial of various lines and several routes during the previous fifteen years. The overland route by way of Egypt seemed by far the best for the Australian mails.

It was soon to be made even more useful by the addition of a canal connecting the Mediterranean and the Red Sea. Many were the prophecies that it would not be dug, and that, if it were, the Canal would be of doubtful value to the British. The P & O viewed the scheme with misgiving, as it would end the P & O monopoly, and even might bring ruin to the Company, according to the official historian of the Line. The judgement of Anthony Trollope is a strongly worded British appraisal. He wrote in 1862:

'All mankind has heard much of M. Lesseps and his Suez Canal . . . I have a very strong opinion that such a canal will not and cannot be made, that all the strength of the arguments adduced in the matter are hostile to it, and that steam navigation by land will and ought to be the means of transit through Egypt.'[2]

---

[1] *G.P.O. Records* (N.Z.). Folder for 1860; *Votes and Proceedings* (N.S.W.), 1858-9 II, 470. Also an anonymous pamphlet *Government Subsidies and the Postal Services with India, China and Australia* (rev. ed., 1879), 23. It was published in the interests of the Orient Line, when it was trying to break into the P & O monopoly. It will be cited as *Orient Pamphlet*.

[2] Cable, op. cit., 160-1 for the worries of the P & O; Trollope, *The West Indies and the Spanish Main* (5th ed., 1862), 319.

The Canal, Trollope notwithstanding, was opened in November 1869. The P & O's *Delta* was one of a long cavalcade of sixty-eight vessels that went from Port Said to Suez on a leisurely three-day journey through the desert. By 1869 the Canal Company was nearly bankrupt. Would it fail after all? In 1870 less than 500 vessels passed through the new waterway. However, the use of the Canal was such a saving of time and expense as compared with the voyage around Africa that the Canal Company began to prosper. In 1875, nearly 1,500 vessels used it, and four out of five were flying the British flag.

Soon British opinion began to change with regard to the value of the Canal, so much so that the British Government sought an interest in the Company. In 1875 the Khedive of Egypt was in such financial difficulties that he decided to sell his large block of Canal shares. Benjamin Disraeli, Prime Minister at the time, purchased them for the British Government in a coup that 'outgeneralled the French', to use his own words. Disraeli's consuming urge was not the route to Australia, but the passage to India. He believed that 'our interest in its [the Canal's] maintenance and proper management is much greater than that of any other European power'.[1]

What effect had the completion of the Canal on the carriage of mail across Egypt? When a new contract was arranged with the P & O in 1867, mail by Canal did not seem likely. In 1869 when the Canal was ready, the Secretary of the Post Office asked the P & O 'whether it was likely that their vessels would go through the Canal within the next three years'. The Company, which was then building additional docks at Alexandria, replied that it was 'most improbable'. In the early years of the Canal, ships took as much as eighty hours in going between Suez and Port Said, as they had to travel slowly and only during daylight. The British Post Office hesitated, naturally, to change the mail route from the railway to the Canal because the crossing by railway was very much quicker. The Egyptian Government had improved the railway line when the Canal was nearing completion so as to compete with its rival. By the time the Canal was ready for use, the average time for the mail crossing by rail was just under fourteen hours. When Edmund Creswell, a Post Office surveyor, was sent to Egypt in the early seventies he made the crossing by rail and also by water. The railway journey took only twelve hours; the Canal crossing in the P &

[1] Hoskins, op. cit., 473-6; Monypenny & Buckle, *The Life of Benjamin Disraeli* (1929), V, ch. xii.

O's new steamer *Peshawar* took fifty-three hours, 'during eleven of which we were aground'.[1]

The P & O, even though it would have preferred to have no waterway across Egypt, soon found it necessary to adjust its services to the Canal. Before it was opened in 1869, the trade with the East by way of Egypt was largely a monopoly of the British P & O and the French Messageries Maritimes. These companies, aided by large subsidies, were 'alone able to maintain a fleet of steamers east of Suez', according to Mr Creswell. The opening of the Canal, however, brought about an 'entire revolution in the trade with the East'.

Even the picturesque tea clippers were outdated, as tea carried by steamships through the Canal vied to be the first to arrive in England with the annual new supply of tea. Alfred Holt complained bitterly at this time of the preference granted the P & O. Holt was dispatching a steamer to India every twelve days by the Canal. He wrote in June 1873: 'One of my steamers is at this moment competing with an extra cargo ship of the P & O to bring the first cargo of tea to London . . . The P & O can easily arrange to have a small extra mail-bag on board to obtain precedence through the Canal.' Mail steamers still have precedence over vessels carrying general cargo.

British mail went by the Canal for the first time in 1873 when the Post Office permitted the heavier and slower mails by way of Gibraltar to go all the way by ship. Not until 1888 did the Post Office agree to the carriage of all the through mails across Egypt by ship. By then the mail service with India, China and Australia had, at last, received its modern character.

---

[1] *P.O. Records*, 396Z/1874, 11N/1887; Creswell's *Report* of December 10, 1868 and another of April 4, 1873. In the latter *Report*, he stated that the *Indus* was four days in a passage that was prolonged because the French mail steamer *Irawaddy* was stranded and blocked the passage.

18

BRITISH MAILS CROSS THE PACIFIC

NEW ZEALAND was the chief advocate of a mail service with England across the Pacific. Its location over a 1,000 miles south-east of Australia meant a slow and unreliable communication by way of the Cape of Good Hope or Suez. The extreme distance of New Zealand from the homeland struck Anthony Trollope when he journeyed to the south Pacific in the seventies. After crossing from Australia, he wrote: 'I was struck with the peculiarity of being in New Zealand . . . New Zealand had come up in my days, and there still remained for me something of the awful distance—for New Zealand is, of all inhabited lands, the most absolutely anti-podean to Greenwich.' Trollope it should be added, very soon felt at home. Well he might, since no settlement has remained more British, even though so far removed.[1]

Captain Cook had made a thorough study of the New Zealand coasts in the eighteenth century. No extensive settlements, however, took place before 1840. The systematic colonization scheme of Edward Gibbon Wakefield, which had been tried out in South Australia in 1836, was extended to New Zealand shortly after. Although the islands had been the scene of some missionary activity among the Maori, and whalers had made use of the New Zealand harbours, it was only after migration began on a large scale in 1840 that the British Government gave serious attention to the islands. The capital was set up in the north part of North Island, first at the Bay of Islands and later at Auckland.

The New Zealand Company, fathered by E. G. Wakefield, sent its settlers, not to Auckland, but to the south end of North Island, to Port Nicholson on which Wellington, the present capital, is located. This landlocked and extensive harbour is entered from Cook Strait, which separates the North from the South Island. Nelson at the west end of the Strait was an early settlement as was New Plymouth on the south-west coast of the North Island. The

[1] *Australia and New Zealand* (1873), II, 321.

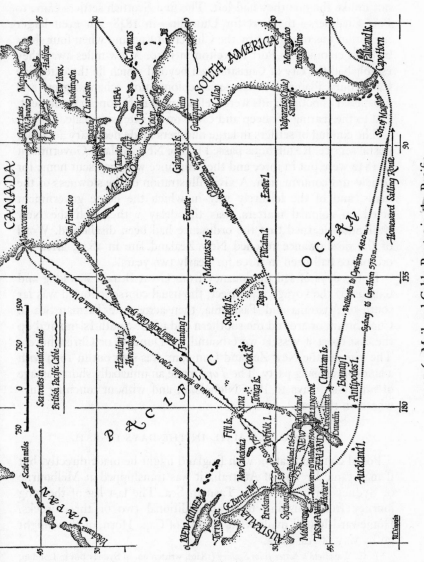

MAP 6. Mail and Cable Routes in the Pacific.

principal settlements in the South Island, apart from Nelson, were centred at Christchurch, half-way down the east coast, and at Dunedin farther to the south where Scottish migrants found a land not unlike the one they had left. The first Scottish settlers came to Port Chalmers—the port for Dunedin—in 1848. An even larger migration was organized by the Church of England when four ships brought colonists to Port Lyttelton in 1850. A few miles away they established the city of Christchurch beyond which lie the extensive Canterbury Plains. These special colonization schemes grew and prospered as both islands were well adapted to European settlement, and to the rearing of sheep and cattle on an extensive scale.

The coming of settlers in large numbers made necessary a regular postal service. Regulations passed by the New Zealand Government in 1842 were put in force and the ordinance was then sent home for review and confirmation. A vivid illustration of the slowness of the mails, and of the leisurely way in which the home government acted on colonial matters, was the delay with which the New Zealanders learned that the ordinance had been disallowed. Word of the disallowance reached New Zealand late in 1843, after the ordinance had been in force for nearly two years.

In the days of sail the journey from Great Britain was long and tedious. If the voyage was direct, the usual course followed was far south of Australia and Tasmania, then across the Tasman Sea to Cook Strait, or around the southern end of the South Island and up the east coast if vessels were bound for Dunedin or Christchurch. The *Tory* of the New Zealand Company was sent out in 1839 with a land-purchasing party. The *Tory* made an unusually short passage of ninety-six days to Port Nicholson, and without touching anywhere on the way.[1]

NEW ZEALAND MAIL IN THE DAYS OF SAIL

Postal communication with England might be made directly, but if mail came by way of Australia it was transhipped at Melbourne or Sydney for crossing the Tasman Sea. The last leg of the long journey from England took an additional two or three weeks. Homeward-bound mails went by way of Cape Horn, or they might go by way of Australia.

[1] E. G. Wakefield's *Letter from Sydney* (1829), written not in Sydney but in London, inspired the colonizers. Several of his brothers shared his interest in New Zealand; Captain Arthur Wakefield was killed by the Maori in 1843; Colonel W. H. Wakefield went out in the *Tory*, and was the founder of Wellington; he died there in 1848. E. G. Wakefield later migrated as well.

Internal communication was troublesome from the first because the settlements were so widely scattered. Their only communication with each other was by sea, for overland journeys were difficult owing to the rough nature of the country, the almost impenetrable forests, and the hostile attitude, on occasion, of the Maori. With these internal communications we are not here concerned, save to observe that the scattered settlements added greatly to the difficulties of mail delivery. In the early decades it was not uncommon for news or mail from Wellington or Nelson, intended for Auckland, to reach Auckland by way of Sydney. New Zealand was Australia over again on a smaller scale.[1]

The voyages of the early emigrant ships will make clear the time that the settlers had to wait for letters in the days of sail. Over 800 migrants left Britain in the autumn of 1840 to make their homes in or near Wellington on the shores of Port Nicholson. Each of the first five vessels on which they came took over 100 days; the *Aurora* 125 days, the *Oriental* 137, the *Bengal Merchant* 102, the *Duke of Roxburgh* 125. The *Adelaide* reached Wellington after 173 days at sea. It is not surprising to learn that the *Adelaide*'s passenger list was increased by five births on this long voyage.[2]

The first ships to bring Scottish settlers to Dunedin in South Island—it was in 1848—were the *John Wickliffe* and the *Philip Laing*, requiring 118 and 134 days respectively. Christchurch received its first large body of emigrants in 1851. They had left at the same time, September 1850, on four ships after a farewell luncheon at Gravesend, given by Lord Lyttelton. Three of the four, the *Charlotte Jane*, the *Randolph* and the *Sir George Seymour*, reached Port Lyttelton at the same time in just under 100 days. The *Cressey*, which carried the mail for those already there, took 110 days.[3]

In the previous year the *Lady Nugent* had brought the agent of the Canterbury Association, John R. Godley, to prepare the way for the settlers. Charlotte Godley, his wife, has left a very readable account of life in New Zealand a century ago. Her *Letters* well picture the yearning for mail and the seemingly endless waiting for

[1] D. Robertson, *Early History of the New Zealand Post Office* (1905), 30; A. O. Thomson, *The Story of New Zealand* (1859), II, 216. By sea Auckland and Wellington are 600 miles apart by the west coast route, and twice as far by the east coast. Dunedin is 400 miles south of Wellington by sea.

[2] The *New Zealand Journal*, published in London by the Company, furnishes contemporary accounts. See, e.g. I (1840), 223, 245-6, 391, etc.

[3] op. cit., XI (1851), 329, 358, etc.

word from home, caused not only by the great distance but by
further tiresome delays as letters were carried from one port to
another. She wrote three months after her arrival: 'If I let myself
think too long together of the time it is since we have heard . . . I
am tempted to wish N.Z. had gone completely under the sea before
I was born.' The first letters for the Godleys arrived eight months
after their departure from England. They came by way of Auckland,
'with which', she wrote, 'there is, from here, very imperfect communication'. News according to Charlotte Godley, was 'always four
months and generally six months behindhand'.[1]

The coming of mails by steam was not of great help. When the
Duke of Wellington died in mid-September 1852 the news went out
to Australia by the new steamship mail lines. Yet the inhabitants of
Wellington, New Zealand, first knew of the Great Duke's death in
January 1853. Official mourning was thus delayed for four months
in the city named in his honour.

In 1854 a steam service was extended across the Tasman Sea.
The first vessel hired on a regular schedule was the *William Denny*,
plying between Sydney and Auckland. This barque of 600 tons and
200 horsepower was joyously received in Auckland on her first trip
from Sydney in July 1854. Many Aucklanders took a trial ride on
'the gallant ship as she speeded down the harbour'. The service was
monthly, the *William Denny* leaving Sydney on the arrival of the
English mail; she was always to proceed to sea within six hours after
the mail was on board. This service was primarily for Auckland and
was paid for by the government of the Auckland Province. The
William Denny carried cargo as well as mail and passengers. In
September 1854, for instance, she brought '23 horses and 4 heifers
and 80 tons of general cargo as well as the English mails'. Unfortunately, this first steam service was brief; the vessel was wrecked on
North Cape in March 1857.

The mail service between Sydney and Auckland was of little use
to Wellington and of less value to the settlements on South Island.
Consequently Wellington arranged in June 1857 for the steamship
Marchioness to give Wellington a monthly service with Melbourne.
The *Marchioness* did well enough if the English mail arrived on
time. In October 1858, however, she returned from Melbourne
without the English mail 'owing to the non-arrival of the *Australian*

---

[1] *Letters from Early New Zealand by Charlotte Godley* (Christchurch, 1951), 59, 86,
123, 127. When the Godleys returned to England at the end of 1852, they first went to
Sydney, whence the *Angelsey* took them home by way of Cape Horn in 106 days.

which was thirteen days overdue at Melbourne when the *Marchioness* left'.[1]

The southern New Zealand settlements naturally resented the special arrangements made by Wellington and Auckland for the English mails. Because of the insistent demand for a better mail service for the widely scattered communities, the central government finally arranged in 1859 for an interprovincial (domestic) service to be combined with an intercolonial connection with Australia across the Tasman. Henry Sewell, the Colonial Treasurer at the time, who was in England in 1857, contracted for a service with a shipping Line that took the name of the Intercolonial Royal Mail Steam Packet Company. The service began late in 1858. Contact with the P & O was made at Sydney. From there, the Intercolonial mail-packet went to Nelson, where the mails for Wellington, Canterbury and Dunedin were transferred to another vessel. The packet from Sydney then proceeded to Auckland by way of New Plymouth. As Henry Sewell put it: 'By this arrangement all the provinces will have the opportunity of receiving and answering letters in the shortest possible time.'

Much contention, nevertheless, went on between the provinces as each hoped to improve its mail service. By the end of 1859 Auckland once again had a direct service with Sydney, and the rapidly growing southern provinces obtained a direct service with Melbourne. There was even talk of separating the North from South Island, and making them into two colonies, largely because Auckland, the capital, was at the northern end of North Island. Separation was avoided, however, by making Wellington the capital in 1865, and improving the steam services between the various ports. A direct service was set up between Dunedin and Australia when the Province of Otago had a gold rush in the early sixties.[2]

At best, communication with the mother country by way of Australia was distressingly slow. Australians, even in Sydney where the outward P & O journey ended, could reply to their British letters by the returning mail-packet. New Zealanders, even in Auckland, could not, because of the additional journey across the Tasman Sea, since the round-trip voyage between Sydney and

[1] *G.P.O. Records* (N.Z.) for ep. of September 9, 1854 from the Colonial Secretary of Sydney to the Colonial Secretary, Auckland; and folder for 1857; *A.J.H.R.* (N.Z.), 1861, Dl, p.15 *A.J.H.R.* signifies Appendices of the Journal of the House of Representatives.

[2] *A. J.H.R.* (1860), D5, p.10; (1861), Dl, pp. 4, 12–17; *1st Rep. P.M.G.* (N.Z.), 1860); W. P. Morrell, *The Provincial System in New Zealand* (1952), 112–20 for the views of the southerners.

Auckland could not be made in less than ten days; the return mail for Britain left Sydney eight days after the arrival of the mail from Southampton. Australians could receive replies to their letters within five months; New Zealanders could not. One of Auckland's newspapers complained: 'We have been made utterly subservient to the dictates of Australia. It is high time that New Zealand should be placed on an equitable footing with the other colonies. In postal matters we are at the fag end of an imperfect chain.'[1]

THE PANAMA ROUTE

The obvious alternative to this 'imperfect chain' was mail communication across the Pacific to Panama. Not only would the route be shorter, but by it New Zealand would receive the mail first instead of last. From the earliest days of colonization the settlers had dreamed of a Panama route. Hope had been aroused when the Royal Mail began a service between England and the West Indies just as New Zealand was being settled. E. W. Stafford, at a dinner in 1857, recalled the time of his arrival in the colony fifteen years earlier (1842): 'I can well remember that the first house I entered after landing . . . was that of the late Captain Wakefield . . . I can well remember that, in discussing the future of New Zealand (a topic seldom omitted at that table), his remarking as he pointed to a map of the world which hung behind his chair, "Before we have all died, there will be communication by steam between this country and Great Britain by way of Panama." '[2]

The New Zealand Company had dangled before the eyes of prospective migrants the hope of faster communication by the Panama route. Their *New Zealand Journal*, published in London, looked forward to a connection of New Zealand with the Royal Mail: 'It is calculated that the course of post [the time from sending a letter to receiving an answer] will be at the most only five months and a half.' When the Pacific Steam Navigation Company began running vessels south from Panama to Valparaiso, the Colonists had some thought of making a connection with that Line at Valparaiso, but a direct service to Panama was soon seen to be much more desirable. The Directors of the New Zealand Company even

[1] Auckland *New Zealander* July 12, 1862; *Parl. Deb.* (N.Z.) 3rd & 4th Parls., p. 92, being speech of Crosbie Ward on November 24, 1864; *A.J.H.R.*, 2nd sess., 3rd Parl. D3, p. 9.
[2] The speech was made in Auckland. Stafford was head of the ministry at the time. For the quotation, see the Nelson *Examiner* for February 25, 1857.

sought tenders for such a Line. They held that the route 'between
New Zealand and the west coast of the Isthmus of Darien, whence
the passage to Chagres is by no means difficult' would result in
regular communication with England in seventy days. This route
was hailed by the Company as the 'Vision of Columbus Realized.'[1]

When the Jocelyn Committee of 1851 made its first report to the
British Parliament, it paid some attention to a possible Panama
route. The Committee reported that the Pacific Steam together with
the West Indian Royal Mail were planning a line from Panama to
New Zealand and Sydney by way of Tahiti. The route, according
to the Committee, would offer a regular and sufficiently rapid postal
communication, and afford passengers a route comparatively free
from storms, and that it would at the same time bring the 'rising
colony of New Zealand into the main line of communication'.

Projectors made several other suggestions in the early fifties.
Nothing came of a project of the Australasian Direct Steam Navigation Company (1853), nor one by Samuel Cunard for a Pacific
service that would forestall possible American efforts to capture this
route. The most likely offer was made by the so-called Australasian
Pacific Mail Steam Packet Company, which had on its provisional
board representatives of both the Royal Mail and the Pacific Steam.
The management of the Royal Mail seems to have been more
fearful of the designs of Samuel Cunard than of the Americans,
fearful that the 'astute Canadian had something up his sleeve'.
Screw-driven steamers were actually being built in 1853 for the
Australasian Company, and given such suggestive names as *Kangaroo*, *Emeu* [sic], *Black Swan* and *Dinornis* (the extinct New
Zealand moa). The *Kangaroo* was expected to take off for Sydney
late in 1853, but the hopes of New Zealanders were again disappointed. This *Kangaroo* never saw Australia, as the Crimean War
offered safer profits for the newly built ships. The *Emeu* and the
Kangaroo were taken over by the British Admiralty, and the other
two were sold to the French for troop transports. The disgusted
colonists learned in July that the proposed Pacific route was abandoned after 'they had fed us for two years with hopes'.[2]

After the Crimean War the Royal Mail continued to show an
interest in the Pacific mail route to New Zealand. A representative
of the Company, Champion Wetton, visited the south Pacific in

[1] *New Zealand Journal*, I (1840), 31; II (1841), 109, 114, 153; IV (1843), 123.
[2] *1st. Rep. S.C. on Steam Communication with India* (1851), pp. iv, viii, 212; Auckland
New Zealander May 21, November 23, December 14, 1853; July 12, 18, 1854.

1857 where he was wined and dined. Prime Minister Stafford made the statement, quoted earlier in this chapter, at a banquet held for Wetton when he visited Auckland. The Royal Mail, however, preferred to give its support at that time to the weak European and Australian Line via Suez rather than venture a service from Panama.

The British Post Office was not at all sympathetic with the colonial desire for a Pacific mail service. It is true that in 1858 when tenders were being sought for a new Suez service the Admiralty declared that it planned to call for tenders for a steam communication via Panama in addition to the Suez service. The Post Office was so strongly opposed to the probable increase in expenditure that a long minute of September 1858 by Rowland Hill questioned the need for a Pacific Line when none of the packet Lines south of the Equator carried sufficient mail to repay the postage. In addition, the small amount of correspondence with New Zealand—but 6 per cent of the Australasian mail—did not deserve special consideration. Victoria was the colony according to Rowland Hill, whose wishes should be respected, for her mail-load was over two-thirds of the whole. Rowland Hill suggested that additional packets should be placed on the Suez route, if a monthly service was too infrequent.

New Zealand finally opened the route to Panama on her own initiative. The successful arrangements were largely the work of a young enthusiast named Crosbie Ward who had migrated from Ireland to Canterbury in 1852. Six years later he was representing Lyttelton (the port for Christchurch) in the General Assembly where he showed a keen interest in better mail service overseas. In 1861 Crosbie Ward became Postmaster-General of New Zealand, and late in the next year went to England to arrange, if possible, for a Panama Line. In London, Ward was joined by the representative of New South Wales, Edmund Hamilton, in seeking from the British Government a promise to use this route. But neither the Post Office nor the Treasury was willing to assume this additional expense. In June 1863 a large delegation supported Ward and Hamilton in an interview with W. E. Gladstone, then Chancellor of the Exchequer. Crosbie Ward pointed out the growth in Pacific trade, and the impossibility of New Zealanders replying to mail by the next packet that left Sydney for England. He believed that the 'close monopoly' of steamship traffic in the Indian Ocean would be broken by a Pacific Line, and asserted that New Zealand was 2,000 miles nearer Great Britain by Panama than by Suez, and that the shorter route would bring New Zealanders within 48 days of

England, and Sydney 54. Ward also declared that New Zealand's share of the south Pacific correspondence, which had been but 6 per cent in 1857, was now 16 per cent.

Gladstone was not impressed. He objected, as one would expect, to the additional expense. Melbourne's large share of the mail and its nearness by way of Suez were the chief reasons for opposing the Panama route. Clearly Gladstone had been briefed by Rowland Hill.

When Crosbie Ward failed to gain the co-operation of the home government he invited tenders on behalf of New Zealand. One by the General Screw was rejected on what was alleged to be the small steam power of its vessels. The other came from the Intercolonial Line already serving New Zealand, and was more acceptable, possibly, for that reason. A contract resulted on December 17, 1863. The service was to be monthly, the time for each voyage across the Pacific to be no more than thirty days. The New Zealand terminus was to be selected by the Company; much to the disgust of Auckland, the Intercolonial chose Wellington rather than Auckland, as being more central and nearer Sydney.[1]

Crosbie Ward's achievement, strangely enough, was not acceptable to the New Zealand Government. The Ministry that had sent him to Great Britain as Postmaster-General with power to act had fallen forty-eight days before Crosbie Ward signed the contract for the Panama Line. He had done so in good faith, as the time for communications between New Zealand and Great Britain then took much longer than forty-eight days. It serves as another illustration of the need for faster communication. Ward was also accused of exceeding his instructions when he agreed to a contract calling for a subsidy of £63,000 a year, when New Zealand's standing offer was for only £30,000. Ward replied to this criticism when he returned to New Zealand by showing that the ending of the present expense of the Suez service would bring the colony's expenditure within the £30,000 limit. At long last the Government in power accepted the contract after the provinces of Wellington and Canterbury had offered to take care of any expenditure above £30,000. Dr Featherston, the Superintendent of the Wellington Province, went to Australia to obtain the co-operation of the east-coast colonies. Neither Victoria nor Queensland was willing, but New South Wales

[1] For the negotiations of Ward and Hamilton, *A.J.H.R.*, 4th sess. 3rd Parl., Dl, 11; *Report* of the Colonial Secretary (N.S.W.) of June 25, 1863. One factor that favoured Wellington as the port for the Pacific Line was that Port Nicholson had the only lighthouse at that time along the New Zealand coasts.

agreed, partly because of the real value to that colony of a Pacific Line, and partly out of chagrin at the leading place of Melbourne in the services by way of Suez. New South Wales joined New Zealand only if Sydney was to be the western terminus of the main-line steamers. On this understanding New South Wales contributed half of the cost for a revised contract that called for £110,000 a year. The enlarged Intercolonial Line was renamed the Panama New Zealand and Australia Royal Mail Company.[1]

The four vessels for the Panama Line were built in Great Britain. The *Kaikoura*, the *Ruahine* and the *Rakaia* were each of 1,500 tons and 450 horsepower; the *Mataura* was of 1,700 tons and 450 horsepower. The *Ruahine* was equipped with two screws, the first ocean-going steamer to be so fitted. The Company was determined to make good on the longest non-stop run ever undertaken by a steam vessel.[2]

The *Kaikoura* began its journey from Sydney on June 15, 1866, after reaching Australia by way of the Cape of Good Hope. She had accommodations for 200 passengers, and carried 1,000 tons of coal for the long voyage. The *Kaikoura* took seven days to cross the Tasman Sea, a rough beginning, as a bad storm smashed her starboard lifeboat and swept overboard the greater part of the livestock intended for consumption on the voyage across the Pacific. Wellington welcomed the new liner with enthusiasm. Visitors to the ship admired the 'magnificent saloon containing five large tables with a piano at one end and a library at the other', and marvelled at the 'capacious ice-house, capable of containing a ton of ice'. A dinner and a ball fittingly emphasized the opening of the Line. The Wellington *Independent* for June 23rd was printed in blue instead of black ink with the statement that the date of the *Kaikoura*'s arrival 'will in future be marked as a red-letter day in our calendar'.

The vessel reached Panama in twenty-five days. Her passengers and mail, after crossing the Isthmus by the railway, left for England on the *Tyne*, awaiting them at Colon. On the return trip the *Kaikoura* reached Wellington August 25th bringing British news and mail that had left the mother country fifty-four days earlier. After the laying of the Atlantic submarine cable late in the same year, news could be cabled across the Atlantic and sent to Colon, news

---

[1] *5th & 6th Reports P.M.G.* (N.Z.); *A.J.H.R.*, 6th sess., 3rd Parl. (1865), Dla, pp. 8–14, being papers on the Panama contract.
[2] Lawson, Will, *Steam in the South Pacific* (1909) ch. V; *8th Rep. P.M.G.* (N.Z.).

that was ten days later than the departure of the mail from South-ampton.[1]

A well-known British statesman used the Line in its first year. Charles Dilke, who went around the world in 1866-7, recorded his impressions of the various English-speaking countries in his very readable *Greater Britain*. After crossing the United States he went by ship to Panama and thence 'in one of the ships of the new Colonial Line, for Wellington in New Zealand, the longest steam voyage in the world'. The *Rakaia* carried him to Pitcairn Island, which was reached on the sixteenth day, and thirteen days later the liner reached the 'great sea-lake of Port Nicholson'.[2]

For two and a half years the Panama Line carried on with remark-able regularity. The mail was due in Southampton in less than sixty days after leaving Sydney. Mail for the colonies left England on the 2nd, was scheduled to leave Panama on the 23rd, and to reach Well-ington fifty days after leaving England, and Sydney nine days later. It was a saving for Sydney of four days over the route by Suez and Southampton. If the Suez route via Marseilles and through France is compared with the time of the Panama route, the time was about the same. The minimum cost of a letter to Southampton either way was 6d. If a letter was routed through France, the charge was about double.

The long voyage was a tax on the bunker capacity of the vessels. The *Mataura*, largest of the four liners, used 36 tons of coal every twenty-four hours. It was noted with astonishment at the time that such a vessel, making a voyage of nearly 7,000 miles at a 10-knot speed, could do so without having to store 'a single coal on deck'. Coal hulks at Panama were supplied with coal brought out from Great Britain. To ease the bunkering, the Line arranged in 1867 for a coaling station at the French-held island of Rapa, located about half-way between Panama and Wellington, and about 1,000 miles north-west of Pitcairn. Five acres of land on Rapa were leased for ninety-nine years.[3]

The voyages of the Panama Line ended after two and a half years. Although the vessels were satisfactory and kept well to schedule, they usually carried few passengers and little freight. The supposed

[1] Wellington *Independent*, June 23, August 25, November 20, 1866.
[2] *Greater Britain* (1870), 234-7.
[3] Wellington *Independent*, January 6, February 23, 1867, January 28, 1868. Pitcairn, directly on the shortest route between Wellington and Panama, was not usable as a coaling station because of no harbour. For descriptions of both Rapa and Pitcairn, see T. Heyerdahl, *Aku-Aku* (N.Y., 1958), 329ff. Today vessels of the New Zealand Line using the Panama Canal, regularly stop at Pitcairn if the weather permits.

unhealthiness of Panama was played up by opponents of the route. Fear of yellow fever also had an effect, as an outbreak had occurred at Panama in 1866 and at St Thomas during the next year. On one voyage the *Mataura* reached Wellington with 100 boxes of mail and only sixty-six passengers. In October 1867 the *Rakaia* brought twenty-three passengers; in June 1868 the *Ruahine* forty-one. When Charles Dilke continued his voyage from Wellington to Sydney, the *Kaikoura* carried only one other passenger. In the first eight months—sixteen voyages—the liners had but 500 passengers in all. The chief reason given for the ending of the service was 'the almost total absence of passenger traffic'.

Another reason for the lack of patronage, apart from the unhealthiness of Panama, was the irregularity of the liners of the Royal Mail to and from Colon. Not infrequently the late arrival of the Royal Mail ships prevented vessels of the Panama Line from leaving for New Zealand on schedule. The Royal Mail services had been seriously deranged in October 1867 by a severe hurricane that hit St Thomas. The Panama Line, of course, was completely dependent on the Royal Mail connection to make its through service attractive. The *Rakaia*, leaving Wellington in December 1868 carried the last mail to Panama, and then went around Cape Horn into the Atlantic.[1]

Despite its short career, the Panama Line had set a precedent for the carriage of mails across the south Pacific. The time taken by a letter between New Zealand and Great Britain had been reduced to less than two months. The Panama route had proved that a 7,000-mile passage across the Pacific could be made easily and regularly by steam. Above all, the experience had so sharpened the demand for faster mails that another route across the Pacific was soon in use.

SERVICE VIA SAN FRANCISCO

In 1869 the New Zealand Parliament considered at length a possible route by way of the United States. San Francisco was the obvious replacement for Panama, since the first transcontinental railway across North America had been completed to San Francisco

---

[1] *10th Rep. P.M.G.* (N.Z.); *13th Rep. P.M.G.* (N.S.W.). The *Sydney Morning Herald* asserted that the Royal Mail, by withdrawing its financial support, 'might almost be said to have killed the Panama Line'. The four vessels were taken over by the Royal Mail as a result of a forced bankruptcy, and were soon running under new names in the Atlantic. Bushell, op. cit., 95-97, does not recognize New Zealand's part in setting up the service, nor attach any blame to the Royal Mail for the failure of the Panama Line.

in that very year, 1869. E. W. Stafford, the Prime Minister of New Zealand, was certain that this route would soon be a great commercial highway for commerce with Europe, because of the rapid crossing of North America by rail, and the use of the fast Cunard steamers on the Atlantic. Stafford blamed the colony of Victoria for the collapse of the Panama Line: 'Victoria arrogated to herself the position of Queen of the colonies, and was determined to favour no scheme which does not make Melbourne the first and last port of arrival and departure.' A satisfactory alternative seemed likely.

Another prominent advocate in New Zealand of better postal communications overseas was Julius Vogel. Born in England, he had come to Melbourne in the gold rush of the fifties, and moved on to Otago when gold was discovered there ten years later. Vogel entered New Zealand politics in 1869, and for the next thirty years was one of New Zealand's leading statesmen. He became a vigorous advocate of communication across the Pacific, both by ship and cable; he was even in favour of annexing Samoa as a port of call for the San Francisco mail service. Julius Vogel became Postmaster-General in the Fox Ministry that succeeded Stafford's in 1869. With one slight exception he held that office for the next seven years, keeping the portfolio even when he was Prime Minister.

In 1869 a Committee reported to the New Zealand House of Representatives that the route via San Francisco was, beyond all comparison, the best. In addition to being the fastest route to the mother country, it would open direct communication with the United States and Canada, instead of having to send mail to America by way of Great Britain. As to cost, the Committee believed that it would not much exceed the present expenditure via Melbourne. Mail could reach San Francisco in three weeks, cross the United States in six days, and take nine or ten more to cross the Atlantic. Allowing two days for stoppages at Tahiti and Hawaii, the mail should take less than forty days.[1]

A contract between the New Zealand Postmaster-General, Julius Vogel, and the United States consul in Sydney, Hayden Hezekiah Hall, provided for a monthly service between Sydney and San Francisco, with calls at the Bay of Islands or Auckland in New Zealand and at Honolulu. The estimated mail time between Sydney and London was forty-four days, and Mr Hall expected it to be lower 'when the Line is well established'. The promoter had

---

[1] *Parl. Deb.*, (N.Z.), V, 15-18; *A.J.H.R.* (1869), E2, pp. 4-9. The American Continent had been spanned by telegraph since 1861.

no ships, but chartered vessels being used along the Australian coasts. The Hall Line never really got going; it ended in March 1871.

Julius Vogel next arranged for a successor to the Hall Line when he went on a trip to England by way of the United States. The contractor was W. H. Webb, a prominent New York shipbuilder and architect. Webb at least had a number of steamships available for immediate use—large side-wheelers that were built to serve as troop transports in the American Civil War. They were afterwards in the West Indian trade, and later went around to San Francisco in search of more profitable charters. Webb's Line was to run through from San Francisco by way of Honolulu, and after reaching Auckland the vessels were to continue down the New Zealand coast with stops at Wellington and Port Lyttelton before terminating the voyage at Port Chalmers in Otago. Mr Vogel thus hoped to satisfy the demands of the various provinces for a share of the benefits. Some of the vessels were to cross the Tasman from Auckland to Sydney. The Webb steamers, bearing such names as *Nebraska*, *Nevada* and *Dakotah* were wooden paddle-wheel steamers of 2,000-3,000 tons—of great size for that day. They were better adapted, however, for river and coastal traffic than for long runs on an ocean the size of the Pacific, especially as this vast expanse of water seemed at times decidedly misnamed. If an engine broke down, there was insufficient auxiliary sail to move vessels fitted with cumbersome paddle boxes. The *Nebraska*, leaving Sydney in April 1873, made the last voyage.[1]

Thus far Vogel's efforts had been anything but successful. In the meantime New South Wales was showing greater eagerness for a Pacific Line that would free her from dependence on the P & O via Melbourne. New South Wales had given notice to terminate the contract with the P & O because of 'the loudly expressed wish of the Community that some satisfactory service via Fiji and San Francisco be entered into'. Matters came to a head at the Colonial Conference held in Sydney in 1873. There, to the great chagrin of New South Wales, the Government of Victoria announced that it had made a contract with the P & O for a continuance of their Australian service—with a difference. By this contract the main-line vessels would terminate their voyages at Melbourne, and not at Sydney as formerly. One need not be surprised that it was now 'necessary for New South Wales to adopt some decisive and independent course

[1] *A.J.H.R.*, (1870), E4, pp. 3-13; *12th Rep. P.M.G.* (N.Z.), and the *13th* and *14th* as well.

if she wished to maintain a leading position as the oldest of the Australian colonies'. New South Wales, now under the vigorous leadership of Henry Parkes, was prepared for cordial co-operation with New Zealand.[1]

Finally, in the mid-seventies, a satisfactory mail line resulted from the co-operation of New South Wales and New Zealand. Henry Parkes, the Prime Minister of New South Wales, was responsible for an offer by the American Pacific Mail Line. Parkes opened his visit to the United States in 1874 by speaking at a public meeting in San Francisco on the value of a trans-Pacific Line, not only for the British colonies in the south Pacific but for America as well. He also made plain the disappointment of the British Pacific colonies with such American contractors as Hall and Webb. The representatives of the Pacific Mail Line who heard the 'very able speech of Mr Parkes' were so impressed that the Postmaster-General of New South Wales soon received an offer from the Pacific Mail 'to carry on this service'. The letter added, 'Knowing that your experience with American lines had not been satisfactory, we are the more anxious to demonstrate that this Company is able to establish permanently such a service.'[2]

The contract of 1875 for the Pacific mail service provided for five screw-driven steamers. Sailings were every fourth week with stops at Honolulu and Fiji. The vessels were to fork alternately at Fiji for New Zealand and for Sydney; if a main liner went on from Fiji to Sydney, the mail and passengers for New Zealand changed to another vessel, and if the liner went on to New Zealand, the Australian mail and passengers were transferred. The New Zealand service included several calls down the east coast before reaching the terminus at Port Chalmers. The contract was not wholly American, as John Elder & Company of Glasgow furnished two of the vessels, the *Zealandia* and the *Australia*.

The transfer of mail and passengers at Fiji was soon found

---

[1] *17th* and *19th Reps. P.M.G.* (N.S.W.). The latter *Report* includes a summary of the efforts to date to set up a Pacific mail service. Henry Parkes, Prime Minister of N.S.W. from 1872 to 1876, was as much interested in Imperial communications as Julius Vogel.

[2] *A.J.H.R.* (1875), 33-43; *21st Rep. P.M.G.* (N.S.W.). The American Pacific Mail had been active for over a quarter of a century, first as a coastal line. A trans-Pacific service by way of Honolulu to the Orient had been started in 1866 with the use of 4,000-ton wooden side-wheelers. By the mid-seventies the Pacific Mail had changed to screw-driven steamers. The paddle-wheel vessels of the Pacific Mail were the last great ocean steamships not screw propelled. Cunard's last paddler had been built in 1862, the last for the P & O in 1864, and the last for the Royal Mail in 1865. See J. H. Kemble 'Side Wheelers across the Pacific', in *American Neptune*, II, 5-38 (1942).

inconvenient, and often unpleasant because of the tropical conditions. The contract was modified, in consequence, to provide for direct runs via Auckland to Sydney. New Zealand was to take care of its own coastal service. The subsidy, originally £89,250, was reduced to £72,500, of which New South Wales paid £40,000 and New Zealand £32,500.[1]

The revised schedule proved the beginning of a satisfactory Pacific mail route to the mother country. The vessels were punctual. The homeward mails from Auckland had been delivered in London, on the average, in less than forty-one days, one delivery being made in the 'unprecedented' time of thirty-eight days. The prophecy of a fast Pacific service for New Zealand had come true through the efforts of E. W. Stafford, Crosbie Ward, Julius Vogel and Henry Parkes, among others. Initially a New Zealand venture, the Pacific mail service had been finally put on a sound basis with the co-operation of New South Wales.[2]

When the first settlers came in 1840 the mail took well over 100 days between England and New Zealand. Thirty-five years later distant New Zealand was only one-third as far from the homeland so far as letters and travel were concerned. The use of the Pacific route, along with constant improvements in steamship design and in the efficiency of the marine engine had made the difference.

[1] *A.J.H.R.*, 1st sess., 6th Parl. (1875), F3, p. 46; *23rd Rep. P.M.G.* (N.S.W.).

[2] Sydney continued to have a service via Suez as well as San Francisco. By the mid-seventies the Sydney mail via Suez went by railway between Sydney and Melbourne, and all the Suez mail was being sent overland through France via Brindisi. The *20th Rep. P.M.G.* (N.Z.) gives the following tabulation of mail times to and from London from March 1878 to March 1879.

Via San Francisco	Sydney	Melbourne	Wellington	Auckland
outward (days)	46·67	49·25	43·83	40·92
inward	45·33	48·50	43·42	40·33
Via Brindisi				
outward	42·	39·92	48·46	51·61
inward	47·61	44·54	55·46	58·69

19

THE HANDLING OF OCEAN MAILS
A CENTURY AGO

WHEN the foreign mail services out of Falmouth were turned over to the Admiralty in 1823, it was assumed that ten-gun brigs would carry the mails to Portugal and the Mediterranean, to the West Indies and South America, and across the north Atlantic to Halifax. The mails would be at least as regular as they had been and they would also be safer, for naval brigs were not likely to be easy victims of privateers in the next war.

The expected did not happen. Uninterrupted years of peace followed the downfall of Napoleon. Within fifteen years the marine engine was pushing ships over the open ocean. The result was a drastic change in the handling of the mails going overseas. With the rapid rise in emigration and the surprising increase in trade, the mail routes of 1823 expanded into a vast network to serve world-wide commercial and industrial needs, and to bring closer the extensive colonies of settlement within a growing Empire. As the Committee, headed by Lord Canning, put it in 1853: 'When it became requisite to dispatch the mails by steam . . . the Government had to call in a new class of packets.'[1]

Under the new arrangements the Post Office suggested the times for the departure of the mails, but the Treasury and the Lords of the Admiralty largely dictated the terms of the contracts. The Treasury, of course, had the deciding voice in the amount of the subsidies, the Admiralty the chief influence in the character and the handling of the packets. The change to steam meant a rapid growth in the subsidies. Too often the contracts and the size of the subsidies were arranged through the Admiralty without competitive bidding. The Canning Committee of 1853 was very critical. The subsidies, it reported, had become a very serious charge on the public revenues, for the total had risen to £863,140 annually, and

[1] *Rep. Com. on Contract Pkts.*, (1853), 1.

'demands were continually being made for a large increase'. They found that the actual sea-postage amounted to little more than half the cost. The Committee strongly believed in the freedom of trade, but found that the 'existence of highly subsidized companies prevents unassisted competition, hinders the development of private resources and the progress of improvement'.

What was wrong? Were the so-called subsidies of postal services really intended for non-postal purposes, as the Committee seems to have inferred—for political ends in the national interest, and, in particular, for the needs of the Admiralty? The Admiralty certainly benefited from many non-postal clauses in the contracts. It insisted that the vessels meet structural qualifications that would fit them to carry the largest guns in case of war. Mail-packets had been used during the Crimean War for the transport of men and supplies to the eastern Mediterranean, a use that had led to the withdrawal of steam postal services with Australia, and the cancelling of a proposed line to New Zealand just as it was ready to begin. The Canning Committee was opposed to such practices. To them it was 'false economy' to give a 'military character to postal vessels', since the demand for mail steamers should be greater, not less, on the outbreak of war.[1]

Every vessel used for carrying mail had to meet a rigorous Admiralty survey of its hull, and be capable of acceptable speeds on a measured course. The Admiralty even insisted—a surprising requirement at this time—that the steam packets must be built of wood, although iron steamships were already gaining great favour. In reply to a request from the P & O that they might construct their mail steamers of iron, the Admiralty wrote on June 24, 1850 that no vessels would be accepted for postal contracts 'if built of iron or any other material offering so ineffectual a resistance to the striking of shot'. In reply, the Secretary of the P & O gave reasons for the Company's preference for iron. Ships built of iron had greater buoyancy and, therefore, a greater speed, as well as increased room for mails and cargo. They would also be safer, as such a vessel 'can be effectually divided into a number of perfectly water-tight compartments'—an impossibility in a wooden vessel because of 'her working in a seaway'. The Admiralty was not impressed, for in a brief reply of January 29, 1851, they informed the P & O that 'my Lords see no reason to alter their decision'.[2]

---

[1] ibid., 3-9. Lord Canning was Postmaster-General at the time.
[2] *Parl. Ret.*, 86/1851.

A usual clause in the Admiralty contracts required a mail vessel to carry a naval agent. He was to see that the details of the contract were met, especially that the mail-bags and boxes were properly housed. Although the Admiralty agent aboard might well have been replaced by a postal officer, the agent was useful. He made regular reports at the end of each voyage to the general packet agent at Southampton, and copies were forwarded to the Admiralty and to the General Post Office. About sixty naval agents were used on the mail-packets at the mid-century. Some of the home Lines, which were also under the Admiralty after 1837, had an agent aboard each vessel, including the Holyhead-Dublin service and that to the Channel Islands. An agent was particularly valuable on routes where the mail-ships had to stop at a succession of ports—on such complicated services as those of the Royal Mail in the West Indies and on the Lines east of Suez. Agents were aboard the mail vessels in the Mediterranean, on those along the east coast of South America, and even on the vessels of the Pacific Mail that went along the west coast of South America. The reports of the agents often furnish vivid accounts of the mail-carrying practices of a century ago.[1]

The Admiralty agents afloat were naval lieutenants retired on half pay, who welcomed the additional compensation for the duty on board. The life at sea was congenial, and the agents enjoyed the authority vested in them. They were required to be 'in all respects capable [physically] of proceeding to any port of the world to which you may be ordered'. One newly appointed agent received the following standard instructions from Captain Patey:

'You are to repair on board the packet *Poonah* at this port on the 20th inst. and proceed to Alexandria, thence overland to Suez where you will join the first contract mail-packet not having a naval agent, on the Suez and Calcutta Line, upon which Line you will continue to be employed until further notice . . . taking especial care that no time be lost by you in the receipt and delivery of the mails . . . You are personally to attend to this duty and examine the boxes, bags, etc., in detail with the lists, & make yourself acquainted with their addresses and dispose of them accordingly.

[1] Forty volumes of these manuscript letters, dated between 1855 and 1870, have been preserved in the Post Office Record Room. They include the letters forwarded from Southampton, where Charles Patey of the Royal Navy was the Superintendent, and also letters from the G.P.O. in London to Patey with instructions for the agents aboard the packets. The report of the Canning Committee (1853) gives the names of the agents at that time. Two-thirds of the fifty-eight agents were assigned to lines that used Southampton as a home port. The letters will be referred to as *Epp. Adm. Agts.*

'On arrival at the different ports, after having delivered the mails, you are to wait upon the British Admiral or Senior Naval Officer afloat . . . and present him a list of Her Majesty's ships and foreign vessels fallen in with, together with any information of importance or of public interest . . . You are to be very particular to insert the movements of all ships of war British and foreign in your journals. At the conclusion of each voyage the following documents are to be made up and immediately transmitted to me, abstract of journal in duplicate, return of voyage speed in duplicate, lists of mails received and delivered.'

The agent on board was to see that the correct speed and course were maintained, that the mails were properly housed under lock and key, that the vessel was not in danger from too large a cargo or from improper loading. He might remonstrate with the captain if he felt it necessary. This was usually done formally in writing instead of by a personal interview. Friction between the agent and the commander of a vessel was not infrequent. The agent was sensitive as to his status and often tried to make the most of his appointment. It was a welcome opportunity for those who might have failed, through circumstances or lack of ability, to rise very far in the Senior Service. The commander of the packet felt that his authority was weakened by the presence of the agent on board.

The naval agents had the final decision as to proceeding to sea or putting into harbour, or stopping to assist any vessel in distress. The agent was to have a first-class cabin with appropriate furniture, and to be victualled as a chief cabin passenger without charge 'for his passage or victualling'. His servant was to have accommodations suitable to his station. The agent was to be taken to and from shore 'in a suitable and seaworthy boat of not less than four oars . . . with effectual covering for the mail bags'. Thackeray in recounting his *Journey from Cornhill to Cairo* in 1844—he was on the P & O *Iberia*—wrote a diverting description of an agent landing the mail at a port of call. Lieutenant Bundy left the ship in full dress, 'a sabre clattering between his legs', wearing a cocked hat 'ornamented with a shining gold cord'. Although dressed fit to command a frigate, Lieutenant Bundy took the mails ashore 'in a little squat boat with royal standard aft and a man-of-war's pennant forward'.[1]

That the captains disliked the agents is evident; their petty

---

[1] For Thackeray's account of other experiences on this voyage, see above, p. 163n. The other quotations are from the P & O contract of January 1, 1853.

differences were often unduly magnified. The naval agent on the Royal Mail *Clyde* complained of the treatment he received on a voyage from St Thomas to the Spanish Main in 1859. When the *Clyde* was in the harbour of Kingston, Jamaica, he asked for a boat to pay an official visit to the American Commodore. The men assigned to the boat 'were not dressed in blue entirely . . . There was no uniformity in their dress, some had blue, others dirty jumper things . . . The indignity was too clear to pass unnoticed.' Agent Bushell on the *Seine* complained in 1865 that the Master at Arms came to his room at 11 p.m., and told him to put out his light 'and not to go to bed until it was done'. Bushell felt that this was an indignity 'to which officers of my rank are never subjected on one of Her Majesty's Ships of War'.[1]

AGENTS EAST OF SUEZ

We learn something of the conditions aboard the mail ships a century ago from the complaints of the agents as to the accommodations for themselves and their servants. When the agent on the P & O *Behar* in 1861 sought to improve his servant's quarters—'a very good man, a native, and in my service a long time'—the agent was told that his servant was provided with accommodation 'under the forecastle with the native crew and servants attached to the ship'. Another agent sought better treatment for his native servant who was described as an 'educated and consistent Christian'. The reply came that the place for his chest was under the forecastle 'where the other native servants sleep . . . I may mention', added the captain, 'that he has had a blanket given him for which he appears to be ungrateful.'[2]

Nor were the cabins that were assigned to the agents always satisfactory. The agent on the P & O *Northam* wrote back to Capt. Patey: 'The cabin set apart on board the *Northam* is so small that literally I cannot turn in it . . . and certainly the worst and smallest in the ship. It is a disgrace to the service that a Commander or any officer in the Royal Navy should be treated with such gross indignity.' Agent Webber had also complained some years earlier of the room he had on the *Northam:* 'In it I can neither read nor write nor sit.' Webber had to use the saloon table for writing his reports. It was only cleared at seven bells (10 a.m.) and at 'three bells the

---

[1] *Epp. Adm. Agts.*, May 25, 1859, April 27, 1865.
[2] ibid., May 30, 1861, December 12, 1863.

table cloth is laid for dinner and from that hour until ten the next morning I cannot put pen to paper'. To make writing almost impossible the saloon was full of noise, 'emanating from French creoles, negro servants and questionable children'. Another agent's room was immediately over the screw: the cabin 'is in a constant state of vibration at sea, and in harbour full of coal dust'. The agent on the *Victoria* of the E & A Line had a cabin without furniture, with 'a tube for ventilation from the engine room close to it'. It was not possible to use the room 'under full steam in the Tropics'. Another complained of his cabin, the one aft in the saloon 'where the vibration was so great that it was impossible to write'.[1]

The agents were also sensitive regarding their allowance of drink, and some seem to have over indulged. Chief cabin passengers on the P & O vessels were allowed daily a pint of port and one bottle of malt liquor. The agent on the *Jeddo* in 1862 reported from Suez that, in warm climates, he seldom touched any wine but claret. On asking for it, he was refused. Compelled to have recourse to port, 'I asked for a second glass of port and was told that the allowance had been consumed.' When information reached Southampton in 1862 that some of the agents drank so much as to interfere with their duties, inquiries were made of the other agents. One replied that he had heard of the 'insobriety of a naval agent on the Australian Line and another on the Calcutta Line'. He added: 'I have been repeatedly shocked to hear passengers, people on shore and officers of the Packet Company's vessels speak in the most derisive terms of some of my brother officers who have so tarnished our cloth over so large a sphere of ocean.' One agent, Reynolds by name, was forced home by his brother officers. Lieutenant Hamilton—'report speaks very strongly against him for the same fault'—was forced to resign. He even had to pay for his passage back to Southampton.[2]

The mails, mostly in metal-bound wooden boxes, were supposed to be stored in the mail room, the key of which was hung in the agent's cabin. As the vessels were seldom over 2,000 tons, there was frequent complaint as to the smallness of the mail rooms. This was especially true on the packets east of Suez, particularly on the route to Australia. Agent Webber reported that the *Northam*'s mail room would not hold more than a third of the 700 boxes of the Australian mail; the remaining 400 were on the 'orlop deck mixed with the

[1] ibid., May 4, 11, 1859, October 24, 1863, September 7, 1866, February 15, 1868. The vessels were not large according to modern standards: the *Behar* registered 1,603 tons; the *Northam* 1,330.

[2] ibid., September 8, November 28, December 6, 1862; March 13, 1863.

cargo, though the mail bags, parcels and Admiralty packages have been placed for further safety in the bullion room'.[1]

Complaints as to the mail space also included references as to their improper location. They were supposed to be convenient of access at ports *en route*, and easy to empty in case of disaster at sea. Thomas Goss complained that the *Madras*, off Sydney, had a mail room so far aft that it was difficult to stow away parcels coming 'on board at the later places we touch at'. He added that the rats up to Point de Galle very much injured some of the letters. To prevent this happening again, Goss recommended that the room be lined with zinc or lead. The various committees of inquiry also came to realize this inadequate housing. The Secretary of the P & O told a Committee in 1866: 'The space occupied by the mails is a very serious matter. What were originally mail rooms in the steamers are now not sufficient in size.' This was a decided understatement. An agent on the run between Suez and Colombo reported in the sixties that the 'mail rooms of none of these steamers are capable of holding one-third of the boxes'. Sometimes a mail room was put to other uses. An agent reported in 1869, on the outward voyage to China in July, that the *Travancore's* mail room was 'partially occupied by opium'.[2]

Sorting out the boxes at junction points and delivering the right ones at the various ports was slow at best. One way of hastening the delivery was by various markings of the boxes. Those holding letters were marked with the letter 'L' to distinguish them from boxes containing newspapers. The boxes with letters were always to be landed first. Often, however, they were not well marked. We learn from a report of 1863 that 'those from New Zealand are often most carelessly marked . . . hastily stamped with the Post Office seal, which stamps are frequently broken and the inscription illegible . . . It is often impossible to tell them, particularly when they are transferred at Galle by night . . . and the time bills are the only guide by which the necessary lists can be made out.' An agent complained in the same year (1863) that the labels—this was at Chagres—were of thin parchment, some half torn off 'and the remainder much defaced by cockroaches'. Metal labels were suggested.

There was complaint at this time because of confusion and delays

---

[1] ibid., April 28, July 27, 1859; April, 3, 1860.
[2] ibid., April 30, 1860, January 20, 1865; November 3, 1869; *Rep. S.C. on East India Communication* (1866), 66.

in the delivery of mail boxes to the Australian colonies and to the naval squadron in the south Pacific. Frederic Hill wrote from London in 1857 that the boxes for the south Pacific would be more clearly marked. They were to be distinguished by stripes; the 'stripes on each box shall vary in colour', according to the colony to which each was sent. Those for Geelong (near Melbourne) and for Queensland (still a part of New South Wales) were to be further distinguished from those for Melbourne and Sydney respectively: 'The stripes in each case might be of the same colour, but in the case of Geelong and Queensland there should be two stripes instead of one.' The colours were not named, though we learn that the mail boxes for Mauritius were marked with green stripes. Mail for the squadron in Australian waters was also sent in boxes distinct from those for the colonies 'as is the case for China'.[1]

The postmasters on duty east of Suez make reference to moveable letter boxes aboard the ships. The postmaster at Calcutta in 1861 reported that 'the Moveable Letter Box placed on board . . . between Suez and this Port has been unlocked and in no way secured except by a piece of tape tied around and sealed . . . On the passage from Madras to this Port, the above mentioned box was broken open and I have failed to find by whom done.' In 1864 the authorities in London received a complaint from the Chamber of Commerce in Singapore that 'the agents of late have refused to allow the posting of letters . . . in the moveable boxes on board, on the ground that they were intended for the passengers'. Frederic Hill replied that there was no objection to their general use. The naval agents were put right as to the purpose of the boxes: 'In placing moveable boxes on board the China mail-packets, it was not his Lordship's intention to restrict their use to passengers . . . There is no objection to letters being placed in boxes by the public at Singapore up to the time of the packet's departure.'

Moveable maritime letter boxes had been used in the cross-Channel boats since 1843. According to a convention with France they were 'to afford the inhabitants of the ports of the two countries every facility for the dispatch of letters'. The moveable letter box was also in use on the French and British packets in the Mediterranean, and they were issued for packets east of Suez in 1858. The boxes were taken to the postmaster at each port of call, to be opened

---

[1] ibid., October 10, 1860; April 17, 1861; March 18, August 10, September 24, 1863; May 30, 1864; *Letter* of Frederic Hill to the P.M.G. of New Zealand of October 6, 1857.

and empties. The naval agents were instructed 'to see that the boxes are properly locked and brought on board the packet to which you are attached before the departure from each place'. West of Egypt a stamp indicating date and place of arrival was put on by the postmaster. The letters 'M.B.' (B.M. *bôite mobile* where the port of arrival was French) indicated the use of the box. Letters so stamped are rare even for Malta, and they do not seem to have been issued for use east of Suez.[1]

Many of the reports give the various causes for the failure of the packets to meet the contract schedule. The marine engines of that day were often found unequal to the work, especially on the long Australian run. The round trip between Sydney and Suez, nearly 17,000 miles, was 'too great for a steamer to perform without repairs'. The *Emeu* on a voyage from Australia to Suez in 1859 broke down near Mauritius. As only one engine was working on this paddler, she was 'all the time going round and round outside [the harbour], fearing to stop in case the single engine should happen not to go over the centre'. The *Granada*, another paddle-wheel steamer of only 560 tons, proceeded to Aden with the *Emeu*'s mails; they must have taxed the *Granada*'s hold, for this mail was made up of 375 boxes and bags, and weighed 50 tons. When the *Alma*, a 2,000-ton screw-driven steamer, grounded between Suez and Aden in 1859, the mail had to be hastily removed. The agent reported: 'The time bills, my Journal and the list of the mails are all under water in the cabin but myself have seen the mails passed from the mail room into the boats and landed . . . I feel confident nothing is missing'. The *Bengal* broke down in the same year on the way from Aden to Point de Galle when the cogs on the driving wheel were 'suddenly carried away'. The screw could not be disconnected, because of the 'great quantity of water coming through the after flange'. The packet finally limped into port under sail.[2]

The agents often reported the use of slow vessels. An agent on the Bombay Line to Hong Kong wrote in 1859 that the *Malabar* had exceeded the contract time by over four days: 'I do not consider her to be a safe vessel in heavy weather from her deep and sudden plunging in a seaway.' He gave notice that another vessel must be

---

[1] ibid., November 4, 1861; March 1, 1864; April 29, 1867. See also O. G. Bowlby, 'Maritime Moveable Boxes' in the *Philatelist and Postal Historian* (London), XVI, 40ff. and 75ff. (1949); A. W. Robertson, op. cit., D35-38.

[2] *Epp. Adm. Agts.*, April 15, June 10, 28, 1859. In the early steamers various devices were tried to free the vessel from the 'drag' of the screw when the ship was using sail; feathering the screw, and raising it out of the water on a jointed shaft were two of the ways.

provided for the return journey. His forebodings were only too well founded. In 1869 the *Malabar* was wrecked near Point de Galle when one of her passengers was Lord Elgin. The agent wrote: 'Owing to the suddenness of the wreck, the great bulk of His Lordship's luggage, papers, etc., have been lost'. The *Ripon* was found next year to be unequal to the required speed of 10 knots. In 1862 the *China* was reported as 'totally incompetent'. She had taken the place of the *Jeddo* 'in order to accommodate a larger number of passengers'. One of the worst cases was the overloading of the *Nemesis* at Suez in 1860. In addition to a full passenger list, the Captain took on, at the last moment, 180 French soldiers bound for China. No wonder the *Nemesis* lay 'so low in the water that the ports on the weather side must remain closed'. In that trip down the Red Sea several passengers died from the oppressive heat, and the mails were delayed. On another occasion, the P & O steamer *Columbian* remained a day and a half beyond contract time at Suez waiting for its general cargo, although the mails were on board. The Admiralty agent finally wrote to the Captain 'to proceed to sea immediately and he did so'.[1]

The Australian service was irregular, not only because of occasional breakdowns, but on account of the large amount of coal needed by the engines of a century ago. The *Northam* was reported in 1859 as hardly able to go from Mauritius to the first Australian port—King George's Sound—because of 'insufficient bunker space'. The fuel required for the long voyage was taken on, usually at Aden. The *Columbian*, also in the year 1859, was at Aden over thirty-eight hours taking on 850 tons of coal. The *Geelong*, a screw-driven steamer of but 1,800 tons, left Galle for Australia in April 1857 with 436 tons of coal in the bunkers, 238 tons in the main hold and 176 tons in the after hold. The agent thought it worthy of notice that 'no coals have ever been placed on deck'. This was unusual. The Secretary of the P & O Line, replying to a criticism that coals were commonly put on deck for the long Australian run, wrote that coal was sometimes put in bags on deck for about two days' use only, and was always used first. Frederic Hill at the G.P.O. retorted that so recently as December last (1865) the *Bombay* left Galle for Sydney with five days' coal supply on her upper deck. The naval agent aboard the *Bombay* in reporting this, observed that 'if the vessel got into a cyclone, the power of man

[1] ibid., June 10, October 29, December 26, 1859; September 5, 1860; May 29, 1862.

could not save her'. This long run caused so much concern in 1862 that Frederic Hill forbade the use of any P & O vessels for the Australian service until they had been surveyed at Southampton.[1]

THE ROYAL WEST INDIAN MAIL

The service to the West Indies also had its shortcomings. The long transatlantic runs between Southampton and St Thomas, and between Southampton and Brazil, were a strain on the steamship engines of a century ago. From St Thomas various branches served the other islands, the mainland of South and Central America, and even the Mexican port of Vera Cruz. The most important run ended at Colon (Chagres), the terminal of the recently completed railway. The mails that were carried across the Isthmus to Panama on the Pacific might go south on the British Pacific Steam Navigation Company's ships, or north on the American Pacific Steam Line to California, or in the late sixties, to New Zealand and Australia on the short-lived Colonial Line.

Unlike the P & O, the West Indian Line was never troubled by the great size of the mails. The chief difficulty was the proper co-ordination of its many branches, and also keeping to time in a region subject to difficult weather conditions. The route from St Thomas to Colon was the most important in the Caribbean, but it appears to have been not uncommon for the mail connections at the Isthmus to be missed or delayed. The *Clyde* left St Thomas on a Thursday in 1859 and hastened to Colon so as to arrive before Sunday, 'a day on which the Panama Railway Company will not at all times run a train, not even for our mails'. In 1865 the *Solent* reached Colon twenty-seven hours late, landing the mails one hour after the train had left for that day. This meant, of course, a delay for the departure of the Pacific mails from Panama. In 1862 the packet agent at Colon was warned to have the mails ready at the stated time for the packet departing for St Thomas. The agent, a Mr Cowan, was told that the recent delay was not the first one, and that he would henceforth be held 'wholly responsible'. Two years later the *Tyne* left Colon without the mails from the south Pacific,

---

[1] ibid., June 10, November 8, 1859; April 24, 1860; March 25, 1866; April 7, 1867. The difficulties of this route were so well known as early as 1851 that, when bids were asked for, the P & O was unwilling to accept 'the killing penalties of running to time'. The E & A took the contract instead, and failed miserably. See above, p. 196.

though we do not know whether Mr Cowan was to blame. The mails that did not catch the *Tyne* left later on an American packet bound for New York whence the Cunard Line carried them to England. Frederic Hill at the G.P.O. wrote the Superintendent of Packets at Southampton that these mails from the Pacific, 'as it happened reached this country on the same day on which they would have arrived by way of St Thomas'.[1]

The need for an efficient service from the Isthmus was partly because of the 'treasure' that came to Panama from the west coasts of the two Americas. On one occasion the *Medway* was held up for twenty-four hours waiting for specie valued at $2,000,000. The agent stationed at Colon had asked the Admiralty agent on the *Medway* to permit the delay. The latter was agreeable, since the 'present threatening aspect of affairs in Europe' required the delivery of this large amount of treasure without delay.[2]

The reports contain much criticism of the inadequate vessels of the Royal Mail. The agent on board the *Eider* asserted in 1865 that she was not fit even for branch lines in the West Indies. On one occasion the *Eider* started from Colon for St Thomas twelve hours before schedule, and even so was late in arriving. The agent reported: 'She is so crank that she cannot carry sail without burying the lee paddle wheel so deeply that the vessel's speed is affected.' The *Trent* was reported in 1860 as making a day's run of but 119 miles on 33 tons of coal.

Occasionally the ships of the Royal Mail were put to non-postal uses by the Admiralty. In 1862 the British consul at Havana required the *Thames* to transport supplies to Mexico for the British Division of the occupying Allied Forces. The supplies consisted of 82 mules and their harness, 270 bales of hay and 5 tons of Indian corn.[3]

The American Civil War (1861-5) had a direct effect on the region served by the Royal Mail. The 'Trent Affair' of November 1861 appeared likely to endanger the peaceful relations between Great Britain and the United States.

Captain Charles Wilkes of the American war vessel *San Jacinto* was cruising in West Indian waters when he heard that Messrs Mason and Slidell—two representatives of the Southern Confeder-

[1] ibid., May 14, 1859; November 9, 1862; March 4, 1864; June 20, 1865.
[2] ibid., May 23, 1859.
[3] ibid., February 14, 1860; March 24, 1862; July 8, 1867. In 1867 the Admiralty agent wrote from Vera Cruz that the Emperor Maximillian [sic] had been shot on June 18th.

acy on their way to Europe—had reached Havana and were about to embark on the Royal Mail steamer *Trent*. Captain Wilkes decided to intercept them. He was a bold, even headstrong, naval officer of long experience.[1]

The *San Jacinto* took up a position in the Bahama Channel to wait for the *Trent*. On November 8, 1861 the *Trent* was halted by a shot 'immediately across our bows', according to the report of the naval agent, Richard Williams. The *Trent* had left Havana the day before with the mails, a large amount of specie, as well as numerous passengers. The executive officer of the *San Jacinto* boarded the *Trent* in order to obtain the two Southerners, their luggage and any dispatches found 'in possession of those on board the steamer'. The boarding officer was instructed by Captain Wilkes to do his duty 'with all the delicacy and kindness possible'.[2]

Although this incident is one of the best known in the American Civil War, it may be worth while to observe the part played in it by the naval agent, Richard Williams. He reported that the boarding officer asked Captain Moir for a list of the passengers. It was refused. Thereupon the Admiralty agent supported the Captain of the *Trent* by formally protesting the boarding of the mail steamer: 'Sir, on board this ship I am the representative of Her British Majesty's Government . . . and in distinct language I denounce this as an illegal act, an act in violation of international law, an act indeed of Piracy.' When the boarding officer, Lieutenant Fairfax, beckoned to the *San Jacinto* for a further force, the two Southerners came forward voluntarily. Nothing could be done to prevent the seizure of the two men as the *San Jacinto*, according to the report of Williams, was 'on our port bow about 200 yards off, the Ship's Crew at Quarters, the Ports open and the Tompions out'. The agent's report concludes: 'Sufficient time being given for such necessaries in the shape of clothing which they might require . . . these Gentlemen were forcibly taken out of the ship . . . At 8.40 p.m. we parted company and proceeded on our way to St

---

[1] Charles Wilkes joined the American Navy in 1818, three years after the end of the war that had been caused, in part, by the British claim that they had the right to search a neutral vessel. In 1830 Wilkes was put in charge of the division of instruments and charts of the U.S. Navy, and eight years later headed a large surveying expedition to the Antarctic, in which they discovered the Antarctic Continent. The part discovered by the expedition still bears the name Wilkes Land.

[2] ibid., November 9, 1861 for the Admiralty agent's report. T. L. Harris, *The Trent Affair* (Indianapolic, Ind., 1896) goes into the incident at length. A better balanced account of the incident and the diplomatic aftermath is furnished by E. D. Adama, *Great Britain and the American Civil War* (1925), ch. VII.

Thomas.' On the agent's arrival at St Thomas, a copy of his report was forwarded to Sir Alexander Milne.[1]

News of the stopping of the *Trent* created a tremendous furor in Great Britain when the *Trent* reached England at the end of November. Richard Williams was lionized, and appears to have greatly exaggerated the affair. He was reported to have embroidered his account at a dinner in December by saying that American marines rushed at Miss Slidell with fixed bayonets, and that he, Williams, had just time 'to put my body in between'. Anti-Union sentiment was so aroused that the British Ambassador in Washington was instructed to give the United States seven days in which to free the two Southern commissioners. Troops were embarked for Canada as a precaution. Two of the transports that carried them were the Royal Mail's *Magdalena* and *Parana*. Another transport was the *Adriatic*, an American built side-wheeler, formerly of the Collins Line, but under British ownership at this time. On her paddle-boxes the Stars and Stripes were still emblazoned.

An observer of the effects of the incident in America was Anthony Trollope. He was then in the United States on post-office business and in addition, seeking information for a work published in the next year under the title *North America*. Trollope had crossed the Atlantic in August 1861 on the Cunarder *Arabia*, via Halifax to Boston. When he reached Washington late in the autumn, William Seward, the American Secretary of State, was about to reply to the British demand. In fact, Mr Trollope was dining with Secretary Seward on the day the decision was made to release the two Confederate envoys. Trollope had feared there might be war. 'I was preparing myself for a quick return to England,' he wrote, and added: 'Our grievance was that our mail-packet was stopped while doing its ordinary beneficient work . . . and our mail-packets were not to be stopped with impunity.' The released envoys continued their journey to Europe in January, embarking at St Thomas on a mail-packet for Southampton. The voyage was resumed after an eight weeks' interruption.[2]

---

[1] No physical force was needed to remove the Confederate agents. They hoped that their seizure would advance the Southern cause in Great Britain and on the European Continent. After Mason and Slidell were taken aboard the *San Jacinto* they were treated almost as guests, even eating at the Captain's table.

[2] Trollope's *Autobiography* (1950), 163-6; and his *North America* (1862), II, ch. 11. Trollope mistakenly refers to Wilkes as a commodore. The Royal Mail was later used by a much-sought Confederate, General John C. Breckenridge, who had been Secretary of War. After the war was over, he managed to escape to Havana where he took passage on the Royal Mail's *Shannon*. See A. J. Hanna, *Flight into Oblivion* (Richmond, Va., 1938), 232.

One other American 'piratical' act was recorded by another British mail agent. In 1864 the American sloop of war *Wachusett* seized the Confederate commerce destroyer *Florida* in a Brazilian harbour. Captain Napoleon Collins of the *Wachusett* attacked the *Florida* at night when most of her crew and officers were ashore, towed her out of the neutral harbour of Bahia, and sent her to the United States. The Admiralty agent on board the *Magdalena*, on the Brazilian mail route at the time, gave a vivid report of the capture. It was based on information from Captain Morris of the *Florida* and his purser: 'These officers are now on board this ship, taking passage to Southampton.' The report indicated that there was great excitement and indignation in Bahia: 'It is supposed that the Chamber of Commerce of New York has offered a reward of $500,000 for the capture of the *Florida*.'[1]

The naval agent's role when a vessel was in distress is illustrated by the wreck of the *Duncan Dunbar* a year later. In October 1865 this sailing ship, outward bound for Sydney, was wrecked on the Rocas Reefs, some 200 miles from Pernambuco, and well off the Brazilian coast. The crew and passengers, 117 in number, were transferred to a narrow spit of sand, with supplies of food for several days. The Captain thereupon rigged one of his boats and went to Pernambuco to seek assistance. There he found the Royal Mail packet *Oneida*, about to leave for Southampton. On his asking for help, the naval agent aboard the *Oneida* gave his cordial consent for this deviation from its course. Those marooned on the sand spit had waited for ten days before they boarded the *Oneida*. They reached Southampton in November, nine weeks after the *Duncan Dunbar* had left for Australia.[2]

The *Trent* proved to be so inefficient as a mail carrier that she was withdrawn in 1865—'no longer to be employed in the contract mail service'. The Royal Mail, in fact, had been using old ships too long in an area where it was not easy at best to keep up to schedule. Hurricanes, earthquakes and yellow fever almost stopped the West Indian service in 1867. When yellow fever broke out in Jamaica, the packets bound for Colon ceased to stop at Kingston, and when yellow fever hit St Thomas as well and an earthquake shook the island in addition, the services were about at a standstill. To make the Royal Mail's plight still worse, the *Rhone* and the *Wye* were lost

[1] *Epp. Adm. Agts.*, October 16, 1864. The *Florida* had destroyed over fifty American merchantmen. The American Secretary of State apologized for the 'unauthorized' act.

[2] Bushell, op. cit., 112-114, 257. The *Oneida*, formerly of the E & A Line to Australia, had been taken over by the Royal Mail in 1858.

in the hurricane of October 1867. All this we learn from the reports of the naval agents. They must have found service in the Caribbean as trying as did the agents who travelled on the mail-ships east of Suez.[1]

The Admiralty agents, whose reports have been used to reveal the mail-carrying conditions a century ago, were continued on some lines for a time after the Post Office resumed control of the packet services in 1860. They were withdrawn first from the Calcutta Line where the mails were 'entrusted to the care of the Commander as was done for some years without inconvenience on board the Cunard packets'. The mail contracts after 1860 regularly contained a paragraph headed, 'Masters to take charge of the mails if required.'

In 1853, Captain Patey, the Superintendent at Southampton, wrote to London suggesting changes in the handling of reports. He proposed that much time and expense could be saved if his agency at Southampton was transferred to London, and the naval offices were discontinued at the 'outstations' of Dover, Holyhead and Liverpool. By 1870 the reports regarding the services at sea were sent directly to the Controller of the Packet Services in London.[2]

SORTING AT SEA

Even before 1860 the Post Office put marine sorters on board some lines where, of course, they would replace the naval agents. Sorting on sea routes was but an extension to ships of a practice used for many years on the main railways of Great Britain. The Irish mails between Holyhead and Dublin were sorted by 1860 on board the mail-packets as well as on the trains to and from Holyhead.

Outside the British Isles, ship sorting was first tried on the homeward-bound packets between Alexandria and Southampton, where it was regarded as 'very satisfactory'. Later it was put to use on the outward voyages between Suez and India. In 1868 the Post Office introduced sorting on the outward voyages of the P & O to Hong Kong. Marine sorters of the Hong Kong Post Office came aboard the mail-packets at Singapore to sort on the voyage up the China

---

[1] *Epp. Adm. Agts.*, June 20, 1863; March 31, May 31, June 30, November 23, 1867; January 11, 1868. For a full account of this disaster, see Bushell, op. cit., 118-22.

[2] *Epp. Adm. Agts.*, September 5, 1860; December 30, 1863 (for Captain Patey's letter). In this letter he wrote that the contract packets at the time numbered 141, and that they received subsidies of nearly 1,000,000 sterling per annum.

Sea. On the arrival of the P & O mail ship at Hong Kong, the letters going on the packet could be immediately transferred to a sorter who had them in charge on the voyage to Shanghai. The use of marine sorters on this route was so satisfactory that it continued for many years.

When sorters were proposed for the Cunard liners, to sort mail on the return trips from America, Samuel Cunard objected. It might do in the Mediterranean, he wrote, or in a mild climate, but 'our ships have no spare decks, and the mails which are in large bags are locked up in the mail room under hatches . . . We frequently make a passage when it would be impossible to open the hatches on any day without great risk from shipping at sea.' The Postmaster-General replied that a room could easily be furnished that would not require the opening of the hatches, and that, in any case, the sorting would be done only on the homeward voyages. As so often happened, the Treasury sided with Mr Cunard.[1]

The attempt to use sorters on the ships of the Royal Mail Line was a disastrous experiment. It was proposed in 1867 for the homeward-bound packets leaving St Thomas. By this plan the mails would be bagged for their various land routes by the time the liner touched at Plymouth to disembark the mails. The work on shipboard was to be performed by a postal officer and his assistant. Unfortunately for the first two men chosen, this experiment began just as yellow fever was raging in St Thomas. When the two sorters died at sea the plan was suspended. After another short trial, it was abandoned. Sorting on the railway between Plymouth and Bristol was found quite adequate for the West Indian mails.[2]

Such were some of the practices in use on the packets in the sixties of the last century.

[1] 4th Rep. P.M.G. (1858), 21; 7th Rep. (1861), 7; Parl. Ret. 84/1859, 2nd sess.; Epp. Adm Agts., January 18, 1868. And see article by Colonel Webb and J. D. Riddell in the Philatelist and Postal Historian, XXXVI, 252ff., where the marine sorter hand-stamps of the Hong Kong Post Office are shown.

[2] Epp. Adm. Agts., April 24, August 15, October 31, 1867; April 30, 1868; April 6, 1869.

H*

20

THE CARRIAGE OF OCEAN MAIL—
1860-85

THE year 1860 marks the beginning of a new stage in the handling
of the mails sent overseas. For more than three decades the packet
services had been under the direct control of the Admiralty. Steam
had taken the place of sail during that time. The general adoption
of the screw propeller was causing the disappearance of the paddle
wheel on the high seas, and sails as well ceased to be an essential
part of the equipment for an ocean liner. After 1860 the advances in
mail carrying under Post Office control were so remarkable that the
earlier decades soon seemed remote.

A brief survey of the services as of 1860 will enable us to ap-
preciate the changes that were at hand. Although the home services
were carried on at a small expense, the routes overseas continued to
be a heavy financial burden, with one exception. The cross-Channel
services out of Dover more than paid for themselves. The packets
went to Ostend three days a week, and to Calais daily except
Sunday. The mails via France had become very important, particularly on account of the heavy Indian and Australian mails that
came very largely by the overland route. So important were they
that the Dover contractor had to provide special packet-boats for
the mails from the East that came to Calais, in case they arrived in
Calais at times that did not fit the regular schedule.

In 1860 the P & O had a monopoly of the Mediterranean services
and the mail lines beyond Suez to India, Hong Kong and Australia.
The original route to the Iberian Peninsula was to be discontinued
in 1862 when the railway connection through France made mail-
packets unnecessary. In 1869 the P & O received subsidies that
amounted to over £400,000 a year.

The Cunard Company held the British contract for the North
American mails. A weekly service alternated between New York,
and a route that still went to Boston by way of Halifax. The Cunard

234

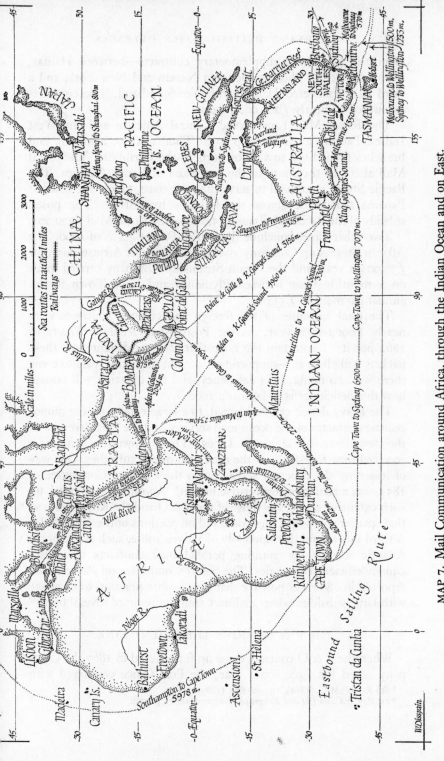

MAP 7. Mail Communication around Africa, through the Indian Ocean and on East.

Company had three supplementary contracts—between Halifax, Bermuda and St Thomas; between Nassau and New York, and a third that connected Halifax with Newfoundland. The contracts amounted to nearly £200,000 a year.

The Royal Mail Line served Central America and the West Indies. Packets made the trip to St Thomas twice a month, and branches fanned out to various ports in the Caribbean. The Royal Mail also had the route to the east coast of South America. The Pacific Steam continued to serve the west coast, taking the mails at Panama that came across the Isthmus by railway. The postal subsidy of the Pacific Mail was £25,000, of the Royal Mail £270,000.

Two other Lines conclude the British Packet list as of 1860. The African Steamship Company visited various West African ports for £30,000 a year, and the Union Steamship Company carried mails on a monthly basis between Plymouth and Cape Town for an annual payment of £33,000.

The total subsidies of the foreign and colonial contracts were nearly £990,000 a year. As the Postmaster-General's *Report* of 1862 put it: 'I entertain the hope that at some distant time these packets will all be self-supporting . . . but for many years to come there will, no doubt, be a deficiency, and the question will remain how this deficiency is to be made good.'[1]

The heavy deficit can be blamed, to a large extent, on the monopolistic character of the ocean mail services and the great strength of the few favoured shipping Lines. Three powerful companies received over four-fifths of the total paid out in subsidies. One way of lessening the expense, according to the Canning Committee of 1853, was a return to competitive bidding. Another was to break up such extensive services as those of the P & O and the Royal Mail, so that smaller shipping Lines could bid on portions of these networks. A third was to end the monopoly of a given route, such as the north Atlantic seaway, by granting parallel mail contracts to several equally efficient companies. The Select Committee on Packets that reported in 1860 was positive that it was quite practical to dispense with large subsidies where ordinary traffic supported several lines.'[2]

THE P & O VERSUS THE ORIENT LINE

When the P & O contract came up for renewal in 1867 the Company asked for £500,000 a year; the Post Office countered with

[1] *8th Rep. P.M.G.* (1862), 19; *9th Rep.* (1863), 17-22.
[2] *1st Rep. S.C. on Pkt and Telegraph Contracts* (1860), p. xvii.

£400,000, to be increased, if necessary to give the Company a
6 per cent profit. In 1870 this sliding scale was removed by setting
the subsidy at £450,000. When the contract was up for renewal in
1874, the Company asked that the mails be allowed to go through
the Canal, which had been in use for five years. The Post Office was
opposed, and with good reason, as the Canal route was much slower
than the crossing by railway. The Post Office, however, finally
permitted the 'slow' mails, coming all the way to Egypt by water
from Southampton, to use the Canal. A lowering of the subsidy to
£430,000 accompanied the partial use of the Canal. The P & O
complained that it had been 'hardly dealt with' in this new contract.
It denied the view of 'doctrinaires' that a 'mail service should be
measured merely by the postage it earns, instead of by its commercial and political importance'.[1]

When the contract again expired at the end of the seventies, the
Post Office returned to competitive bidding, in the hope of lowering
the subsidy still further. Of the four bids received, only two offered
a complete service to India and the Far East, the P & O and the
Ocean Steam Ship Company of Alfred Holt. This Holt Line of
Liverpool had pioneered in producing effective cargo carriers,
screw-driven iron steamers with vastly improved engines. In 1874
the various Liverpool shipping Lines had petitioned Parliament
against the renewal of the P & O contract, but without success. The
bid made by Alfred Holt's Line in 1879—for the service to India
and China—was £338,000, over £30,000 less than that of the P & O.
The Post Office would have accepted the lower bid, but the influence
of the India and Colonial Offices decided the Treasury to stay with
the P & O Line. It was not so much a question as to the size of the
bid, as a preference for the P & O Company—'old friends who had
faithfully performed their contract for a lifetime'. At least the
contract had been lowered by some £60,000.[2]

The contract of 1879 brought several changes. All the mail now
went by way of France and Italy, via the Italian port of Brindisi, and
across Egypt by railway. The Line to Calcutta was discontinued at
this time, all Indian mail using the port of Bombay on the west
coast, as it now had railway connections with the east coast. The
service was weekly to Bombay and fortnightly to Shanghai by way

[1] *34th Annual Rep.* of the P & O (1874); Cable, op. cit., 164-5; *Orient Pamphlet*, 10-11.
The blow could not have been very serious, as a 7 per cent dividend was declared for
the year ending in September 1874.

[2] Contract of February 7, 1879; *Tr. Min.*, February 12, 1879. This contract did not
include the Australian branch, now in colonial hands. For Holt's Line, see F. E. Hyde,
Blue Funnel, A History (1956), 25-27, 37.

of Ceylon, Singapore and Hong Kong. Point de Galle in Ceylon,
which had long been the port of call, was replaced by Colombo. A
drastic change was made by the P & O at home when the terminus
of the Line was moved in 1880 from Southampton to London. This
was done, partly to meet the competition for cargo, and partly to
avoid the cost of rail carriage between London and Southampton,
and the possible damage to shipments that went by rail and had to
be transhipped at the port.

Something akin to victory from the viewpoint of the Post Office
came when the P & O contract was renewed in 1888. By this agreement the Suez Canal was at last put to use for all the mail through
Egypt. Night travel through the Canal was now possible by the use
of electric headlights. They were first used in 1886 when a vessel of
the P & O had the distinction of being 'the first steamer with an
electric apparatus for the purpose of navigating the Canal at night
time'. The subsidy by this contract was lowered substantially from
£360,000 to £265,000, and yet an improved service was provided. The
rate of speed between Brindisi and Bombay was to be 12½ knots.[1]

Another way of cutting down packet expense was to arrange with
the colonies to share the cost of their mails overseas. Even before
1860 the Indian Government was required to pay half the net loss
on its routes, including the Line that went east to Hong Kong.
This was justified on the ground that both India and Great Britain
profited equally from the services. From the viewpoint of India this
was certainly a debatable point. In 1878, for example, India contributed £107,000 towards the deficit on the P & O contract. When
all mail for Great Britain was dispatched from Bombay, the Indian
Government obtained relief from paying towards the costs of the
Line to the Far East, but the colonies of Ceylon, Singapore and
Hong Kong still shared the deficit.[2]

As early as 1855 the Australian colonies had been approached on
the matter of sharing the costs. They were not unwilling as the gold
rush had brought great prosperity. Beginning with the year 1875,
the British Post Office carried the mails at its own expense a part of
the way—to three 'junction' points, whence they continued under
colonial contracts. These 'junctions' were Singapore for a Queensland Line via Torres Strait, San Francisco for the Pacific Mail Line
to New Zealand and New South Wales, and Ceylon for the P & O
service to the southern Australian colonies. The decision to give the

---

[1] Contract of March 18, 1887; *33rd Rep.* (1887), 4; *P.O. Records* 11N/1887.
[2] *6th Rep. P.M.G.* (1860), 55; *9th Rep.* (1862), 17-19; *24th Rep.* (1878), 34-35;
Parl. Ret., 405/1867.

colonies the responsibility for the services from Ceylon came just as there was growing ill feeling between Sydney and Melbourne, especially as Victoria, of which Melbourne was the capital, was by that time more important postally to the British Post Office because of its larger mails. And the colony of Victoria, had emphasized its superiority by making a contract secretly with the P & O in 1874.

One outcome of the colonial rivalry was the use of the Pacific for mails of the colony of New South Wales; another result was the contract by New South Wales with a Line that would carry mails to Great Britain by going west. The new rival of the P & O was the Orient Steam Navigation Company. It had been founded by James Anderson, who had come up to London from Aberdeenshire. His ships at first were sailing clippers. When the Company changed to steam in 1877, it first tried out ships chartered from the Pacific Steam Navigation Company, bearing such names as *Lusitania*, *Chimborazo* and *Cuzco*. The vessels were later purchased when several shipping firms combined to back the new steam Line to Australia. The first vessel, the *Lusitania*, reached Australia by way of the Cape of Good Hope in a few hours over forty days. In October 1879 the *Cuzco* made the fastest passage on record, in 37 days and 10 hours, considerably better than the average time for the mails by the P & O—51 days out and 48 home. The Orient Line, which soon abandoned the Cape route in favour of the Suez Canal, provided a regular service every four weeks.

The Orient Company presented a heaven-sent opportunity to New South Wales, with the result that the colony made a contract with the Line in 1883, by which the cost was based on the size of the mails; letters were carried at the rate of 12s a lb. In order to save time, New South Wales sent the mails to Melbourne by railway, to be taken aboard the Orient liner that had previously left Sydney with passengers and freight. The Line agreed to land the mails at Plymouth thirty-nine days later. The services were so arranged as to alternate with the P & O, giving Australia a competitive fortnightly service by way of Egypt. The foolish and rather petty rivalry between Sydney and Melbourne, along with the competition of two shipping Lines, had greatly improved the Australian mail service.[1]

[1] The *Orient Pamphlet*, already cited, was published in 1879 to press its effort to get a postal contract. See *Votes and Proceedings* (N.S.W.), 1878-9, V, 867; 1868, IV, 1034; 1883-4, IX, 553. When the Orient Line debarked the mail in the Mediterranean to cross overland to Calais, it used the port of Naples. The railway between Sydney and Melbourne had been joined at the border in 1878, the gauge in N.S.W. *not* agreeing, of course, with that in Victoria.

ATLANTIC ROUTES

In the meantime, interesting changes were taking place on the Atlantic. In 1860 the South African colonies were receiving mails via the Union Steam Ship Company's vessels at the rate of £33,000 a year; ten years later it was lowered to £20,000. A decisive change came in 1872 when the Union Company attempted to obtain a long renewal of its contract on terms that would give more effective competition with Donald Currie's Castle ships. The scheme failed, and in 1878 the self-governing Cape Colony took over the control of its mail services. Parallel contracts with the Union Line and Donald Currie gave an alterating weekly service. Competition had brought lower rates of postage and a greatly improved connection with England.

The colony renewed contracts with the two lines for the rest of the century, every contract containing a clause forbidding the combination of the two shipping lines. In 1883, payment on the basis of postage was replaced by fixed subsidies at £25,000 a year for each Line. When the Castle Line changed its home port in 1891 from Dartmouth to Southampton, it was preliminary to another change—the combining of the two Lines in the last year of the century. The mail service was henceforth performed by the Union-Castle Mail Steamship Company.[1]

The West Indian mails had been carried at a heavy loss ever since the Royal Mail was founded; in 1860 the subsidy amounted to £240,000 a year, much more than twice the sea-postage earned on this mail route. Yet this contract had been renewed for eleven years in 1858. This inheritance from the Admiralty was so expensive that the Post Office advertised for tenders as the contract neared its end, hoping that competition might lessen this 'heavy drain upon the public purse'. Among the several tenders, the only possible substitute was the Liverpool and West Indian Steamship Company of Alfred Holt. He offered, in 1862, to give a monthly service for the postage, or a fortnightly one if the postage was not less than £24,000 annually. Holt concluded his offer by observing that the 'system of subsidies' prevented the extension of steam navigation.[2]

The outcome of the competitive bidding was a continuance of the

---

[1] Murray, op. cit., 75, 109, etc. The contracts of 1893 were the first that did not include the clause forbidding combination.

[2] *21st Rep. P.M.G.* (1875), 11; *Parl. Ret.* 408/1863. In 1864, Alfred Holt transferred his shipping interests to the Far East, as we have already learned. See above, p. 237.

Royal Mail contract at a reduced cost. The Royal Mail agreed to accept an annual payment of £172,914, a large reduction even if it still far exceeded the postage. Mails were carried fortnightly between Southampton and St Thomas in just over fourteen days, and reached the Isthmus of Panama in twenty-one days. In order to cut down the deficit, the Post Office decided to have the West Indian colonies share half the cost, a practice already in use east of Suez. Although it may have been reasonable to expect mature self-governing colonies like those in the south Pacific to share the postal deficits on ocean mail, one may well question the application of the principle to the undeveloped colonies, politically speaking, in the West Indies.[1]

The Post Office again renewed the Royal Mail contract in 1869 at the same figure, partly because of the 'unparalleled losses' suffered by the Company in the West Indian hurricane of two years earlier. This extension also included the service of the Royal Mail between Southampton and the east coast of South America. Hitherto, the main-line packets on that route had stopped at Rio de Janeiro, where mail and passengers had to be transferred to another vessel for Montevideo and Buenos Aires. In 1869 the mail-packet that left Southampton began going the whole way to Argentina. A somewhat similar change occurred on the West Indian route when the Royal Mail made Colon, not St Thomas, the terminus of the transatlantic liners.[2]

When the Royal Mail contract came up for renewal in the mid-seventies it was at last brought somewhat more in line with the other postal contracts. The annual subsidy for the West Indies became £86,750, and the South American service to Argentina was put on a poundage basis, 2s 6d per lb. for letters and 3d a lb. for newspapers. The Postmaster-General was able to report in 1873 that this service was almost self-supporting. T. A. Bushell, in his official history of the Royal Mail, agreed; he wrote regarding this change that the 'spacious days of Admiralty control were now at an end, and in future the business was to be conducted on strictly commercial lines'.[3]

---

[1] *Parl. Ret.*, 92/1865; 274/1865. The colonial share of the deficit came to about £30,000. It might be added that the preference for the Royal Mail over the Holt Line was partly because the West Indian colonies favoured the Royal Mail.

[2] Bushell, op. cit., 123-4. According to the *17th Rep. P.M.G.* (1871), the deficit in 1870 was £116,350; in 1871, £110,950.

[3] *Parl. Ret.*, 212/1870, 48/1874; *21st Rep. P.M.G.* (1875), 11; Bushell, op. cit., 124-6. By 1876 the time between Southampton and St Thomas had become about eleven days.

THE CUNARD MONOPOLY

The changes in the north Atlantic were more remarkable than any we have examined thus far.

In 1860 the Cunard Company had the exclusive contract with the British Post Office for the transatlantic mails. The Allan Line, subsidized by Canada, was also carrying mails between British North America and Great Britain.

Just as Mr Cunard was obtaining the renewal of his contract in 1858, the Irish were making a strong bid for a packet service from some port in Ireland. This seemed reasonable since Ireland was nearer than Great Britain to North America. It irritated the Irish that their transatlantic letters had to go eastward to England before going westward across the Atlantic. As far back as 1851 the agitation for an Irish packet port had led the Admiralty to appoint commissioners to examine the eligible harbours. Of the nine ports surveyed, those of Cork and Galway were recommended as the best for mail-packets. Cork's harbour (Queenstown, now Cobh) was praised as the safest of all 'to run for in a gale of wind'. Galway found favour because the Aran Islands largely protected it from the Atlantic swell. But the west coast of Ireland was considered dangerous, especially in winter.[1]

As an Irish port for transatlantic mails, Galway was the first to be tried out. The stimulus for its use came from the strong desire of western Ireland to have a port, and to this was added the wish of Newfoundland for a direct connection with the British Isles. Newfoundland felt that it deserved a better service than the branch from Halifax. It seemed a hardship to the islanders that a Cunard liner frequently passed in sight of St John's, the capital of Newfoundland, on its way to Halifax. Halifax was over 500 miles to the west, whence the mails were brought back to Newfoundland. Were there a direct service to St John's, the mails would only take six or seven days instead of two weeks to a month by way of Halifax. The colony felt its isolation the more keenly since it had been granted self-government in 1855.

To meet the desires of Newfoundland, the Cunard Company offered in 1857 to give a direct service from Liverpool by ships that would terminate their voyages at St John's. The Company was not

---

[1] *Rep. Commrs. . . . . as to the Proposal for an Irish Packet Station* (1851). The mileage to New York from the various ports was given as follows: from Southampton 3,069 miles; from Liverpool 3,013; from Cork 2,780; from Galway 2,731.

willing to slow down the through services to America by a stop at St John's—the transatlantic competition was too keen for that. But the Admiralty and the Treasury were not prepared to add a special service for Newfoundland only.

New hope came to Newfoundland and Galway in 1858 when the ships of the Lever Line began a passenger service across the Atlantic from Galway. John O. Lever of Manchester had been carrying on a profitable business by taking emigrants to the new world. He now sought additional profit by a mail subsidy, and proposed to stop at St John's Newfoundland, on the way. A telling argument for this arrangement was the use that could be made of the call at St John's for sending telegrams to North America. As soon as a telegram reached St John's by ship it could be telegraphed to the American Continent, and reach its destination days ahead of messages sent all the way by ship. This attractive feature of the Galway service had been made possible by the laying of a cable between Great Britain and Ireland in 1851, and another that connected Newfoundland with Nova Scotia on the American mainland. Attempts at laying a transatlantic cable in 1857 and again in 1858 had not succeeded.[1]

Because of the strong backing of the Irish members in Parliament, and of the desire to give Ireland more recognition, the Admiralty and the Treasury were willing to grant Lever a mail contract. The Post Office, to whom the suggestion was referred, had serious doubts as to the regularity of the service because of the heavy fogs and the dangerous coasts, and it looked on the Galway proposal as based primarily on 'political rather than postal considerations'. Then too, according to the Post Office, it would only take mail from the Cunard Line which was already heavily subsidized. Nor were the Canadians agreeable. They even offered the alternative of having their Allan Line ships stop at St John's, and do so for the postage to be obtained from the Newfoundland mails. That would have been an excellent solution, except that the Allan Line was a Canadian Company and was already running in competition with Cunard for the transport of American and Canadian mails. Despite the doubts of the Post Office, the Government awarded a mail contract to the Galway Line for a fortnightly service to New York and Boston by way of St John's for a subsidy of £78,000 a year. The

---

[1] *Parl. Ret.*, 230/1869. For the Galway project, see *1st Rep. S.C. on Pkt. and Telegraph Contracts* (1860), 425ff. For the Atlantic cable, successfully laid in 1866, see below, ch. 22.

Company set about building 'paddle-wheel vessels of the greatest power' to insure regularity. Motives political rather than postal were back of a new transatlantic mail line.[1]

Mr Lever's Atlantic Royal Mail Steam Navigation Company was never able to live up to its imposing title. The *Connaught*, the first vessel ready for the crossings—they began in 1860—had such a light draught, according to the Admiralty agent on board, that she was almost unmanageable. On her second voyage she was lost off the port of Boston. The *Hibernia* proved so unseaworthy in her trials that she had to be strengthened. The third vessel to be delivered, the *Columbia*, was a year late, and was so unfit to meet the terms of the contract that she took seventeen days instead of seven in reaching St John's. Nor was the fourth vessel, the *Anglia*, fast enough to meet the contract terms. Mr Lever chartered or purchased other vessels in the hope of carrying on. The *Indian Empire* proved to be completely out of her element in the north Atlantic. The most successful vessel of the Line was the *Adriatic*, the large wooden paddle-wheel steamer that had formerly belonged to the American Collins Line. She was bought in 1861.[2]

The Galway Line gave such poor service that the Post Office suspended the contract in the spring of 1861. The Line was allowed to try again in 1863, but the lack of vessels brought the adventure to an end in 1864. John Lever's scheme to use Galway was a miserable failure. It ruined numerous shareholders.[3]

The attempt to use Galway as a transatlantic port for mail had one permanent result. Other companies that were fearful of the effect of this new Line on their business decided to make use of an Irish port on their way between Great Britain and America. The Allan Line replied to the use of Galway by stopping at Londonderry for Irish mails and passengers. The Cunard Company, previously very much opposed to an Irish port of call, decided to stop at

[1] ibid., pp. x-xiv, 33, 144. The *2nd Rep.* of this Committee of 1860 was given over to investigating a scandal connected with otbaining the contract—the Galway 'job' as one member of the House of Commons termed it. For a good summary, see Bonsor, op. cit.

[2] *Epp. Adm. Agts.*, April 11, 20, 1861; March 14, September 29, 1863.

[3] *6th Rep. P.M.G.* (1860), 56; *Parl Ret.*, 60/1863 and 433/1863; *Epp. Adm. Agts.*, January 20, 1864. The use of the *Adriatic* is of some interest. After serving the Galway Line, the *Adriatic* seems to have ended a checkered career as a hulk on the west coast of Africa. She was one of the last ocean-going wooden paddle-wheel steamers. It is odd that the *Adriatic* should have been pictured on a United States postage stamp in 1869—on the 12 cent green of the first American pictorial issue—12c (6d) being the rate at the time for a half-ounce letter crossing the Atlantic. The *Adriatic* had not been American owned since 1861, was thirteen years old in 1869 and by then already out of date. The stamp shows the *Adriatic* on a stormy sea, presumably carrying transatlantic mail, long after she had ceased to do so. See illustration facing p. 193.

Queenstown, the harbour for Cork, and the Company did this without seeking additional subsidy. The Cunard packets serving Halifax and Boston began calling at Queenstown in 1859, the New York packets in the spring of 1860. This stop proved very useful to the Post Office. British mails that were twenty-four hours later than those taken aboard at Liverpool, could overtake the liner at Queenstown by crossing from Holyhead and going from Dublin to Cork by railway. The call was a boon to Ireland; American letters no longer travelled eastward across the Irish Sea before beginning their westward transatlantic journey.[1]

The failure of the American Collins Line and the collapse of the Galway project did not end attempts to cut into the Cunard monopoly. William Inman, member of a British firm acting as agent for the old sailing liners, decided to start a new Line of steamships. His first vessel was the iron screw steamer *City of Glasgow*. To it were soon added other 'City' ships, named after such places as Philadelphia, Washington, Brussels, London, New York and Paris. The original transatlantic terminus was Philadelphia, but in 1856 it was changed to New York. From the beginning, the City ships proved both comfortable and fast, so comfortable that they were soon carrying more travellers than any other line.[2]

When the American Collins Line ceased running in 1858, Mr Inman began using the Collins Line sailing days from Liverpool. As he put it before the Committee of 1860: 'We immediately took the Collins Line mail day and asked for the mails, and the Cunard Company immediately put on a steamer against us for the same day and under our rates.' He wrote to the Treasury in 1858 that his Company 'have more than once offered to carry Her Majesty's mails for the ocean postage'. When the Galway Line wangled a contract, Inman vigorously protested. It will be recalled that, just at this time, the Cunard Company obtained a long renewal of their contract, although it had several more years to run. Although Mr Inman made no direct accusation, his meaning was clear when he asserted that 'postal contracts have been made use of by others to endeavour to drive us off the ocean'.[3]

---

[1] *1st Rep. S.C. on Pkt. and Telegraph Contracts* (1860), p. xiv; *Parl. Deb.*, 4th ser. cxxi, 208.

[2] The Company's official name was the Liverpool, New York and Philadelphia Steamship Company. The fleet included the *Kangaroo* from 1854 to 1870, the *Kangaroo* that was to have started a Line to Australia. Mr Inman claimed that his Company was the first to carry on 'ocean screw steaming with success'.

[3] *1st Rep. S.C. on Pkt. and Telegraph Contracts* (1860), 127, 215, etc., and *Parl. Ret.*, 230/1859, 41-46.

THE BLUE RIBAND

Although the Inman Line was not driven off the ocean, it did not obtain a mail contract at this time. Yet Mr Inman's fast screw steamers had to be given some consideration when the Cunard contract expired in the late sixties. Inman's *City of Paris* won the western record in 1867, taking it away from Cunard's *Scotia*, the last side-wheel steamer used by the Cunard Company. Two years later the *City of Paris* raced the screw-driven Cunard liner *Russia* in an exciting crossing. They left New York within an hour of each other, the *Paris* reaching Queenstown in just under 8 days and 20 hours. It was a near thing, for the *Russia* took only forty-five minutes longer. In 1869 the *City of Brussels* made the homeward run in the record breaking time of seven and a half days.[1]

When the Cunard contract came up for renewal in 1868, the Post Office was set on lowering the high subsidy of £170,000. The United States Post Office, for one thing, had been paying for their mail carriage eastward—since the failure of the Collins Line in 1858—on the basis of the amount of mail that was carried. The postal administrations of the United States and Great Britain had finally agreed, in 1867, to lower the rate on a transatlantic half-ounce letter from 1s (24 cents) to 6d (12 cents). Moreover, twenty-five first-class steamers were in the Atlantic service at that time, of which only six were Cunarders. In addition to the Inman ships, the Anchor Line gave a weekly service from Glasgow, and two German lines, the Hamburg American and the North German Lloyd, stopped regularly at Southampton. It seemed high time that competition was put to use.[2]

When the Post Office sought tenders on the basis of the sea postage, Inman made a bid but the Cunard Company held out. Later the Cunard Company denied that this refusal was intended to put the Government 'into a corner'. The Post Office was clearly in a corner, nevertheless, when Inman changed his mind and joined with the Cunard Line in offering to share the services on a fixed-subsidy basis. The collusion of the two principal British Lines came as a blow to Post Office Headquarters, who found it wise to submit

---

[1] Bonsor, op. cit., 17; A. J. Maginnis, *The Atlantic Ferry* (1893), 45. The *Scotia*, built in 1862, of 3,871 tons, was capable of 14 knots by the lavish use of coal. She made her last voyage in 1875. A witness before the *Sel. Com. on Mail Contracts* of 1869 (p. 2), declared, 'There is only one vessel that crosses the Atlantic now that is not a screw; she is the *Scotia*, an old boat now.'

[2] *Parl. Ret.*, 115/1867; *Rep. S.C. on Mail Contracts* (1869).

to the patriotic desire for the two principal British Lines. They
received seven-year contracts for three sailing a week from Liverpool, two by Cunard and one by Inman, at annual subsidies of
£70,000 and £35,000 respectively. The Post Office at least had the
satisfaction of lowering the transatlantic contract by £60,000. As
the postal rate was now but 6d on a half-ounce letter, the sea-
postage accounted for only about a third of the payments to the two
Lines.[1]

The Committee of 1869 was curious about the collusion of Cunard
and Inman, since they had been in bitter opposition for years.
John Burns of the Cunard Company said that they 'had been
fighting Mr Inman for the last twenty years, but they got tired of
the competition'. They agreed to work together 'because our trade
was being eaten into by foreigners . . . and because our country
was not supporting us against foreign competition'. When Mr
Inman took the stand he was asked some very embarrassing
questions—why had he changed his mind when he had held for
years that a subsidy was not essential? He, as well, referred to the
encroachments of foreign companies, even though he admitted their
steamers were built 'side by side with ours on the Clyde'. (He was
alluding to the North German Lloyd, whose ships were British
built and largely manned at this time by British crews.) When
pressed as to why he joined with the Cunard Company in asking for
a subsidy, all he would say was 'We prefer to have something
settled . . . to have a regular service . . . to put "royal mail
steamer" on our ships . . . I cannot give any other reason.' What
had been Cunard versus Collins was now Cunard and Inman
against the field of some half-dozen vigorous competitors, including
several British-owned Lines.[2]

The contest for the blue riband of the Atlantic, as well as for the
passengers and for the mails, became even more intense in the
seventies. Another competitor, the White Star Line, began its

---

[1] *15th Rep. P.M.G.* (1869), 10; *17th Rep.*, (1871); *Parl. Ret.*, 106/1859. The one
concession to the other Lines was the arrangement with the North German Lloyd for
carrying American mail once a week from Southampton for the postage only. The whole
business was thoroughly examined by the Select Committee of 1869, appointed to
'inquire into the Mail Contracts with Messrs Cunard and Company and with Mr Inman'.
Numerous witnesses told the Committee that a fixed subsidy was quite unnecessary.
It was learned that the North German Lloyd was carrying the mail for the German
Federation for the postage only. Several British Lines offered to carry letters for 1d an
ounce. See pp. 17, 23-32, 49-50, 54-60, 105 of the *Report* of 1869.

[2] *Rep. S.C. on Mail Contracts* (1869), 106-16, 125-32. The excuse of foreign compe-
ition was a fixed idea with Sir Samuel Cunard, who had died in 1865, and much more
appropriate as an excuse in the fifties than in the late sixties.

career in 1871. Thomas H. Ismay of Liverpool had entered the shipping business a few years earlier by purchasing the flag and goodwill of the White Star clippers in the Australian trade. His iron clippers did well enough on that route, but he decided to enter the more attractive transatlantic business. His Line, The Oceanic Steamship Company, became known as the White Star from the flag flown by his ships. His fleet was newly built by the forward-looking firm of Harland & Wolff of Belfast. The Company's pioneer liner was the *Oceanic*, which made her first crossing in March 1871. Other early White Star liners bore such names as *Baltic*, *Atlantic*, *Republic*, *Adriatic* and *Britannic*. They were about 4,000 to 5,000 tons in size, with standards of comfort that made them great favourites for travellers.

Mr Ismay made clear that his ships were out to win the blue riband. In 1872 the *Adriatic* won the record from Queenstown to New York by the first passage under eight days. In 1876 the *Britannic* lowered the record to 7 days and 14 hours. Clearly the White Star was making it difficult to justify the continuance of fixed mail subsidies to Cunard and Inman only, if the fast carriage of the mails by British lines was the Government's intention. Cunard was being hard pushed, not only by the White Star, but by Inman, the North German Lloyd, and the up and coming Guion Line.[1]

The Post Office made another effort in 1876 to put the cost of the ocean service on a postage basis. When the two contracts expired at the end of the year, the Post Office announced that it intended to forward American mails on fixed days every week, and to pay for their carriage at the rate of 2s 4d per lb. for letters, and 2d per lb. for newspapers. The announcement referred to a similar arrangement

[1] Originally Mr Ismay planned to use the names Pacific and Arctic for his ships, but they were laid aside because of the tragic losses of the two Collins liners *Pacific* and *Arctic*, still a fresh memory. The *Britannic* was the first screw steamer of over 5,000 tons, with the exception of the gigantic *Great Eastern*. The *Great Eastern* of over 18,000 tons, launched in 1858, was never a success, despite the fact that she was equipped with paddle wheels *and* a screw. The Guion Line of Liverpool started in 1866. The *Arizona* of this Line made a passage from New York to Queenstown in 7 days and 8 hours in 1879. See Bonsor, op. cit., for details on the various lines.

The craze for speed and for the coveted blue riband brought out more clearly than ever the commendable care of the Cunard Company. The first Inman liner, the *City of Glasgow*, had a short life; she disappeared in 1854 on a voyage to New York with 480 on board. Two years later, the *City of New York* was wrecked, but no lives were lost. In 1870 the *City of Boston* 'went missing'; the crew and passengers numbered 177. The year 1875 brought two more serious disasters. The *City of Washington* was wrecked off Nova Scotia, but all on board were saved. Not so fortunate was the *Atlantic* of the White Star Line, wrecked on the way from New York to Halifax with the staggering loss of 546 out of 862 on board.

of the United States Post Office, and to rates as fixed by the Postal Union. The Postmaster-General, Lord John Manners, added that he hoped to receive the 'cordial support' of the shipping Lines. Some were far from cordial. The White Star refused at first to consider carrying mail on this basis, although the Cunard and Inman Companies grudgingly agreed. On the other hand, such Lines as the North German Lloyd, the Guion Line and the Anchor Line were cordiality itself. They were delighted with what was hailed in Parliament as a 'free trade policy'. Cunard, Inman and the North German Lloyd (from Southampton) carried mail once a week under the new plan. The Guion Line gave a third weekly service from Liverpool until it was replaced by the White Star in April. The Anchor Line ships even began calling at Londonderry (Moville) in northern Ireland in order to pick up Irish mail and passengers. This scheme of the Post Office lasted for a year and the results should have pleased both the Government and the public. In 1877 the cost of the American mail service dropped 75 per cent, from £105,000 to £28,000.[1]

Sad to relate, the Postmaster-General did not win the battle, even though he had won the first skirmish. The Cunard Company, according to a speaker in the House of Commons, hungered for the good old times, and induced the Inman and White Star Companies in November 1877 to unite with Cunard in refusing to carry the mails on a month-to-month basis. The Post Office, consequently, had no option but to abandon its plan. The three Lines soon demanded an increase in the rates on the ground that the service was run at a loss, whatever that may mean. The rate, as a result, became 4s a lb. for letters and 4d a lb. for newspapers. For various reason the Post Office had fallen 'into the hands of what was known as the Liverpool Shipping Ring'. The Postmaster-General, Lord John Manners, who was accused in Parliament of being 'lax and squeezable', replied that he had not abandoned the plan, but that it had abandoned him.[2]

---

[1] *23rd Rep. P.M.G.* (1877), 21; *Parl. Ret.*, 92/1878; *Parl. Deb.* H.C., 3rd ser., ccxxxviii, 1635-6, a debate brought about in the House of Commons by George Anderson of Glasgow: he moved that 'the time for monopoly in the American mail service has passed'.

[2] *Parl. Deb.*, loc. cit., *24th Rep. P.M.G.* (1878), 23; *Parl. Ret.*, 92/1878; and the official *The Post Office, an Historical Summary* (1911), 55, for the reference to the Shipping Ring. It grew out of an agreement of several companies to charge the same rates and to grant rebates to 'loyal' shippers using Lines of the 'Ring'. This means of control was later examined by the Royal Commission on Shipping Rings (1909). See also *S.C. on Steamship Subsidies* (1902), 151.

The subsidies for the north Atlantic mails led to continuous deficits during the eighties as the principle of monopoly was resumed. When the agreement with the three companies expired at the end of 1886, another try by the Post Office resulted in lower rates for two services a week only, via Queenstown, with Cunard and White Star, by now the favoured lines. The attempt to put the American service on a poundage basis had failed.

How does the profit and loss account stand as of 1885, after a quarter century of effort to make the mail services self-supporting? The Postmaster-General declared in 1886 that some Lines showed heavy losses, on others they were slight, on still others they were nil. The three Australian routes were under colonial control, with no loss to the British Post Office. The same could be said of the service to South Africa. Nor were the Dover routes any more of a concern than they had been in 1860. The deficits were negligible on the Lines to the east and west coasts of South America. The three companies giving the most trouble in 1886 were the same ones that worried the Postmaster-General in 1860. The West Indian Line was in the 'red' some £63,000, the North American service showed an annual deficit of £59,000, and the P & O cost the British Post Office over £223,000 despite the colonial sharing of the contract expenses.[1]

Some progress has been made in the twenty-five years. The principle of paying for ocean mails by weight was more generally accepted, and was in use on many of the routes. The monopoly of the three great shipping Lines had been loosened. Mechanical improvements had made the service far better—the screw had replaced the paddle, iron and now steel were in use for the hulls of the mail liners. A steamer of 3,000 tons had been large in 1860. The *Teutonic* (9,984 tons) and her sister ship, the *Majestic*, built in 1889, had the look of the modern liner, with their straight stems and the abandonment of sails. And the latest liners were faster than ever before. The marine engine had become a compound engine, with improved boilers and cylinders and pressures, with greater economy in the use of coal, and with better prospects of keeping to schedule for far places.

The Post Office still faced a large 'deficiency' in the mail services overseas. This is not so serious as it may appear. The strong demand for cheaper ocean postage was already having some effect, tending to raise the deficit temporarily as concessions were made on postage

[1] *32nd Rep. P.M.G.* (1886), 30-31. The total deficit in that year was £347,000.

rates. The formation of the Universal Postal Union in the seventies had brought a general lowering of ocean mail rates. By 1886 the desire for cheaper ocean postage within the Empire, even Imperial Penny Postage, could no longer be ignored.

21

OCEAN PENNY POSTAGE

❧ ❧

PENNY postage for Great Britain's domestic mail began in 1840. It came almost as a revolution, largely because of Rowland Hill's famous pamphlet, *Post Office Reform*. The change was accepted reluctantly by the officials at St Martin's, but it was so generally welcomed that official opposition was pushed aside. The uniform penny rate for a half-ounce letter applied only to mail both sent and received *within* the British Isles. This did not mean a land service only, for the mail between Great Britain and Ireland had to be carried across the Irish Sea, and to other nearby islands. The Orkneys, the Shetlands and even the Channel Islands also enjoyed the penny rate.

The contrast between a low postage in the British Isles and the high cost of sending a letter to a nearby foreign country or a distant colony was startling. The announcement of uniform penny postage in 1840 warned the public that 'Colonial Letters if sent by Packet [will be] Twelve Times, if sent by Private Ship Eight Times the above Rates.' The packet rate of 1s and the ship-letter rate of 8d were retained at a time when large numbers of emigrants were leaving for British North America, the United States, and the far distant colonies in the south Pacific.

In his pamphlet of 1837 Rowland Hill had proposed that foreign and colonial letters might be charged at only twice the suggested inland rate, that is, 2d. 'There is perhaps scarcely any measure', he wrote, 'that would tend so effectually to remove the obstacles to emigration, and to maintain the sympathy between the colonies and the mother country . . . as the proposed reduction in the postage of colonial letters.'[1]

Yet the 2d charge for outgoing colonial and foreign letters was never seriously pressed by Rowland Hill. A change in the rates for foreign letters would have required new treaties with

---

[1] Rowland Hill had been Secretary of the Colonial Commissioners for South Australia before he turned to postal reform.

other Governments. The colonies, of course, would have welcomed with enthusiasm a twopenny rate with the mother country. But the overseas possessions were far removed from Great Britain, and postal services to them were already so highly subsidized that nothing was done. When Rowland Hill became Secretary to the Postmaster-General in 1846—to ensure the success of his plan—he did nothing to extend it to the colonies. Hill was principally concerned with keeping down the cost of 'my plan' so that his optimistic forecasts of its financial effects would work out.

Yet the desire for a cheap colonial rate, even penny postage all the way, persisted. The well-known Mulready pictorial envelope, issued officially in 1840, seemed to imply its extension overseas. On the face of the envelope Britannia was pictured seated on a throne in the centre of the design with a lion at her feet. From her island she appeared to be spreading her benevolent rule to distant shores where emigrants, Chinese, Indians and negroes were awaiting winged messengers to be seen carrying letters over the intervening seas.

A cheap colonial rate had many advocates in the forties. Dr George Gregory, a witness before the Committee that proposed uniform penny postage, was an advocate of penny postage to the colonies. It would be an inestimable blessing, he said, one that would bind them more closely to the mother country. The Free Traders, of course, favoured fewer restrictions on communication and on the interchange of goods. The international peace movement, strong at the time, hoped that closer bonds between the nations would prevent war. In Britain a Colonial Postage Association kept before the public the ideal of cheap ocean postage.

ELIHU BURRITT

Unexpected assistance came from an American who crossed to Britain in 1846 to work for 'human brotherhood'. Elihu Burritt was the humble native of a village in Connecticut, happily named New Britain. There he was apprenticed to a blacksmith, but Burritt was so avid of learning languages that he became known as the Learned Blacksmith. While in England to push his League of Universal Brotherhood, Burritt conceived the idea that the extension overseas of Britain's domestic penny postage would be a valuable ally of the peace movement. His advocacy of universal penny postage was warmly welcomed in the British Isles. The propaganda methods used in the penny-postage movement ten years earlier were revived. Numerous petitions were sent to Parliament. Burritt advocated ocean penny postage before sympathetic audiences in every large town in the United Kingdom. Placards were put up in railway stations and other public places. One effective device was the issue of propagandist envelopes bearing symbolic pictures. One issued by Bradshaw's—already known for its railway guides—pictured a side-wheel steamer on whose mainsail was inscribed 'The World's Want and should be Britain's Boon—an Ocean Penny Postage'. James Valentine, later renowned for his pictorial postcards, also co-operated. On one of his envelopes showing a paddle-wheel steamer, the word MAIL appeared in large letters on the paddle box where the liner's name was usually displayed, and the envelope carried the exhortation: 'Britain from Thee the World expects an Ocean Penny Postage to make her Children one Fraternity.'[1]

Elihu Burritt was in Britain for much of the time during the next quarter century. He issued a number of pamphlets. One, entitled 'Ocean Penny Postage, Its Necessity Shown and its Practicability Demonstrated', was printed in London about 1846, the year that Rowland Hill entered the Post Office as a permanent official. According to this pamphlet, ocean penny postage meant a charge for the ship carriage, which would be in addition to the domestic penny postage in Great Britain and the internal rate of the receiving colony or foreign country. This would make the cost of a half-ounce letter at least 3d, 'where there are now charges of 1s for these three services'. Burritt cited the low cost for carrying newspapers; a copy of *The Times*—it then weighed 3 ounces—could be sent to New Zealand for 1d. This meant that over half the contents of the mailbags were already under the penny postal system. He believed that 'England alone of all the nations can give the world an Ocean Penny Postage'. And he held that it would be without additional expense, as the clandestine use of the mails would end, and the increasing migration would rapidly multiply the number of letters going overseas. In this pamphlet Burritt urged Rowland Hill 'to expand the Penny Post to the compass of the oceans, and he may live to see half the entire correspondence of the world pass through England, and by England's ships to all the sea-divided habitations of men'.

Another of Burritt's pamphlets, 'An Ocean Penny Postage. Will

[1] These pictorial envelopes have attracted collectors. See Robson Lowe, op. cit., I, 248ff; see illustration facing p. 257.

it Pay?' (published in London in 1851) made much of the 'absurd anomaly' of a charge of 10d for a letter from London to Paris, whereas a letter from London to Edinburgh—a much longer distance—went for 1d. Indeed a letter could go for 1d from the Channel Islands to the Shetlands, a journey of 1,000 miles including two long passages by sea. The tenpenny rate was an absurdity.

Possibly his best-known pamphlet, 'The Proposition of a Universal Penny Postage' (London, 1853), gave particular attention to the anomalies of the transatlantic mails. Burritt wrote that there were ship owners who would carry letters across the Atlantic for 1d. He believed that the ending of the Cunard and Collins monopolies would be a great saving to the post offices and the citizens of the two countries. By his calculation penny postage would at least quadruple the number of letters. Nor did he forget the colonies: 'A strong and widespread expectation has been created that this great boon will be conceded by the British Government . . . The labouring classes of the people, who supply chiefly the great stream of emigration, are especially animated with this expectation'. Elihu Burritt concluded his appeal in this pamphlet by warning that 'no partial concession will tend to quiet the earnest desire . . . for the reduction of the ocean transit service to the uniform charge of one penny'.[1]

The propaganda that started in the mid-forties reached its height in the next decade. Members of all political parties gave their hearty support. In 1853 delegations even visited the Prime Minister, the Chancellor of the Exchequer and the Postmaster-General on behalf of ocean penny postage. The Government, however, was unwilling to take so drastic a step.[2]

THE LOWERING OF COLONIAL RATES

The widespread desire for cheaper postage to the colonies

---

[1] See Merle Curti, *The Learned Blacksmith* (N.Y., 1937), ch. II.

[2] Elihu Burritt was the U.S. Consul at Birmingham from 1865 to 1870. He died in 1879 in his native town, just six months before the death of Rowland Hill. In the month of Burritt's death the *Illustrated London News* published the portrait and an obituary of 'this remarkable American lecturer who came to England about thirty-three years ago'. It referred to his 'scheme of ocean penny postage which has not yet been realized' but, it added, 'We believe there is no insuperable difficulty about it, whenever governments are disposed to find leisure for such useful tasks, instead of cultivating the seeds of international hatred and jealousy.' See issue for March 1879. In less than two decades sea postage became what Burritt hoped it would be and what Rowland Hill regarded as unattainable.

brought but a half-hearted response from the Government. Rowland Hill, contrary to his original suggestion of 1837, now held that the demand for ocean penny postage was based on a 'false analogy'. Varying distances at home might be disregarded. But a great increase in letters could not be expected by a sharp lowering of the oversea rates on long routes 'where in the nature of things the answer is slow'. The expensive subsidies, however, were the real causes for his reluctance, along with a fear of the adverse effect of lowered rates on his financial prophecies. The proposals of Burritt would make sense, wrote Rowland Hill, when contractors will carry letters to India or Australia for the same charge as to Glasgow or Aberdeen.

Mr Hill, nevertheless, advised the Postmaster-General that there should be some reduction in the colonial rates. He was very conscious of what he called 'the association for obtaining a low rate of transmarine postage', and he feared 'that the Government might be placed in the dilemma of having either to resist a popular demand, or to submit to a very serious loss of revenue.' Accordingly, Hill suggested a lowering of the varying colonial rates from about 1s to 6d. His main purpose, in his own words, was to prevent the public demand from gaining 'troublesome force'.[1]

The lowering of colonial rates at the mid-century appears to be the direct result of propaganda for ocean penny postage. A charge of 6d began to apply in 1853. The lowered rate was not immediately effective to all the colonies but by 1858 the annual *Report* of the Postmaster-General announced that the rate of 6d applied to every colony, and that the ship-letter rate to all parts of the world was also lowered to 6d where it had been higher.[2]

One of the worst anomalies was a basic charge of 10d on a letter to France. It became even more absurd when a letter could travel from Britain even to Australia for 6d. Treaty negotiations in the early sixties finally led to an agreement on a new rate of 4d. Another anomaly was created when the rate to Canada was lowered in March 1854. By this change a half-ounce letter to Canada cost 6d, if it went directly to Canada, whether the packet-boat was British or Canadian.

---

[1] See the autobiographical *Life of Rowland Hill*, II, 241-2. In the same volume, p. 319, Rowland Hill takes pains to correct the impression, given by Miss Mitford, that Burritt's interest in penny postage had preceded his own. Burritt graciously replied to a letter from Rowland Hill that such was not the case.

[2] *4th Rep. P.M.G.* (1858), 20, 25. A decade later the Post Office returned to the shilling rate for South Africa, and even raised the rate to 1s for the Australian colonies as of July 1, 1864, if the letter went by way of Southampton, and to 1s 4d if via France. But the colonial outcry soon cancelled the change.

The American 'Learned Blacksmith' Elihu Burritt an ardent advocate of Universal Brotherhood and Ocean Penny Postage. *Source: Illustrated London News*, March 1879, lxxiv, 297.

Sir John Henniker Heaton, M.P., who was successful in obtaining a penny-postage rate for the Empire. *Source:* Mrs. Adrian Porter, *Life and Letters of Sir John Henniker Heaton,* (Her father) 1916.

A propaganda envelope on behalf of ocean penny postage, issued in Great Britain by James Valentine. *Source:* A. W. Robertson, *A History of the Ship Letters of the British Isles,* 1955.

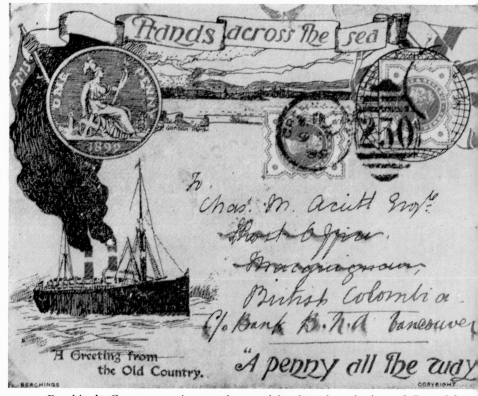

Beeching's Commemorative envelope, celebrating the winning of Imperial Penny Postage (1898). It shows an ocean liner of the time. *Source:* A. W. Robertson, *A History of the Ship Letters of the British Isles,* 1955.

But if a Canadian letter crossed on the Cunard Line, as often happened, and went through the United States, an American transit charge was added to make the total 8d. This increased the confusion, for a letter sent from Britain to the United States cost 1s, 4d more than if sent to Canada by way of the United States.[1]

Efforts to lower the postage rates between Great Britain and the United States led to long negotiations. For some time the two Post Offices could not agree on how much of the total postage should be assigned to the ocean carriage. In 1859 the American Postmaster-General proposed a reduction of the total postage from 24 cents to 12 cents (1s to 6d), the ocean carriage to be assigned 7 cents, the internal postage in the United States 3 cents, and the British internal charge to be what it actually was, 1d (2 cents). The Postmaster-General of the United States considered 3 cents as little enough for the American portion of the rate as a letter might travel 3,000 miles in America; the domestic rate at the time was 5 cents up to 300 miles, and 10 cents for greater distances. Rowland Hill wanted 4 cents assigned to the sea carriage, since the subsidy paid the Cunard Line 'much exceeded the postage', as he put it. Not until 1867 did the two Post Offices agree on a combined rate of 6d for a letter sent across the Atlantic; the new rate went into effect on the first day of 1868.[2]

A charge of 6d for transatlantic mail was far from meeting the wishes of those wanting ocean penny postage; if large subsidies hindered cheap ocean postage, the Government should use ships that were willing to carry letters at cheaper rates. This was brought out in evidence before the Committee of 1869 that inquired into the recent contracts with Cunard and Inman. The two Companies had combined to obtain a fixed subsidy in reply to the request of the Post Office for bids on the actual mail carried. The Committee reported there was no longer any need for fixed subsidies. The National Steamship Company of Liverpool, through its Director, James Robinson, bid for the mail to the United States both in 1867 and 1868, and agreed to do it for 1d an ounce so that the Government need charge only 1d a letter. Stephen Guion, head of the Guion Line, also told the Committee that he would carry the

---

[1] A. D. Smith, *The Development of the Rates of Postage* (1917), 87; *Life of Rowland Hill*, II, 183, 211.

[2] *6th Rep. P.M.G.* (1860); *14th Rep.* (1868). The United States had lowered its internal rate in 1863 to 5 cents, a step that aided the agreement. Each country made arrangements for sending its mail to the other country.

I

mail to New York on terms that would assist 'in the inauguration of penny postage'. But the Treasury rejected both offers.[1]

THE UNIVERSAL POSTAL UNION

The initial step in the world-wide lowering of mail rates was not taken in Great Britain. The prelude to the Universal Postal Union was a suggestion of Montgomery Blair, the Postmaster-General of the United States in the Cabinet of President Lincoln. In August 1862, he wrote to the principal governments in Europe suggesting a meeting in Paris to discuss international postal practices. The rates, according to Mr Blair, were particularly confusing to residents in the United States and their overseas correspondents; in some cases as many as six different rates were in use between the United States and a foreign country, depending, of course, on the route put to use. This was largely because of variations in sea postage and transit rates. Fifteen governments sent delegates to a conference in Paris. The articles of general agreement included recommendations for a uniform basic weight, that transit charges through a country should never be more than half the domestic postage, and that the ocean postage should be no greater than the actual cost of carrying the mail.

Five years later Heinrich von Stephan of the North German Union called for a congress to organize a postal union, but it had to be postponed on account of the Franco-Prussian War. In the early seventies the invitation was renewed by the Government of Switzerland, with the result that a conference met at Berne in September 1874.

The Berne Congress led to a surprisingly large body of agreement on many controversial matters. Letters were to be charged a basic minimum rate of 25 centimes ($2\frac{1}{2}$d or 5c.), for a letter weighing 15 grams ($\frac{1}{2}$ ounce). If mail was carried a greater distance than 300 miles by sea, the carrying country might add a surtax of half the general Union rate. Each postal administration was to retain the postage it collected.[2]

The advantages were so obvious that non-European countries soon sought admission, and the European nations with overseas

---

[1] *Rep. S.C. on Mail Contracts* (1869), pp. v, 55-56, 60. See also above, p. 246 for this Committee. The National Line had been founded in 1863, the Guion Line in 1866. McCalmont, op. cit., regarded the abandonment of the contract system as 'necessary for the founding of an ocean penny postage'. See p. 143.

[2] See A. D. Smith, op. cit., 263ff.

empires also wished their colonies included. When India applied for admission in 1875, another Congress convened in Berne to discuss the entry of colonial territories, and it accepted the membership of British India, and all the colonies of France, Spain and Holland. Such additions naturally raised the question of the additional charges for letters travelling long distances by sea. The French proposed that the current high subsidies should *not* be the basis for the Union rate, as they were obviously intended for commercial, political and naval ends. As a result, the Congress decided that the country whose ships carried the mails could add a surtax equal to the full domestic postage—not half as proposed in 1874.

Although India was admitted in 1876, the British Empire as a whole did not join the Union. Any British colony wishing to enter the Union was required by the home government to reconsider the proportion of the packet charges borne by the colony and the mother country. The first self-governing British colony to join was the Dominion of Canada—in 1878. The federation of the British North American colonies a decade earlier had made united action easy. Canada's own mail line across the Atlantic as well as her nearness to the United States made her admission desirable. Newfoundland, which was not part of the Canadian Dominion at this time, joined the Union in 1879, and by 1881 all of the British West Indies and the West African colonies were Union members. By this time *all* the colonies of France, Spain, Portugal, Denmark and the Netherlands were included in the Union.[1]

Voting rights seemed so important that a state was given an extra vote when all her colonies joined the Union. When Canada became a member, she naturally insisted on having a vote, but the Union was opposed to a third British vote. Instead, Great Britain gave her colonial vote to Canada.

The other self-governing British colonies did not join the Union during the first decade. Cape Colony and Natal had just taken over their own postal arrangements. Nor were the Australian colonies in a position to join; sharp rivalries had created such deep differences, that, by this time, the colonies in the south Pacific were served by four mail Lines. The Postmaster-General of South Australia declared that Australasian colonies were prevented from entering the Union by the great cost of several separate mail services 'which

[1] Membership in the Union meant new stamp denominations for Great Britain and Canada. The first British 2½d stamp appeared in July 1875. Canada had issued a stamp in 1857 marked 'Canada Packet Postage', valued at 6d, which was the overseas rate at the time, but in October 1875 the Dominion of Canada issued its first 5c. (2½d) stamp.

the rival interests of the colonies, it was thought, made necessary'.[1]

The Postal Union so revolutionized charges by sea and land that the British sixpenny rate to the colonies was decidedly outdone by the twopence-halfpenny rate between the European countries and their colonies. Yet the British rate of 6d remained the colonial rate for some time after Great Britain and many of her colonies had entered the Union. Henniker Heaton, the leading advocate of imperial penny postage stated in Parliament, in 1887, that nine-tenths of the British colonies received letters from the mother country costing more than 2½d at the same time that letters from France and Germany travelled the same routes at the lower rate. The only British colonies having the basic Union rate of 2½d in 1887 were Gibraltar and Malta in the Mediterranean, and Canada and Newfoundland across the Atlantic. The basic rate to the West Indies and India was 4d, and to Cape Colony, Australia and New Zealand 6d. The anomalies are explained in part, at least, by the annual deficit on the British ocean mail services—at this time nearly £350,000.

The British colonies in the south Pacific were slow in entering the Postal Union. They feared that reductions might be made in their ocean rates, possibly forced by Germany and other European countries who were eager for the further lowering of rates at sea. And there was also the matter of voting rights. The Australian colonies and New Zealand wished for more than one vote for their group. In 1885 at the Lisbon Congress, their entrance was the subject of discussion, but the Congress was willing to grant only one vote to the group of seven colonies.

Their admission finally came in 1891 at the Vienna Congress. During a preliminary postal conference of the colonies in Sydney in that year, there was a strong desire to enter the Union, but they still sought adequate voting rights—adequate meaning two or three votes at least for the group. But the south Pacific colonies finally joined the Union in 1891, even though the Congress was unwilling to give them more than one vote.

When the Australian colonies and New Zealand entered the Postal Union most of the British colonies were included. The Postmaster-General of Great Britain announced in 1892 that all the colonies had joined save Cape Colony, British Bechuanaland,

---

[1] *Rep. P.M.G.* (So. Aust., 1884), 106; *Rep. P.M.G.* (N.Z., 1892). Additional votes for states with colonies seemed necessary to protect them against any drastic lowering of rates for ocean carriage.

St Helena 'and a few other unimportant parts of the Empire!'
Cape Colony entered in 1895. When the six Australian colonies
federated at the turn of the century, the Commonwealth of Australia
still shared one vote with New Zealand, which had refused to join
the Commonwealth. Finally at the Rome Congress in 1906, New
Zealand was granted a separate vote as one of Britain's self-governing
Dominions.[1]

A PENNY ALL THE WAY

Despite the general reduction of sea postage that followed the
spread of the Universal Postal Union, ardent advocates still sought
the lowering of imperial postage to 1d. The most persistent and
successful was Henniker Heaton. In the mid-sixties he had migrated
from Kent to Australia where he worked for a time in the bush and
later engaged in newspaper work in Sydney. After an absence of
twenty years he returned to England with his Australian wife. His
tireless efforts were especially powerful after his election to Parliament from Canterbury, which he represented for over a quarter of
a century.[2]

In season and out, Heaton sought the extension of uniform
penny postage within the Empire. Rowland Hill had regarded
Burritt's idea as based on a false analogy, and the Post Office had
countered his proposals by lowering the colonial rate to 6d. This
did not satisfy Heaton, however, for he could not see why penny
postage should any longer be bounded 'by the seas that wash our
coasts'. He was rebuked again and again by officialdom for his
meddlesome interference.

In a series of open letters, Henniker Heaton gave his reasons for
extending penny postage to the most distant colonies. His reasons
were not new. The cost of ordinary freight to Australia, he wrote, is
but 40s a ton, but the charge for letters is £1,792 a ton. As to
newspapers, the lower rates are recognized, since a newspaper,
weighing 4 ounces, could be sent to the ends of the earth for 1d,
while a letter of the same weight would cost 4s. Long distances
should not greatly increase the cost of carriage: 'Indeed, for the
same sum which it costs to convey a letter between London and

[1] *38th Rep. P.M.G.* (1892); *41st Rep.* (1895); *Rep. P.M.G.* (N.Z., 1906). The writer
has used an unpublished official report in the P.O. Records, London, of October 22,
1886, entitled *The British Colonies and the Postal Union* 'being a brief account of the
reasons which have hitherto deterred the Australian and South African colonies from
joining the Union'.

[2] See *The Life and Letters of Sir John Henniker Heaton* (1916) by his daughter Mrs
Adrian Porter.

I*

Dublin, they can be conveyed between London and Sydney.' As to the high subsidies paid the mail lines, Heaton underlined the well-known fact that most of the subsidies were for purposes 'entirely different from those for which the Post Office exists'—for maintaining a merchant fleet, encouraging faster communication and for the support of naval policy. He repeated a statement made by Lord Monteagle in Parliament as far back as 1842 that the 'expense of the packet service had no more to do with penny postage than the expense of the war in Afghanistan . . . It was not right to place the expense of the packet services to the account of the Post Office.' Despite the large subsidies, Heaton felt that the quarter of a million emigrants who were leaving the 'Old Country' every year deserved the best possible communication with 'home'.[1]

The Golden Jubilee of 1887, commemorating fifty years of the reign of Queen Victoria, did not bring the extension of penny postage. Cecil Raikes, the Postmaster-General, regarded the extension as a very distant prospect. A Jubilee issue of postage stamps came out in that year, in which ten different denominations appeared, from a $\frac{1}{2}$d to 1s, but a 1d stamp was *not* included, strange as it may seem. Three years later, in 1890, the fiftieth anniversary of domestic penny postage was widely acclaimed. In the celebrations, Mr Raikes alluded to those who 'sometimes wish to pose as postal reformers' and to their ineffectual arguments in behalf of imperial penny postage. Their agitation, he declared, was 'but a bubble that merciless logic has burst'.

Henniker Heaton was not silenced by the failure of his efforts in the eighties. A move in the right direction was the extension in 1891 of the twopence-halfpenny rate to all parts of the Empire. The Chancellor of the Exchequer pointed out what a great sacrifice this was—the loss of £100,000 a year in addition to the deficit 'already incurred by Great Britain in this branch of the business'. The annual *Report* of the Postmaster-General added that the 'people were well content that our colonies should enjoy the same rate (that is, 2$\frac{1}{2}$d) as the rest of the world'.

The Imperial Federation League, which was very active at the close of the century, strongly urged imperial penny postage. It regarded the recent lowering of colonial rates to the Postal Union level as a hindrance to the efforts of the League to extend penny postage to the whole Empire. Robert J. Beadon, writing in 1891,

[1] See *Parl. Deb.*, H.C., 3rd ser., lxiv, 321 for the Monteagle statement; and *Parl. Ret.* 34/1887 for Heaton's open letters to the Postmaster-General.

regretted that Chancellors of the Exchequer should be unwilling to surrender postal revenues because they wished 'to squeeze every penny they can get out of a tax, which, as is said, nobody feels and which, therefore . . . loses the Government no votes'. Beadon's proposal included an imperial penny stamp, not to take the place of other penny stamps completely, but to be used for emphasizing the unity of the Empire.[1]

The Queen's Diamond Jubilee was another celebration that might well have been graced by the gift of imperial penny postage. Imperial feeling was running high at the time. Joseph Chamberlain, Secretary of State for the Colonies, had become a convert to the 'easiest communication within the Empire'. He even suggested, in speaking before the Colonial Conference in that year, that we should 'make any sacrifice of revenue that may be required to secure uniform penny postage throughout the Empire'. But the Jubilee did not include the concession. Instead, there was some thought of lowering the domestic rate to a ½d, but this would have made the imperial twopence-halfpenny rate more glaring. As a substitute, the domestic penny rate was rather unnecessarily enlarged to cover a 4-ounce letter.

In 1897 the next Postal Union Congress was held in Washington. At the sessions there was some discussion among the British delegates of lowering the rate within the Empire to 2d. Canada, however, preferred to go even further than a reduction within the Empire to 2d, and to extend her own domestic three-cent rate to the Empire as a whole. After the Washington Congress was over, Canada decided to take the step. William Mulock, the Postmaster-General of Canada, announced that Canada would send a letter weighing 1 ounce to any part of the Empire for 3 cents (1½d), the new rate to begin on January 1, 1898. This was a startling decision, and unwelcome to the British Post Office and to the various colonies in the southern hemisphere. The British Post Office persuaded Canada to postpone her proposed reduction, pending an imperial postal conference called to meet in London during the summer of 1898.

The post-office departments of the Australian colonies held a preliminary conference in Hobart at which the colonies agreed to oppose the lowering of the rate even to 2d. The Hobart conference

[1] 37th Rep. P.M.G. (1891), 6; 38th Rep. (1892), 9; R. J. Beadon, Uniform Imperial Postage (1891). The Post Office magazine, St Martin's-le-Grand (III, no. 7) roundly condemned Mr Heaton's efforts in a series of articles on 'The Post Office and Mr J. H. Heaton'.

was sure there was no great demand in the colonies for a reduction, even though 'certain distinguished gentlemen in England have interested themselves in postal matters'. When the Australian Conference sent a telegram to Ottawa opposing any reduction, Postmaster-General Mulock replied that Canada would welcome an intercolonial uniform rate, but if that were not possible, she would like to reduce her outgoing rate to all parts of the Empire, while conceding like freedom of action to all other parts. He added that 'existing postal rates constitute a serious grievance considering the Canadian geographical and commercial position'.[1]

The Westminster Postal Conference of 1898 came to a surprising conclusion, despite the announced position of Great Britain and the Australian colonies. Mr Mulock, it appears, had strong encouragement from Joseph Chamberlain. At the first meeting of the Conference the delegates of Great Britain brought out the familiar arguments against lowering the rate. William Mulock, however, was not deterred; he even proposed a penny rate for the parts of the Empire ready to receive it. The British Postmaster-General, the Duke of Norfolk, then attempted to obtain a compromise on a twopenny rate. But at the third meeting of the Conference the attitude of the British delegates had completely changed. Their twopenny idea was dropped, and full support was given to the proposal for imperial penny postage. Joseph Chamberlain, it would seem, had been responsible for the change of view. Penny postage for the Empire, so long sought by Henniker Heaton, was begun on Christmas Day of 1898, save for Australia, New Zealand and Cape Colony where arrangements were not yet complete. A pictorial envelope, issued in 1899, pictured a modern mail steamer with red funnels, and on the envelope were the words 'Hands across the Sea. A Penny All the Way'.[2]

The next step in this series of changes was in New Zealand. Joseph Ward, the Postmaster-General since 1891, had been inspired by Henniker Heaton as early as the mid-eighties. In 1892 Ward's desire to establish internal and external penny postage led

[1] *Votes and Proceedings* (Queensland), 1898, I, 653ff. The agents of the Australian colonies in London were directed to oppose firmly the lowering of the rate. It should be added that Canada was proud of not using the Post Office for the gathering of revenue.

[2] For an account of the Conference, see Mrs Porter, op. cit., 179. It would appear that the Government planned to introduce the lower rate on the Prince of Wales's birthday (November 9th), but it was delayed because of the Queen's feelings. A story, often retold, states that when the Postmaster-General informed the aged Queen of the change to take place on the Prince's birthday, she asked in her most icy tone, 'And what prince?' The Duke of Norfolk was equal to the occasion: 'The Prince of Peace, ma'am, on Christmas Day.' See *St Martin's-le-Grand*, VIII, 372.

the New Zealand Parliament to authorize it 'whenever desirable'. The Government decided to inaugurate penny postage on the first day of the new century, January 1, 1901. As Ward put it: 'The beginning of the new century will fittingly mark the event . . . and prove an epoch in the history of the colony.' It was more than imperial penny postage, for the Postmaster-General of New Zealand announced that the new rate was to be universal—that any postal administration in the world could have a New Zealand letter for 1d. Ward took especial pleasure in telegraphing the news of this decision to Henniker Heaton.[1]

Henniker Heaton had several other occasions for satisfaction after 1898. During the first decade of the new century he set himself the task of obtaining penny postage with the United States. The fear of the Post Office that the change would result in a heavy loss was countered by an offer from two of Mr Heaton's friends, Lord Blyth and Andrew Carnegie, to guarantee the Post Office against any loss for the first five years of penny postage with the United States. Although their offer was not accepted, penny postage between Great Britain and the United States began in 1906. In the first year of penny postage with the United States, the number of letters increased by 25 per cent.[2]

Australia, by now a united Commonwealth, gradually came into line. In 1902 Australia agreed to accept letters for 1d from any place within the Empire. Letter postage from Australia to Great Britain was lowered from 2½d to 2d in 1905, and finally in 1911 Australia established the penny rate for letters leaving Australia as well as for those coming in. Little wonder that when Henniker Heaton returned from a visit to Australia in 1912, he found that he had been created a baronet. On his return he was lauded as one who 'had done more to draw the Empire together than all the speeches of all the statesmen'. He had become the latest and one of the most effective of a long line of reformers who have contributed to the growing usefulness of postal communication in a world that was more closely knit than ever before. The British Postmaster-General in 1912 announced that 'penny postage now embraces the whole of the British Empire save Pitcairn Island'.[3]

---

[1] At the Postal Union Congress in Rome (1906), Joseph Ward urged the delegates to replace the general twopence-halfpenny rate, in use since 1875, by 1d. The Congress did not comply, but at this Congress New Zealand was finally and fittingly given a separate vote in the Postal Union, after a heated debate and a narrow majority of two votes.

[2] *54th Rep. P.M.G.* (1908), 1; *55th Rep.* (1909), 3.

[3] Mrs Adrian Porter, op. cit., 340-7; *Commonwealth Parl. Papers* (Aust. 1911), II, 1125.

22

CHANGING COMMUNICATIONS—
1886-1918

IN the latter half of the nineteenth century, the Post Office made efforts—narrated in the previous chapter—to obtain cheaper postal rates for letters going overseas, efforts that were largely successful.

It was also a time when the Post Office was striving—to a large extent in vain—to lower the high subsidies paid to the selected shipping Lines, and to spread more widely among the various British steamship companies the contracts for carrying the mails. The Post Office had sought to base the cost for sending mails overseas on the actual amount of mail that was being carried. The Anchor Line, which had not been successful in its efforts to share in the transport of the Royal Mail, wrote the Postmaster-General in 1884 on behalf of 'Free Trade in Mail Carrying', in which it expressed regret at the practice of ever larger mail subsidies paid year after year to a few favoured Lines that had been selected from a large number capable of fast transatlantic travel.[1]

The free-trade views of the Anchor Line found little favour. The 'veiled' subsidies remained as a heavy charge against the Post Office while serving at the same time to strengthen the chosen companies. To justify their selection, these Lines built ever larger and larger ships. It is hardly necessary to add that in this way they increased their earning power as well. By 1895 the subsidies paid by the Post Office totalled over £730,000 annually, but the actual loss was cut down to about £430,000 by the sea-postage and by repayments from the Dominions and the colonies for their proportional shares of the subsidies. The payments went principally to four lines, the P & O, the Cunard Company, the White Star and the West Indian Royal Mail.[2]

[1] *Parl. Ret.*, 99/1885, being 'the whole correspondence with various domestic companies regarding conveyance of mails to North America', pp. 46-47.
[2] *42nd Rep. P.M.G.* (1896), 52-53.

Early in the present century (1902) a Select Committee on Steamship Subsidies examined once again this perennial question. The Committee reported that a 'general system of subsidies other than for services rendered is costly and inexpedient'. The view, also held by the Post Office, came out clearly in the evidence of Sir Spencer Walpole, the Secretary of the Post Office in the nineties. He told the Committee that if particular Lines and particular routes were favoured it was a handicap to the 'rest of the trade . . . There is not that free competition that I should like to see.'[1]

The older practice of including Admiralty clauses in the contracts was revived in 1885 after a quarter century of disuse, revived at a time when hostilities with Russia seemed likely. Henceforth important mail contracts—those with steamship companies having vessels of great power—were submitted to the Admiralty, and clauses were included that allowed the Admiralty, in case of war, to buy or hire the fastest vessels of the contracting mail lines. The selected vessels were to carry Admiralty 'fixtures' so as to be converted quickly into armed cruisers. Such ships were required also to carry officers and men that were, in part at least, in the naval reserve. In 1900 these provisions for Admiralty subsidies applied to eighteen of the fastest ships of the various mail Lines. Thirty others might be called on if needed.[2]

International tension was gathering strength at this time as the great powers became more and more concerned with colonial and economic expansion. France, Germany and the United States were strong competitors in a field where Britain had held the leading position for a century. A powerful Germany was picking up colonial holdings, often adjacent to those held by Great Britain and France. A German fleet was in the making, and seemed to require efforts on the part of Britain to hold a position on the high seas comparable with the extent of its world-wide commerce and its global communications. A clause that was included in every postal contract made this clear: 'The speed of the British ships shall equal the highest speed of the foreign mail ships on the same route.' The century of the Pax Britannica was nearing its end.

The British steamship Lines had shown a remarkable improve-

---

[1] *Rep. S.C. on Steamship Subsidies* (1902), pp. iii, xxv, 151-3. The word 'subvention', also in use at the time for subsidy, was regarded by the Committee 'as the same as a subsidy, but it is thought to be more euphemistic and to create less prejudice'.

[2] ibid., pp. x, 34, being the evidence of Captain F. C. D. Sturdee. In 1900 the Admiralty was making annual payments to the mail companies of £77,000 in addition to the large grants through the Post Office.

ment, as a result of international competition. Sir Thomas Sutherland of the P & O testified before the Select Committee of 1902 on the progress made by his Company. In the last twenty-five years the time required between London and Bombay had been lowered from twenty-two to just over fourteen days. In 1878 the time needed on the overland route between London and Melbourne had been forty-eight days; in 1900 it had been lowered to less than thirty-two days. Sir Thomas asserted that the speed of his ships in 1900 was 50 per cent better than a quarter of a century earlier.

In 1904 an Inter-Departmental Committee on the Eastern Mail Service reported on the best means for speeding the mails to the Far East and Australia. The Committee, despite the glowing report of Sir Thomas Sutherland, believed that the speed of the P & O vessels should be increased. The Line had been required to run its ships at no more than $14\frac{1}{2}$ knots, the same rate as the ships of the French Messageries Maritimes and of the North German Lloyd serving the East. A Mail Service Committee of 1904 recommended that the P & O vessels on the India route should maintain a speed of 16 knots, because of the 'general desire for acceleration', and also suggested that the Admiralty clauses and assistance be continued in the P & O contracts, even though the Admiralty had just decided to subsidize only those mail vessels capable of 22 knots. The contract with the P & O of 1907 followed the recommendations of the Committee by requiring speeds of 16 knots on the Brindisi-Bombay route.[1]

Other mail Lines showed similar improvements in speed. By 1900 the Union-Castle ships were taking seventeen days between Southampton and Cape Town. On the south Pacific route by way of San Francisco, there was a striking improvement. In 1875 the Pacific Mail Line gave a service that carried the mail between London and Sydney in just under fifty days; by 1889 the mail on this route took under forty days; by 1900 it had been lowered to just under thirty days. When the Panama Canal was opened in 1914, New Zealand had an alternative route, but it was not so fast as that by San Francisco. By the end of the century New South Wales and New Zealand found it worth while to use another trans-Pacific route—to Vancouver and across Canada by railway to the Atlantic.[2]

The north Atlantic crossing, as one might expect, was the most

[1] ibid., pp. x, 10, 233-4; *Rep. of Mail Service Com.* (1904), 2-6; *Parl. Ret.*, 311/1907.
[2] *Rep. S.C. on Steamship Subsidies* (1902), 56; *Rep. P.M.G.* (N.S.W.) for 1875, 1889, 1900.

competitive. Here British and foreign Lines had contended for decades. The rivalry compelled the two British subsidized Lines, Cunard and the White Star, to improve their ships and the speed with which they made the crossing. In 1891, the White Star's *Teutonic* of nearly 10,000 tons, had won the blue riband by a record run between New York and Southampton of five days and sixteen hours at a speed of over 20 knots. Two years later the Cunard Company was again in the lead with its new *Lucania* of 12,950 tons; she crossed in five days, eight and a half hours; and she retained the lead until 1897. In that year the *Kaiser Wilhelm der Grosse* took over, only to be beaten in 1903 by the faster German liner, the *Deutschland*. The Germans retained the blue riband for most of the first decade of the new century.

In the meantime the Cunard Company was preparing to meet this foreign challenge. In 1903 it agreed with three government departments, the Post Office, the Admiralty and the Board of Trade, for the building of two gigantic liners that would be capable of 25 knots. The contract was expensive. A postal subsidy of £68,000 supplemented one from the Admiralty of £180,000 a year, in addition to strong financial assistance from the Government for the building of the vessels. Obviously the contract was for much more than mail carrying.

The result of these arrangements was the building of the *Lusitania* of over 30,000 tons, and the *Mauretania* of 31,938 tons. In 1907 the *Lusitania* retrieved the blue riband from Germany by a transatlantic voyage of just under five days. This was soon followed by the fastest voyage yet of the *Mauretania*; she crossed the Atlantic in four days and eleven hours at an average speed of 26 knots. By this time the largest Cunarders were driven by quadruple screws and oil-burning turbines. The *Mauretania* kept the record for more than twenty years, to the chagrin of the German companies. The largest Cunarders were of such size at this time, more than 800 feet from stem to stern, that the Company suggested a change in its mail contracts, so that the larger vessels would no longer have to stop at Queenstown. The request was granted.[1]

The rivalry for the Atlantic speed record led, in 1912, to one of the greatest of marine disasters. The White Star Line, not to be outdone by Cunard or the Germans, commissioned Harland &

---

[1] For data on the blue riband, see Bonsor, op. cit., 590-3, and *Lloyd's Calendar 1950*, 403; the two volumes are not in entire agreement. For the Queenstown call, see *Cd. 7007* (1913). The Cunard Company declared that their largest liners faced undue risks in entering the harbour of Queenstown (Cobh).

Wolff of Belfast to build two twin liners that would be larger and faster than anything afloat. The *Olympic* and the *Titanic* were the result. The *Titanic*, over 46,000 tons, started on her maiden voyage from Southampton to New York in April 1912. As every reader knows, she did not complete the trip. Several hundred miles south-east of Newfoundland the *Titanic* struck an iceberg while steaming at an excessive speed at night through an area known to contain icebergs. Supposedly unsinkable, she foundered with the loss of over 1,500 lives. It is not so well known that an enormous load of mail went down with the ship—3,366 bags of letters besides numerous bags of parcel mail. A much more serious loss for the Post Office was the drowning of the five sorters on board, John R. Jago Smith and James B. Wilkinson of the British Post Offices and their three American colleagues.[1]

The steamboat had been the accepted carrier for fast overseas mail for three quarters of a century, from the time of the pioneer voyage of the *Great Western* in 1838. After the First World War super liners such as the *Olympic* and the *Mauretania* were to be surpassed by the Queens. The *Queen Mary*, over 80,000 tons and a fifth of a mile long, was over sixty times the size of the *Great Western*. In 1936 the *Queen Mary* crossed in just under four days; two years later she again lowered the record to three days and twenty hours at a speed of over 31 knots. She kept the record until 1952 when it was won by the *United States* in a crossing that took less than three days and a half. By this voyage she won back for the United States a blue riband that it had not held since the days of the Collins liners a century earlier.

Despite the further lowering, year after year, of the north Atlantic record, the primacy of the steamship was endangered by other forms of communication. It had been the postal practice for years to use land carriage wherever possible. As early as 1880, for instance, the Post Office decided that all the mails via the Suez Canal should go overland through France rather than all the way by sea via Gibraltar.

[1] Lord Mersey's Committee made a careful study of the disaster, reporting that 'the loss of the ship was due to collision with an iceberg and the excessive speed at which the ship was being navigated'. At the time, Lord Charles Beresford stated in Parliament that 'as any seaman knows the ship was going too fast in dangerous waters'. When Herbert Samuel, the Postmaster-General, was asked in the House of Commons about the speed of the *Titanic*, he replied that mail ships were required 'to use their best endeavours to complete the voyage within the shortest possible time consistent with prudent navigation'. A bronze tablet in the Southampton Post Office commemorates the devotion of the five 'sea-post officers'. See *P.O. Records*, Eng. Min., 18060/14; *Parl. Deb.*, H.C., 5th ser., xxvii, 1206; xxxviii, 1582; xlii, 62, 81.

The mails between Britain and various Pacific ports is another example of steamship limitations. The route by way of San Francisco became worth while for the colonies of New South Wales and New Zealand as soon as the American transcontinental railways connected San Francisco with New York and the Cunard Line. Although actually longer than the route by way of Suez, it was able to compete with the route via Egypt by the use of 3,000 miles of land carriage. For the same reason mails by the Canadian Pacific Railway to Vancouver made that route feasible by the end of the century for mails between Great Britain and Hong Kong and other ports in the Far East. As early as 1891 this Canadian route was used to shorten by ten days the course of the Hong Kong mails as compared with the all-sea route via Singapore. The Eastern Mail Committee of 1904 even suggested that mail for China might well use the recently opened railway across Siberia.[1]

CABLE AND WIRELESS

Another form of communication overseas had developed to world-wide proportions before 1914. Although no substitute for surface mails by ship, the submarine telegraph often paralleled the steamship routes and supplemented the letter mails. The electric telegraph began to spread in England at the opening of Queen Victoria's reign, just at the time that the marine engines were driving the paddle wheels of the first ocean steamships. Telegraph lines soon extended to more distant points, and joined the seaports with London. The extension of the telegraph lines to the ports naturally led to the idea of the submarine telegraph. John W. Brett and his brother Jacob even formed a company in the mid-forties to establish 'a telegraphic communication from the British Isles across the Atlantic . . . and establishing electric communication with the colonies'.[2]

A less grandiose scheme of the Bretts was the English Channel Submarine Telegraph Company. A cable was laid from Dover to the French coast in 1850. The first line had but a brief life, for a French fisherman fouled it with his anchor, and then chopped it in two, thinking it was a particularly tough form of seaweed. A second and successful cable was laid across the Channel in 1851.

[1] *Rep. Eastern Mail Service Com.* (1904), 4; *33rd Rep. P.M.G.* (1907), 8.
[2] Non-British readers may or may not need to be reminded that the British and other Commonwealth post offices include the responsibility for communication by telegraph, cable, telephone and wireless as well as by letter-mail.

After a submarine telegraph had connected Great Britain and Ireland in 1853, the way was opened for a mail contract with the Galway Line. A chief feature of the scheme which had much to do with its acceptance was the sending of telegrams to Galway whence they were to be carried on the shortest Atlantic crossing to New-foundland, and from there by telegraph to the neighbouring Continent.[1]

The most ambitious undertaking of the fifties was a submarine cable all the way across the Atlantic from Ireland to Newfoundland. A British engineer, F. E. Gisborne, was the leader in the project, and a wealthy New York capitalist, Cyrus W. Fields, gave financial support in this symbolic joining of Europe and America. The first attempt, in 1857, failed as the cable broke 300 miles west of Valentia (County Kerry), Ireland. In the next year the two cable-laying ships met in mid-ocean for another attempt, spliced their cables, and then one steamed east and the other west. The telegraph was successfully laid and the first communication by cable across the Atlantic occurred in August 1858. But the line was weak from the beginning, and went 'dead' in October.

A third attempt in the sixties succeeded; in September 1866 Ireland and Newfoundland—America and Europe—were per-manently connected by submarine telegraph. No longer could delays in communication bring about confusion and disagreement such as was possible, for example, in 1812 when decisions that might have kept the peace could not be known in time to prevent a declaration of war by the United States against Great Britain.

Soon other private British companies were laying cables eastward towards India, China and Australia. By 1870 India was in telegraphic communication with London. From India lines soon extended to Singapore whence branch cables went to Hong Kong, and south-east to Australia. By October 1872 a land telegraph stretched across Australia to the south coast, thereby connecting Adelaide and the south-eastern colonies with the mother country.

As early as 1887 Sandford Fleming of Canada had spoken before a colonial conference in London on the value of a cable across the Pacific for strengthening the bonds of Empire, and making the more distant colonies independent of foreign nations in their telegraphic communication with London. It was some years, however, before Britain and the interested colonies could agree on the proportion of

---

[1] G. R. M. Garratt, *One Hundred Years of Submarine Cables* (1950), 4-8. For the Galway Line, see above, pp., 242ff.

expense each should bear in its maintenance. It was ready for use in 1902. Two lines, one from Brisbane in Australia, the other from New Zealand joined at Norfolk Island. Thence a single cable stretched north-eastward to Fiji, from there to Fanning Island, and from this tiny base near the Equator the last link in the connection with Canada was laid in one continuous uninterrupted stretch past Hawaii to British Columbia 3,500 miles away. From there Canadian land lines carried telegraphic messages across the Continent. This cable was state owned, and operated by a Pacific Cable Board on which Great Britain and the various Dominions were represented. The first chairman of the Board was Sir Spencer Walpole.[1]

By 1914 British cables girdled the earth. This world-wide system added greatly to the value of the surface mail communications and became even more valuable when the surface routes were hindered or closed by the world war that began in 1914.

Already, however, other means of communication supplemented the telegraph and the submarine cable. The telephone had been used since the 1870s. It soon became so useful that the Post Office telegraphs in Great Britain were losing business to the country-wide Post Office telephones and the various private telephone companies. As a result, the Post Office took over the private telephone lines in 1912. Although international telephone cables were laid across the English Channel, it was to be some time before telephone conversations were possible across the intervening seas and oceans.[2]

Of even greater value was the development of communications without the need of wires whether on land or over the sea. The age of electricity was bringing change after change. If one could communicate without wires, it would indeed bring in a new era.

The use of wireless communication had been tried successfully in the later decades of the nineteenth century, but only over short distances. W. H. Preece, later the Engineer-in-Chief of the Post Office, had sent messages between Southampton and the Isle of Wight as early as 1882. In 1895 wireless communication had been made between Morven on the west coast of Scotland and the nearby Isle of Mull.

During these years Mr Marconi was carrying on promising experiments in Italy. He came to England in 1896, where Mr Preece, now Engineer-in-Chief, gave him every assistance. Soon the distance for wireless communication began to lengthen. In 1899

[1] See Garratt, op. cit., 32-33; George Johnson, *The All Red Line* (Ottawa, 1903); *A.J.H.R.* (N.Z.), F8, 1-2.
[2] *The Post Office, an Historical Summary* (1911), 88-100.

messages were sent for the first time across the Channel. The next important victory of wireless was on the Atlantic. After Marconi erected a station at Poldhu in Cornwall, he went across to New-foundland to test signals across the Atlantic. This was in 1901 when he had the satisfaction of detecting signals across 3,000 miles of open ocean.[1]

An obvious use for the early wireless was the sending of signals between ship and shore, and from ship to nearby ship. Marconi made experiments in 1902 while on a voyage to America—in the *Philadelphia* of the American Line—and was able to receive and transmit messages between the ship and the Isle of Wight, and later to receive on shipboard, tape recordings from as far as 1,500 miles away.

Little wonder that the Government showed a keen interest in this new form of communication. It led to an Act of 1904 that put wireless under Government control. Before the end of the decade the Government had purchased from the Marconi Company and from Lloyd's Corporation all the coastal stations in Great Britain. In 1906 an international congress in Berlin drew up a Radio-tele-graphic convention that regulated the use of this new medium in much the same way that the Universal Postal Union had set up controls for international surface mails thirty years before.

British passenger and mail ships as well as those of other nations were soon required to have wireless equipment for essential com-munications while at sea. A well-known use of wireless in 1910 illustrates its value, a use that aroused wide interest. Dr Crippen had left Britain that summer to avoid arrest following the murder of his wife. He and his typist, dressed as a boy, fled to Antwerp where he engaged passage for Canada in the Canadian Pacific liner *Montrose*. Crippen and his shipmate, who had registered as Mr Robinson and son—a seemingly safe pseudonym—were soon suspected by the Captain as the couple that was wanted. The Captain thereupon sent a wireless message to Liverpool. The next day Chief Inspector Dew left Britain on the *Laurentic*; she was expected to reach Canada ahead of the *Montrose*. The race was won, for the Inspector, disguised as a pilot, was able to arrest Crippen and his companion before the *Montrose* docked.

Wireless also enabled vessels to communicate at sea in case of need, for the custom of the sea had always been to give ships in

---

[1] R. H. Vyvyan, *Wireless over Thirty Years* (1933), 23–31. The agreed signal was the letter 'S'—three dots.

distress every assistance possible. This was brought out vividly in 1912 when the *Titanic* called for aid after striking an iceberg. Several ships heard the calls and rushed to the scene of the disaster, but the first one arrived only after the *Titanic* had disappeared.

By the opening of the First World War an Imperial Wireless Chain was in prospect. A Select Committee on the Marconi Agreement was appointed in 1913 because of the urgent need for establishing a chain of stations in view of the danger of war. The Committee was to examine the existing systems of long-distance wireless telegraphy as to their capacity for continuous communication 'day and night over land and sea for distances of between 2,000 and 2,500 miles'. The war that began in the next year postponed the creation of an Imperial Wireless Chain.[1]

BEGINNINGS OF AIR MAIL

More revolutionary in its effects on the older forms of communication was the carriage of mail by air. The desire to fly like a bird had been the dream for centuries. Even before the French Revolution of 1789, 'free balloons had been flown in France. The best known use in the nineteenth century for their carriage of mail was a service out of Paris when it was surrounded by German forces in 1870. The balloon, of course, was not very reliable, as winds might carry mail out of Paris to any point of the compass. The only way of sending mail into the besieged city was by the use of homing pigeons. But the messages were more like telegrams than letters.

As the balloon became more highly developed, it was used in Britain to amuse the public by the carriage of souvenir mail. An early and curious flight with mail occurred in Beckenham, Kent, as part of the village celebration of the Coronation of King Edward VII and Queen Alexandra in August 1902. The promoters of the Beckenham celebration thought that a balloon post would be more attractive than mere ascensions. Accordingly, some 300 picture postcards were overprinted 'Beckenham Celebration—Dispatched from the Clouds by Balloon Post'. Those who bought cards addressed them and put on the necessary postage. They were then

[1] *Rep. S.C. on Marconi Wireless Telegraph Co., Ltd.*, (Cd. 6781) pp. v, 36. Before 1914 cables and wireless communications overseas were largely under the control of private companies, save for the Pacific Cable. In 1920 the Transatlantic Cable, the Pacific Cable, and various private companies were merged as Imperial and International Communications, Ltd., better known as Cable and Wireless. In 1950 Cable and Wireless were taken over by the Post Office, supplementing its control of internal communications by telegraph and telephone. See the official *The Post Office, 1950*, 4-6.

done up in bundles of 100 each and put in three separate bags. An attached label requested the finder of a bag to deliver the contents to the nearest post office. If the finder sent the label to the Secretary of the Beckenham Organising Committee, his reward was 5s.

The winds carried this 'free' balloon towards Dover, and the bags were dropped in Kent. Soon the balloonists were out over the Channel, and fearful that they might not reach the French coast after 'delivering the mail'. Fortunately they just reached a beach to the north of Calais.[1]

The balloon was the forerunner of the airship. If a balloon could be guided, that is dirigible as well as machine driven, it might be practicable as a carrier of regular mail. Attempts at directed flights had already been tried in Germany where Ferdinand von Zeppelin was the most persistent advocate of the balloon-like airship. Not until 1910 did the Government in England see fit to appropriate money for an airship programme, but little progress had been made in the adoption and development of the airship by 1914.

By the opening of the present century some advance had been made in the use of a flying machine that was heavier than air, and also fitted with an internal combustion engine. The first successful flight anywhere was in 1905 when the Wright brothers, Orville and Wilbur, were able to make a sustained flight on the sand dunes off the coast of North Carolina in the United States. The first flight was modest indeed; a frail contraption of wood and wire, weighing about 600 lb. including the pilot, flew for less than a minute and for a distance of only 850 feet.

During the following decade considerable progress was made in the size of the machine, and in the length of sustained flight. In 1909 the first airplane to cross the Channel was a machine of 25 horsepower that carried Louis Blériot from Calais to Dover in thirty-seven minutes.

Two years later, in September 1911 a series of flights took place between Hendon and Windsor—it was another Coronation year. The promoters of these flights obtained the permission of the Post Office to carry letters and cards that bore the words 'First U.K. Aerial Post by Sanction of H.M. Postmaster-General'. The flights, some twenty in all, were over but a short distance, a journey of some 20 miles that even the pre-war machines could make in fifteen minutes. The airplanes carried souvenir mail in covers provided for the flights, and they were given a special cancellation.

[1] John Pringle, *Early British Balloon Posts* (n.d. c. 1925).

To some it seemed like a game of make-believe; to others it was not only a means of celebrating the Coronation of King George and Queen Mary, but the beginning of a new era in communication. The magazine *Flight*, which defended the project, admitted that the airplane was not likely to take the place of orthodox methods of mail carrying; it preferred to leave such speculations to H. G. Wells. Yet the Post Office had given its official sanction to a series of flights. Only after the First World War, however, would civilian air-mail flights become a regular part of the postal service.[1]

FOREIGN SERVICES IN WAR TIME

Three years later the country was at war with Germany. The conflict sharply divided the pre-war attempts at finding new forms of communication from their post-war uses. Military necessity was to push forward the evolution of aircraft so rapidly that flying was to make astonishing advances after the war.

As soon as the war began the Post Office naturally turned its attention to military as well as civilian needs. The cross-Channel cables, for example, became of the utmost importance for keeping in touch with the armies in France. So valuable were the cables to France that ten new telephone and telegraph cables had been laid before the war came to an end. Even parts of the former German cables in the Channel were put to British use. More surprising was the diversion of the German cable to New York; it was made into an additional transatlantic line of communication after the ends had been fished up and landed at Penzance, Cornwall, and at Halifax in Nova Scotia.[2]

Wireless communication was rapidly improved by the necessities of war, but all private or civilian use of wireless was forbidden. All the stations and all apparatus came under the control of the Post Office.

It need hardly be said that the foreign mail services were greatly disorganized by the war. The times of transit were no longer because of the use of indirect routes and by the closing of some ports to shipping. The fast overland route through France and Italy had

[1] S. J. Field and H. C. Baldwin, *The Coronation Aerial Post* (1934) was written from the philatelic point of view. H. G. Wells had already published speculative novels with such arresting titles as the *First Man in the Moon* and the *War in the Air*. It was the *Manchester Guardian* that regarded the flights as a game of make-believe. See *Flight* for September 25, 1911.

[2] Sir Evelyn Murray, *The Post Office* (1927), 200ff. E. C. Baker, *History of the* (Post Office) *Engineering Department* (1939) is one of the official 'Green Papers'; see p. 23.

to be abandoned. The surface mails reverted to the all-sea route via Gibraltar if going or coming from the Near East, a route that had not been of much importance since 1880. The mail services to India became fortnightly once again. The P & O ceased to serve Australia, but the Orient Line continued the carriage of Australian mails by using the all-sea route around Africa. During the war, considerable Australian and New Zealand mail came and went by way of Vancouver and San Francisco.

The taking over of steamships by the Admiralty during the war meant, according to the Postmaster-General, that 'many of the packet companies have been unable to fill their contractual obligations'. This was certainly an understatement. Mails were often kept in port after embarkation, awaiting a favourable time for departure. Many of the finest liners that had been doing regular mail runs before the war became victims of the submarine.

Probably the most widely remembered sinking was that of the giant Cunarder *Lusitania*. In May 1918 she fell victim to a German torpedo off the Old Head of Kinsale, Ireland, when she was almost home from New York. Nearly 1,000 persons lost their lives. Although much mail was lost because of submarine attacks on British liners, it happened that the *Lusitania*'s mail was not large on her last voyage. She was carrying the mail that had been specially endorsed for the *Lusitania*; the American liner *New York*, leaving about the same time, carried most of the European mail. Yet the *Lusitania* had aboard sixty-three bags of mail—about 147,000 letters—and while at sea she received three more bags, two from the *Caronia* and one from H.M.S. *Glory*. The records show that the mails lost by the sinking of the *Lusitania* included four dispatches from the Governor of Bermuda to the Colonial Office. They were sent in a weighted bag that would cause them to sink in case of disaster at sea, a revival of the custom used in sailing-packet days a century earlier when the mail-bags were weighted with pigs of iron if a packet was likely to be captured.[1]

To avoid complete loss of important mails, they were distributed among the vessels that were taking the same route. Writers were encouraged to adopt the centuries-old device of sending duplicates, even triplicates, at separate times and by different routes. The only mail service relatively free from hazard was that for the prisoners of war. Not within the memory of the oldest resident had the mails going overseas been so disrupted.

[1] *P.O. Records*, Pkt. Min., 139/15; *Rep. P.M.G.* (1915-16), 7-8; Murray, op. cit. 208.

23

MAILS TAKE TO THE AIR

✦✦✦

THE return of peace in 1918 brought intense relief and gave deep satisfaction to a generation that had never before experienced a general war. The Post Office could give its attention once again to civilian needs.

Yet the post-war world was so different from that of five years earlier that even mail carrying could hardly be the same. The life-and-death struggle of war had so hastened the development of aircraft that now mails might well use the airways. Sir Evelyn Murray, Secretary of the Post Office, wrote that air mail by 1919 'had gradually secured a footing as a valuable adjunct to the ordinary mail service for urgent communication'. Although Sir Evelyn admitted that prophecy was a dangerous pastime, he was on safe ground in foreseeing that 'Imperial postal communications may well have entered upon an entirely new phase, the results of which it is difficult even to forecast.'[1]

The experimental Coronation Air Mail of 1911 between Hendon and Windsor was not followed by further attempts until the summer of 1918 when the Royal Air Force established a service to the Army Post Office in France. In the spring of 1919 the R.A.F. began another run between Cologne and Folkestone, carrying the mails for the British Army of Occupation. As yet, however, aircraft were not reliable for regular flights if the weather was bad, nor was it safe as yet to fly by night.

In the meantime the Government was so impressed by the rising importance of air travel and communication that several important decisions prepared for the future. In 1917 the Government set up a Ministry of Air. At the Peace Conference in Paris an Air Convention had been drafted and signed by the representatives of twenty-six countries. The Convention affirmed the sovereignty of each state over the air space above its territories, as well as the freedom of 'innocent passage' by the aircraft of other contracting states. Rules

[1] op. cit., 64, 218.

of the 'road' were even worked out. It was the opinion of the
Convention that aircraft should keep to the right in passing each
other, that airplanes should always give way to airships and balloons,
and that airships should always yield the right of way to balloons.[1]

The probable growth of air travel was so likely before the war
came to an end that a large and representative Civil Aerial Transport Committee was appointed in 1917 to make a thorough study of
the whole matter, especially from the international viewpoint.
They agreed that no technical difficulties would prevent the carriage
of mails and passengers, that there would be a great demand for air
services after the war, and that it was extremely important that
Great Britain so prepare for the greater use of aircraft as to be 'first
in the field in the matter of aerial transport'. The Committee
considered at some length the particular uses of both the airship and
the airplane. The airship was believed at the time to have a range of
about 1,000 miles without landing, but that the range of the airplane
was only half that distance. The airship also had a greater load
capacity, but its speed of travel was considerably slower than that of
the airplane—not more than 60 miles an hour. The Committee
concluded that the airship was likely to have a marked advantage
over steamships as to speed 'save in contrary winds'. And the airship, if speed was not the material factor, would offer advantages
'over the aeroplane in the way of comfort and the ease of navigation'.
The Committee urged immediate action, as some of the Allies were
already starting experimental air services. It proposed the formation
of a special branch under the Air Ministry for 'civil aerial transport'.
As a result a Department of Civil Aviation was set up in 1919
within the Air Ministry. The relative value of the airship and the
heavier-than-air machines was soon to be put to the test.[2]

THE FIRST AIR SERVICES

An agreement in September 1919 with France for a service

---

[1] *Convention* regulating air navigation (Cmd. 670, 1920); *The Approach towards a
System of Imperial Air Communications* (1926), 23ff., 48. This elaborate 'memorandum'
was prepared by the Air Ministry for the Imperial Conference of 1926. It will be cited
as *Memorandum*.

[2] *Rep. Civil Aerial Transport* (Cmd. 9218, 1918), 11, 15, 42-3. Lord Northcliffe was
chairman of the Committee, but his departure to America on Government business led
to the appointment of Major John Baird as chairman. The Committee had some sixty
members, including Sir Sefton Brancker of the Air Ministry, G. Holt Thomas head of
the Aircraft Mfg. Co. and builder of the De Havillands, Lt.-Col. J. T. C. Moore-
Brabazon, the pioneer aviator; J. D. Siddeley; and H. G. Wells. Sir Evelyn Murray
represented the Post Office.

between London and Paris opened the first regular airmail service overseas. The British Line that carried the mails to Paris was Air Transport and Travel Ltd., which had been organized by Holt Thomas, with Sir Sefton Brancker as one of its directors. As a carrier of the mails, Air Transport and Travel was regarded as a trial service, for the Post Office was not at all sure that the flights would be regular or useful. The Company's machines were capable of carrying but two passengers, in addition to the pilot, and only a small amount of mail and luggage. The letter fees for this first service were made unusually high. A special air charge, including express delivery, was set at 3s 6d the ounce, in addition to the ordinary charge for surface mail. The Post Office was feeling its way rather haltingly, for it still continued to regard an airborne letter as 'something more akin to a semi-urgent telegram than to ordinary correspondence'.[1]

The air fee was so high that it did not attract much business. In the first few months only about forty letters daily—a mere handful—were carried across the Channel by the one daily service. But in April 1920 the Company began sending two services across each day, and in May 1920 the fee was lowered by the Post Office to 2s per ounce in addition to the ordinary postage of $2\frac{1}{2}$d. The express delivery charge of 6d was to be paid only in case that service was wanted. Letters to be sent by air to Paris had to be enclosed in an outer cover addressed to the 'Postmaster Croydon'. The necessary postage was to be affixed to the inside envelope, on which the sender was to write the words 'Air Mail' or 'Air Mail Express' at the upper left-hand corner of the envelope to indicate the service desired.

Despite the small use of this first airline overseas, the Government decided to renew the contract in the spring of 1920. Air Transport and Travel was again the successful bidder. In July 1920 the fee was cut drastically, the rate being lowered from 2s to 2d, in addition to the ordinary surface rate. At the same time the Post Office hoped to attract business by making it much simpler to send letters by air. On August 9, 1920 the Postal Services Department informed the Postmaster at Croydon:

'Instructions will appear in tomorrow's *Post Office Circular* concerning the use of special blue labels bearing the words "By Air

---

[1] The quotation is from Frederick Williamson, *The Air Mail Service* (1934). The author was soon to be Director of the Postal Services. This volume was the first of a useful series of 'Green Papers' issued by the Post Office.

mail", which are in the future to be affixed to all packets intended
for transmission from this country by air mail . . . It is anticipated
that the labels will be a sufficient indication to sorters that the
correspondence to which they are affixed is intended for transmission by air . . . There will, accordingly, no longer be any need for
the public to enclose air mail packets in covers addressed to you.'

The *Post Office Circular* of August 10th was the first one to include
a separate Air Mail Leaflet. They were to be stocked in all Head and
Branch offices for distribution 'with discretion' to all persons likely
to use the services. All mail bearing the special blue label was to be
'circulated to Croydon'. This use of blue labels in 1920 to distinguish
air mail has since become universal.[1]

At this time the Post Office began to use other air lines as well as
Air Transport and Travel for carrying mails to the nearby Continent.
Handley Page had three separate routes—to Paris, to Brussels and
to Amsterdam. Instone Air Lines began a service to Paris in 1920.
In April 1922 Daimler Hire Ltd., also opened a London-Paris
service. But the air lines were not prospering. Air Transport and
Travel had even gone into liquidation, and none of the others was
doing well.

As air traffic grew, the adequacy of airfields was naturally questioned. Handley Page preferred to use Cricklewood, although the
chief London airfield until 1920 was Hounslow, but in that year it
was reoccupied by the R.A.F. It was just at this time that the Air
Ministry decided to make Croydon the London Terminal Airport
for traffic to and from the Continent. Croydon seemed preferable to
Hounslow because the aircraft would not have to cross 'a densely
populated portion of the London suburbs'. By the late twenties
Croydon was enlarged and rearranged so as to handle a traffic that
was constantly growing. As early as 1923 there was talk of the need
of additional airfields for London. Sir Sefton Brancker, the Director
of Civil Aviation, even suggested the possible use of Hyde Park! In
speaking before the Third Air Conference in 1923, he said: 'We may
be able to turn Hyde Park into an aerodrome, but I think it will take
ten years to break down our conservative public opinion . . . Then
we shall be able to use Hyde Park.'

Not until 1923 was a permanent system of subsidies worked out

---

[1] *P.O. Records*, Pkt. Min., 110/20. The French had also organized a company to
furnish passenger and air services on this route. As in the case of surface transport, air
mail from Paris went ordinarily by French aircraft.

to aid the struggling companies that were serving the Continental centres. Sir Samuel Hoare, Secretary of State for Air, appointed a Civil Transport Subsidies Committee to advise on the best method of subsidizing air transport. The Committee, headed by Sir Herbert Hambling, proplsed that a new company be formed by combining the four operating companies. The successor was to have a monopoly of British subsidies for air transport to Europe. In addition to working the routes already in use, the new company was to improve and lengthen the lines of air travel, and ultimately to extend the air services to points within the Empire. The recommendation led to the organization of Imperial Airways in 1924.[1]

After Imperial Airways had been formed as the 'instrument' for spreading British commercial air transport, it began to extend services beyond Europe. There was one exception, however, for aircraft were as yet not capable of regular flights across the Atlantic to America. Attempts had been made just after the war to pierce this ocean barrier. Lord Northcliffe, as early as 1913, had offered a prize of £10,000 for the first direct non-stop flight over the north Atlantic, but the war soon intervened. In 1919 the prize was re-offered, and a number of venturesome British airmen crossed to Newfoundland by ship to seek the award. Not only was the shortest Atlantic crossing between Newfoundland and Ireland, but the prevailing winds made flights eastward more likely to succeed. Hawkins and Mackenzie Grieve set off in May 1919, but failed when their airplane came down some 700 miles west of the Irish coast, but both they and a bag of souvenir mail were saved.

Success crowned the efforts of another pair of airmen in the following month. John Alcock and Arthur Whitten Brown, in a bi-plane powered by two Rolls-Royce engines of 375 horsepower each, only just managed to reach Ireland. Their airplane, after a flight of sixteen hours nosed down into a bog near the Clifden wireless station to the north-west of Galway. Alcock and Brown were handed the award by Winston Churchill, Secretary of State for War and Air, and they also received knighthoods for their achievement of the first crossing of the Atlantic by air. Their mail of 197 letters was duly delivered, most of it ultimately landing in the

---

[1] *Proceedings of the 3rd Air Conf.* (1923), 32; *Memorandum* (1926), 23-24, 64ff. *Rep. Com. of Inquiry into Civil Aviation* (1938), pp. ii, 39-40. The financial assistance to Imperial Airways was liberal—£137,000 a year for the first four years, then tapering off and ending after ten years. The total subsidy of £1,000,000 was to be repaid when the Company reached a profit-earning condition. See also Robin Higham, *Britain's Imperial Air Routes 1918 to 1939* (London, 1960), pp. 72ff.

albums of collectors. The flight had made only too clear that a regular air-mail service along the route of the north Atlantic seaway was still some distance in the future.[1]

On the other hand, Imperial routes by way of Egypt to South Africa and the Far East seemed much more favourable for early air-mail development, since there were no such long stages as the non-stop flight across the Atlantic to Newfoundland. Air-conscious Australia was particularly eager for such communication, and far away New Zealand would benefit immeasurably by an air-mail service. In 1919, the same year that Alcock and Brown had made their successful flight, the Australian Government offered a £10,000 prize for the first flight between England and Australia. It would have to be made in stages, of course, but the terms required its completion within thirty days. Two airmen, Ross and Keith Smith, left Hounslow on November 12, 1919. After many adventures and some maddening delays, they reached Port Darwin on December 10th—with fifty-one hours to spare!

The first British air-mail flights to the east of Europe were between Egypt and Baghdad. Just after the war the R.A.F. had carried on a regular service for official passengers between Cairo and Baghdad, a distance of over 800 miles. They also carried mail soon after the first flight in 1919. The long journey, much of it over desert, was regarded as an excellent experiment in 'long-distance flights in a hot climate'. Every journey was made by a pair of airplanes, partly for protection, partly to ensure that the mail went on if one of the machines had mechanical trouble. There were a number of stops on the way, and the speed was only about 75 to 85 miles an hour. Yet this service was a decided saving in time. Surface mails between London and Baghdad usually took a month, but the Cairo-Baghdad air service cut the time down by nine or ten days. This pioneer route was used by the R.A.F. for over five years, until it was taken over by Imperial Airways in 1926, as part of the route to India.[1]

THE AIRSHIP

During the twenties when the air service to the East was under

[1] Harry Harper and Robert Brenard, *The Romance of the Flying Mail* (1935), 28-36; R. E. R. Dalwick and H. C. H. Harmer, *Newfoundland Air Mails 1919-1939* (1953). Both mails of these pioneer flights were accompanied by way-bills of the Newfoundland Post Office. The original Vickers Vimy used by Alcock and Brown is now in the Aeronautical Museum in South Kensington, London.

[1] Roderic Hill, *The Baghdad Air Mail* (1926), 31-32, 39-44; *Memorandum* (1926), pp. v-vii. The original letter rate for the R.A.F. Service was 1s the ounce, plus the ordinary postage. It was later lowered to 3d.

development, there was still considerable question as to the relative value of the airship and the aeroplane. Would not the airship, for instance, be better for long-distance journeys? Alcock and Brown had only just made the crossing of the Atlantic, and the flight to Australia in 1919 had been by numerous stages. G. H. Scott, a member of the Second Air Conference (1922) was sure that 'a satisfactory system of aerial transport can only be established by both airships and airplanes working together . . . Unless the airship is used it is difficult to see how imperial communications can be improved.' Sir Samuel Hoare in speaking to the Imperial Conference of 1926 stated that 'the airplane and the airship are really complementary'. He admitted that the large airship was a fragile structure, but he told the Conference that much progress had been made in giving it rigidity and improving its safety. One great advance, according to Sir Samuel Hoare, was the invention of the mooring mast by which an airship could be 'easily moored without the risk involved in pulling a structure 700 feet long into a shed'.[1]

In 1919 the *R 34*, carrying a souvenir mail, had made a successful transatlantic flight. It went by way of Newfoundland to New York in June under the command of Major G. H. Scott; the return crossing in July took only seventy-five hours. On the strength of this successful experiment, the American Government agreed to purchase a similar airship, the *R 38*. The *R 38*, however, foundered in August 1921 during trials that were preliminary to her expected transatlantic journey. All her personnel—forty-five British and American officers and men perished. This halted airship construction for a time.

Two years later the British Government revived the airship programme on an even grander scale. Two airships were authorized. The *R 100* was to be built at Howden in Yorkshire by the private Airship Guarantee Company; the *R 101* was to be constructed at Cardington by the Air Ministry. They were over 700 feet long, about the length of the latest and largest ocean liners.

According to Sir Samuel Hoare, they were not mere copies of the German Zeppelins: 'The structure of both the airships that are being built will be incomparably stronger . . . than airships that have been built in the past.' The construction of one by the Air Ministry, of the other by a private company, was to provide com-

[1] ibid., pp. viii-ix; *Cmd.* 1619 (1922), being the Proceedings of the 2nd Air Conference, p. 74.

petition in design and to ensure that a 'purely accidental failure of one ship will not terminate the whole programme'. The two airships were to have a cruising speed of 60 to 70 miles an hour, and flights of some 4,000 miles without refuelling. The cost was about £500,000 each.

They were several years in the building. The *Report* of 1929 on the Progress of Civil Aviation announced that they were well on, and that tests would be made in September. The *R 100* was to make its first long journey overseas to Canada, the *R 101* to India by way of Egypt. They were designed to carry 100 passengers and 10 tons of mail.[1]

The first flights of the two airships took place in 1930. The *R 100* succeeded in crossing the Atlantic to Canada, reaching Montreal on August 1st. She did the trip in seventy-nine hours. The writer remembers vividly watching the *R 100* sailing majestically eastward above the St Lawrence as she began the return journey. The 700-foot airship could be distinctly heard and seen on an evening that was beautifully clear. She looked unreal, as though a great ocean liner had soared out of the water for a crossing of the Atlantic.

The *R 101* began her long flight to India on October 4th. She carried several well-known passengers. Air Vice-Marshal Sir Sefton Brancker was aboard; he had long been Director of Civil Aviation in the Air Ministry. And the Secretary of State for Air, Lord Thomson, was also a passenger. He had held the same Cabinet post in Ramsay Macdonald's first Ministry in 1924 when the airship programme was started. Lord Thomson hoped, apparently, to share in a convincing demonstration that would put the airship services within the Empire on a firm and lasting basis. Unfortunately the journey had hardly begun when the *R 101* crashed in a storm near Beauvais, France, in the early hours of the next morning. Of the fifty-three passengers aboard, forty-seven lost their lives, including Sir Sefton Brancker and Lord Thomson.

This disaster seemed such a reflection on the airworthiness of the dirigible that the airship programme was dropped, even though Sir Samuel Hoare had said that a purely accidental failure of one of the two ships would not end the use of airships. The *R 100* despite

---

[1] *Deb.* H. C., 5th series, cliii, 375; ccxxvi, 1036; *Memorandum* (1926), 10-16; *Rep. on Civil Aviation 1928* (1929), 27; *Rep.* (1930), 25-26. The well-known novelist Nevil Shute [Norway] recorded, in his autobiographical *Slide Rule*, his participation in the building of the *R 100* at Howden. 'It was generally agreed', he wrote, 'that the airplane would never be a suitable vehicle for carrying passengers across the oceans, that airships would operate all the long-distance routes of the future.'

her successful transatlantic round trip, was never flown again. The general financial depression that began about this time may have been a contributing reason for concluding the use of airships. Yet as late as 1935 Sir Frederick Williamson of the Post Office still hoped that the airship was only in a state of 'suspended animation', that in the future high-speed airships would fly night and day along the main routes, airplanes being used for feeder purposes.[1]

IMPERIAL AIRWAYS

For several years after Imperial Airways became the 'chosen instrument' for British services overseas, it was concerned chiefly with extending its routes in Europe where the British Company was faced by strong competition from continental airlines. Actually air transportation of passengers and mails to the Continent was not much faster as yet than that by surface routes. The machines were confined by flights by day because of the lack of facilities for journeys at night.

The agreement made with Imperial Airways in 1924 required not only the upkeep of the existing European services, but the development of any extensions that would be approved by the Air Ministry. As time went on and the airplane increased its range, the Empire was more and more regarded as the appropriate field for long-distance flights. If the conquest of the air had ended British insularity, there might be compensation in developing air routes that would bring the distant Dominions and colonies nearer the centre of the Commonwealth. In 1926, accordingly, a second agreement was made with Imperial Airways for a service between Egypt and India. This route seemed to merit first attention because of the great size of its mail, greater than that of any other part of the Commonwealth save Canada. India, too, lay on a route that would make extensions worth while. To the east was Malaya whence services might diverge to Hong Kong and to the Australias and New Zealand to the south-east, along trade lanes and mail routes already served for many years by the ocean liner and the submarine telegraph.

Imperial Airways expected to open an Indian route within two

---

[1] *Deb*. H.C., 5th ser., ccxliv, 855; cclxii, 2008, 2067; *Memorandum* (1926), 15; Williamson, op. cit., 18. The disuse of airships was wise, even though a Zeppelin succeeded in making a round-the-world flight in 1929. The Germans also started a regular transatlantic service in 1936, but it ended when the *Hindenburg* burst into flames when landing at Lakehurst, New Jersey in 1937.

years. The first flight of a weekly service actually left Croydon at the end of March 1929, and reached Karachi seven days later. The journey was by air to Paris, thence by train to Brindisi, whence an airplane was again used to Egypt, and from Cairo the flight went on to Karachi by way of Basra at the top of the Persian Gulf. By the end of 1929 the air service had been extended to Delhi, and by the end of 1933 the service went by way of Calcutta and Rangoon to Singapore.[1]

In 1929 when the first British air services had extended to India a noteworthy Congress of the Postal Union met in London. This was the first Congress to consider the carriage of mails over the territories of the Union members. Two years earlier the European nations had made preliminary regulations for their air services at a meeting held at the Hague; these arrangements, with but slight changes, became part of the general agreement of the worldwide Postal Union. Freedom of transit was guaranteed throughout the entire territory of the Postal Union members. Air letters that were to be charged an additional rate must be uniform in all countries. Air mails were to be delivered with the utmost rapidity, at least by the first general delivery after they were landed. On every air letter a special *blue* label was to be affixed or a similar stamped impression bearing the words 'Par Avion', with a translation such as 'By Air Mail' in the language of the country of origin. The British Post Office set up bright blue pillar boxes in the principal urban centres to popularize the new world wide airmail. The first ones were erected in 1930, and they were in use until 1938 when the 'All-up' Scheme made them unnecessary.

Soon many countries began the issue of special air-mail stamps for publicity purposes. This did not appeal to the British Post Office. It held that the best publicity was a 'simple procedure, and a quick, cheap and regular service'.[2]

At this time a new Imperial route was extending southward from Cairo towards Cape Colony and Natal. A west-coast route was not feasible because of the few British colonies, and on account of their unimportance postally speaking. East Africa, on the contrary, had a

---

[1] Williamson, op. cit., 4-5; *Rep. Com. of Inquiry into Civil Aviation* (1938), 40-41; *Rep. on Civil Aviation 1928* (1929), and those for 1929, 1932, 1933.

[2] Williamson, op. cit., 9. For the blue label, see Art. 22 of the 'Provisions for the Conveyance of Letters by Air' in the *Report* of the Congress of 1929. The British Post Office celebrated the meeting of the Congress in London by issuing a set of six commemorative stamps. Five were from the ½d up through the 2½d, and they were sold in large quantities. The sixth stamp was valued at £1, and was rarely seen by the general public. It was criticized as being intended for sale to collectors.

continuous stretch of British colonial territory, and it was believed that a route down this side of Africa would add much to the mail load because of the great advantage of air mail where the surface mails were irregular and slow in transit. The route had reached Kisumu on Lake Victoria by March 1931. From there it was extended by way of Nairobi, the capital of Kenya, to Northern Rhodesia. The completed route to Johannesburg and Cape Town was in use early in 1932.[1]

Australia is a Commonwealth in which air services have been very popular. The stretches of a vast continent, the location of scattered centres of population along the coasts, the lack of adequate roads and railways had led to an effective network of air lines by the time Imperial Airways had reached Singapore. The Line known as Quantas (Queensland and Northern Territory Aerial Services) joined with Imperial Airways to form Quantas Empire Airways for the linking of Australia with Singapore. This route was in regular use before the end of 1934. It completed an air connection of over 13,000 miles between London and Australia—the longest air route in the world up to that time.

By the end of the thirties amazing progress had been made. Within five years after the first air-mail journey to Karachi regular services were in working order over the length of Africa and to Australia by way of India. Imperial Airways was well named, for it had drawn the Empire-Commonwealth closer together than ever before. The services on the main route and their feeders along the way were so regular that the airplane could fairly stand comparison with the railway train and the steamship.

The number of flights along these routes also increased as well as the speed of the machines and the amount of mail that was transported. The saving in time was phenomenal. Mail by air to Delhi, for instance, now took less than six days—a saving of more than eleven days over the fastest surface carriage. By 1934 Singapore was receiving its London mail by air in eight and a half days, a saving of over thirteen days by the ships of the P & O. The mail to Sydney by air took thirteen days, less than half the time required for the surface carriage. Surface mails now reached Cape Town in seventeen days by the Union-Castle Line, but air mail required only ten days.[2]

At first the rates for air mail varied widely, depending on the distance the mail was carried. The basic weight was set at half an

[1] *Rep. on Civil Aviation 1932* (1933), 66-67.
[2] *Rep. on Civil Aviation 1934* (1935), 127.

ounce rather than the basic weight of one ounce in use for the European air mail. A half-ounce letter between London and Karachi cost sixpence, one to Kenya 7d. The letter rate to Cape Town was set at 1s, that for Singapore 11d. To arrive at the total minimum cost of an air-mail letter, the writer had to add the ordinary surface postage of 1½d.

In 1934 the numerous variations in the cost were simplified by having the same flat rate to all countries that were about the same distance from England. By this 'zone' system, letters to and from Australia cost a flat rate of 1s 3d, the half ounce, the flat rate including the former additional surface charges. Regions somewhat nearer Britain, such as South Africa, Kenya, India and Ceylon were in the zone where the basic rate was 6d. A nearer group, including Egypt, Palestine, Iraq, Syria and Persia had an air-mail rate of 3d. Clearly letters by air had ceased to be considered as 'semi-urgent telegrams'.

The services grew more and more popular with every passing month. The amount of air mail jumped in the same way as domestic surface mail when uniform penny postage replaced varying rates in Britain in 1840. By 1930 the mail traffic by air totalled 30 tons. Every year saw it mount. In 1933, it reached 85 tons; in 1934, 122 tons; in 1935, 187 tons. Postal communication had entered upon a new phase.[1]

THE ALL-UP SCHEME

Imperial air mails were reorganized in the late thirties just as a new war seemed in the offing. After long discussion between representatives of the Post Office, the Air Ministry and Imperial Airways, an Empire Air Mail Scheme was ready for announcement. Sir Philip Sassoon, the Under-Secretary of State for Air, informed the Commons in December 1934 of the new arrangements. The time schedule was to be improved, with a substantial increase in the frequency of the service. A thorough development of the ground conditions were to make it possible to fly by night as freely as by day.

Most astonishing of all was the decision to carry *all* of the first-class mail by air. Even more gratifying was the change in rate. Up to

[1] *Rep. on Civil Aviation 1935* (1936), 14; Williamson, op. cit., 14; D. O. Lumley, *Air Mail Operation* (Green Papers, no. 23) describes clearly the handling of air mail at this time.

this time the Imperial surface rate had been a uniform 1½d for an ounce. The new 'all-up' rate was set at 1½d but for a half ounce only, with no special fee for conveyance by air. Sir Philip Sassoon estimated that mail between London and India would take two days, two and a half days between London and East Africa, four days for mail to the Cape and also to Singapore, and seven days for letters between England and Australia.[1]

The Scheme was only possible by a large financial outlay. The agreement called for an annual subsidy to Imperial Airways of £900,000 for the carriage of the mails. As this would be cut down by contributions from the participating territories, the total cost to the British Post Office would be about £525,000 a year. The decision to face an initial loss was not regarded as a change from the position held by the Post Office, that subsidies should not exceed the actual postal income. The losses, it was hoped, would be more than matched during the fifteen years the agreement was to run.

The contract that was drawn up in June 1937 foresaw the possibility of war, for various clauses were included in the contract that are strikingly similar to the Admiralty provisions in the ocean mail contracts. Government freight and officials were to be carried at reduced rates, although the mails were always to have priority. His Majesty's aircraft were to have free use of the airfields and the harbour facilities used by the Company. The 'Admiralty' clauses included the requirement that the Company's airplanes were to be at the disposal of the Government in time of emergency.[2]

The drastic lowering of air-mail rates overseas, far greater than 'anywhere else in the world', was intended to secure British supremacy in the air. The Company was to use the very latest models of aircraft. The new air liners and flying boats weighed about 18 tons each, and were powered by four engines with a total of about 3,000 horsepower. They were to travel at a speed of 200 miles an hour, and could keep to the air for 800 miles without refuelling. Imperial Airways claimed to be the pioneer in the use of large aircraft, to be 'the first air transport company in the world to employ twin-engined, then three-engined and now four-engined airliners, and the first to operate the big flying boat'.

The Scheme included a much larger use of flying boats than landplanes, as the flying boat was more suitable over territories in

[1] *Deb.* H.C., 5th ser., ccxcvi, 1328-31.
[2] *Empire Air Mail Scheme* (Cmd. 5414, 1937); *Agreement* with Imperial Airways, June 9, 1937.

which airfields were difficult to construct and maintain. Night flying was to be a regular part of the programme. The Ensign air liner and the Empire flying boat were to make transport by air 'a normal means of locomotion and not an adventure'. Passengers were to sleep aboard, according to the Company's arrangements, 'but will come ashore in the evening for dinner while the chairs are being moved and stowed away, and the bunks fitted in their places'. The forecast added that 'All these steps are being taken in order that the mail shall be carried punctually and regularly.'[1]

The Scheme opened in June 1937 on the route to South Africa, with three flights a week between England and Kisumu, and two a week between Kisumu and Durban. Durban had become the terminus in South Africa by a change of the route that now went along the east coast. The first flying-boat service to India began in February 1938. Four flights a week were scheduled between England and Karachi and two flights weekly on to Singapore. Ceylon was joined to Karachi by a feeder service. By July 1938 the third stage was reached by the opening of the service to Australia. An inaugural ceremony was attended by ministers of the various governments when the first flying boat started on its long journey from Southampton to Australia. In September a branch line connected Hong Kong with the main line at Bangkok. By that time five mails a week were going between England and India, and three to Australia.

The last link in the long communications chain to the south Pacific was the flying-boat service between Australia and New Zealand, a distance of 1,200 miles over the Tasman Sea. The Company organized to fly the mails across the Tasman was Tasman Empire Airways Ltd., or TEAL, as it is usually called. For distant New Zealand, the new service by TEAL would be 'incomparably more important than any [advance] yet recorded in the history of overseas mail communications'.

New Zealand, however, did not have the air service across the Tasman for some years after it was in regular use between England and Australia. For some time ships continued to carry the mails across the Tasman for this last leg of the Empire Air Mail Scheme. The flying boats for the service between Sydney and Auckland

[1] *The Empire Air Mail Programme* (n.d., c. 1937), a pamphlet issued in behalf of Imperial Airways. When the new Ensigns had been delivered, it was found necessary to correct the inadequacies of their engines. See Lord Reith, *Into the Wind* (1949), 338; Higham, op. cit., 85-87, 289-94.

were so slow in arriving that it was April 1940 before they began a regular air service.[1]

All in all, however, it was an astonishing accomplishment. In the short time of two years a fast service by air, carrying all the first-class mail, had begun numerous regular flights. It received widespread approval. During the twelve months ending in 1937—before the Scheme had begun—the total number of letters and parcels sent abroad by air had been 20,000,000. In the next twelve months when only the first stages of the Scheme were in use, the amount of mail had doubled. In the year ending March 31, 1939, it doubled again. The daring change to a Scheme 'unique among the air services of the world looked to have an even more successful future as further extensions could be made, provided the world remained at peace'.[2]

The only important parts of the Commonwealth not yet included in the All-up Scheme were the Dominion of Canada, the Colony of Newfoundland, the British colonies in the West Indies, and some scattered islands in the southern hemisphere.

Even by the late thirties aircraft were not sufficiently developed to span the Atlantic with any regularity. The first flight across the Atlantic by a heavier-than-air machine carrying a commerical load was made in July 1938. The *Mercury* went by way of Newfoundland to Montreal and on to New York, and returned to Britain by way of the Azores and Lisbon. The commercial load was only half a ton. As early as 1937 Imperial Airways began a weekly service between Bermuda and New York, a route used by the first regular trans-atlantic liners. A Lisbon-London service began in January 1939 by non-stop airplanes between the two capitals. There was even a suggestion at the time that a direct crossing between Ireland and Newfoundland would start soon, but that the northern route would not be used during the winter months. The flying boat *Caribou* made the first flight westward on what was hoped to be a regular

---

[1] *Rep. on Civil Aviation 1938* (1939) for the details of the service. The New Zealand Post Office and Government were disappointed at the delays in their air service. See the writer's *History of the New Zealand Post Office*, ch. XIX, for a fuller account of the Tasman services.

[2] *Deb.* H.C., 5th ser., cccl, 1015; [Cadman] *Com. of Inquiry into Civil Aviation* (Cmd. 5685, 1938), pp. ii, 39-47. The *P.O. Commercial Accounts* furnish the record of growth for the financial years ending March 31:

1922-3	Letters and parcels by air overseas	153,000
1934-5		7,535,000
1935-6		10,792,000
1936-7		20,645,000
1937-8		40,362,000
1938-9		91,233,000

service, made it in August 1939 just as the war was about to end the peace-time carriage of international mails.[1]

A further change in the organization of the overseas air services came on the eve of the war. In 1938 a Committee of Inquiry, of which Lord Cadman was chairman, made a thorough investigation of Imperial Airways, and also of British Airways, which had been organized in 1936 to take charge of the European routes formerly under Imperial Airways. The Committee admitted that Imperial Airways had achieved 'considerable efficiency', but that it had failed to co-operate as fully as 'we should have expected from a Company heavily subsidized and having such important international and imperial contacts'. The Committee recommended, therefore, that the two official overseas airlines should have a chairman who could give his whole time to the work, and that the two airlines should be more closely 'tied in' with government. As a result, Woods Humphery, the chairman of Imperial Airways, was replaced by J. C. W. Reith. Lord Reith came over from the BBC, which he had organized and guided skilfully during its first fifteen years. Following the Cadman Report and because of the darkening international sky, British and Imperial Airways were united as a public corporation, somewhat similar to the BBC. It was named, at Lord Reith's suggestion, British Overseas Airways Corporation, BOAC, as it is usually called. The Act of Parliament creating BOAC required that the chairman and the deputy chairman be appointed by the Government.

By 1939 it was clear that a new air age was in the making. From a hesitant use of airmails across the Channel, a new Empire Air Mail Scheme had developed. To the older ocean services by steamship, had been added a new type of mail and passenger carrier that was using, in the words of Lord Reith, the 'unbroken ocean of the air'.[2]

---

[1] *Rep. on Civil Aviation 1938* (1939), 17; *Civil Air Transport Service* (Bermuda-New York), being Cmd. 5870, 1939; *Deb.* H.C. 5th ser., cccxv, 1731-4; cccxli, 1549. For the beginnings of the Atlantic All-up Scheme, see Lord Reith, op. cit., 343.
[2] *Rep. Com. of Inquiry on Civil Aviation* (1938), pp. viii, 15-16; *Rep. on Civil Aviation 1938* (1939), 7; *Deb.* H.C., 5th ser., cccxxxvii, 39-40; cccxli, 453-5; Reith, op. cit., 329, 337. Lord Reith was transferred early in 1940, to the Ministry of Information.

24

THE SECOND WORLD WAR AND AFTER

THE severest test ever faced by Britain began when the Second World War opened in September 1939. After the Nazis had overrun the Netherlands, Belgium and France, they proceeded to attack the British Isles by air. Although the attacks failed, they showed clearly that the conquest of the air had ended any insular security that Britain had enjoyed in the past. The war that lasted for nearly six years disorganized the highly developed and world-wide postal services. In fact, one of the first casualties of the war was the 'All-up' postal arrangement for nearby Europe. Since 1935 European first-class mail had been dispatched by air whenever this was quicker than by a surface route, and it had been carried at the ordinary surface rate of $2\frac{1}{2}$d for the first ounce. All this ended with the outbreak of war as most of the termini on the Continent were closed by the Nazi occupation. Surface mails to the Near East and beyond by way of the Mediterranean were in partial use only until Italy entered the war in June 1940. After that, shipping in general followed the much longer route around Africa. The Suez Canal was more vulnerable than ever before, now that wars were waged in the air as well as on land and sea.

The Empire Mail Scheme—begun with such high hopes ten years earlier—was also wrecked when its most important section, between London and Cairo, was no longer usable. The Ministry of Air requisitioned civilian aircraft, and their manufacture was discontinued. So far as BOAC was concerned, it became a part of the Royal Air Force Transport Command.[1]

A regular transatlantic weekly service by flying boats had been started by BOAC a month before the war opened. The *Caribou* and the *Cabot* that made the first flights were presently 'on loan' to the Air Ministry—and were soon wrecked. Their 'loan', in Lord Reith's opinion, was a mistake, for they would have done more good in the mail service overseas. A civilian air service was tried for a

[1] *Deb.* H.C., 5th ser., cccc, 308; Reith, op. cit, 345-6.

time with the co-operation of Pan American Airways, since the
United States did not enter the war until December 1941. Clippers
flew between New York and Lisbon via Bermuda, and a British
service connected Lisbon and London. The schedule was supposed
to be weekly, and the time between New York and London was set
for two weeks from collection to delivery. The air mails, however,
were delayed on occasion as much as three weeks. This was much
longer than the usual time for surface mails crossing the Atlantic by
ship during war-time. An attempt was made to route the mail for
India and the Far East by way of the Atlantic. The letters were
superscribed, 'Via North Atlantic and Transpacific Air Service'.
The charge was almost prohibitive: 5s as a basic rate was four times
the ordinary air rate of 1s 3d. It was suspended when the United
States was drawn in. The public had strongly criticized the Post
Office for even collecting an air-mail surcharge for this transatlantic civilian service.[1]

The fastest ocean liners were soon put to war purposes under the
Admiralty clauses of the mail contracts. This resulted, of course, in
slower mails overseas, made even slower by the use of devious
routes. The Cunard Company, which had absorbed the White Star
in the mid-thirties, had two gigantic liners available for the Admiralty. The *Queen Mary*, which had won the blue riband three
years before the war by a crossing in less than four days, and the
Queen Elizabeth, her slightly larger sister—launched just before the
war began—were used effectively as transports. Many other
vessels that had been carrying the Royal Mail were similarly
employed.

The surface route around Africa grew in value with the closing of
the Suez Canal to civilian traffic. Even mails for Cairo and the
Middle East were taken all the way around Africa by what came to
be known as the 'horseshoe route'. The Union-Castle Line that had
furnished a weekly schedule between Cape Town and Southampton
was hampered during the war as the best steamers of the Line were
diverted to transport service or otherwise used by the Admiralty.
For example, the *Dunvegan Castle*, a motor vessel of over 15,000
tons, became an armed merchant cruiser, only to be torpedoed and
sunk in August 1940. The *Warwick Castle*, 20,000 tons, was torpedoed in November 1942. The *Pretoria Castle*, ready for the mail

---

[1] By September 1941, BOAC had begun to run a frequent military service to Canada,
the aircraft using Prestwick in Ayrshire as the British base. See *P.O. Circular*, Mat 21,
1941; *Deb.* H.C. 5th ser., ccclvii, 1179; ccclxvii, 891; ccclxix, 273; ccccxx, 1847.

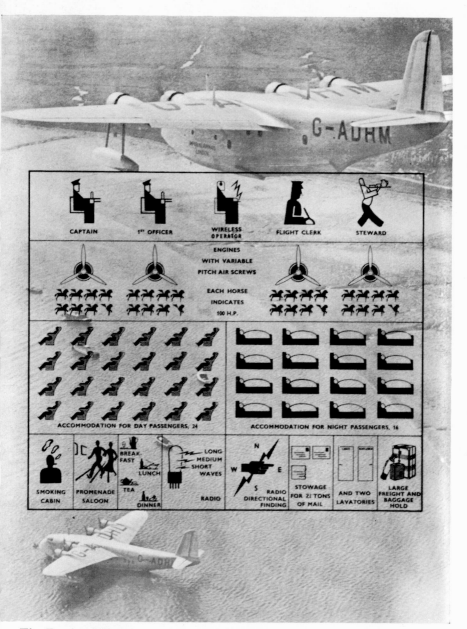

The Empire Flying boat of the All-Up Service, 1937, picturing the various accommodations, including 'stowage for 2¾ tons of mail'. *Source:* G.P.O. A pamphlet *The Empire Air Mail Programme*, 1937.

The Post Office promotes th[e] airgraph, 1943. *Source:* G.P.O.[...]

Airgraph sent by Winston[...] Churchill to General Smut[s] when the service was opene[d] to South Africa in Septembe[r] 1942. *Source:* G.P.O. Record[s]

service the year the war opened, was turned over to the Admiralty and converted into an aircraft carrier.

The withdrawal of fast mail ships especially affected the carriage of seaborne mails by the roundabout route to Egypt. Little wonder that it took eleven weeks to carry mails to and from Egypt. This slow service naturally increased the uneasiness at home, as military forces in the Middle East were built up to meet the menace of the German thrust into the Mediterranean. The discontent was justified. A soldier took at least eleven weeks to reach Egypt if sent around Africa by transport. A letter sent back home telling of his safe arrival took as much time again, resulting in a delay of five months before his relatives at home could learn that he had reached the eastern Mediterranean. One is reminded of the days of sail a century earlier when news of emigrants to Australia and New Zealand took about as long in coming from the south Pacific.

THE AIRGRAPH

The widespread anxiety caused by the long delay in receiving news from the Forces in the Middle East was somewhat relieved after a year and a half of war by a fast air-mail service that could be sent by military aircraft. The airgraph letter was devised as a light-weight communication that could go by military airplanes already loaded with priority cargo and official dispatches. Airgraph letters were photographed and then sent home as negatives on microfilm. When they reached London they were used to print letters that were delivered in the ordinary way by the Post Office.

The idea of an airgraph was not altogether new. Something slightly similar had been used in the Franco-Prussian War of 1870. Besieged Paris might send letters out by balloon, but such carriers could not bring letters in. Instead a pigeon post carried the mail from Tours to Paris. The photographed messages—the limit was twenty words—were enclosed in a pellicule attached to the wing of a pigeon. If the bird got through, the message was thrown on a screen by a lantern, and an observer took it down.[1]

In the First World War, Sir Percy Girouard of Armstrong-Whitworth had proposed that messages might be sent by film so a to save cargo space, but the proposal was not tried out. By 1930 Kodak had devised a successful apparatus for photographing in

[1] This pigeon post into Paris was expensive; a letter mailed in Britain for Paris cost the sender 5s a word. It was more like a telegram. See above, p. 275.

K

miniature various documents of the size of bank cheques. Before the war this process was in use by the large London banks to record their cheques and other documents, and it was employed by the Post Office Savings Bank and some other departments of the Post Office for preserving important records. Before the Second World War, Eastman Kodak together with Imperial and Pan American Airways had formed a Company called Airgraphs Ltd., to use microphotography for air mail, but the Company had not actually carried out the idea before the Second World War began. In 1940 Lieutanant-Colonel Moore-Brabazon, Minister of Transport and a Director of Kodak, again brought forward the idea.

The Post Office investigated the airgraph at first as a possible solution for the long delay in communication between the Forces in the Middle East and Great Britain. Kodak Ltd., of London with works at Harrow, was prepared to set up such a service quickly. Kodak already had an establishment at Cairo and at other possible centres for the airgraph service, as well as technical staffs in London and overseas. After the Company had agreed to prepare airgraphs, the Post Office worked out adequate security arrangements, and the Foreign section of the Post Office in London took care of the necessary mail procedures. The first airgraphs from Cairo to London were on their way in April 1941.[1]

The Post Office worked out a special form, 8 by 11 inches, on which could be written about 450 words by typescript or half that many by hand. The writer then wrote the name and address of the person to whom the letter was sent in captial letters in a 'box'. The accumulated forms were next photographed in a series on 16mm film. It was possible to record on every 100 feet of film, 1,600 airgraph letters—later raised to 1,700 by closer spacing. The developed film, weighing but 5 ounces including the container, was then dispatched by air to London. On its arrival the film was used to print the letters on a continuous run of photographic paper, each airgraph message being enlarged sufficiently to make it readable. The letters were next cut apart, folded and inserted in an envelope with a 'window' to show the address as originally written. They were then ready for delivery.[2]

The first shipment of airgraphs from Cairo to London left on

[1] The writer is indebted to an unpublished account by E. C. Baker, Archivist of the Post Office, on 'The Airgraph Service, 1941-1945' in addition to other materials in the P. O. Record Room on this interesting mail. See also *Britain's Post Office*, 272-4.

[2] Messrs John Dickinson & Co., of Tottenham, were able to modify their envelope machines so as to produce the envelope, insert the airgraph and seal the envelope, all in one operation; one machine could handle 8,000 per hour.

April 21, 1941 and reached London three weeks later. It was not as yet possible to send airgraphs from London to Cairo, since Cairo did not have the necessary equipment and materials for printing the airgraphs and preparing them for delivery. The service was at first for Forces mail only; the prepaid charge was 3d an airgraph. The airgraph had the great advantage over surface mail and even the ordinary airletter in that it went all the way by air. The route used was the regular military supply route between England and Cairo—south to Khartoum from Cairo, thence across the desert and the Nigerian jungles to Takoradi on the Gold Coast. From Takoradi the aircraft proceeded to London via Lisbon. Fortunately a feeder air route between Khartoum and West Africa had been laid out before the war.

The small space occupied by the film made it possible for the Post Office to obtain room in aircraft that were certain to be well filled by priority cargo. Any odd corner was put to such use. A film of 1,600 to 1,700 letters was a different matter from that number of ordinary letters; they would have filled two mail-bags and have weighed about 70lb. instead of 5 oz. The original airgraph letters were kept until it was known that the microfilm had been received. Occasionally the letters had to be re-photographed. The flying boat *Clare*, for example, was lost in December 1942; her cargo included 65,000 airgraphs—thirty films weighing about 12 lb. On learning of the loss, the letters were re-photographed, and they were delivered with but a fortnight's delay.

The next step in the spread of the service was the equipment of Cairo and other centres with the necessary machines and film and photographic paper. By August 1941 Cairo was able to receive as well as send airgraphs. The first shipment to the Middle East included a letter from Queen Elizabeth to General Sir Claude Auckinleck, Commander of the Middle East Forces.[1]

By this time the service was faster; the time between London and Cairo had been lowered to less than three weeks. So successful was the use of airgraphs that over 8,000,000 flew this route before the end of 1941.

Extensions of the service were soon undertaken. Developing and printing machines and quantities of film were sent to various places in the Dominions and the colonies, wherever they would serve the Forces overseas. Soon airgraph mail was available at Johannesburg, Bombay, Calcutta, Melbourne and Wellington; before the end of the

---

[1] For a reproduction of this letter, see *Britain's Post Office*, p. 273.

war other centres were set up in Nairobi, Colombo, Naples and Toronto. Algiers and later Naples were airgraph stations for mail to and from the British North African Forces. For a time it seemed likely that Cairo would cease to be an airgraph terminus, but this was prevented by the defeat of the Central Powers in North Africa. Malta was never used as a centre because of its exposed position. Singapore was captured by the Japanese just as it was about to be opened for airgraph mail; the equipment was actually on shipboard when Singapore fell, but it was diverted to Bombay. An airgraph station often served a much larger area than the country in which it was located. Such stations as Toronto, Melbourne and Wellington were of great value for airgraph mail between the Dominions and their expeditionary forces. After the United States entered the war, the same sort of mail was used for the American Expeditionary Forces; it was known as V-mail.[1]

The airgraph for Forces mail was such a boon that there was soon a widespread desire to use it for civilian mail. This was conceded in May 1942. The original charge for the civilian airgraphs was 8d, but in August 1944 the postal charge was lowered to 3d.

The service was of incalculable value. In 1942 after a number of new centres had been opened in addition to Cairo, 61,000,000 airgraphs were successfully delivered. In the next year the annual total rose to 135,500,000. There was some decline in 1944 with the return of more normal conditions for carrying mail overseas, yet nearly 100,000,000 were handled in that year. The airgraph service came to an end in the summer of 1945 after about four years, during which the Post Office had transmitted over 350,000,000 airgraphs. The peak was reached in March 1943 when 1,500,000 left London in one week. The total weight of all the airgraphs was 50 tons instead of 4,500 tons for same number of ordinary letters.[2]

[1] The following table lists the beginning of the airgraph service from and to certain areas. In every instance it was begun for the Forces and later extended to civilians.

To Britain from			From Britain to	
Middle East and East Africa	Apl.	1941	Aug.	1941
Canada and Newfoundland	Oct.	1941	Aug.	1942
India and Ceylon	Feb.	1942	May	1942 (via Cairo)
			Sept.	1942 (direct)
New Zealand	Feb.	1942	April	1943
Australia	Feb.	1942	June	1943
Algiers (BNAF)	Apl.	1942	March	1943
South Africa and the Rhodesias	May	1942	Sept.	1942

[2] The cost of the service was miscalculated at the outset. The contract with Kodak was made on a fixed rather than a cost-plus basis; it was set much too high because the Post Office believed that the service would not exceed 3,000,000 airgraphs a year. So

THE AIR-LETTER FORM

Early in 1942 the Post Office made another effort to save air space by introducing the 'thin' postcard for Forces mail, also at a cost of 3d. The air-mail postcard as well as the airgraph were sent all the way by plane. Ordinary air letters went partly by ship to the 'Continent of Africa' (presumably Takoradi), and from there as occasion offered.

The general desire for a closed light air-mail letter that would have preferential handling similar to that granted the 'thin' postcard and the airgraph was met by the introduction of the air-letter form. An announcement in October 1942 informed the public that 'a new light-weight air-letter service at a postage rate of 6d, normally providing communication by air throughout . . . will shortly be introduced to take the place of the 'thin' postcard, which will then be withdrawn'.[1]

The air-letter form hardly needs description since it is still in general use—a sheet of thin blue paper that was the size of a 'thin' postcard when folded and sealed. Unlike the postcard, its contents were private. At first this 'closed' form had no stamp impressed upon it. Postage stamps totalling 6d were to be affixed to the form before it was issued to the public over a post-office counter. Not until June 1943 was the form issued with a printed 6d stamp. Headquarters in London informed the postmasters that 'stocks of unstamped air-letter forms should be used up before the stamped forms are brought into use'.[2]

The familiar blue air-letter form was first used by the British Post Office as a convenient light closed letter for the Forces. When sold for general use, it made such inroads on the airgraph service that the ending of the airgraph came as no hardship to the public. The air-letter form had come to stay. When the war with Germany came to an end in the summer of 1945 the Post Office announced

---

great was the payment to Kodak that the Company would have made 65 per cent profit, if it had not refunded £130,000 in 1942. For the years 1943 and 1944 the voluntary refunds totalled £530,000. See the *Manchester Guardian* of February 20, 1945, and the *Accountant* of March, 2, 1945.

[1] *P.O. Circular*, October 7, 1942. It actually began on November 25th. One reason for preferring a closed form over the airgraph and the postcard was the dislike of handing in open mail at the local post office! Airgraphs could, of course, be sent directly to the Foreign Section, London.

[2] In some countries air-letter forms are sold without the stamped impression. The New Zealand Post Office, for example, sells the unstamped forms at $\frac{1}{2}$d each, since the rate to nearby Commonwealth states and colonies is less than the standard charge of 8d.

that the familiar blue air-letter form could be used for civilian communication to most Empire and other overseas countries. It was even made available aboard British ships in 1950, to be sent on its way by air at the ship's next port of call.

The folded air-letter form gained such wide public approval that it has since been generally adopted by postal administrations throughout the world. The Congress of the Universal Postal Union held at Brussels in 1952 provided for its general use. The front of the folded form was to bear the word *Aerogramme* and a similar indication such as 'Air Letter' in the language of the country where it was purchased. The Postal Union described this new kind of airmail as a 'sheet of paper suitably folded and gummed, the size of which in that form shall be that of a postcard'. The rate was to be the same as for an 'unsurcharged [that is, a surface] letter of the country of origin'.[1]

THE REVIVAL OF PEACE-TIME SERVICES

In 1945, BOAC could for the first time really enter on a civilian air-mail programme. But the service was not simply a continuation of that which had begun shortly before the opening of the war. When the Labour Party was returned to power in the General Election of 1945, Clement Attlee's Ministry was determined to push forward the air services. The Labour Party continued the Ministry of Aircraft Production and added the Ministry of Civil Aviation.

The Attlee Government also decided to break up the single corporation that had been in charge of all the air services overseas. BOAC was to fly the imperial routes in use before the war, and to have under its care those that would be developed on the highly competitive north Atlantic route. A second corporation, British European Airways (BEA) was put in charge of the services to Europe and within the British Isles. A third corporation was created to open up the field of British aviation in South America. This was considered important because of the 'long and close relation with the states of that Continent'. There was to be no wasteful and subsidized competition, as the air services were to become self-supporting as soon as possible. The Civil Aviation Act (8 & 9 Geo. VI, ch. 70)

---

[1] *P.O. Circular*, October 7 and November 25, 1942; June 16 and September 22, 1943; July 11, 1945; *Report* of the UPU held at Brussels, Art. 5 of the 'Provisions for Air-Mail Correspondence.' Each postal administration was to fix the charge for its own air-letter form.

also set up a Transport Advisory Council. The directorates of the three corporations were to be appointed by the Ministry.[1]

The older airfields had been outdated by the growth of the services and the ever increasing size and power of the airplanes. Hendon and Heston, Cricklewood and Croydon might have satisfied the needs of earlier decades, but they were now inadequate. Changes had already begun during the war, when Prestwick had been developed for war-time use. As early as 1941 it was the regular port of departure for a frequent service to Montreal. By 1949 all the air correspondence posted in Scotland for the United States and Canada was sent from Glasgow directly to Prestwick.

London, however, remained the main centre for Britain's international mails. After the war, Northolt was used for civilian traffic until 1954. By that time the new London Airport, begun in 1943, was ready to receive planes. This ambitious project, extending along the Bath Road beyond Cranford, replaced the earlier airports on a scale considered necessary for the future. The principal runway is nearly as long as the distance between the GPO and Hyde Park Corner. This immense airfield dwarfs those thought sufficient thirty years earlier when it was seriously suggested that Hyde Park should be taken over as an airfield.

The overseas air routes were again put to use after the war, and the mails soon became larger than ever before. By the fifties, BOAC was running three services a week on the South African route, several each week to India, and carrying mails twice weekly between London and Sydney. Quantas was in 'parallel parntership with BOAC on the 'kangaroo' route. The north Atlantic services to New York were seven to nine times weekly, and three to four a week between Britain and Montreal. In the financial year ending March 31, 1948, BOAC carried nearly 2,000 tons of mail. This 'uplift' was paid for on the basis of 'ton-miles', that is by multiplying the weight by the distance the mails were carried. British South American Airways Corporation did not long remain separate, but was merged with BOAC in 1949, with the result that there were, once again, but two 'chosen instruments' for carrying British air mails overseas.

British European Airways, organized in 1946, reported in 1952 on

[1] *Report on British Air Transport* of the Ministry of Civil Aviation (Cmd. 6605); *Rep. on Br. Air Services* (Cmd. 6712). Annual grants for the first two years were not to exceed £10,000,000, and were then to be reduced. It was expected that, ultimately, the air services would be self-supporting.

its first five years. In the year ending March 31, 1948, it carried 1,800 tons of mail. Four years later, the tonnage had quadrupled, of which about two-thirds went overseas. This rapid increase is partly explained by the revival in 1948 of the pre-war programme of sending 'by far the greater part of the letters posted in this country for Europe by air without extra charge', that is, at surface rates. By 1960 BEA's carriage of mails had risen to nearly 8,000 tons annually.

The 'uplift' for BOAC had more than doubled by 1960 to well over 4,300 tons. Its 'ton-miles' were far greater than that for BEA because of the greater length of the BOAC routes. The 'ton-miles' for BOAC were over 9,000,000 in 1950; ten years later they were about 22,500,000.[1]

Nor should one forget the part played by the less spectacular but time-honoured steamship Lines. It was the old story repeated. In the early nineteenth century the steam-driven mail ships had replaced the sailing packets because the steamship was more regular and faster than the packets that depended on the whim of the winds. Constant improvement over the years had made the steamship a very satisfactory carrier of the overseas mails. By 1939 they were larger and faster than ever—the Queens were great hotel-like monsters of 80,000 tons, and capable of more than 30 knots, and an Atlantic crossing in less than four days.

Nevertheless, the airplane was challenging the steamship's monopoly even before the beginning of the Second World War. Yet by 1939 the mail taken overseas by ship was still more than twice the amount that went by air.

After the return of peace the airlines carried an ever increasing amount of the mails sent overseas. The pre-war All-up Scheme had shown the possibilities of air mail. The war-time airgraph and the cheap air-letter form had revealed its adaptability. By the mid-fifties—for the year ending March 31, 1955—the correspondence sent by sea numbered 234,000,000 items, and the number of items carried by air overseas was also 234,000,000. The rate of increase, however, was not the same for the two services. If this total is compared with the number of postal items carried in the last year before the war, mail by sea had increased 5 per cent, but mail by air had increased 150 per cent. If the comparison is based on weight,

---

[1] For a tabulation of the mail tonnage and the 'ton-miles' of the two Companies, see the Appendix. The figures are based on the official *Post Office 1950* and the annual reports and accounts of the two airlines.

the surface mails by steamship were still much bulkier, for by far the larger amount of printed papers, newspapers and the bulky parcel mails went overseas by ship. On the other hand, the cost of carrying the mails by air was very much higher than by the older surface routes. Since the end of the war in 1945, the cost of conveying the mails by air has more than tripled to over £10,000,000 a year, and the cost of conveying an item of mail overseas by air is nearly three times the expense of sending it by ship.

This was discouraging, since the Government had expected the two sponsored air lines to be self-supporting in the long run. The Post Office, in particular, wished to avoid 'veiled subsidies' that would result in higher mail charges to the public. Yet there always remained the demand for carriers that could compete effectively on an international basis for passengers and the carriage of freight as well as for the transport of the mails. The highly competitive services required ever faster and more luxurious airliners on the routes from Britain to Europe, to the Commonwealth countries and especially for crossing the Atlantic. In the late fifties the most advanced engines were no longer using propellers. A Comet flew from Hong Kong to England in the overall time of twenty-two hours at a speed of nearly 500 miles an hour. In the same year (1958) a Comet crossed from London to Gander in less than six hours, the fastest transatlantic run up to that time by a British civil airliner.

With the introduction in 1958 of the turbo-jet engines, it looked as though a new Blue Riband was to be sought by the various national companies doing a transatlantic mail and passenger business. The so-called Jet Age had introduced another change, and the most spectacular, in the speeding up of the mails that were sent overseas. The trend seemed clear. The use of a new and faster form of communication overseas can now link London and Sydney in much less than a week. An airliner can cross the Atlantic, not in four days but in almost as many hours. What a change from even a century ago when a letter from London to Paris took at the best twelve to fourteen hours on the way, and mail from London to New York was a fortnight *en route*. Letter mails now travel over the seas at a speed undreamed of by Roger Whitley and Benjamin Franklin, or even by Elihu Burritt and Rowland Hill a century ago.

The most recent revolutionary change in British communication overseas is the laying of a chain of submarine cables. When completed it will encircle the globe.

K*

Submarine telegraph cables had even spanned the Atlantic a century ago. Telephones, however, were limited to land lines, and to one conversation at a time over a single wire. The first submarine telephone cable from the British Isles to the nearby Continent was laid across the English Channel shortly before 1914.

During the first half of this century long-distance telephone conversations were possible by the use of wireless equipment. The first transatlantic conversation by wireless occurred in 1925. But this form of communication was very limited by its almost prohibitive cost.[1]

The surprising change now going on is the laying of a British telephone cable system, 32,000 miles long, that will draw the Commonwealth nations closer together than ever before. Foreseeing that the existing telegraph and radio network could not long meet the growing demand for long-distance communication, a Commonwealth Telecommunications Conference meeting in London during 1958 planned a submarine telephone cable that would connect Great Britain, Canada, Australia, New Zealand and southeast Asia. By that time scientific advances had made direct dialling possible even across continents by the use of co-axial cable or by the installation of microwave radio repeaters where the terrain was very irregular. Electronic amplifiers, built into submarine cable at intervals somewhat greater than the distance separating Dover and Calais boost the human voice over thousands of miles along what might well be called communication highways. The technical requirements were worked out by research engineers from the British Post Office and Cable and Wireless under the leadership of Mr R. J. Halsey, CBE, Director of Research in the British Post Office.

The first link in this round-the-world telephone chain was opened in December 1961 by a cable across the Atlantic. This Canadian transatlantic telephone, known as CANTAT, entered the Atlantic at Oban in Scotland and emerged on the north coast of the Canadian Province of Newfoundland. After crossing to Corner Brook on the west coast it again submerged to reappear at Grosses Roches, Quebec, on the south shore of the St Lawrence. From there the main telephone highway will continue westward by the use of coaxial cable and microwave relay towers. CANTAT can carry numerous conversations along one wire at the same time, and in

---

[1] *See* above, pp. 273 ff.

perfect secrecy. Electronic repeaters keep the human voice clear and strong all the way across the Atlantic.[1]

By mid-1962 another section of this global telephone cable was laid between Sydney in Australia and Wellington in New Zealand, a distance of 1,242 miles; by means of fifty repeaters about 26 miles apart it provides for eighty speech channels. This was the first section of the Commonwealth Pacific Telephone cable, known as COMPAC. By the end of 1963 it had gone northward from New Zealand by way of Fiji, Fanning Island and Hawaii to Vancouver. In general COMPAC follows the route of the Pacific telegraph cable that was first put to use in 1902. The Pacific telephone cable does not, however, by-pass Hawaii; there it connects with an American telephone cable that emerges at Oakland in San Francisco Bay.[2]

The extension of British communications overseas has been a constant growth from the days when a 'Postmaster-General for Foreign Parts', over three centuries ago, saw to the proper carriage of mails by small boats between Dover and Calais. Since then the carriage of British mails has spread across all the oceans to every continent by surface transport and by the airways. It has been supplemented by the development of radio and by submarine telegraph and telephone cables. The time-honoured mail service will carry on, of course, and should continue to improve in effectiveness as new needs have to be met with the passing of the years.

Future growth in the varied postal services overseas will depend on whether the nations can unite in preserving the ways of peace on a shrinking globe.

---

[1] Such a telephone cable had been laid across the Atlantic five years earlier. It also landed in Newfoundland and reached the mainland of North America by way of Nova Scotia. This project was jointly carried out by the communication agencies of Great Britain and Canada, along with the American Telephone and Telegraph Company. In the United States, the Post Office does not have charge of communications by telephone and telegraph.

[2] At the time of writing, the telecommunications link overland in Canada is going forward. For the most part, microwave repeaters erected on high towers will serve to join the Atlantic and Pacific cables. A third link to connect Australia with south-east Asia is under active consideration. SEACOM, as it is called, will go by way of Cairns in Queensland to Singapore with a spur to Hong Kong from Jesselton in North Borneo. A fourth main section is intended to go westward from Singapore to England. This joint enterprise is in charge of a Board made up of representatives of the four partners who share in the project.

APPENDIX

I

❧

The packets captured during the American Revolution, and their captors so far as they are recorded. In the dating, the months are shown in Roman numerals. This tabulation and those for the wars that began in 1793 and ended in 1815 are based on official records, principally *F.L.B.*, *T.L.B.*, *Pkt. Min.* and *Pkt. Rep. Bks.* Packet names are occasionally duplicated, indicating that the captain continued the service with his ransomed packet or a replacement.

Date	Packet-boat and Capt.	Station	Captor, if known
1777			
6 ii	Swallow (Newman)	Falmouth	Am. priv. *Reprisal*
2 v	Prince of Wales (Bossom)	Harwich	Am. priv. *Surprize*
28 vii	Weymouth (Flyn)	Falmouth	Am. priv. *Oliver Cromwell*
16 xii	Duke of Cumberland (Mitchell)	St Augustine	
1778			
25 vi	Le Despencer (Pond)	New York	Am. priv. *Nancy*
17 viii	Duke of York (Dashwood)	Falmouth	Fr. frigate
18 ix	Harriott (Spargo)	Lisbon	Am. priv. *Vengeance*
20 ix	Eagle (Nichols)	Lisbon	Am. priv. *Vengeance*
31 x	Dashwood (Burnaby)	Falmouth	
1779			
7 i	Weymouth (Buckingham)	Falmouth	
17 iv	Prince of Orange (Story)	Harwich	
18 vi	Earl of Bessborough (Shrieve)	Minorca	Fr. xebeck
vi	An Ostend Packet-boat	Dover	
13 vii	Diligence (Clark)	off Pensacola	

13 vii	*Prince Frederick* (Beauvoir)	Dover	
11 viii	*Dashwood* (Roberts)	Falmouth	4 Am. privs., retaken by H.M.S. *Perseus*
12 viii	*Halifax* (Boulderson)	Falmouth	
25 viii	*Sandwich* (Hill)	Falmouth	2 Am. privs., *Dean* and *Boston*, retaken by H.M.S. *Romulus*
9 ix	*Comet* (McDonogh)	off Pensacola	
23 xi	*Hanover* (Willard)	Dover	Fr. priv.

1780

7 iii	*Hillsborough* (Parry)	Holyhead	2 Am. privs., *Black Prince* and *Black Princess*
8 iii	*Bessborough* (Goddard)	Holyhead	2 Am. priv., *Black Prince* and *Black Princess*
12 v	*Prince Frederick* (Beauvoir)	Dover	a 'Frenchman'
21 v	*Hillsborough* (Blackhall)	Falmouth	Am. priv.
23 v	*Carteret* (Newman)	Falmouth	4 Am. privs.
7 viii	*Mercury* (Dillon)	Falmouth	3 Am. privs.

1781

19 i	*Prince Frederick* (Beauvoir)	Dover	a 'Frenchman'
28 i	*Comet* (McDonogh)	off Pensacola	recaptured
9 iii	*Lord Howe* (Jeffery)	Falmouth	Am. warship *Thorne*
16 iii	*Anna Teresa* (Crosby)	Falmouth	Am. priv.
10 iv	*Diligence* (Clark)	off Pensacola	Fr. warship
3 vi	*Prince of Wales* (Hearne)	Harwich	
23 vi	*Mercury* (Dillon)	Falmouth	recaptured
8 viii	*Diligence* (Steele)	off Pensacola	
24 viii	*Comet* (McDonogh)	off Pensacola	Am. priv. *Pilgrim*
24 viii	*Queen Charlotte* (Clarke)	Falmouth	Fr. warship *Glorieux*
23 xi	*Eagle* (Richards)	Falmouth	

1782

| 23 i | *Prince William Henry* (Peters) | Falmouth | 2 Am. privs. |

5 ii	*Courier* (Boyton)	Dover	
19 iii	*Grenville* (Nankerville)	Falmouth	Am. priv., recaptured
15 vii	*Speedy* (D'Auvergne)	Falmouth	2 Fr. frigs., recaptured
15 vii	*Swift* (Nichols)	Falmouth	2 Fr.frigs. recaptured
16 x	*Antelope* (Kempthorne)	Falmouth	ransomed from French

APPENDIX

II

Packet-boat losses during the French war of 1793-1802. The *Rep. on Mr Palmer's Agreement* (1797), 109, furnishes some of the data for this tabulation. The French captured all of the packet-boats save the *Duke of Clarence*, taken by a Spanish privateer. Some of the names of the French vessels as they appear in the Post Office records are obviously misspelled.

Date	Packet-boat	Station	Captor
1793			
ii	*Dispatch*	Dover	
24 xii	*Arab*	Corunna	Frig. *l'Insurgente*
1794			
23 iv	*Expedition*	Lisbon	Frig. *Thames*
24 vii	*King George*	Lisbon	Frig. *Unité*
19 ix	*Antelope*	America	French squadron
23 ix	*Thynne*	Lisbon	French squadron
1795			
19 i	*Queen Charlotte*	W.I.	Frig. *Republic*
10 ii	*Tankerville*	Am.	'War vessel' *La Fille de Patriot*
14 iii	*Princess Royal*	Yarmouth	
7 iv	*Prince William Henry*	W.I.	Frig. *La Vengeance*
1796			
5 vi	*Prince of Orange*	Yarmouth	
10 vi	*Tartar*	Am.	*L'Aigle* and another brig
17 viii	*Princess of Brunswick*	Corunna	*Adventure*
30 ix	*Active*	W.I.	Priv. *Voltigeur*
x	*Duchess of York*	Corunna	
1797			
27 ii	*Princess Elizabeth*	W.I.	Priv. *Actif*
10 iii	*Sandwich*	W.I.	Priv. *Dugay*
28 iii	*Swallow*	W.I.	Priv. *Triumph*
2 vii	*Grantham*	W.I.	Priv., retaken by H.M.S. *Tamar*
10 viii	*Dolphin*	Yarmouth	
25 x	*Union*	Yarmouth	

10 xii	*Countess of Leicester*	Am.	Priv. *l'Insurgente*
1798			
11 i	*Prince Ernest*	W.I.	Priv. *Belliqueux*
15 i	*Prince Edward*	W.I.	Priv. *La Dennis*
9 ii	*Portland*	W.I.	Priv. *La Julie*
20 iii	*Roebuck*	W.I.	Priv. *Braave*
31 iii	*Swallow*	Am.	Priv. *Braave*
27 v	*Princess of Wales*	W.I.	Priv. *Tiger*
vi	*Prince Adolphus*	Lisbon	Priv. *La Tesse*
27 vii	*Duke of York*	W.I.	Priv. *La Confiance*
1799			
29 iii	*Carteret*	W.I. and Am.	Priv., retaken by Am. frig. *Constitution*
8 iv	*Chesterfield*	W.I. and Am.	Priv. *Mars*
26 xi	*Lady Harriott*	Lisbon	Priv. *Mars*
7 xii	*Westmorland*	W.I.	
22 xii	*Adelphi*	W.I.	Priv. *Grand Buonaparte*
1800			
26 ii	*Princess Royal*	W.I.	Priv. *Courier*
7 iii	*Carteret*	W.I.	Priv. *Bellona*
16 iii	*Jane*	W.I. and Am.	Priv. *La Vengeance,* retaken by H.M.S. *Argo*
4 v	*Princess Charlotte*		Priv. *l'Ariage,* retaken by H.M.S. *Hussar*
6 v	*Marquis of Kildare*	Lisbon	Priv. *Ransom,* retaken by crew
11 v	*Princess Amelia*	W.I.	Priv. *Grand Decidie*
29 vi	*Dolphin*	Yarmouth	Priv. *Buonaparte*
28 xii	*Duke of Clarence*	W.I.	Sp. priv. *El Fuerte Castra*
1801			
25 v	*Earl Gower*	Lisbon	Fr. priv. *Télégraphe*
5 vi	*Phoenix*	Am.	Fr. priv. *Psyche,* retaken by H.M.S. *Naiad*
8 vii	*Lady Arabella*		Fr. priv., *Raton,* retaken by H.M.S. *l'Oiseau*

In addition, ten West Indian mail-boats were taken during this war.

APPENDIX
III

❦❦❦

The Falmouth-based packet-boats that were captured during the Napoleonic War and the War of 1812. An asterisk indicates that the crew of the packet-boat received awards for the defence of the vessel, even though it was in vain.

Date	Packet-boat and Capt.	Station	Captor
1803			
31 vii	*King George (Yescombe)	Lisbon	Fr. priv. *Reprisal*
10 ix	Duke of York (Fenner)	Lisbon	Fr. priv. *Dinant*
1804			
25 iv	*Duke of Marlborough (Bull)	W.I.	Fr. priv. *Gen. Erneuf*
13 v	Duke of Kent (?)	W.I.	Fr. priv. *Sans Pareil*
1805			
16 v	*Queen Charlotte (Mudge)	Am.	Fr. priv. *l'Hirondelle*
26 v	Earl of Leicester (Bell)	W.I.	Fr. priv. *la Bellona*
14 vi	Lord Charles Spencer (Cotesworth)	Am.	Fr. priv. *Vaillant*
vi	*Chesterfield (Blight)	W.I.	Sp. brig. *La Serena*
7 viii	Prince of Wales (Todd)	Lisbon	Sp. priv.
1806	no captures		
1807			
12 xii	*Duke of Montrose (Dyneley)	W.I.	Fr. priv. *La Confiance*
1808			
18 xi	Duke of Marlborough (Bull)	Lisbon	Fr. priv. *La Josephine*
1809	no captures		
1810	no captures		
1811			

4 ix	*Swallow* (Morphew)	W.I.	Fr. frig. *La Clorinde*
29 x	*Chesterfield* (Gibbon)	Am.	Fr. priv.
1812	no captures before the U.S. entered the war.		
6 viii	*Prince Adolphus* (Boulderson)	W.I.	Am. priv. *Gov. McKean*
15 ix	**Princess Amelia* (Moorsom)	W.I.	Am priv. *Rossie*
15 x	*Swallow* (Morphew)	W.I.	Am. frig. *President*
23 xi	**Townshend* (Cock)	W.I.	Am. privs. *Tom* and *Bona*
11 xii	*Nocton* (Naylor)	Brazil	Am. frig. *Essex*
1813			
4 iv	*Mary Ann* (Caddy)	Gibraltar	Am. priv. *Gov. Tomkins*
14 iv	**Express* (Quick)	Brazil	Am. priv. *Anaconda*
21 iv	**Ann* (Britton)	W.I.	Am. priv. *Yorktown*
24 vi	**Manchester* (Elphinstone)	Am.	Am. priv. *Yorktown*
10 vi	*Duke of Montrose* (Blewett)	Am.	Am. frig. *President*
28 vi	*Lapwing* (Elsworthy)	Corunna	Am. priv. *Rattlesnake*
26 ix	**Morgiana* (Cunningham)	W.I.	Am. priv. *Saratoga*
22 xi	**Lapwing* (Furze)	W.I.	Am. priv. *Fox*
25 xi	*Little Catherine* (Blewett)	Passages	Fr. frigs. *Sultane* and *l'Etoile*
13 xii	*Duke of Montrose* (Vivian)	Brazil	Fr. frig. *Sultane*
1814			
27 i	*Carteret* (Carne)	W.I.	Fr. sloop-of-war *Halcyon*
16 ii	*Townshend* (Cock)	Brazil	Fr. frig. *La Clorinde*
13 v	*Little Catherine* (Richards)	Brazil	Am. priv. *Herald*
2 vii	**Princess Elizabeth* (Forrestdale)	Gibraltar	Am. priv. *Harpy*
1815			
8 ii	*Lady Mary Pelham* (Graham)	W.I.	Am. priv. *Kemp*
27 ii	**Princess Elizabeth* (Forrestdale)	Brazil	Am. priv. *America*
15 iii	**Windsor Castle* (Sutton)	Am.	Am. priv. *Roger*

In addition, twenty West Indian mail-boats were taken during the war.

APPENDIX

IV

❧

The Falmouth packets, used for carrying ocean mails, as of 1827. They had been under Admiralty control since 1823. Of the thirty-nine sailing packets in the service at that time, eighteen were holdovers from the post-office régime. They are indicated by an asterisk in the list. The remainder were naval sloops of war. The first five were used on the Lisbon station, being those of the senior commanders. The list of the packets and their commanders is taken from R. Thomas, *History of the Town and Harbour of Falmouth* (Falmouth, 1827). See above, p. 111.

1 *Duke of Marlborough* (John Bull)	21 *Rinaldo* (Moore)
2 *Magnet* (Porteous)	22 *Plover* (Jennings)
3 *Duke of Kent* (Lawrence)	23 *Cygnet* (Gooding)
4 *Stanmer* (Sutton)	24 *Kingfisher* (Poore)
5 *Sandwich* (Schuyler)	25 *Goldfinch* (Walkie)
6 *Marchioness of Salisbury* (Graham)	26 *Zephyr* (Church)
7 *Lord Hobart* (James)	27 *Hope* (Wright)
8 *Redpole* (Bullocke)	28 *Sphynx* (Passingham)
9 *Queensberry* (Hannah)	29 *Eclipse* (Griffin)
10 *Nocton* (Morphew)	30 *Dore* (Forster)
11 *Lord Melville* (Furse)	31 *Osborne* (Leslie)
12 *Francis Freeling* (Cunningham)	32 *Lady Wellington* (Lugg)
13 *Countess of Chichester* (Kirkness)	33 *Mutine* (Pawle)
14 *Camden* (Tilly)	34 *Sheldrake* (Ede)
15 *Princess Elizabeth* (Scott)	35 *Tyrian* (Dwyer)
16 *Lady Mary Pelham* (Cary)	36 *Duke of York* (Snell)
17 *Lady Louisa* (Figg)	37 *Skylark* (Aplin)
18 *Frolic* (Barron)	38 *Hearty* (Jewry)
19 *Swallow* (Baldock)	39 *Myrtle* (Sison)
20 *Emulous* (Croke)	

APPENDIX

V

✥

Mail carried by air, 1950-62, by the two official lines, BOAC and BEA. The tabulation shows the uplift in tons and the ton-miles of the two services. Based on the *Annual Reports* and *Accounts*, and on information furnished by E.V. Dolby, Air Mail Adviser for BEA and BOAC.

Year ending March 31st	BOAC Uplift in tons	BOAC Ton-miles to nearest thousands	BEA Uplift in tons	BEA Ton-miles to nearest thousands
1950	2,003	9,075,000	4,168	1,835,000
1951	2,272	11,806,000	5,249	2,096,000
1952	2,895	15,316,000	6,489	2,452,000
1953	3,110	15,975,000	6,289	2,541,000
1954	3,366	17,269,000	6,582	2,601,000
1955	3,407	17,263,000	6,964	2,919,000
1956	3,815	18,887,000	7,895	3,646,000
1957	4,145	21,132,000	7,541	3,623,000
1958	4,103	20,201,000	7,465	3,600,000
1959	4,064	20,802,000	7,669	4,058,000
1960	4,363	22,551,000	7,848	4,001,000
1961	5,548	29,488,000	8,850	4,215,000
1962	5,810	30,074,000	9,325	4,091,000

APPENDIX

VI

❦

Mail carried overseas by ship and by air for the last full year before the Second World War, and for the post-war years. The tabulation shows the number of items posted and the cost of their conveyance. Based on *P.O. Commercial Accounts* and the *Appropriation Accounts, Revenue Departments*.

Year ending March 31,	Total items Posted by Surface Mail	by Air Mail	Cost of Conveyance by Surface Mail	by Air Mail
1939	214,000,000	91,000,000	£ 607,480	£ 963,930

Reports were suspended during the First World War.

Year ending March 31,	Total items Posted by Surface Mail	by Air Mail	Cost of Conveyance by Surface Mail	by Air Mail
1946	Reports suspended		1,178,050	3,028,660
1947	332,000,000	220,000,000	1,019,800	3,381,410
1948	250,000,000	182,000,000	1,307,460	4,044,850
1949	230,000,000	153,000,000	1,293,240	3,905,000
1950	201,000,000	170,000,000	1,457,280	5,011,600
1951	204,000,000	168,000,000	1,645,800	5,788,750
1952	213,000,000	202,000,000	1,996,470	8,018,800
1953	215,000,000	211,000,000	2,269,420	7,939,830
1954	218,000,000	224,000,000	2,453,230	8,404,090
1955	234,000,000	234,000,000	2,611,120	8,720,480
1956	235,000,000	239,000,000	2,787,660	8,444,500
1957	253,000,000	271,000,000	2,864,860	9,136,680
1958	245,000,000	258,000,000	3,072,880	9,051,210
1959	199,000,000	238,000,000	2,757,220	9,647,960
1960	197,000,000	248,000,000	2,831,290	9,588,390
1961	198,000,000	275,000,000	2,704,440	10,192,300
1962	188,000,000	281,000,000	2,659,000	10,576,471

BIBLIOGRAPHY

The titles, listed in several groups, do not include all the works used or appearing in the footnotes but only those that were of considerable value. Citations are shown in square brackets where a short title was more convenient. Manuscript and printed documentary materials are, for the most part, in the Record Room of the GPO Headquarters Building, London.

MANUSCRIPT SOURCES

Admiralty Agents, Letters of (40v., 1855-79) [Epp. Adm. Agts.]
American Letter Book (1775-83)
Archives, New Zealand, in the GPO Record Room, Wellington
Cotton-Frankland Correspondence (the 1st joint Postmasters-General, 1691-)
Dispatches to the Govs. of New South Wales (Mitchell Library, Sydney)
Establishment Books P.O., from 1747
Falmouth Letter Books (8v., 1704-9, 1778-81, 1810-24); the others have not survived [Fal. L.B.]
Gardiner, Thomas, General Survey of the Post Office (1677) in the Dartmouth Papers, British Museum
General Accounts, P.O. [Gen. Accts.]
Minutes, P.O.
Packet Minutes, P.O. [Pkt. Min.]
Packet Report Books, P.O. [Pkt. Rep. Bks.]
Palmer, John, Papers of (Comptroller-Gen. of the P.O., 1786-92)
Peover Papers (The Letter Books of Col. Roger Whitley, Dep. P.M.G., 1672-7)
Postmaster-General's Minutes, listed by years in various series, as, e.g. [Pkt. Min. 447L/1860]
Receiver General's Entry Books, P.O. [Rec. Gen. Entry Bks.]
Reports of P.O. Commrs. James and Smith, sent to the south Pacific in 1844 [Rep. James & Smith]
Reports of the Postmasters-General, not printed before 1854 [Rep. P.M.G.]
Treasury Letter Books, P.O., beginning in 1706 [T.L.B.]
Walsingham, Papers of Lord (P.M.G., 1787-94)

DOCUMENTARY AND OFFICIAL PRINTED MATERIALS

Acts of the Privy Council of England (1890-) [Acts. P.C.]

Annual Reports and Accounts of BOAC and BEA, the former from 1950, the latter from 1953

Annual Reports on the Progress of Civil Aviation (1929-)

Appendices to the Journals of the House of Representatives, New Zealand [A.J.H.R.]

The Approach towards a System of Imperial Air Communications (1926) [Memorandum]

Baker, E.C., *History of the [P.O.] Engineering Department* (1939)

Calendar of Letters and Papers . . . Henry VIII (1852-1910)

Calendar of State Papers (1856-) [Cal. S.P.] in various series, America and West Indies; Domestic; Home; Venetian; Treasury Books and Papers [Tr. B & P]; and Treasury Papers [Tr. P.]

Circulars, P.O.

Command Papers, numbered in series, as e.g. [Cd. 7007, Cmd. 670, etc.]

Commercial Accounts, P.O.

Commonwealth Parliamentary Papers (Australia)

The Empire Air Mail Scheme (1937)

Historical Records of Australia, v. xxiv (1925)

Lumley, D.O., *Air Mail Operation* (1936)

Parliamentary Debates, New Zealand

Parliamentary Debates, U.K. cited as, e.g. [Deb. H.C., 5th ser., xlii, 62]

Parliamentary Returns, listed by number and year, as e.g. [Parl. Ret., 464/1846]

The [official] Post Office, reports for 1934, 1950, 1951

The Post Office, an Historical Summary (1911)

Reports of the Royal Commission on Hist. MSS. (1870-)

Reports of the Postmasters-General overseas, as, e.g. [Rep. P.M.G., N.Z.]

Reports of the Postmasters-General, U.K., printed from 1856 to 1916

Williamson Frederic, *The Air Mail Service* (1934)

Votes and Proceedings of the various Australian Colonies

REPORTS OF PARLIAMENTARY AND OTHER COMMITTEES AND COMMISSIONERS
(in chronological order)

Com. of H.C. to Enquire into Certain Abuses of the Post Office (1787), stimulated by Lord Tankerville, P.M.G., 1782-86 [Rep. Com. Tankerville]

Commrs. of Enquiry, the 10th Rep. (1788) on the Post Office. The unpublished Observations on this Report by the P.O. are cited as [Observations]

Commrs. of Finance, the 7th Rep. (1797) on the P.O.

Com. on Agreement made with Mr Palmer (1797, reprinted 1807)

Commrs. of Revenue, the 22nd Rep. (1830) on the pkt. establishment

Com. on Management of the Post Office, the 6th Rep. (1836) on pkt. stations

Select Com. on Steam Communication with India, Lord W. Bentinck, Chairman (1837)

Sel. Com. on W.I. Mails (1841)

Commrs. to Inquire Respecting Port . . . for Steam Vessels . . . to the West Indies and other Places (1841) [Commrs. on Channel Port]

Secret Com. of House of Commons on the P.O. (1844)

Sel. Com. [of New South Wales] on Steam Communication with England (1846)

Sel. Com. on Halifax and Boston Mails (1846)

Sel. Com. on Contract Packet Service (1849)

Sel. Com. on Steam Communication with India . . . and Steam Communication between England, India, China, Australia, New Zealand or any of Them (1851), Lord Jocelyn, Chairman

Commrs. Appointed to Inquire as to . . . an Irish Packet Station (1851)

Com. on Contract Packets (1853), Lord Canning, Chairman

Sel. Com. on Packet and Telegraph Contracts (1860)

Sel. Com. on Mail Contracts . . . with Messrs Cunard . . . and Mr Inman for the Conveyance of the Mails . . . to the United States (1869)

Sel. Com. on the Cape of Good Hope and Zanzibar Contracts (1873)

Sel. Com. on Steamship Subsidies (1902)

Com. on the Eastern Mail Service (1904)

Com. on Civil Aerial Transport (1918)

Com. on Civil Air Transport Subsidies (1923), Sir Herbert Hambling, chairman

Com. of Inquiry into Civil Aviation (1938), Lord Cadman, chairman

SECONDARY WORKS

London is the place of publication unless shown to be elsewhere. Some volumes are included, even though their worth needs some qualification, as indicated where cited.

Albion, R.G., *Square Riggers on Schedule* (Princeton, 1938)

Babcock, F.L., *Spanning the Atlantic* (N.Y., 1931)

Beadon, R.J., *Uniform Imperial Postage* (1891)

Bonsor, N.R.P., *North Atlantic Seaway* (Prescot, Lancs., 1955)

Bowen, F.C., *A Century of Atlantic Travel* (Boston, 1930)

British Almanac and *Companion to the Br. Almanac* (1826-)

Burritt, Elihu, *Ocean Penny Postage*, Its Importance Shown (1846?) *An Ocean Postage*. Will it Pay? (1851?)
The Proposition of a Universal Penny Postage (1853?)

Bushell, T.A., *Royal Mail*, a Centenary History of the Royal Mail Line (1939)

Butler, R.L., *Doctor Franklin, Postmaster General* (Garden City, N.Y., 1928)

Cable, Boyd [Ernest A. Ewart], *A Hundred Years of the P & O* (1937)

Clark, Wm. B., *Ben Franklin's Privateers* (Baton Rouge, La., 1956)

Coggeshall, George, *The History of the American Privateers* . . . in the Years 1812, '13, and '14 (4th ed., N.Y., 1861)

Cotton, Sir Evan, *East Indiamen*, ed. Sir Charles Fawcett (1949)

Curti, Merle, *The Learned Blacksmith* [Elihu Burritt] (N.Y., 1937)

Dictionary of National Biography [D.N.B.], of Am. Biography [D.A.B.]

Ellis, K., *The Post Office in the Eighteenth Century* (1958)

The Empire Air Mail Programme (1937)

Fellowes, Capt. William, *A Narrative of the Loss of* . . . *the Lady Hobart on an Island of Ise in the Atlantic Ocean* (1803)

Garratt, G.R.M., *One Hundred Years of Submarine Cables* (1950)

Gay, Susan E., *Old Falmouth* (1903)

Government Subsidies and the Postal Service with India, China and Australia (rev. ed. 1879) Cited as [Orient Pamphlet]

Hamilton, J.H., *The "All-Red" Route*, 1893-1953 (Victoria, Br. Col., 1956)

Hays, C.D., *Remarks upon the Proposed Establishment of Steam Communication with the Australian Colonies* (1847)
Steam Communication with the Australian Colonies, with a Comparison of Different Routes (1849)

Heaton, John Henniker, wrote numerous articles on universal and imperial penny postage that appeared in the *Contemporary*, the *Fortnightly* and the *Nineteenth Century* during the quarter century before the First World War

Robin Higham, *Britain's Imperial Air Routes* (1960)

Hill, Roderic, *The Baghdad Royal Mail* (1920)

Hill, Sir Rowland and G.B. Hill, *Life of Rowland Hill* (2v., 1880)

Hoskins, H.L., *British Routes to India* (N.Y., 1928)

Jerningham, Frederick, *Steam Communication with the Cape of Good Hope, Australia and New Zealand* (1848)

Kemble, J.H., *The Panama Route, 1848-1869* (Berkeley, Calif., 1943)

Lawson, Will, *Steam in the South Pacific* (Wellington, 1909)

Lubbock, Basil, *The Western Ocean Packets* (Glasgow, 1925)

McCalmont, Robert, *Some Remarks on the Contract Packet System and on Ocean Penny Postage* (1851)

Maclay, E.S., *A History of American Privateers* (N.Y., 1899)

Martineau, Harriet, *Autobiography* (2v., 1877)

Monk, E.V. and E.T. Winter, *Air Mail* (1936)

Murray, Sir Evelyn, *The Post Office* (1927)

Murray, Marischal, *Union-Castle Chronicle*, 1853-1953 (1953)

Norway, A.H., *History of the Post Office Packet Service* . . . 1793-1815 (1895)

Pering, Thomas, *Inquiry into the System of the Post Office* (1815)

Porter, Mrs Adrian, *Life and Letters of Sir John Henniker Heaton* (1916)

Preble, G.H., *A Chronological History of Steam Navigation* (N.Y., 1893)

Rainey, Thomas, *Ocean Steam Navigation and the Ocean Post* (N.Y., 1858)

Reith, Lord, *Into the Wind* (1949)

Robinson, Howard, *Britain's Post Office* (1953)

Robinson, Howard, *The British Post Office*, A History (Princton, 1948)

Smith, A.D., *The Development of the Rates of Postage* (1917)

Smith, William, *History of the Post Office in British North America*, 1639-1870 (1920)

Stanhope, Lord Charles, *A Discourse, shewing the True State* . . . *of the* . . . *Postmaster General of England* (1637)

Thomas, R., *History of the Town and Harbour of Falmouth* (Falmouth, 1827)

Trollope, Anthony, *An Autobiography* (1883)

Trollope, Anthony, *Australia and New Zealand* (1873)

Trollope, Anthony, *The West Indies and the Spanish Main* (1859)

Trollope, Anthony, *North America* (2v., 1862)

Vyvyan, R.N., *Wireless over Thirty Years* (1936)

BRITISH MAILS OVERSEAS FROM THE PHILATELIC VIEWPOINT

Dalwick, R.E. and C.H.C. Harmer, *Newfoundland Air Mails*, 1919-1939 (1953)

Field, E.J. and N.C. Baldwin, *The Coronation Aerial Post*, 1911 (1934)

Lowe, Robson, *Encyclopaedia of British Empire Postage Stamps* (4v., 1948-1962)

Pringle, John, *Early British Balloon Posts* (cir. 1925)

Robertson, Alan W., *A History of the Ship Letters of the British Isles* (1955)

Sidebottom, J.E., *The Overland Mail* (1948)

Staff, Frank, *Transatlantic Mail* (1956)

Studd, M.A., *Paquebot and Ship Letter Cancellations*, 1894-1951 (1953)

INDEX

Aden, port of, acquired (1839), 160–1.
Admiralty, use of naval vessels for mails, 95, 109; Falmouth service transferred to the Admiralty (1823), 111, 217; and home services as well (1836), 123; relation of, to Post Office, 217–8; required packets with wooden hulls, 218; agents of, aboard packets, 219 ff.; packet control returned to P.O. (1860), 144, 234; mail steamers as a naval reserve, 267; Admiralty clauses in air-mail contracts, 291.
Admiralty agents, their duties, 219–221; use of, on Royal Mail, 152, 227–8; east of Suez, 220, 222; dislike of, by captains, 221; agent stationed at Southampton, 232; withdrawal of, 232.
Adriatic, paddle-steamship, largest Collins liner, 141; bought by Lever Line, 244; carried troops to Canada, 230.
air mail, balloon as predecessor, 275; early air trials, 276; a Ministry of Air (1917), 279; opening of service to Continent, 280–1; founding of Imperial Airways, 283; first transatlantic flight (1919), 283; opening of route to India, 284; trial of airships, 285–6; air mail to Africa, 288; to Australia, 289; lowering of rates, 290; All-up Scheme (1937), 291; use of the blue labels for, 288; opening of regular Atlantic service, 293; Lord Reith, head of BOAC, 294; use of airgraphs, 297–300; of air-letter forms (aerogrammes), 301–2; separation of BEA for European services, 302, 304; subsidies for, 305, 317.
Alexandria, steam packets to (1835), 161; land route from, to Suez, 167.
American sailing liners (1818–1840), service opened from Liverpool, 114; use of, by Harriet Martineau, 115, by Tyrone Power, 131, by Charles Dickens, 136, by Emerson, 137; handling of mail on, 115–6.
Amsterdam, postal relations with (1660), 27–8.
Anchor Line, 246, 249, 266.
Anderson, Arthur, of P & O, 164, 167, 175.
Antelope, sailing packet, victory over Fr. privateer (1793), 70–1.
Antwerp, imperial exchange at, 18, 19, 21, 26; rates to (1711), 39.
Atlantic Royal Mail Steam Navigation Co., see Lever Line.
Auckland (New Zealand), 203–4, 216.
Australia, difficulties of mail service to, 185; visit of Br. P.O. commissioners to (1844–5), 187; unsatisfactory sailing packets, 189; various routes from England, 189–91; opening of P & O services (1851), to, 191; Australian Royal Mail Line via Cape, 191–3; General Screw started service in 1853, 194; return to sailing packets, 195; European & Australian Line via Egypt (1865), 196; P & O via Mauritius, 197; colonies in, join U.P.U., 260; imperial penny postage (1911), from, 265; regular air services from England, 289.

Bahama Is., 49, 69, 124.
Barbados, service to, 50; capture of two packets near, 54; first call in W.I. at, 57, 60, 106, 124.
Bermuda, 94, 107, 156.
Bishop, Col. Henry, P.O. contractor (1660–67), 25–6.
Blue Riband of Atlantic, early rivalry for, 246–8; German competition for, 269; regained by Cunard Line, 269; won by *United States*, 270; by air, 305.
Boston, Mass., a port for American sailing liners, 115, 125; Cunard service to, 134–5, 234.

Brancker, Sir Sefton, Director of Civil Aviation, 280–2; death of, in loss of airship *R 101* (1930), 286.
Brazil, sailing packet service to, opened (1808), 93–4; stamping of mail from, 85; great length of voyages to, 94, 102; voyage of *Lady Mary Pelham* (1813) to, 101–3; route to, 124; steam service to, by Royal Mail, 150–1.
Brindisi, packet port, 237.
Bristol, first N.Y. service from (1709–12), 38; desire for packet boats at, 60; sought steam packet service to Ireland, 121; pioneer voyage of *Great Western* from, 127; launching of *Great Britain* at, 137; tender for Atlantic services, 138.
Britannia, Cunard liner, first regular voyage of Line (1840) by, 135; Charles Dickens crosses on, 136.
British & American Steam Packet Co., charter of *Sirius* by, 127; its *British Queen* to N.Y. (1839), 129; the *President* lost at sea (1841), 129–130, 136.
British European Airways (BEA), organized (1945), 302–4, 316–7.
British Overseas Airways Corp. (BOAC), 294, 302–4, 316–7.
Buckingham, J. S., on smuggling in packet boats, 64; on capture of *Lady Harriott*, 74n.
Bull, Captain James, his *Suffolk*, 48, and *Grantham*, 73–4.
Bull Captain John succeeds father (1798), 74; smuggling on his *Duke of Marlborough*, 80; duel of, with H.M.S. *Pinafore*, 87.
bullion, carriage of, by packet boats, 35, 91, 101n; sending of, to London, 83.
Burritt, Elihu, 253–5.

cable, submarine, laid across Channel (1850), 271; to Ireland, 272; across Atlantic, 272; across Pacific (1902), 273; Cable & Wireless, 275; use of, during First World War, 277; submarine telephone cables, 306–7.
Calais, foreign mail via, 1, 15, 25, 30, 59, 117, 234.
Canada, mails to (1765) via N.Y., 48; via Nova Scotia, 146; pioneer steam voyage from, to London, 125–6; Cunard service to, and its withdrawal, 136, 146; direct services by Allen Line (1856), 147; member of U.P.U., 259; varied rates, 258; Far East mail via, 271; terminus of Pacific cables at Vancouver, 273, 307; voyage of airship *R 100* to, 286.
Canning, Lord, P.M.G., 142; criticizes Royal Mail, 152; on expensive contracts, 167, 217–8.
Cape Colony, route via, to India, 172; packet service to (1815–19), 108–9; steam packets to, 173; service to, arranged by colony, 182; lowered rates, 259; air-mail service to, 289.
Carteret, Lord, P.M.G. (1771–89), 62–3.
Castle Mail Packets Co., founded by Donald Currie, 176; competitor of Union Line, 179; contract with Cape Colony, 182; home port, Dartmouth, later Southampton, 179, 183; combined with Union Line (1899), 240.
Ceylon, see Colombo.
Chagres, at Atlantic end of Panama crossing, 149, 152, 154–5.
Channel Islands, packet service to (1780s), 68; renewed in 1793, 68, 77; services to, after 1815, 117; steam packets to (1820s), 122.
Charleston, S. Carolina, 48–9, 53, 71, 149.
Chusan, P & O mail packet, pioneer voyage of, to Australia, 191–3.
coffee houses, use of, for collecting ship-letters (1818–1840), 114–5.

323

Coke, Sir John, 20, 22.
Collins, E. K., N.Y. ship owner, his Dramatic Line of sailing ships, 115; his steamship line (1850), 139–41, 147.
Colombo, replaces Point de Galle as P & O port, 238; air service to, 292, 300.
Cork, Ireland, 60, pioneer transatlantic steam voyage from, 127.
Corunna, Spanish packet port, 32; rates to (1711), 39; service to, ended (1713), 40; and reopened briefly (1803), 91.
crews of sailing packets, on Harwich route (1689–97), 30; smart and pension money for, 33, 46; pay of (1700s), 45–6; victualling of (1689), 34; in 1750s, 46. 50; difficulties of, on W.I. route, 48–9; size of, in Napoleonic War, 79; failure of revolt of (1810), 81; protections of, against press gangs, 81–2; desertions from, 81–2.
Croydon Airport, use of, for European mail, 281–2, 288, 303.
Cunard, Sir Samuel, early career of, 107, 124, 131–3; defends use of N.Y. as terminus, 138; claims of, denied by P.O., 142–3; interest of, in a Pacific route, 155; death of (1864), 144.
Cunard Line, founded, 133; Quebec branch of, 134, 137; first liner to cross Atlantic, 135; service of, to N.Y. begun (1848), 138; subsidy of, 133–4, 139, 142, 234; adoption of ship's lights by, 141; service of, regular, 152–3; career of *Unicorn*, 134, 155; change from paddle wheels to screw (1850s), 215, 246; use of Queenstown (Cobh) harbour, 242; defence of its monopoly, 247; combined with Inman Line, 257; objection of, to sorting at sea, 233; use of ships of, in First and Second World Wars, 278, 296.
Cuxhaven, port for Harwich packets (1793–1802), 68, 75, 117.

Dartmouth, use of, as packet port, 151, 179.
De Quester, Matthew, Foreign Postmaster (1603–31), 17–21.
dispatch service by sailing vessels, to Bordeaux, 91; to Bermuda, 94, 107; to Corfu, 106, 124; to Minorca, 40, 42–3; to West Africa, 173–4.
Donaghadee, Irish packet port, 40, 117.
Donald Currie & Co., see Castle Mail Packets Co.
Dover, earliest packet port, 15, 18, 26; extravagance at (1774), 61–3; closed during Continental wars, 30, 75; size of packets at, 26, 59; steam packets, 117, 120, 234.
Duke of Marlborough (Captain John Bull), sailing packet, 80, 87, 313.
Dummer, Edmond, Surveyor of the Navy, 30; translantic service of, (1702–11), 35, 37.
Dunkirk, a mail service to, 15, 25, 30.

East India Company, early mails by ships of, 108; objections of, to mail, 109; huge floating hotels of, 158; length of sea voyages of ships of, 159; regular calls at Cape Town, 172; use of Aden by, 160; retains Bombay-Suez route, 166, 190. See India.
Egypt, route across, 161–2, 167ff.; transit administration of, 163, 169; completion of Suez Canal (1869), 197–8; Br. mails via Canal, 199, 238; first airgraphs from, 298.
Enterprize, pioneer voyage of, to India (1825), 126, 159.
European & Australian Line, 196, 222.

Falmouth, becomes packet port (1689), 32–3; list of agents and duties at, 33–4; map of harbour, 41; Benjamin Pender succeeds Stephen Bell as agent, 63, 71; service from (1793–1802), 70–4; Saverland, agent at

Falmouth—*continued*
(1810–21), 77–8; packets at, transferred briefly to Plymouth (1810), 81; packet fleet at, in 1810, 78; in 1827, 111; in 1836, 123; superseded by Southampton, 151.
Fellowes, Captain, at Falmouth, 77; loss of *Lady Hobart* (1803), 97–8; transfer of, to Holyhead, 77n, 98.
Finlay, Hugh, P.M.G., Br. N. America, 55, 58.
First World War, foreign service during, 277–8.
Flushing (Falmouth Harbour), 41, 80.
Flushing (Flanders), 20, 22, 24, 26–7, 30.
Foxcroft, Thomas, Dep. P.M.G. in N. America, 49, 55.
France, postal service with, 19, 24, 26; after 1782, 59; short route to Far East through, 163–4, 234; postal convention with (1839), 165; rate to, lowered (1860s), 256.
Francis Freeling, sailing packet, carried bullion, 83, 91; important voyage of, to America (1814), 107.
Franklin, Benjamin, Dep. P.M.G. in N. America, 44, 49; voyage of, in packet boat, 45; dismissal of, as Dep. P.M.G. (1774), 55; privateers sent out from France by, 53.
Freeling, Sir Francis, Secy. of the P.O. (1789–1836), 64, 79, 186; reflections on the service (1819), 103–4; doubtful of value of steam in W.I., 106–7; opposed transfer of packets to Admiralty, 110, 122; his opinion of Waghorn's schemes, 159, 162.

Galway, port of Lever Line, 242–5.
General Screw Steam Shipping Co., first steam line to Cape Colony, 173; contract for service to India via Cape, 174–5; service via New Zealand (1853), 194; tender for service to New Zealand (1863), 209.
General Steam Navigation Co., mails by, to Continent, 123.
Gibraltar, taken, 34, 40; mail service to, begun in 1717, 42; growing value of, after 1800, 91; terminus of first P & O service, 164; eastern route via, 165, 237.
Gothenburg, packet port in Napoleonic War, 75, 117.
Grantham, sailing packet, contract for hire of (1768), 49–50; ownership of, 64; capture of (1797), 73, 311.
Great Britain, pioneer iron screw vessel, 137; use of, to Australia, 194.
Great Western, early paddle-wheel steam packet; pioneer voyage to N.Y. of, 127–8; use of, as mail liner, 131; addition of, to fleet of Royal Mail (W.I.), 151.
Great Western Steamship Co., tender for Atlantic service (1839), 132; objection of, to Cunard monopoly, 137–8.
Guion Line (Liverpool), 248–9, 257.

Haliburton, T. C. (Sam Slick), his *Letter Bag of the Great Western*, 135.
Halifax (Nova Scotia), Packet port after 1782, 58; packets to, in winter, 78, 107–8; importance of, after 1803, 94; route to (1816), 107–8; service to, in 1860, 234; *Tyrian*, sailing packet, returns from (1839), 131.
Hamburg, early postal service to, 20, 24; during 1793–1802, 75; steam service to, 123.
Harwich, early service from, to Netherlands, 25; service regular from (1660), 27–9; packet boats in use at (1689–97), 30; during Am. Revolution, 59; services from, discontinued (1790s), 68, 75; replaced by Yarmouth (1793–1802), 68; after 1815, 117, 123.
Heaton, Sir John Henniker, advocate of lower colonial postage, 261–2; of the penny rate to the U.S., 265.

Helvoetsluis (Hellevoetsluis), packet port for
  Harwich service, 27–8; Harwich packets
  captured at (1803), 75; steam packet, *Curaçao*,
  from, to W.I., 125. See Netherlands.
Hill, J. R. & Co., agents for special services via
  France and Egypt, 163.
Hill, Sir Rowland, 119; his opinion of Royal
  Mail Line, 157; opposed a Pacific service to
  New Zealand, 208; against grant of ocean
  penny postage, 252–3; lowered colonial rates
  to 6d, 256.
Hoare, Sir Samuel, interest of, in air service,
  285–6.
Holland, see Netherlands.
Holt Line (Ocean Steamship Co.), 237, 240.
Holyhead, packet port, 40, 53, 59–60; service
  from, after 1782, 69; after 1815, 118; during
  war of 1793–1802, 77; steam packets at, 118–9,
  122.
Howe, Joseph, interest of, in service to Halifax,
  131–2.
Howth, Irish packet port after 1815, 118–9.

India, mail to, in East Indiamen, 108–9; desire
  of, for steam communication, 159; overland
  route to, 160–1, 165–8; Bombay chief mail
  port of, 237; pays part of Far East subsidy,
  238; air mail to, 288–91.
Inman Line, its 'City' ships, 245–6; joins with
  Cunard against P.O. 247, 257.
Ireland, mail service to, from Scotland (1711),
  40; from Holyhead, 53, 59; route from
  Milford Haven to, 59; Galway and Queenstown as packet ports, 242–5, 269.
Isle of Man, steam packet service to, 121–2.

Jamaica, packet service to, 36, 46, 50, 57; laxity
  of p.m. at, 58, 62–3; service to, difficult (1793–
  1802), 69; stamping of letters from, at
  Falmouth, 85, 106; steam service from, to
  St. Thomas, 124; beginning of Royal Mail
  Line calls, 149; preference of Trollope for,
  156.

Kaikoura (New Zealand Line), pioneer voyage
  of, to Panama, 210–12.
King George's Sound (Western Australia),
  important port for mail ships, 185, 191, 196–7.

Lady Hobart (Captain Fellowes), last voyage of
  (1803), 97.
Lady Mary Pelham, figure head for, 78; engagement of, with privateer *Globe* (1813), 101–3;
  long voyage of, to Brazil (1814), 94.
letters, without covers, 24n; stamped where
  mailed, 36; handling of, in W.I. (1790s), 57–8;
  incoming, stamped at Falmouth, 85; loose
  letter bag on packets (1820), 105; movable
  mailing boxes for, on packets, 224; boxed for
  shipment, 225; new adhesive stamps for
  lowered rates overseas, 259n; adhesive air-
  mail stamps, 288.
Lever Line (Galway Line), beginnings of, 242;
  ships of, inadequate, 244; purchase of *Adriatic*
  by, 141, 244; collapse of (1864), 244–5.
Lisbon, beginnings of service to, 34, 39–40, 42;
  packets weekly to (1787), 59; service to,
  irregular (1793–1802), 69; during Napoleonic
  War, 89, 91; Lord Byron to, by mail packet,
  92; regarded as the senior service, 111, 123;
  steam line to, 164.
Liverpool, port for Am. sailing liners, 114–6;
  made a steam packet port, 121–2; paddle-
  wheel steamer *Savannah* crosses Atlantic to,
  125; Shipping Ring at, 249.
Lusitania, loss of mail on, 278.

mail packets, see packet-boats.
mails on sailing packets, care of, sinking of, if in
  danger, 33, 42, 45, 52, 96–7, 100, 103; fumigation of, 84; stamping of, at Falmouth, 85;
  use of private signals, 87; staggering of, 88,
  278; attempted escape by fast sailing, 99, 103.
mails overseas, size of, in 1674, 28; in 1705, 35;
  to W.I. (1788), 58; on Milford route to
  Ireland, 60; to Australia (1844), 188–9.
mails, regulations for overseas, by Ordinance of
  1654, 23; by Act of 1660, 24; Instruction of
  1662, 25; with Amsterdam (1668), 28; at
  Falmouth, 34; by Act of 1711, 39–40; by Act
  of 1765, 47; instructions to postmasters in
  W.I., 57–8; by treaty with France (1784), 59.
mails on steam packets, handling of, storage of,
  219–220, 222–3; marking of boxes holding,
  224; sorting of mails on board, 223; mailing
  boxes aboard, 224.
Malta, packet service opened to, 91; steam
  packets to, 124; from, to Alexandria, 161.
Manley, John, early contractor for postal service,
  23.
Marseilles (Marseille), postal service via, 42;
  short route to India via, 162–3, 165.
Melbourne (Australia), 184, 186, 188, 191, 195,
  204–5, 214, 239, 299.
merchants, approved messenger for Merchants
  Strangers, 17; for Merchant Adventurers,
  17–20; complaints of, concerned with W.I.,
  57, 73; desire of, for packets to Halifax, 107.
Milford Haven, Packet service from, to Ireland,
  59–60, 69, 77, 117; station at, converted to
  steam, 121–2.
Minorca, 40, 42; service to, ended (1783), 43.
Montagu (Captain Norway), 85; engagement
  with privateer *Globe* (1813), 101–3.

Naples, port of, used by Orient Line, 239.
Netherlands, early service to, 20, 24, 27–9;
  importance of (1689–97), 30; rates (1711), 39.
  See Helvoetsluis.
Newfoundland, early service to, via Halifax, 124;
  route to, from Galway, 242–3; offer of Allan
  Line to serve, 243; member of U.P.U., 259;
  Submarine telephone cable (CANTAT) to,
  308.
New South Wales, early service to, irregular,
  184; sailing packets to, 187–9; mail across
  Pacific, 214; subsidy offer, for steam service,
  195; contract of, with Orient Line, 239.
New York, early request for service to, denied,
  39; brief Warren service to (1709–12), 38; rates
  to (1711), 39; reopened (1755), 44–5; crucial
  voyages from (1811–13), 94–5; service to,
  after 1815, 107; Am. sailing liners from,
  114–6, 124; Admiralty sailing packets discontinue service to (1828), 115, 124; *Sirius*
  and *Great Western*, to, 127–8; Cunard Line to
  (1848), 138.
New Zealand, beginnings in, 200–4; an intercolonial mail line, 205; contract for line to
  Panama, 207–210; discontinuance of, 212;
  mails via San Francisco, 213; co-operation of
  New South Wales with, 215–6; member of
  U.P.U., 260; P.M.G. Ward proposes universal penny postage, 264–5; air mail service
  from, to England, 292.
Nieuwport (Newport), mails to Antwerp via, 26.
Nova Scotia, 58, 94. See Halifax.

ocean postage, penny rate of 1840 not extended
  to, 252; penny proposed by Robert McCalmont, 143; anomalies in, 252; attitude of
  Rowland Hill toward, 253; Burritt's interest
  in cheap, 253–5; lowering of British, to 6d,
  256; Heaton's advocacy of penny rate, 261–2;

ocean postage—*continued*
Canadian proposal of 1½d (3c), 263; Westminster Conference on, 264; imperial penny postage (1898), 264–5; penny rate to the U.S. (1906), 265.
Ocean Steamship Company, see Holt Line.
Orient Steam Navigation Co., rivalry of, with P & O, 239.
Ostend, mail service to, 26, 59.

Pacific Steam Navigation Co. (Br.), service of, to Valparaiso, 153, 206; mail contract with, 154; subsidy of, in 1860, 236.
Pacific Steam Navigation Co. (U.S.), service of, from Panama to California, 155; contract of, with New Zealand and New South Wales, 216, 268.
packet agents, at Helvoetsluis (1660s), 28; at Lisbon (1805–15) acting as Army Postmaster, 91; Capt. Patey at Southampton, 232.
packet-boats, sailing, early Continental services, 26, 28, 30; from Falmouth (1689), 33; size of early, 28, 30, 35, 65–7; ownership of, 49, 63–4, 73; bottoms sheathed with copper, 51–2; losses during Am. Revolution, 308–11; smuggling in, 64–5, 79–80, 85–6, 110; limited tonnage of, 66–7, 78; losses during French war (1793–1802), 311–2; during Napoleonic and Am. wars, 313–4; shortage of, in 1802, 73; dilatory captains (1790s), 75; each a distinctive flag, 77; naming of, 78; pratique and quarantine of, 84; accommodations of, as of 1815, 105; as of 1835, 123; replaced by steamship lines, 132ff.; times taken by transatlantic sailing liners to N.Y., 44, 94, 114.
packet-boats, steam, introduction of, at Holyhead (1821), 119; on Dover-Calais route, 120; at Milford and other home stations, 121–2; on line to Malta, 124; times taken by early steam packets to N.Y., 126–7, 135.
paddle wheels, use of, for ocean-going ships, test of, 173; praise of Trollope for, 157; last used on Cunard Line, 246; use of, on Pacific, 214–5.
Palmer, John, Comptroller-General of Mails (1788–92), 57–9.
Panama, Royal Mail service to Chagres, 149, 152, 154–5; importance of crossing, 154; railway built to, 156; visit of Trollope to, 155–7; interest of New Zealand in, 207–11; Colon as Atlantic port of, 155–6, 227; Panama Canal, 268.
Passenger vessels as competitors of packets, 30, 118–9, 123.
P & O (Peninsular & Oriental Steam Navigation Co.), organization of, 165; Southampton home port of, 152; early route of, 163; into Mediterranean (1837), 164; east of Suez (1844), 166; opposed to Suez Canal, 169–70; Trollope's suspicions of, 171; tender for Australian service (1847) by, 190–1; during Crimean War, 194–5; service to Australia via Mauritius and later Ceylon, 197; postal subsidy of (1853), 167; in 1860, 234; in 1867, 237; in 1888, 235; mail agents on ships of, 219–226; home port changed to London, 238; marked improvement of, 268.
Plymouth, 32; Falmouth packets at, briefly (1810), 81; interest of, in packets, 151; early port of Union Steamship Co., 177; used by Orient Line, 239
portmanteaus (portmantles), 22; care of, at Falmouth, 86, 105. See mails, care of.
Port Patrick, mail service from, 40; size of packets at, 59; service from, after 1815, 117; converted to steam, 121–2.
Portugal, postal service to, see Lisbon.
Princess Elizabeth (Captain Kidd), 91; carried Lord Byron to Lisbon, 92.

privateers, attacks of, on packet-boats (1777–1782), 50–6, 308–10; in French war (1793–1802), 170–4, 311–313; in War of 1812, 99–103, 314.

Qantas (Queensland & Northern Territory Aerial Services), joint service of, with Imperial Airways to Australia, 289; in cooperation with BOAC, 303.
Quebec, a mail for, 107; launching of *Royal William* at, 125; Cunard Line branch to, 133–4.
Queenstown (Cobh), use of, as port by Cunard Line, 242; large liners avoid, 269n. See Cork.

rates, overseas postal, in 1654, 23–4; in 1660, 24; charges by number of sheets, 23–4; to W.I. in 1702, 35; in 1711, 39; to N.Y. in 1711, 39; to Cape and India in 1815, 109; on ship-letters raised, 112; between G.B. and U.S., 246, 257; lowering of, to colonies, 256; under U.P.U., 258; Br. colonial rates lowered, 260; penny postage to Empire, 264–5; airmail, 281, 288, 290. See also ocean postage.
regulation of overseas mails, see mails, regulation of.
Reith, Lord, head of BOAC (1938), 294.
Rotterdam, postal regulations with, 27; steam service to, 123.
Royal Mail Steam Packet Co. (W.I.), merchant interest in, 148; first contract, 149; criticism of, 152; said to be established for political purposes, 157; interest of, in Pacific route, 211–212; mail agents on ships of, 221; subsidy of, in 1860, 236; end of high subsidies, 241. See West Indies, Panama.
Royal William, transatlantic crossing of, from Canada, 125–6, 132.

St. Thomas (West Indies), packet port, 106, 124, 227; Trollope visits, 156; Cunard Line to, 236.
San Francisco, port for south Pacific mails, 213, 238, 268, 271.
Savannah, steam paddle-wheel ship, early transatlantic voyage of, 125.
Saverland, Christopher, 64, 68; agent at Falmouth (1810–21), 77–8; packet shortage reported by, 79; handling by, of revolt of crews, 81; urges service to Cape of Good Hope, 109; death of, 111.
schooners, in Br. Navy (1813), 70; as Am. privateers, 103.
screw propeller, early use of, in *Great Britain* (1843), 137; early troubles with, 225; early use of, by General Screw and Allan Line, 147, 174; paddle wheels superseded by, 246, 250.
Second World War, use of fast liners in, 296; airgraphs, 297–300; air-letter forms (aerograms), 301–2.
ship-letters, gratuity to captains for, 24, 39–40, 112; avoidance of the Post Office by, 113; rates on, raised, 112; sending of, on Am. sailing liners, 114–6; uniform 6d rate for (1858), 256.
Singapore, 189, 190–1, 238, 289, 292.
Sirius, steam vessel, pioneer voyage of, to N.Y., 127, 132.
Skinner, Captain John, heroic action of, on Halifax route (1798), 72; transfer of, to Holyhead, 77, 120.
smuggling, see packet-boats.
soldiers, carried free on packet-boats, 26, 28, 50; letters of, at penny rate, 85.
Southampton, as chief Channel port, 149, 151–3, 183, 238, 256.

South Australia, 185, 192, 259.
Spain, mail service with, via France, 26, 30–1; brief use of Cadiz as packet port, 91. See Corunna.
Speedy and *Swift*, two sailing packets, mysterious capture of (1781), 53–4.
stamps, see letters.
Stanhope, Sir John, Master of Posts under Elizabeth I and James I, 17, 19–20.
Stevens, Captain, of *Lady Mary Pelham*, 77–8, 103.
Suez Canal, early plan for, 168; Br. objection to, 168; opening of, 197–8; use of, by Br. mail ships (1873–   ), 199; night travel by, 238; use of, during Second World War, 296.
Sydney (Australia), 184, 186–7, 191, 204, 214, 216, 239, 289.

Tankerville, Lord, P.M.G. (1780s), efforts of, to reform postal services, 61–2.
Tasman Empire Airways (TEAL), 292. See New Zealand.
Tasmania, 184–5; early mail from (1815), 186.
telegrah, submarine, see cables.
Thomson, Lord, Secy. of State for Air, death of, in loss of airship *R 101*, 286.
Titanic, loss of mail on (1912), 270, 275.
Todd, Anthony, Secy. of the P.O., (1768–98), 61–4.
Toulmin Line of sailing packet to Australia, 187–9.
Tour and Tassis, Counts of, postmasters in Holy Roman Empire, 16, 26, 59, 67.
Treasury, relation of, to packet services, 31, 217; the postal service as a source of revenue, 31, 39, 46; assistance of, to Cunard Line, 269.
Trent, steam packet of Royal Mail, 151, 231; stopped by *San Jacinto*, 228–30.
Trinidad, packet service to (1811), 93; mail-boats to, 106.
Trollope, Anthony, Post Office Surveyor, postal visit to W.I. (1858), 155–7; praise of, for paddle-steamers, 157; sent by P.O. to Egypt (1858), 169–71; opposed to Suez Canal, 197; visit of, to New Zealand, 200; on postal business to the U.S. (1861), 230.
Tuke, Sir Brian, first Master of the Posts, 16–7.

Union-Castle Mail Steamship Co., 240, 268, 296.
Union Steamship Co., began as colliery line, 175; starting of Cape service by (1857), 176; service of, extended to Mauritius, 177; proposed service to Zanzibar of, 180–1; contract of, with Cape Colony, 182; subsidy of, in 1860, 236; combined with Castle Line, 240.
United States, basic letter rate of, to Britain lowered to 12c (6d), 257; P.M.G. of, seeks general postal union, 258; penny postage of G.B. with, (1906), 265. See also, New York, Boston, Collins Line.
Universal Postal Union (U.P.U.), formation of, 258; growth of membership in, 259; Australian colonies join the, 260; voting rights in, 259–61, 265; regulation of air mail by, 302.

Vancouver, use of, as mail port by New Zealand and New South Wales, 271; terminus of Pacific Cable (1902), 273; of Pacific telephone cable (COMPAC), 307.
Victoria (Australia), 185, 188, 195.

Waghorn, Thomas, early career of, 159; advocate of route around Africa, 159–160; change to overland route by, 162; activity of, satirized by Thackeray, 163; favoured Torres Strait route to Australia, 190.
Walsingham, Lord, P.M.G. (1787–94), opposition of, to John Palmer, 58; views of, on Lisbon service, 59; on size of packet-boats, 59.
War of 1812–15 with the U.S., opening of, 94–5; losses of packet-boats during, 103, 314; Freeling's reflections on losses during, 103–4.
Warren, William, brief postal service of, to N.Y., 38.
Waterford, Irish packet port, 59–60, 69, 117.
Wellington (New Zealand), 200, 203–5, 209, 211, 299.
Wells, H. G., 277.
West Africa, so-called postal service to, 173–4.
Western Australia, settlement of, 184–5; desire of, for steam packets, 195; King George's Sound first packet port of, 185, 191, 196–7.
West Indies, early service to (1702–11), 35–7; route to, reopened, 43; contracts for mail packets to (1755), 43, 48; difficulties of service to (1775), 48–9; packets to, sheathed with copper, 51–2; rates to, in 1711, 39; in 1765, 47; service to, after 1783, 57; during war of (1793–1802), 69; complaints of merchants on service to, 57, 73; during Napoleonic War, 93; direct packet service to Surinam and Trinidad (1810), 93; use of inter-island mail-boats in, 57, 74, 103, 106; use of steam mail-boats, 123–4, plans of James McQueen for steam service to, 148; contract with Royal Mail, 149–51.
Weymouth, packet port for Channel Islands, 68, 118; use of steam packets at, 122.
White Star, sailing line to Australia, 195; change of, to Atlantic steam line, 247, 249–250; united with Cunard Line, 296.
Whitley, Col. Roger, Dep. P.M.G. (1670s), 26, 39; gratuity for ship-letters introduced by, 24; on service with the Netherlands, 29; proposal of Falmouth as ocean packet station by, 32.
Windsor Castle, sailing packet, 83; courageous action of, in 1807, 98–9; capture of (1815), 103, 314.
wireless, beginnings of, 273; first transatlantic use of, 274; Imperial Wireless Chain projected, 275.
Witherings, Thomas, successor of De Quester as Foreign Postmaster, 21; staffeto post, of, 21; replacement of, 22.

Yarmouth, packet port, replacing Harwich (1790s), 68.